THE SAVAGENESS OF WAR THROUGH THE GROWN-UP EYES OF A CHILD

Long regarded as the greatest Soviet novel of World War II—comparable in stature to Norman Mailer's *The Naked and the Dead* and Jerzy Kosinski's *The Painted Bird*—*Babi Yar* is a vivid and disturbing story of the childhood experiences of a young Russian boy living in the Ukraine at the time of the Nazi invasion.

Out of the searing ordeal of those years, A. Anatoli (Kuznetsov) has created a novel of unsparing truth—a devastating document that, once read, can never be forgotten.

A. ANATOLI (KUZNETSOV)

BABI YAR

THE LONG
SUPPRESSED
VERSION OF THE
COMPLETE
AND UNCENSORED
TEXT OF THE
GREAT RUSSIAN
NOVEL OF
WORLD WAR II

Translated by David Floyd

WASHINGTON SQUARE PRESS
PUBLISHED BY POCKET BOOKS NEW YORK

A Washington Square Press Publication of
POCKET BOOKS, a Simon & Schuster division of
GULF & WESTERN CORPORATION
1230 Avenue of the Americas, New York, N.Y. 10020

ISBN: 0-671-45135-9

First Pocket Books printing December, 1971

10   9   8   7   6   5

PREFACE

When I submitted the original manuscript of this book to the editor of the magazine *Yunost* in Moscow it was returned to me immediately with the advice not to show it to anybody else until I had removed all the 'anti-Soviet stuff' from it. I removed important sections from the chapters about the Kreshchatik, the destruction of the monastery, the disaster of 1961 and so forth, and submitted a milder version in which the sense of the book, though discernible, was concealed.

The manuscript passed through many departments, up to and including the Central Committee of the Soviet Communist Party, and while it was being prepared for publication the multi-stage censorship cut out another quarter of the text: the whole sense of the book was turned upside down. It was in that form that *Babi Yar* was published.

The same fate befell all my earlier works, and the works of other writers too. In the Soviet Union a writer is constantly faced with a choice: either he will not be published at all or he can publish what the censorship will permit.

The manuscript remained in my hands, however, and I continued to work on it. I put back the sections on the Kreshchatik, the monastery and the 1961 disaster, after having improved and re-written them, and I added new facts and made some things clearer. As a result of this the manuscript became so 'seditious' that I was afraid to keep it at home, where I was often subjected to searches, so I photographed it and buried it in the ground, where I hope it still is to this day.

In 1969 I escaped from the Soviet Union, taking with me the films to which I had transferred my manuscripts, including the complete text of *Babi Yar*. I am now presenting it as the first of my books to appear without being submitted to any political censorship, and I wish the present text of *Babi Yar* to be regarded as the only true one.

You have here in one volume the text that has already been published, the sections that were rejected by the censorship, and the passages that I have added since publication, including final corrections for the sake of style. Here is, at last, what I actually wrote.

THE AUTHOR

Editor's Note:
Readers interested in the differences between this complete text of *Babi Yar* and the truncated version passed by the Russian censors are referred to the hardbound edition published by Farrar Straus & Giroux, New York, in which the author's additions and the passages cut by the censors are printed in different type faces. This edition contains the entire text of the author's complete and final version but set in a uniform type face for easier reading.

CONTENTS

PART TWO

PART THREE

BABI YAR

Ashes

This book contains nothing but the truth.

Whenever I used to tell parts of the story to people they would always, without exception, declare that I ought to turn it all into a book.

I have in fact been writing that book for many long years. What might be called the first version was written when I was only fourteen. In those days, when I was just a hungry, frightened little boy, I used to write down in a thick, home-made notebook everything I saw and heard and knew about Babi Yar as soon as it happened. I had no idea why I was doing it; it seemed to me to be something I had to do, so that nothing should be forgotten.

The notebook was labelled BABI YAR, and I hid it away where other people should not set eyes on it. There was an outbreak of violent anti-Semitism in the Soviet Union after the war, which included a campaign against so-called 'cosmopolitanism' and the arrest of a group of Jewish doctors as 'murderers', and it was practically forbidden to mention the name Babi Yar.

One day my mother came across my notebook as she was cleaning the house. She read it, wept over it and advised me to take good care of it. She was the first to say that I ought someday to make it into a book.

The longer I lived in this world the more convinced I became that I had an obligation to do so.

Time and again I set about the task of writing an ordinary documentary novel on the basis of my notes, but without the slightest hope that it would ever be published.

Apart from that, something rather strange happened to me. I had been trying to write a straightforward novel in accordance with the rules of 'socialist realism'—the only guide to writing which I knew and which I had been taught ever since my schooldays. But the truth of real life, which cried out from every line written in my child's notebook, immediately lost all its vividness and became trite, flat, false and finally dishonest when it was turned into 'artistic truth'.

'Socialist realism' requires an author to describe, not so much what really happened, as what ought to have happened, or at any rate what might have happened. This method, false and hypocritical in intention, has in fact destroyed Russian literature, which produced so much that was great in the past. I refuse ever again to follow those rules.

I am writing this book now without bothering about any literary rules or any political systems, frontiers, censors or national prejudices.

I am writing it as though I were giving evidence under oath in the very highest court and I am ready to answer for every single word. This book records only the truth—AS IT REALLY HAPPENED.

I, Anatoli Vasilevich Kuznetsov, author of this book, was born on August 18th, 1929, in the city of Kiev. My mother was Ukrainian, my father Russian. On my identity card my nationality was given as Russian.

I grew up on the outskirts of Kiev, in the Kurenyovka district, not far from a large ravine the name of which— Babi Yar—was known then only to the local people. Like the other parts of the Kurenyovka it was our playground, the place where I spent my childhood.

Later it became famous, suddenly, in a single day.

For more than two years it was a forbidden area, fenced off with high-tension wires which enclosed a concentration camp. There were notices saying that anyone who came near would be fired on.

On one occasion I was even inside the camp office, but not, it is true, actually in the ravine itself, otherwise I should not be writing this book.

We could only hear bursts of machine-gun fire at various intervals: ta-ta-ta, ta-ta . . . For two long years I could hear them, day after day, and even now they still ring in my ears.

Towards the end a heavy, oily column of smoke was seen to rise above the ravine. It hung over the camp for three long weeks.

It was hardly surprising that when it was all over, despite our fear of mines, I went along with a friend to see what was left behind.

The ravine was enormous, you might even say majestic: deep and wide, like a mountain gorge. If you stood on one side of it and shouted you would scarcely be heard on the other.

It is situated between three districts of Kiev—Lukyanovka, Kurenyovka and Syrets, surrounded by cemeteries, woods and allotments. Down at the bottom ran a little stream with clear water. The sides of the ravine were steep, even over-hanging in places; landslides were frequent in Babi Yar. In fact it was typical of the whole region: the whole of the right bank of the Dnieper is cut into by such ravines; Kiev's main street, the Kreshchatik, was formed out of the Kresh-chaty ravine; there is a Repyakhov ravine, a Syrets ravine and others, many others.

On our way we caught sight of an old man, poorly dressed and with a bundle in his hand, making his way from one side ·of the ravine to the other. We guessed by the sureness of his step that he lived thereabouts and had used the path before.

'Please, mister,' I asked, 'was it here they shot the Jews, or farther on?'

The old man stopped, looked me up and down and said:

'And what about all the Russians who were killed here, and the Ukrainians and other kinds of people?'

And he went on his way.

We knew the stream like the palms of our hands. As children we had made little dams to hold it back and we had often swum in it.

The river bed was of good, coarse sand, but now for some reason or other the sand was mixed with little white stones.

I bent down and picked one of them up to look at it more closely. It was a small piece of bone, about as big as a finger-nail, and it was charred on one side and white on the other. The stream was washing these pieces of bone out of some-where and carrying them down with it. From this we con-cluded that the place where the Jews, Russians, Ukrainians and people of other nationalities had been shot was some-where higher up.

We carried on walking for a long time on these bits of bone until we reached the very top of the ravine, and the stream disappeared in the place where it was first formed by the many springs which trickled from the layers of sandstone. It must have been from there that it carried the bones down.

At this point the ravine became much narrower and split

into several branches, and in one place we saw that the sand had turned grey. Suddenly we realized we were walking on human ashes.

Near by there had been a fall of sand, following the rains, which had exposed an angular projection of granite and a seam of coal about a foot thick.

There were goats grazing on the hillside with three little boys, each about eight years old, looking after them. They were hacking away diligently at the coal with little picks and breaking it up on the granite block.

We went up to them. The coal was brown and crumbly, as though it was a mixture of the ashes from a railway engine and carpenter's glue.

'What are you doing?' I asked.

'See here!' And one of them pulled out of his pocket a handful of something which glittered where it was not covered in dirt, and spread it out on his hand.

It was a collection of half-melted gold rings, ear-rings, and teeth.

They were digging for gold.

We walked around the place and found many whole bones, a skull, still not dried out, of someone recently buried, and more pieces of black ash among the grey sand.

I picked up one of the pieces weighing four or five pounds and took it with me to keep. It contains the ashes of many people, all mixed up together—a sort of international mixture.

It was then that I decided that I must write it all down, from the very beginning, just as it really happened, leaving nothing out and making nothing up.

And that is what I am doing, because I know I have to do it, because, as it says in *Till Eulenspiegel*, Klaas's ashes are knocking at my heart.

So the word 'Document' which appears in the sub-title of this novel means that I have included in it only facts and documents, and that it contains not the slightest element of literary invention—of what 'might have been' or what 'ought to have been'.

Part One

The End of Soviet Rule

Soviet Informburo
Evening Bulletin
September 21st, 1941

In the course of September 21st our troops continued to fight the enemy along the whole front. After many days of bitter fighting our troops withdrew from Kiev.*

I saw them running and knew that it was all over. The men of the Red Army in their faded khaki uniforms, some of them with packs on their backs, others without even their weapons, were running in twos and threes through the courtyards and across the back gardens and jumping over fences.

Stories were told later about the soldiers rushing into the houses and pleading for civilian clothes. The women quickly dug out some old rags, the men changed into them in the hope of hiding themselves, and the women stuffed their useless weapons and tunics with badges of rank into the cesspools.

Then it became very quiet. The fighting had been going on for many days, with cannons thundering, sirens wailing and air raids coming one on top of the other. At night the whole horizon had been lit up by flashes and fires. We had slept on our bundles in a trench, with the earth shaking and bits of it falling on our heads.

But now it was quiet—the sort of quiet which seemed worse than any shooting. And we didn't know where we were: still under Stalin, already under Hitler, or were we in a narrow strip in between?

A machine-gun could be heard chattering away very clearly near by, from the direction of the railway embankment.

---

* *Pravda*, September 22nd, 1941. Kiev was surrendered on September 19th and not the 21st, as the bulletin says.

Little branches and leaves were falling off the old elm tree above the trench. I crashed through the entrance-hole and tumbled into the dugout, where my grandfather silenced me and gave me a clout.

We had dug our trench in the garden; it was the usual kind of air-raid shelter—the 'slit-trench'—of those days, shaped like a letter T, six to seven feet deep and about two and a half feet across. There were similar trenches in all the court-yards, squares and streets; the government had appealed over the radio for people to dig them and explained how to do it.

But my grandfather and I had put in several days' work improving the design. We had lined the earth walls with boards, paved the floor with bricks and covered over the top. We did not, of course, have enough timber to do it properly, but we laid some nine-foot boards across the top of the trench and then piled on top of them all the pieces of wood we could find in the barn.

My grandfather had worked it out that if a bomb were to fall on the trench it would, he explained, hit the pieces of wood first and they would cannon off it like billiard balls and the explosion would never reach us. The damned thing would have no hope of destroying such a fortress!

To make it even stronger we shovelled earth on top of the wood and then covered it with turf to camouflage it, so that we had an impressive and clearly recognizable hillock be-neath which, when the entrance-hole was shut, it was as quiet and as dark as the grave.

It was our good fortune that nothing exploded near our trench and that not even a sizeable piece of shrapnel fell there, otherwise all that wood would have come tumbling down on our heads. But at that time we were still unaware of this and were only proud of our handiwork and quite sure we had provided ourselves with a perfect shelter.

Earlier, when we did not have such a fine air-raid shelter, my grandfather, my grandmother and I used to hide from the bombs beneath the bed.

It was an old-fashioned bed, good and strong, and the ends were made of sheets of metal with pictures painted on them in oils—mills, lakes with swans, and castles. We reckoned that if a bomb were to fall it would come through the roof and the ceiling, bounce off the spring mattress and explode. But the eiderdown on top of two quilted blankets would not, of course, let any splinters through.

So that we should not have to lie on the bare floor my grandmother used to spread a blanket under the bed and put some pillows on it, which made it really quite cosy.

Whenever the shooting started and the windows began to rattle from the whine of the dive-bombers, Grandpa would be the first to dive under the bed. He would work his way across as far as possible and squeeze himself up close to the wall. Next I would tumble in and squeeze up to him. And then Grandma, who was everlastingly pottering around the stove, would grab our cat, Titus, and lie down on the outside, protecting us all with her own body. That was how we used to look after ourselves.

Grandpa would say a prayer under his breath and then demand of me crossly:

'Why on earth do you keep on wriggling about, you silly *gomon*? Have you got a worm inside you?'

Once we had finished the construction of our mighty trench we used to take refuge in it in the same order, only now Grandma always had to take the pillows and a blanket with her. (She never left them in the trench, so that they should not get damp.)

Titus the cat had become accustomed to war; at the very first sound of shooting he would rush, tail high, in tremendous bounds across to the entrance to the trench and stay there miaowing with terror in his eyes until he was let in. He knew only how to climb up the hanging ladder and had not learnt how to get down it.

I still don't know where my grandfather came across that word *gomon*. He is dead now, and I forgot to ask him. But it is true that a worm of curiosity was always nagging at me. I used to wriggle out of the trench to watch the planes and see the beastly crosses on them, and I used to try and see the bombs exploding.

But now, when I saw the Red Army men on the run and it became obvious that it was all over, I was frightened—really frightened—at last.

We had a paraffin lamp burning in the trench which smelt badly. My mother (who until now had been on duty day and night in her school) was sitting on a stool, stark terror in her eyes. My grandfather was eating; he always ate when he was

nervous. His grey beard, with two pointed ends, wagged up
and down because he had false teeth and did not chew his
food but munched it, Grandma used to say, the crumbs
dropping into his beard. Grandma was muttering a scarcely
audible prayer and crossing herself in front of an icon of the
Virgin which she had brought into the trench. I myself had
put a nail into a board to hang the icon on. I was very fond
of it; it was my favourite among all the icons my grandmother possessed.

Somewhere in the walls, behind the boards, there was some
quiet rustling and movement; the beetles and the worms and
the busy ants lived out their lives there unseen, utterly indifferent to the war.

But at last the earth had ceased to tremble and fall on
our heads, and it seemed as though, in that ominous silence,
something utterly frightful was about to happen, some explosion such as we had never heard before.

I just sat there, scarcely breathing, waiting for it to
happen . . .

Suddenly there was the muffled sound of footsteps, the
flap over the entrance was lifted, and there stood our neighbour, Yelena Pavlovna, looking strange and quite beside
herself. With joy and wonder and triumph in her voice she
exclaimed:

'What are you sitting there for? The Germans are here!
It's the end of Soviet rule!'

I was twelve years old, and a lot of things were happening
to me for the first time in my life. It was certainly the first
time the Germans had arrived, and I rushed out of the
trench before the others, screwing up my eyes because of
the strong light, and noticed that the world had become
somehow different—like fine weather following a storm—
although outwardly everything seemed to be unchanged.

Yelena Pavlovna was gasping for breath, waving her hands
about, and saying tenderly and happily:

'So young, such a young lad standing there! My windows
look out on to the street. The truck drove off, but he stayed
there, this young one, a good-looking boy!'

I immediately rushed across the yard and skipped over the
fence.

Near the fence which ran round the garden in our Peter-Paul Square there was a low-slung, evil-looking, long-nosed gun standing on fat rubber tyres. And next to it was a German soldier who was indeed very young and very fair, rosy-cheeked, and wearing a remarkably clean and well-fitting grey-green uniform. He was holding a rifle at the ready, and when he noticed that I was looking at him he drew himself up proudly. But he did it in a very pleasant way, as though he was just playing a part.

I had a lifelong friend, three years older than myself, Bolik Kaminsky, about whom I shall have more to say later. He had been evacuated along with other apprentices at the factory school. Well, this German lad was very like my friend Bolik.

You see, I had been expecting absolutely everything: that Germans were terrifying giants of men, swarming over their tanks in gas-masks and horned helmets; and I was shocked to see that this lad was so ordinary, so . . . well, nothing unusual, just like our Bolik.

There he was, showing off, as I too would have been showing off if I had a gun like that.

At that moment came the sound of the outsize explosion that I had been expecting. I caught my breath, hit my chin on the top of the fence and nearly fell off it. And, to his shame, the young soldier went down on his knees, cowering close to the gun in fright.

But, to give him his due, he came to his senses at once, stood up of his own accord and began staring at something somewhere above my head. I turned round and saw broken pieces of wood twisting and floating high in the blue sky above the tops of the trees and falling slowly to earth.

'Ha, so they've blown up the bridge after all, the bloody wastrels!' said Grandpa, coming across to the fence and poking his nose over the top so that he also could have a look at the first German. 'My goodness, what a sight! God Almighty, what hope has Stalin got of fighting them! That's a real army! Not like our poor devils, hungry and barefoot. Just look at the way he's dressed!'

The young soldier really was very well turned out. In newspaper cartoons and Soviet films the Germans were always made to look like ragged beggars and bandits, while

Soviet soldiers were always good-looking, smartly turned out and pink-cheeked.

An angular, box-like, predatory-looking truck drew up in a cloud of dust, turned swiftly round (Grandpa and I followed all this very closely) and some more young German boys, also very smartly turned out and as deft as jugglers, hooked the gun on to the truck in one quick move and hopped on to the running-boards; with them hanging on to each side, the truck shot off at top speed in the direction of Podol.

'Yes,' said my grandfather, quite staggered by all this, and crossing himself with a sweeping gesture. 'Thank the Lord, the rule of the down-and-outs has come to an end, I thought I'd never live to see the day . . . Come on, give us a hand to get these things into the house; everything's damp in the trench. Now we can have a decent life.'

I went rather unwillingly across to the trench. There my mother was handing bundles, cases and stools out of the dark hole and Grandma was taking them and putting them together in a pile. I started to carry them indoors.

We had repeated this operation so many times recently: into the trench, out of the trench, up and down. If only there had been something worth saving, but there was nothing but old, ragged clothes, sheepskin coat from Tsarist days, all patched and moth-eaten, a pair of faded trousers, a few cushions . . . In short, it was not a man's job.

At that moment the head of my second friend, Shurka Matso, peered over the top of the fence. With his eyes almost popping out of his head he called out:

'The Germans are coming down the tramline! Let's go!'

I was off like the wind.

The whole of the Kirillovskaya (under Soviet rule it had been renamed Frunze Street, but the name did not catch on), as far as you could see in both directions, was jammed with trucks and other vehicles. The cars were very angular, with all sorts of things sticking out, netting thrown over them and things hanging down. Every motor-vehicle has its own face, and eyes the world through its headlights indifferently or angrily, with sorrow or surprise. These, like the one that came to take the gun away, had a predatory look. I had never seen such machines in all my life; they seemed to me to be immensely powerful and they filled the whole street with the roar and fumes of their engines.

The bodies built on some of the lorries were like little houses, fitted out with beds and with tables screwed to the floor.

The Germans were staring around out of their vehicles and strolling down the street—clean-shaven, wide awake and very cheerful. It was not, I thought, so difficult to be bright and cheerful in the infantry if, like them, you didn't have to march but rode in trucks! They laughed at anything that amused them and called out something funny to the first of the local people to creep out on to the streets. Dashing motorcyclists in helmets, with machine-guns mounted on their handlebars, swept through between wagons laden with shells and kit-bags.

The heavy weapons were being pulled, as though they were only toys, by enormous bay work-horses such as we had never seen before. With manes the colour of straw, moving their shaggy hooves forward slowly and surely, harnessed together in teams of six, they made light work of drawing the heavy weapons. Our stunted Russian nags, half-dead from lack of fodder, on which the Red Army was retreating would have looked like foals alongside these giants.

The officers in their tall peaked caps with silver braid travelled in dazzling black and white limousines, chatting cheerfully among themselves. We, Shurka and I, caught our breath and scarcely knew where to look next. Then we plucked up the courage to run across the road. The pavements were quickly filling up with people rushing in from all sides. Like us, they first looked at this armada in amazement, then began to smile at the Germans in reply and to try to start up conversations with them.

As for the Germans, practically all of them had little conversation-books which they were quickly looking through and calling out to the girls on the pavement:

'Hey, girl, miss . . . ! Bolshevik—finish. Ukraina!'

'Ukrayéena,' the girls corrected them with a laugh.

'Ja, ja. U-kray-éena! Go walk, spazieren, bitte!'

The girls giggled and blushed, and all the people around were laughing and smiling.

There was a general movement from the direction of Bondar Lane: people's heads could be seen moving slowly

and evenly forward in what turned out to be a procession
of elderly men and women. The old man at the head of the
procession had a white cloth across his shoulder and was
carrying a tray on which was a large round Ukrainian loaf
of bread with a dish of salt on top. The crowd rushed to see
the spectacle, fighting with one another to get to the front.

The old men were late and not quite sure to whom they
should hand the symbols of friendship. So their leader went
up to the nearest white limousine, from which some officers
were viewing the scene in amusement, and offered them the
tray with a deep bow. Shurka and I had lost each other. I was
doing my level best to force my way through to the front.
They were saying something and there was a burst of laughter, and the people at the back asked: 'What did he say?
What did he say?' But the column moved on and I only
managed to see the officer in the passing motor-car put the
bread and the cloth into the back seat.

People around were saying that somewhere near by the
Germans had shouted out: 'Butter, bread!' and had thrown
out a whole case of butter and baskets full of bread right on
to the tramline. Anybody could take it if they wanted it, it
seemed. I rushed around trying to find out where it had been
and finally dashed off in the direction of the bridge over
Vyshgorod Street.

I found no butter and no bread near the bridge. But there
was a fire. A brick house on the corner was burning slowly
and quietly, set on fire by a shell that had gone through the
window. The fence had already collapsed on the flowers
growing close to the house, and people were walking on it.
Two women and a little girl were digging up earth with
spades and throwing it on the fire, because there was no
water. A man stepped out of the crowd of bystanders, took a
stick in his hand and started to hit the panes of glass in the
window with all his might.

A German jumped down from a lorry, aimed his camera
at the scene, going down on his haunches and twisting his
body around, getting photographs of the fire from all angles.

The man clambered through the window and started to
hand the women chairs and boxes of linen from the cup-
boards, and to throw out coats and dresses. Everybody
praised him, and I thought to myself what a brave man he
was.

Troops continued pouring out from under the bridge. The sun was bright in the sky and there was no firing whatever to be heard—only the roar of engines, the rumble of wheels, voices and laughter. After such a long time living in a hole in the ground I just couldn't take it all in; rather weak at the knees, I made my way back home to tell my story.

There in our yard I found a soldier in a grey-green tunic, his gun slung over his shoulder and a rope in his hand, a simple-looking lad, with fair eyelashes contrasting with a forehead burnt red by the sun, who was looking around calmly while my grandfather signed to him to inspect the shed:

'Here is nix, nix, nix; but there, maybe, ist! Better have a look, bitte.'

The soldier went rather reluctantly into the shed.

'They're looking for prisoners,' Grandma explained to me from the porch.

Inside the shed there was a hatch leading down into the cellar. The soldier started pointing at it and saying:

'Matchess, matchess.'

We gave him some matches. He lit one and peered cautiously into the hole.

'Mind the partisans!' said Grandma in a loud and mocking voice.

The soldier jumped back as if stung, swung round and eyed us all with suspicion.

'I'm only joking,' said Gran. 'Go on, go on, don't be afraid. There are no partisans there.'

But the soldier muttered something in his irritation, showed no desire to get into the hole, and pointed sternly at the red flag belonging to the house which we used to have to put out over the door on special days.

'What about that?'

'Yes, yes,' said my grandfather hastily, took hold of the flag and ripped it off the pole. 'Martha—stuff it in the fire right away. But the stick's all right; it'll do for a broom-handle.'

Another soldier came up, also carrying a piece of rope. He beckoned the other excitedly and they both rushed off. Granny signalled to me to come into the house.

'Look, climb up in the loft and hide this away there; wrap it up in a bit of newspaper or something.'

'But what's it for, Gran?'

'Nobody really knows anything, son . . . The Germans have got red flags too, and if they tell us to hang them out we shall have to go and buy some more material. Do as I say, son.'

I understood and clambered up into the loft, crawled over into a far corner and stuffed the paper bundle under a beam. When I let myself down again, covered in cobwebs, Grandma was standing in the doorway with Yelena Pavlovna calling out:

'Dad! Come here quick. They're taking a partisan off.'

Our sunburnt soldier was leading a large, dirty pig down the street, his rope now tied round the animal's body. Another soldier was driving the pig from behind with a long stick, while a group of other soldiers accompanied him, gabbling away amongst themselves.

With much raising of eyebrows and vocal effort Yelena Pavlovna was explaining that the soldiers were not the least concerned to look for prisoners; they were simply looting. They had taken the pig from the Kaminskys; they had stolen some sheepskins; in her house they had looked into the cupboard and under the bed . . . They had taken the pillow-cases from the pillows and, for some reason, a towel off its nail. Her neighbour had not wanted to part with the pig, so they had left a receipt, saying: 'Officer will pay.' It seemed as though we had been lucky not to have had anything taken; perhaps it was because Gramp had used some German words and they hadn't dared.

Gramp was following thoughtfully the progress of the valiant armed procession with the pig.

'Oh well,' he said sternly, 'let's get the things carried back into the trench. Blast their eyes . . . I forgot—it's the right of a victorious army to loot as they please for three days!'

Looting's a Lot of Fun, But You Have to Know How to Do It

Our neighbour went off with the receipt he had been given for the pig down to the school, where the Germans had already set up their headquarters. I hurried after him, thinking that they would get some German money and I would be able to have a look at it.

I stayed by the gate. In the yard he told them what he wanted, then went in through the door. A little later I saw him shoot out of it again with a crash, gesticulating helplessly. The soldiers shouted at him and rattled the bolts of their guns. I was afraid they would start shooting, and made off quickly round the corner.

Troops were still crossing the square, though there were not so many of them as before. But from the market district people were running in all directions, like cockroaches, with bags stuffed full of things, greed and excitement written on all their faces. I realized I was missing something and hurried down to the shopping market.

I found people looting a large footwear shop. The shop-window had been shattered and there were grown-ups inside it, elbowing each other out of the way and trampling the broken glass underfoot. I dashed in after them just in time to see them get their hands on some boxes of shoes and galoshes—my God, what fabulous goods for those days! But while I was forcing my way through, the shelves were stripped, as if a wind had swept them bare, and the crowd stormed off round the corner. I poked around a bit, clambering over other people's backs and bewailing my lot: everybody pinching stuff from under my very nose, yet I couldn't get my hands on anything. They were already snatching bundles of shoe-laces and tins of shoe-polish out of each other's hands.

So I skipped back through the window and out on to the street to have a look round and see whether there wasn't another shop still unlooted. And I saw, to my great annoyance, that while I had been messing around in the shoe shop they had broken into a shop next door selling household goods and were already carting off tins of paint and bundles of shovels and locks.

I rushed in, got to work with my elbows and squeezed my way up to the counter. But there I could see only people's feet trampling down a mixture of putty and whitening. Then I saw some men crowding into an annexe, so I tried to follow them and in the doorway got hit over the head and in the teeth. The pain made me see red, so I ran around and forced my way in between two men; I was so crushed that my ribs creaked, but there at last, right in front of me, was a packing-case that had been broken open.

Inside it, packed in straw, were some beautiful new paraffin lamps without their glasses. I reached out, knocking other people's hands away, and got hold first of one and then of another—and then the lamps were finished.

I was furious, because I realized that my loot was quite worthless. But the shop was now empty and the looters had dashed off elsewhere. I ran outside, and there I nearly howled: they had broken into the haberdashery store which had been untouched when I came along. It looked as though only women were doing the looting there. They were screaming, and the walls of the little shop were shaking.

So this time, twisting and turning like a young animal, I forced my way through and grabbed a box from the shelf. Some women tried to snatch it off me, but I hung on to it like a cat to a piece of meat. They shook the very life out of me, the box broke open and a stream of simple black overcoat buttons poured out of it. Dozens of hands started scooping the buttons up and in my excitement I started to do the same, stuffing them into my pockets—after all, I had more right to them than the others.

I caught sight of some clothes-brushes lying around under our feet, tried to get hold of them and managed to pick up four or five, but dropped one of the lamps, which some greedy woman immediately snatched from under my nose.

I went out on to the street, thoroughly knocked about and unsteady on my feet, to see people dragging bags of salt out of a food store. But by the time I had run across to it there was nothing left but paper and empty boxes.

I was ready to burst into tears. I had never been greedy: I was Grandma's well-behaved, polite little boy. Yet all of a sudden this craze for loot had come over me like a hot avalanche, and I felt a tightness in my throat from greed and excitement.

The main thing was that I realized this was an unrepeatable chance—to be able to go looting with such impunity, so richly and so grandly. But I had missed everything, and by so little! . . . That's what it meant to be inexperienced. 'All right,' I thought, trying to console myself. 'Next time . . .' But when would there be a next time?

Out of self-pity I gathered up from the counters the weights off the scales and carried my booty off home.

People were looking out of their windows and gateways. Our neighbour Pavel Sochava said with heavy irony, so that the whole street could hear:

'So Tolya's been out looting as well. Go and tell Mummy, so that she can give you a good hiding.'

I felt as though I'd had a bucket of cold water thrown over me. I had been so proud to carry my lamp and my brushes, but now I ran into the courtyard as quickly as I could and unloaded my spoils inside the house . . . My mother gasped:

'What on earth is that?'

Grandma looked at the things and shook her head:

'You think we haven't any lamps, son?'

Gramp, on the other hand, backed me up and said approvingly:

'Why shouldn't he? Good lad! The Bolsheviks have taken everything away from the people and sold it back at three times the price. It's all ours. I wish I'd known; now I've missed it! Look at Shatkovsky—he carted off half the food store and got a barrel of sunflower-seed oil up here. What a chance it was! Up here it's us they're looting.'

I learnt that while I had been down in the market six soldiers had come demanding eggs and milk—had poked their noses into everything as if it belonged to them and had taken a lot of potatoes, cabbage and tomatoes . . .

Fine goings on! Whilst some people were looting down there, others were looting up here!

Still shaking with excitement, and encouraged by Gramp's words of approval, I ran off to find Shurka Matso and we

hurried down again to the market together. It was already
empty.

There was nothing to be seen anywhere; it was as if the
whole place had been swept clean. In the shops there was
nothing but paper, straw and broken glass. In the footwear
shop we got into the cash-desk and started winding the
handle of the cash register. We issued ourselves with receipts
for thousands of roubles, went outside and scattered them all
over the street and then, no longer excited, we stood and
watched more and more troops entering the city.

There were heavy tractors and transporters on caterpillar
tracks; and there were columns of soldiers on bicycles and
others on ordinary carts. The ones who had already arrived
and settled in the city were carrying bundles with their
possessions and had their greatcoats slung over their shoulders.

A wind sprang up, blew the straw and paper about and
carried away the fumes from the engines. And the troops
continued marching through. They simply swarmed into the
city; there seemed to be no end to them, and every single
one seemed to have found something to carry away. Such a
peaceful, everyday, prosaic case of looting . . . It was Friday,
September 19th, 1941.

KIEV IN HANDS OF GERMAN TROOPS

Führer's HQ   September 20

The Supreme Command of
German Armed Forces announces:

While operations aimed at the encirclement of Soviet
Armies in the east continued, the assault on Kiev,
capital of the Ukraine, was begun. Following a coura-
geous action to break through strong defences on the
western bank of the Dnieper, our troops entered the
city. From this morning the German military flag flies
over the citadel of Kiev.

The advance to the east from the Dnieper continues
unhalted. We are having important successes in battles
for the defences of Leningrad.*

* *Ukrainskoye Slovo*, September 21st, 1941. The paper was published
in Ukrainian by the occupation authorities.

So This Is the New Life

At about the time when the Germans were taking Kiev the newspaper *Ukrainskoye Slovo* brought out its fifteenth issue, printing it in Zhitomir. It was sold or simply given away free in the streets by people rejoicing in the victory, and my grandfather managed to get hold of a copy. He brought it home as if it were something sacred and was longing to read it.

But what with the small type and the cheap newsprint, like wrapping paper, it was printed on, he just couldn't read it, so he gave me that job while he sat and listened, pondering the sense of it all.

I will reproduce only the paper's headlines:

KIEV IN HANDS OF GERMAN TROOPS
POLTAVA OCCUPIED
OUTSTANDING SUCCESSES AT LENINGRAD
MORE GROUND GAINED BEFORE LENINGRAD
220,000 POUNDS OF BOMBS DROPPED ON PORT OF ODESSA
BIG ADVANCES BY GERMAN FORCES IN BATTLES FOR FOOT-
    HOLD ACROSS LOWER DNIEPER
THE UKRAINIAN PEOPLE FIGHT
REVIVAL OF CHURCH IN KHOLM REGION
DEVELOPMENT OF ART IN ZHITOMIR
'TO KIEV'—A POEM BY YAKOV NAGORNY

. . . Here I am going to make the usual type of digression and tell the history, at least in general outline, of our little family—who we were, what sort of people we were and why.

I myself cannot bear it when this sort of digression occurs in books I am reading. I skip them, and if my digression seems to you uninteresting don't hesitate to pass it over, because the most important part of this book is much farther on.

But if you are interested to learn how a man could yearn

for Hitler to come, read at least the passages about my grand-father.

FYODOR VLASOVICH SEMERIK, my grandfather, hated Soviet rule with all his heart and soul and longed for the arrival of the Germans as liberators, on the assumption that there could be nothing worse in the whole world than the Soviet system.

No, he was by no means a Fascist or a monarchist, a nationalist or a Trotskyist, a Red or a White—he didn't have the slightest idea about such things.

He came from a family of Ukrainian serfs; he was a poor peasant. His social status was that of an industrial worker employed in a town. But in actual fact he was the most ordinary, the smallest, the most hungry and the most intimidated citizen of the Land of the Soviets, which he regarded as no more than his stepmother.

My grandfather was born in 1870—the same year as Lenin, but that was all they had in common. Grandpa couldn't bear to hear Lenin's name mentioned, though he was long dead, along with many of his followers who had also died or been done to death. He reckoned that all our troubles were Lenin's doing, that Lenin had 'played at ruling Russia as if he was playing roulette, lost everything and then gone and died'.

Whenever he said that sort of thing, my grandmother would look about her in horror and exclaim in a voice that could be heard in the courtyard:

'Stop your idle chatter, you stupid man. Good folk are dying, while you, you good-for-nothing, are still hanging around.'

My grandfather was born and grew up in the village of Shenderovka in the Kanev district, in a desperately poor peasant family of eleven children; they lived, according to him, in a tumbledown shack.

As a young man he worked as a farm labourer for German settlers in the Kherson region, having left his family for good. After doing his military service he moved to Kiev in the hope of making a better living, went around from job to job, worked for a time as handyman for a general, married a laundrywoman, then took a job as a tram conductor, and kept dreaming of having his own little house and enough to live on—so that he could eat his fill and not have to worry about the next day. That was the extent of his dreams.

My grandmother and he went without food and without adequate heat, saved up their money kopek by kopek and ruined their young lives, but managed at last to buy a tiny patch of land in the marshes of the Kurenyovka; they reclaimed it with their own hands, and slowly built themselves a wooden shack. Then came the revolution.

It brought them no benefits at all, only more hunger and more fear—and it put an end to all their dreams. Grandpa put no faith in the Bolsheviks' fine words about a heaven on earth in the dim and distant future. He was a very practical man.

After that my grandfather worked for many years as a mechanic on the drainage system in Boot and Shoe Factory No. 4. He would crawl around through the drains in his stinking overalls, and he was even injured while working at a machine—you could scarcely be more a member of the working-class than he was. And throughout those years he never ceased to loathe the rule of the 'tramps and murderers'. 'They don't know how to run things,' he would say.

But what finally reduced him, a former peasant, to a state of utter horror was the enforced 'collectivization' of agriculture, which produced a famine such as no one had experienced before. The building of new factories, the construction of the Dnieper power station, about which so much fuss was made in those years, the conquest of the North Pole and of the skies—all this made no impression at all on my grandfather.

The North Pole was indeed conquered, but when my grandparents at last realized their greatest dream—to own a cow—there was nothing for them to feed it on. The queues for manufactured feeding stuffs were enormous. Next to their cottage, just across the railway embankment, there was a vast, rich meadow going to waste, yet they were not allowed to graze the cow on it. There was no end to the dodges my grandfather got up to or the people he tried to bribe, so as to get hold of some hay. With his sack and a sickle he would scour the whole of Babi Yar and Repyakhov Yar and cut every blade of grass growing under the fences. He didn't drink the milk himself: he sent my grandmother down to the market to sell it. He always remembered that the German landowner for whom he had worked had a cow which gave three pails of milk a day, and he thought that if he could only feed our poor Lyska properly she might also give as much.

He was, on the whole, a great one for getting things done somehow. But a life of repeated failure and grinding poverty had made him into a thoroughly disagreeable and unusually envious man. He envied half the population of Kurenyovka, especially the people who had a decent garden and were able to take whole basketfuls of radishes down to the market. From time immemorial Kurenyovka had relied on its radishes, as well as its suckling-pigs and chickens, and remained deaf to all kinds of scientific, artistic and political developments, demanding from the politicians only one thing: freedom to sell radishes.

In his *Childhood* Gorky quotes this song:

> A beggar hung out his socks to dry;
> Another beggar pinched them.

And so, as I said, my grandfather was an envious man. But he had no hope of catching up with the more successful farmers of Kurenyovka. He had only a very small plot of land, about twenty feet wide, around the cottage and out-building. On the other side of the fence were the allotments belonging to the collectively owned market garden. One night my grandfather dug some new holes and moved the fence a couple of feet over, thus robbing the market gardeners of five or six square yards of land, but the lazy officials in charge of the collective didn't even notice! For a whole week Grandpa was in an excellent frame of mind, full of his achievement, and he started planning to shift the fence over another couple of feet in a few years' time.

In his old age he became terribly quarrelsome. He would pick his neighbour's pears on the quiet, on the grounds that they were hanging over 'his land', he would set about the neighbour's chickens if they wandered across to us, and in this way he managed to quarrel with the whole street.

When he started swearing and spluttering his 'oo-too-too-too' could be heard right down in the market, and they called him 'Semerik, troo-too-too—three buckets of milk.'

Grandpa was so mean that he never drank vodka, never smoked, never went to the cinema, always tried to dodge paying his fare on the trams and wore his jackets and trousers until they were in shreds and fell to pieces on his back. If a hay-cart went down the street and dropped a little as it went, Grandpa would be first out on the roadway to rake it up carefully and carry it triumphantly home.

The cow turned out to be unprofitable and had to be sold. Then Grandpa tried keeping ducks, and I used to go with him down to the pond, where we would splash about with an old basket trying to collect 'duckweed' to feed them on, but the ducks did not do well on it—they were just skin and bones.

Grandpa then switched to keeping hens, which, he said, get around on their own, scratching about and finding their own food. But the hens were so hungry that they pecked up the plants in the vegetable garden and still didn't lay any eggs. Then he got some piglets to eat up the kitchen waste. But Grandpa's piglets grew up long-legged, muscular and wiry, more like greyhounds. And just before the Germans arrived both the piglets went down with the pest and died. We had to bury them.

Grandpa was certainly a very energetic man who would struggle and strive the whole day long from dawn till dusk. But he just couldn't get rich.

There were, however, others about the place who were able to 'live it up': party officials, secret police officers, thieves, informers and various trade-union officials. They went around in official cars, pampered their bodies at Caucasian health resorts, and regularly received secret supplements to their pay, delivered to them in plain envelopes.* For his frightful job of crawling round inside the drains my grandfather received a monthly salary which was only half the price of a cheap suit of clothes. All his life he never owned a proper suit; he died without ever wearing one.

But there were other people to whom the life of Grandpa's family seemed like the joys of paradise. The peasants worked in the collective farms around Kiev as they had worked in the days of serfdom. No, it was even worse. Under serfdom the landowner used to leave the peasants whole days free to work for themselves on their own little plots of land. But in a collective farm a man had no such free days and had no

---

* The practice of giving senior party and government officials sums of money in addition to their salaries, taken from party or other funds, is long-established in the Soviet system. [Tr.]

land of his own. When he turned out to work in the fields he would be credited with one 'workday' by an entry in the register, and in the autumn he would receive some pay for it, or maybe he would receive nothing, or be paid at the rate of one kopek for each workday.

And so, whenever we had visitors, Grandpa had only one topic of conversation: that in the past everything had been fine, people had been well fed and able to get rich, but that the Bolshevik good-for-nothings had ruined everything.

But when in 1937 his friend, old Zhuk, was arrested for telling a stupid joke in a queue and poor Zhuk vanished at once from sight as though he had been drowned, Grandpa got terribly frightened, kept himself to himself and was left with only half a topic—how good things had been in the past.

I suppose there was as much truth in what he said as there was fiction. The 'good' he talked about made sense only by comparison. And by 1937 Tsarist Russia already seemed to my poor grandfather like a paradise of justice lost.

For some reason or other he never recalled the old shack belonging to his father, who had had to rent a piece of someone else's land. He would recall only how marvellously the general had lived and how open-handed he had been. And how low prices had been under the Tsar: five kopeks for a loaf, two kopeks for a herring, while nobody bothered even to look at the dried fish.

The only person he now told about his hatred for the Bolsheviks was God. He would remain for long stretches on his knees in front of the icons, whispering away to himself, telling them something with great earnestness. He knew that God at least would listen to him and not betray him.

Shortly after the beginning of the war a German leaflet fell on to our roof and stuck there on the chimney in the morning dew. Grandpa saw it, put the ladder up and sent me to get it. With some difficulty I got hold of the sodden bit of paper and we proceeded to read it.

The leaflet declared that Germany's mission was to destroy the Bolsheviks and set up a new and just system under which 'he who does not work shall not eat' but, at the same time, 'everyone who works honestly and well will be rewarded according to his merits'. It said that life in the liberated territory was marvellous, that butter cost ten kopeks a pound, bread seven kopeks and a herring three.

Grandpa's eyes looked up to the heavens. It was a message for him personally.

He learnt the leaflet off by heart and only then did he tear it up into small pieces. He was in his seventy-second year and here was hope reborn—it was unbelievable—maybe he would yet be able to graze his cow on the meadow and get three pails of milk a day; maybe there would yet be enough food in the house for the next day and even the day after; and maybe he might even buy himself at last his first suit of clothes.

MARTHA YEFIMOVNA SEMERIK (her maiden name was Dolgoruk), my grandmother, was born and grew up in the village of Deremezna in the Obukhov district in a godforsaken old shack, with scarcely room to move because of all the children.

It was the sort of shack in which Taras Shevchenko, the great Ukrainian poet, who also came from a family of serfs, spent his childhood:

> I cannot call it paradise . . .
> I shed so many tears there,
> My very first tears. And I do not know
> Whether there is anywhere in the world a misfortune
> That this house does not know.

There were so many members of my grandmother's family, some living in Deremezna and Peregonovka, others working as hired labour in Kiev, that I could never work out exactly how many of them there were or how they were related to me: Gapka and Konon, Ganna and Nina, Thoma and Katka, who was not quite right in the head . . . From time to time they would come and see us and Grandma would give one an old skirt, another some worn-out galoshes.

It was only in the case of the feeble-minded Katka that I knew she was my aunt once removed. A bout of typhus had affected her mind and she had taken to begging; she would sit around the churches with a bag in her hand, or go begging round the houses and bring home bits of bread in her bag, which my grandfather would take off her and give to

the pigs, muttering: 'It makes you think, the way these beggars live and how much people give them at Easter!'

I was very fond of Katka; she was like a saint, so inoffensive and good-hearted. If anyone gave her a sweet she
always saved it for me, and sometimes she would go down
to the market and use the kopeks she had collected to buy
me a present—usually a clay whistle in the shape of a horse.
As I grew bigger she did not notice it and went on bringing
me clay whistles, always muttering something unintelligible
to herself . . . Katka died on the street, quietly and unnoticed,
as sparrows die. They took her off in a cart and buried her
somewhere.

At the age of twelve my grandmother went out to work;
she looked after other people's children, worked as a domes-
tic servant and then became a washerwoman. However much
I asked her she would never tell me anything about her young
days nor about her loves, perhaps because all she could
remember was unpleasant.

She was completely illiterate. She distinguished paper
money by the design and colour, and coins by their size.

Because my mother, who was a teacher, had to work a
double shift at her school and, moreover, stayed on to work
after lessons, I was brought up entirely by my grandmother.
She used to wake me up, wash me, feed me, smack me and
amuse me with Ukrainian fairy tales, and at the same time
she kept the fire going, did the cooking, mixed and ground
our food, made the mash for the pigs, chased the cat out,
worked in the vegetable garden and chopped wood. She
always suffered with her back, and from time to time she
would lie down, groaning quietly; but she would soon be up
again and at her work.

She was a gentle, frail person, with the heavy features of
a countrywoman, and she always wore an old, threadbare
shawl or a spotted scarf round her head.

As with my grandfather, she was not at all impressed by
the aeroplanes or airships which were then flying around; on
the contrary, they frightened her. As she was putting me to
bed above the stove, she would tell me:

'Now, when I was a little girl we used to squeeze up
together above the stove, holding tightly to one another,
naked and barefooted and hungry, like worms, and old
Granny, when she was alive, used to say: "Now you sit there

quietly while you can, because the time will come, a terrible time, when the enemy will swarm across the country and all the land will be covered with barbed wire, and there will be metal birds flying in the sky who will peck people with their iron beaks, and that will be just before the end of the world . . ." And our teeth used to chatter with fright and we would pray: "Please, Lord, do not let us live to see such things . . ." But the Lord did not heed us and we have lived to see the day. Everything has turned out as Granny foretold—the wire and the iron birds, and I suppose we shall soon see the end of the world . . .'

It was probably in expectation of this event that Grandma had not the slightest interest in material possessions, and gave away a great deal for the good of her soul. Maybe we could have lived just a little better, but Grandma was capable of not eating herself and yet giving food away to others. She was always going down to the church with kopeks for the beggars, and then she would suddenly decide to make up parcels to send to the hospital or to friends and neighbours.

My grandfather would lose his temper and cry: 'The wastrels! Who do you think you're feeding, when we are short of food ourselves?' But Grandma would simply dismiss him with a gesture of her hand. She would keep out of his way, and the 'wastrels' would dodge out of sight round the corners whenever Grandpa returned from work. And, to avoid quarrelling and committing a sin, Grandma would go down on her knees and pray.

She had a great many icons. There was a whole collection of them in the corner of the room, with a little oil-lamp burning dimly in front of it, little heaps of incense and bunches of grasses and two wooden crosses—one for Grandpa and one for her to have in their hands in their coffins—and little notebooks in which, at her dictation, I used to write down the names of her numerous relatives, noting whether they were 'fit and well' or had 'passed away'.

The centrepiece was a Madonna, severe and suffering and with a fanatical look in her eyes. Even the child in her arms resembled a little angry old man who was saying: 'You mustn't, you mustn't!' They had such expressive faces that if you looked at them for any length of time it gave you the creeps. This icon was in a deep frame behind glass and had a richly gilded *oklad* with some strange flowers with bunches of metal berries on it . . . I wanted terribly to touch those berries, but they were out of reach behind the glass. Whenever Grandma went out to the market I would move a stool across and spend hours staring at those berries, and it was my dream that, when Grandma died, I would at last get my hands on them.

There was also a kindly-looking St Nicholas, with his white beard, a brave St George triumphing over Evil, and at the side there was another Madonna, with golden hair and a tender expression on her surprisingly familiar face. She was smiling, and the child on her knees was rather plump, apparently very pleased with life, his naked body covered with dimples.

Although this was a plain icon, without *oklad*, I was really in love with it. There are a lot of girls like that in Kurenyovka—fair-haired, soft and tender. They fall for the first good-looking lad that comes along; they get married and give birth to the same kind of tubby little children with dimples, but, unfortunately, their beauty soon fades and they grow old. My very first childhood love was the portrait of such a woman in Grandma's icon, and when later, after the war, I became a man, my first love was exactly the same sort of girl in real life.

My father was a revolutionary and a Communist, and my mother was a teacher. For that reason when I was born there was no question of having me christened. But one day, when my parents had gone out to work, Grandma wrapped me up in a shawl and took me off to the church of SS Peter and Paul, where I was immersed in the font. Grandma could not permit me to remain without the prospect of heaven when I died. She revealed this secret only after I was ten years old, when she recalled how I protested and grabbed the priest by his beard. 'There's a little bundle of flesh for you, so small and already joining up with the Antichrists of today!' he said.

Under Grandma's guidance, however, I remained a religious person until the age of six. She used to take me along to the church of SS Peter and Paul, take communion with me, stand me in front of the icons, take my little fist in her own brown, wrinkled hand and teach me how to cross myself and pronounce the magic words which, I believe, she did not herself understand. Because this is how her prayers sounded and how they have remained with me ever since:

'Afather chart in Heaven. Hallowed be Thy Name, Thy Kingdom come. Onearth as it is in Heaven. Givussisday our daily bread, and forgive us our trespassers and liver us from evil . . .'

My grandmother obviously did not know that the mysterious 'Afather' was in fact 'Our Father'. For my part I decided that God was called Afather, that his name shone out in the dark, that Granny was asking him for crusts of bread—'our daily bread'—and I repeated mechanically after her all the mistakes she made.

But then my father got to know about it, was horrified and ordered my mother to snatch me immediately from the claws of 'religion—opium of the people'. My mother, whom I trusted absolutely, had a little talk with me and, most important, said:

'There is no God. People fly up in the sky in aeroplanes and they've never seen any God there.'

I was shaken by this. I immediately passed this devastating argument on to Grandma. She got cross and replied that such godless creatures as aeroplane pilots couldn't expect to see God. I reflected on this and came to the conclusion that it would be better if God showed Himself to them or, if not to all of them, at least to the bravest and most famous airmen in the world, Chkalov or Baidukov,* who could then come back down and tell us all that there is a God; and then the arguments would be at an end. If He was up there sitting on the clouds, why did He hide Himself away, and why in any case did He let such nasty godless people fly about up there, and how, then, could He be said to be almighty?

My grandmother and I started to have long theological arguments which didn't really lead anywhere. She stuck to her opinion and I stuck to mine, but I became less and less ready to accompany her to church, and when I started school I gave up going altogether.

I used to ask my grandfather about it, but he took up a rather cautious position on questions concerning the Divinity. He recalled that when in 1890 he was working as a farm labourer and was called up into the army, he prayed a great deal not to be taken, kissed all the icons in the church, and

---

* Members of the crew of the Soviet aircraft which flew from Moscow over the North Pole to America in 1936. [Tr.]

was taken all the same. Similarly, for twenty years he had been praying for the Devil to come and take the Bolsheviks away, but they were still there. He recognized the force of the argument about the airmen but, whenever he got into debt or wanted to get hold of some feeding stuff, or simply for the sake of having someone to complain to, he would remain kneeling for long stretches, beating his head on the ground and brushing it with his beard, trying to convince the icons, beseeching and pleading with them to bring him a bit of good fortune.

Unlike my grandfather, my grandmother did not have a single enemy—nothing but friends the whole length of the street. They came running to her in trouble and in need and she gave them all good advice, lent them money, resolved their family quarrels, watched over their infants, treated them with herbs for their stomach troubles and got rid of their worms.

She used to have mysterious and unintelligible visions, and she believed in miracles, which the Soviet authorities do not recognize. I also believe in miracles, and once I actually saw one.

I was ten years old. Late in the evening Granny went out into the yard, only to come back at once crying: 'Come, quickly. God is in the sky!'

My mother simply laughed and would not go out as a matter of principle, but Grandpa and I rushed out to look, and there against the black, starlit sky a human figure could be seen shining, looking like St Nicholas. Or rather it seemed to consist of an outline made up of little star-like points close together. For some reason I was seized by such fright that I rushed back inside and hid behind the door. But Grandma was calling me happily: 'Don't be frightened, come quick and cross yourself.' But, choking with fright, I could only peer out from behind the door and see my grandparents standing in the middle of the courtyard, their faces raised up to the heavens and crossing themselves. Later the vision faded and they came back into the cottage, where for the rest of the evening my grandmother seemed somehow radiant and not of this earth, while Grandpa was lost in his thoughts and worried.

To this day I do not know what it was or how to explain it.

Grandma was very good at curing all sorts of ills. She was particularly successful in removing the effects of the evil eye. This illness has no apparent cause; it comes simply because someone has put the evil eye on you. I was very subject to it as a child.

Whenever I was ill, had a temperature, felt sick or had pains in my joints, Grandma would examine me carefully, then pour some holy water from a bottle into a cup and drop a few ashes from the fire into it, to see which ones sank and which stayed on the top. They might show that my trouble was due to brown eyes. We would then go out beneath the clear sky, Grandma holding her hand on my head while she whispered something. All I can remember from these incantations is: 'Let the evil of the brown eyes slip away like water from the goose's back.' And suddenly I would feel better, more at ease, a feeling of well-being would pass through my body, and it seemed as though I had never had any illness at all.

Grandma used to cure malaria, or 'the shivers' as they call it in the Ukraine, and eczema as well. The only thing she could not cure was the pain in her back.

MARIA FYODOROVNA KUZNETSOVA, my mother, was my grandparents' only daughter. Unlike them she did very well out of the revolution. She would have had to become a servant or a washerwoman, but teacher-training courses were started up, and she completed one in 1923, became a primary school teacher, and went on teaching for the rest of her life.

She was very beautiful, well-read and quite talented. She sang and took part in amateur dramatics in the local club, until one day my grandfather began to notice that he was having a lot of attention from the police.

Our local policeman, Vasya Kuznetsov, was always calling on us: one day the street had not been properly tidied up; on another occasion the number on the house had to be changed, and so forth. To cut a long story short, when Vasili was elected a member of the Kiev City Council, my grandfather decided that he would make a very suitable son-in-law—after all, those city councillors could get everything they wanted for themselves.

What a mistake he made!

It was in fact one of the most disastrous mistakes that

Grandpa made in his whole life. To his dying day he was never able to forgive his son-in-law for bringing nothing into the home. Even when Gramp went down to the police-station to re-register the housing record he was made to sit and wait in a queue like everybody else to be received by his own son-in-law. Vasili Kuznetsov was a real Bolshevik.

And in those days he was an honest Bolshevik. In 1937 people like him were dispatched to prison camps or to the other world to the sound of their frantic cries 'Long Live Comrade Stalin!'

He was a real Russian, from Kursk, and in 1917 he had been working at the bench when a pal came up and said: 'Vasya, they're signing up over there for the Red Guards. Shall we put our names down?' 'Sure thing!' said Vasili, and off he went. He routed the upper classes, joined the party in 1918, fought with the partisans in the Ukraine, was put in command of a machine-gun unit, and under Frunze's* command took Kakhovka, captured Perekop and pushed Wrangel† into the Black Sea.

In my eyes he was an exceptional man, and his word for me was law. On one occasion my mother decided to teach me English. We were sitting at a table when my father entered. For a while he watched me learning to say 'mother' and 'father' and then said indignantly to my mother: 'What's this then? Teaching the boy a bourgeois language? Stop it!' And we stopped.

Sometimes he would sing very well in a fine baritone voice and laugh a good deal, but for some reason he would never talk about the past very seriously.

'Well, what was it like there, fighting with the roughnecks in the Crimea?' my grandfather would ask him.

'Not so bad,' my father would reply, with a laugh. 'It's very nice in the Crimea, lots of wine. Once we'd chased out Wrangel and the bourgeois all the wine-cellars were open. We went straight to the vats. I saw one chap swimming in wine up to his very ears, just as he was, with his cartridge-belt and his boots on. I bet one of my pals my revolver that I'd drink a quarter of port.'

---

* Mikhail Vasilevich Frunze, a Bolshevik military leader and People's Commissar for Military Affairs.

† General Peter Wrangel, an anti-Bolshevik military leader in the Civil War.

'Three litres?' said Gramp with a gasp.

'And I drank it.'

'There you are, you see. What can you expect from drunk-ards like that?' said Grandpa contemptuously. 'They drank the whole of Russia away. Tell me, what did your blessed revolution bring you? Just look at the rags you've got on.'

'I was put up for the Order of the Red Banner,' my father would boast. 'It was the very first medal they gave; it had only just been introduced—Frunze and a few others were given it. But at that time we were full of real enthusiasm and we wouldn't make any concessions. We declared: "They had medals under the Tsar, and now you want to hang things on us again? Maybe you want to bring epaulettes back again? We haven't been shedding our blood for the sake of decora-tions." So I just refused. The commissar told me: "They'll throw you out of the party." I replied, in my cups: "To hell with the lot of you if that's the sort of party it is." So they turfed me out.'

'Good Lord! How do you come to be in the party now?'

'Oh, later on I applied to be taken back. They restored my membership. But they wouldn't give me the medal any more.'

'What a fool you were!' said Grandpa, shaking his closed fists. 'You would have got money for it. And what have you got now—just your one-and-only pair of policeman's trousers.'

My father had indeed finished the Civil War stripped of everything. After being demobilized he was sent to Kiev to serve in the police force. On the way there in the train he had a lot to drink and then started to play cards. Still sixty miles short of Kiev he had lost everything, including his commander's uniform, and was left with nothing but his underpants. A kind-hearted official at some wayside station presented him with some threadbare clothes and some peasant boots, in which the former commander of a machine-gun unit appeared before the authorities in Kiev. They issued him with a police uniform, and Vasili began his struggle to stop prof-iteering and to keep the streets clean.

My mother and grandmother were very fond of him and vied with each other to look after him. In their hands he soon put on weight and improved his appearance, and finally, uniting their forces, they made him his first proper suit, with which my grandfather never ceased to reproach him when-ever the occasion arose.

My father's education then consisted of two years at the parish school. He now attended an industrial training course, which he completed in the evenings. Then he left the police force and went to study at the Polytechnic Institute.

He would sit late into the night working on his drawings. But he was taken away from his studies for long periods— sent off to Uman to carry out the collectivization of the farms. My mother went down to see him there and returned quite horrified. After that he took the public examination for his diploma, and took me along with him to see him do it. When he had finished they applauded him. He became a foundry engineer.

At this point he and my grandfather began to quarrel really seriously. My father would storm at him:

'You're going too far, father-in-law, you're trying to make trouble, you're running down the revolution! Look: your daughter got herself an education, and so has your son-in-law, there's plenty of work and there's no profiteering, no competition and no swindling, but there still can be.'

'You're such a clever chap,' said Grandpa with malice in his voice. 'Just let me keep ten cows and pasture them on the meadow.'

'The meadow belongs to the collective farm. If you're fond of cows, go and join the collective.'

'Yes, that's it. You go and do forced labour in your collective farms yourself.'

At this time the differences between my father and my mother came to a head. The cause here was something different—jealousy. My mother was a very jealous person. At that time I understood nothing of what was going on, but sensed that my parents' characters were in conflict. From then on there was nothing but quarrels and tears in the home.

Then all of a sudden I learnt from Grandma that my mother and father had long ago been to court and been divorced but just couldn't make up their minds to part. At last my father tucked his drawings under his arm and went off to work at the car factory in Gorky, where he soon got married again.

It was 1937 when that happened, and later on I spent much time wondering how it was that my father, who was so set in his beliefs, did not get into trouble in that period. In those days there were only two ways a member of the party could avoid trouble—by keeping silent or by informing on others. And my father was suddenly put in charge of the foundry at the Gorky plant and was allowed to have his own flat and a car . . . But this we learnt only from letters. I no longer knew my father as he was then. My mother forbade me to write to him, but she continued to love him and never remarried.

However, when war broke out and it became obvious that the Germans were going to take Kiev, my mother sent my father some desperate telegrams asking him to give us a home. But there was never any reply to them.

My mother wept hysterically at night, and Grandma would console her:

'Never you mind, never mind, Marusya, we shall survive even under the Germans.'

'But what can *I* do under German rule?' my mother would say. 'Teach the children to sing Hitler's praises? I taught them to glorify Stalin; shall I now do the same for Hitler? I shall take little Tolya and go away, whatever happens.'

'But we shall be lost without you . . .' Grandma would reply tearfully.

It was true: the whole family depended on what my mother earned. She was a proud woman and would not apply for alimony from my father, and it was only just before the war broke out that my grandfather wore her down and we began to receive payments from the Gorky Factory; but they stopped when war broke out.

My mother was in charge of two classes in the normal day school, but she often managed to get some extra work in the evening school for adults. She was permitted to do this because she was a very conscientious and able teacher. More than once there was talk of her receiving an award, but in fact they never gave her even the smallest bonus, because she was not in the party. All she received was words of praise and demands for greater efforts. Friends of hers who were also teachers and who joined the party were given free trips to health resorts and fairly sparkled with medals. There was one such woman, without any ability and stupid as a log of wood, who let her class get completely out of hand and was quite incapable of teaching the children anything. She was made a deputy and given important public positions . . . And her class was handed over to my mother to get back into shape. Mother would sit with the children for days on end and spend her evenings correcting their notebooks. But she did not enter the party; to her the very idea seemed preposterous.

She devoted her whole life to the children, but she treated herself as if she lived in a convent. Sometimes some of her evening-school students, grown-up men with moustaches, already in jobs, would call on us with a view to courting her. My grandfather loved this, because they would bring along sausage, tins of food and bottles of drink, and he would chat with them and ask them to get him some nails or whitewash, while my mother would sit with them rather crossly for a minute or two and then go off to bed. The potential fiancés would lose patience and vanish.

More recently my mother had been sitting by the telephone on duty in the empty school, in case there should be an air-raid warning or incendiary bombs. There were no proper arrangements for evacuating teachers; we had our cases packed, but we were unable to leave, and my mother awaited the arrival of the Germans in horror, knowing they would bring nothing good.

TITUS, THE CAT, was my true friend and constant companion throughout my childhood. After some thought I decided that I would be offending against the truth if I did not mention him as a member of our family. For me at least he was always one of the family, and he played quite an important role in my life, as will appear later.

Titus was old and by inclination very affectionate, but on the surface he was restrained and serious. He did not like people to take liberties with him and knew how to distinguish precisely between those who really liked him and those who were only being condescending and trying to ingratiate themselves.

Grandma was very fond of him; but Grandpa hated him with a fierce hatred—because he didn't earn his keep.

On one occasion Gramp put Titus under his jacket and took him by tram all the way to Pushcha-Voditsa, about ten miles and all through woods.

Titus turned up at home again a week later, very hungry, frightened and miserable.

My grandfather was furious, stuffed Titus into a sack,

carried him to the other side of the city, to Demiyevka, and turned him out in the Goloseyev Forest.

Titus reappeared three months later, with a torn ear and an injured paw—he had had to get right across the vast city. After that my grandfather, rather perplexed, left him in peace.

When later I came across the remarkable story by Seton-Thompson about a cat which made its way through towns and across rivers to return to the rubbish bin in which it had been born long before, I believed every word. Cats can do that sort of thing.

Although our cat Titus learnt how to keep out of the way of Nazi aeroplanes in the trench, he had absolutely no idea of politics. He was, so to speak, the most unpolitical of all of us; and this was a mistake, because the new life was going to affect him, too.

That's the sort of people we were before the arrival of the Nazis and of the war in general: quite unimportant, not liable for military service, elderly people, a woman and a little boy—the sort of people, in short, who want war least of all and who nevertheless seem to suffer most from it.

But I have not the slightest intention of going on to prove that it is the women, children and old folk who suffer most from war. There is no need to prove this to anybody. I am going to talk a lot about people, of course, but the intention is least of all—and I underline this—*least of all* to tell a story about all sorts of personal misfortunes.

This book is about something quite different.

'What medals are those?' my grandfather asked as he studied the newspaper published by the Germans.

A whole page was taken up by an article on 'The Ukrainian People's Struggle,' an historical review with pictures of medallions bearing the heads of Prince Svyatoslav, Princess Olga, Vladimir the Baptist, Bogdan Khmelnitsky, Mazepa, Shevchenko, Lesya Ukrainka and Simon Petlyura.

It was an incredible mixture, at which even I, a small boy, stared in amazement. Svyatoslav, Olga and Vladimir were the founders of ancient Rus, at a time when there was no Ukraine or Russia but only Kievan Rus. Well, there was nothing wrong with that. Ukrainians and Russians have

common ancestors to revere. But then . . . Khmelnitsky an-
nexed the Ukraine to Russia. Mazepa wanted to separate
it again. Taras Shevchenko and Lesya Ukrainka were poets
whose praises had been sung by the Soviet authorities. But
Petlyura fought in the revolution for an independent Ukraine
and all his supporters were shot or rotted away in Soviet
prison camps.

'So they now regard Bogdan as a great man?' said my
grandfather in a tone of surprise.

'Yes.'

'That's fantastic! . . . Mazepa . . . Petlyura . . .' Gramp
stroked his beard thoughtfully. 'As for the first one, I don't
know a darned thing about him, that was ages ago, time of
Peter I. But Petlyura I saw with my own eyes—a parasite
and a rogue. The things they got up to here!'

My mother was in the other room altering my overcoat
for the winter. She came in and glanced at the paper.

'I don't believe anything any more,' she muttered. 'It's
some kind of nightmare. There were *no* good Tsars. And
they are all murderers. From Svyatoslav to Stalin.'

'You can forget about Stalin, you stupid woman!' said
Gramp cheerfully. 'Is now and ever shall be, world without
end. There'll be a good Tsar.'

'No,' said my mother. 'Maybe somewhere in Madagascar,
in America or Australia, but not in Russia. In Russia, never.'

I started reading the facts about the revival of the Church
in the Kholm region and the rapid development of art in
Zhitomir. My grandfather listened with great pleasure, nod-
ding his head gravely.

'Very good,' he said. 'The Germans know what they're
doing. Listen to me: when I was a young man and worked
for the German settlers I realized then that the Germans
know how to manage things. They like work and hate lazy
people; whatever you've earned you get. And there's no
thieving with them: when they leave their houses they just
shut them with a latch—no locks at all. And if by chance
they do catch a thief they simply beat him to death. Now
you're going to see there can be real justice in the way
things are run. A real heaven on earth!'

'There won't be anything of the sort,' my mother said in
a rather strange voice. 'And we shall have the Bolsheviks
back again.'

We didn't start arguing with her, because we knew what she was thinking, though she wouldn't say it out loud—that maybe my father, whom she loved and would go on loving to the end of her life, would come back one day.

'My goodness, how lucky you are,' Gramp said to me. 'For us, your grandmother and me, the new life has come only in our old age. And Marusya just doesn't understand anything. But you are lucky, you are young, you have a wonderful life ahead.'

I thought to myself that, after all, I really was young and everything seemed to be going right for me—the new German masters had arrived, and there would be no more thieves and no more locks. And I was filled with a mixture of alarm and surprise in anticipation of the happy days ahead.

'Never mind, to hell with 'em, I don't care what kind of icons they hang up, Petlyura or the devil himself with horns,' said Gramp in a sudden burst of venom, 'so long as it isn't that monster Stalin, that cursed bootmaker, that lousy Georgian, that black-whiskered murderer, and all his troop of beggars! My God, fancy reducing a country like this to such a level. Thousands of people struggle in queues to get a miserable bit of cloth. Under the Tsar I was the very lowest of farm labourers, yet I could have bought whole rolls of such material.'

'He's just the same as he ever was,' sighed Grandma, standing at the stove. 'Did you buy up a lot of it?'

'I could have! I could have bought it. Because it was there to be bought. There was everything! I was only a farm labourer and you a washerwoman, yet we managed to build ourselves a house. Try and build one today. In the past it was only the husband in the family who worked; even with a family of seven he was able to provide for all of them. But under these Bolsheviks the husband works, and the wife works, and the children work, and still they go short. Was it for that that they got rid of the Tsar?'

'It was bad under the Tsar!' I exclaimed.

'Yes, that's what they teach you in school now. But did you ever see those days?'

'The Tsar put people in prison and sent them into exile.'

'Oh, you're a silly little fool,' said Grandpa. 'People are sent to prison and exile at all times. Lenin caused more people to suffer than all the Tsars who went before him. And as for what Stalin did, no Tsar, not even the most brutal despot, ever dreamt of such things. We had people like Ivan the Terrible and Peter, but God apparently decided to send us a man like Stalin only just before the end of the world. We lived to see the day when a man was afraid of his own shadow. There were informers everywhere, and you were afraid to open your mouth. All you could do was shout: "Glory to the party." And the police would slap a fine on you if you didn't hang out a flag on the gate for their holidays and their blasted elections. From early in the morning, when it was scarcely light, they would bang on the windows, shouting: "All out for the elections by six o'clock, it's a national holiday, let's have a hundred per cent turn-out!" I wish my voting could have choked them! They have the nerve to put themselves up as candidates, to give themselves jobs and share everything out between them—and then tell me I've elected them! What an empty farce! Who does well under Soviet rule? The loud-mouthed scoundrel, that's who. He opens his big trap and shouts: "Our great, brilliant, wise leader, our bright sun in the sky, our beloved party which leads the way . . . !" Tra-ta-ta! And for that he gets his money and eats, the crook. They've produced nothing but parasites. For every man who really works there are three to supervise him and another six standing guard over him. And they stuff themselves like geese and ride around in motor-cars. They turned out the rich and they've made themselves even richer. Our great benefactors!'

'Goodness, you talk a lot of rubbish,' said Grandma, huddled up, frightened, in a corner by the stove. 'Keep your voice down; you can be heard right down the street!'

'There you are! I tell you: we've already got so used to talking only in whispers. I don't care if I'm heard! I want to be able to talk out loud sometime before I die. Their rule is already over; their G.P.U. is gone; their cursed secret police have bolted. And I hope Stalin croaks! And I hope their blessed party dies with him! So there! And there's nobody to arrest me any more. The last time I was able to speak aloud was under those bloody bourgeois. For twenty years I've had to hold my tongue. Listen, folks, better have Hitler, better the bourgeois or the Turks, but not those id-i-ots, robbers and murderers!'

'Oh yes, the Turks will do you a lot of good . . . And did you do so well under the old regime?' Grandma sighed. 'Have you forgotten already what your father's shack was like? Under Soviet rule you got a pension; you might at least say thank you for it. And the rich simply gave you the back of their hand.'

'The rich were no good!' Gramp shouted. (Now we're off, I thought, they'll go on arguing again till evening.) 'They were no good, but at least they knew their job. The Bolsheviks shot the rich, but what have they done themselves? Russia was always a wretched country with no real wealth— and there never would be any the way those down-and-outs ran things. And we seem to get what we deserve. We are just cattle to be driven with a stick. We need people like the Germans to teach us. They won't waste time on such nonsense. Do you want to work properly? Then work. If you don't want to, you can go to hell. And those people who have got used to working with their tongues and licking Stalin's arse—the Germans will get rid of them in no time. Praise the Lord, we have survived Thy ordeal, that Bolshevik plague! Come on then, son, read on, what else do they write there?'

I searched through the paper and found an announcement confirming Gramp's words. It said that certain unemployed males, from sixteen to fifty-five years of age, were 'refusing to accept work'. They were ordered to go down and be registered at once.

'Aha! There you are!' said Gramp with an air of triumph, wagging his finger at us.

A Word from the Author

Young people who were born in the 'forties, the 'fifties and later, who did not see or live through any of this—for you, of course, the story I have to tell is pure history.

You do not like the dry-as-dust history you were taught in

school. I don't like it either. It often seems to be no more than a long list of reigns, dates and idiotic battles which I am supposed to be impressed by. On top of that, stories of all sorts of horrors, one dirty trick after the other, stupidities on top of idiocies, until you are ashamed: can the history of civilization really be like that?

There are some entertaining old gentlemen who never tire of asserting that it is your good fortune to have had your youth in a time of peace and that the horrors of war exist for you only in books. You listen to them and you don't listen. You say you are bored. You say: To hell with you and your wars and the chaos in the world which you have brought about yourselves and which you cannot deal with; to hell with the lot of you.

Well said. I know what you mean.

But if out of my little dormer window I were to croak at you: 'Be careful!' will you understand me? I will put out my antennae and try to receive you.

I can hear a lot of music, I hear a lot of singing, the sound of breaking bottles and glass, the roar of motorcycles and then suddenly people chanting 'Mao' in chorus. The polite tones of a policeman asking the hippies to move on: they want to tidy up Piccadilly Circus.

How pleasant it is, after all: to treat all politics of whatever kind with utter contempt, to dance, to love, to drink and sleep and breathe. To live. God give you strength!

The only thing is that I can see from my little window that while some people are loving and sleeping, others are busy making handcuffs for them. Why? That's the question. There are so many would-be benefactors in the world. And they are all determined to shower benefits on the whole world. Nothing less. And for this purpose very little is needed: simply that the world should fit into the design which is taking shape God knows how in their feeble, complex-tortured minds.

They do not scorn politics; they are makers of policy. They make their own cudgel and then bring it down on other people's heads and in this manner they put their politics into practice.

Careful, my friends!

On the basis of my own and other people's experience and of experience generally, on the basis of much thinking and searching, worry and calculation, I say to you: THE PERSON WHO TODAY IGNORES POLITICS WILL REGRET IT.

I did not say I liked politics. I hate them. I scorn them. I do not call upon you to like them or even respect them. I am simply telling you: DON'T IGNORE THEM.

If you have already taken up this book and have had the patience to read this far, I congratulate you, and I would beg you in that case, please do not drop it, but read it to the end.

You see, what I am offering you is after all not an ordinary novel. It is a document, an exact picture of what happened. Just imagine that had you been born just one historical moment sooner, this might have been your life and not just something to pick up and read. Fate plays with us as it wishes—we are just little microbes crawling about the globe. You could have been me; you could have been born in Kiev, in Kurenyovka, and I could now have been you, reading this page.

So here is my invitation: enter into my fate, imagine that you are living in my shell, that you have no other, and that you are twelve, that the world is at war and that nobody knows what is going to happen next. You were just holding a newspaper in your hands with an announcement about people who refused to work. Just now. Right now.

Let us go out on the street. The German military flag is flying over the citadel. The Soviet system is finished. It is a warm autumn day and the weather is good.

The Question of Heaven on Earth

We had a long way to go, right across the city, to Zverinets, which was why Grandma had packed bread, some apples and two bottles of drinking water in her bag.

There were straw and pieces of paper and horse-droppings scattered all over Kirillovskaya Street, because nobody had cleared anything up. All the windows were broken and glass crunched underfoot. Here and there women were standing at open windows, cleaning off little crosses made of paper.

A crowd of people were drawing water from the little stream which flowed out of Babi Yar. They were scooping it up in jugs and glasses and pouring it into buckets. The water wasn't running in the mains, so the whole population had made their way with all sorts of vessels down to the streams and to the Dnieper and were putting bowls and casks beneath the drainpipes to catch the rainwater.

A tramcar was standing on its rails, just where it had been when the current had been turned off. I hopped up inside, ran down between the seats, sat in the driver's place, and started turning the handles and ringing the bell. It was marvellous—to have a whole tramcar to myself and do what I liked with it. Somebody had already screwed out the lamp-bulbs and started to remove the windows.

Tramcars were standing abandoned right along the line, some of them not only without windows but with their seats missing as well.

On the hoardings there were still some Soviet posters with caricatures of Hitler, but in one place German ones had been pasted over them. These included pictures, painted in yellow on black paper, of the happy life now to come—in one, well fed Ukrainian peasants in Cossack dress were shown grazing their cattle; in another, they were sowing seed from a basket in great swinging gestures. They were also shown happily harvesting corn with their reaping-hooks and threshing it by hand, with flails, while in the last picture the whole family were eating at table, beneath a portrait of Hitler decorated with fancy cloths.

Then my eye fell on something next to the poster which made me wonder if I was seeing straight:

JEWS, POLES AND RUSSIANS ARE THE BITTEREST ENEMIES OF THE UKRAINE!

It was in front of that poster that I began to wonder for the first time: What exactly was I? My mother was Ukrainian, my father Russian. So I was half Ukrainian and half Russian, which meant I was my own enemy.

The more I thought about it the worse it seemed. My best friends were: Shurka Matso, who was half Jewish, and

Bolik Kaminsky, who was half Polish. It was a complete mix-up. I went off at once to tell Grandma all about it.

'Don't take any notice of it, son,' she said. 'That's been written by some silly fools.'

All right, perhaps they were just fools. But they hadn't written it, they had printed it. Why should people print such terrible things and stick them on the hoardings?

In Podol the streets were swarming with people who all seemed very worried and very busy; everybody was carrying something or moving sacks of things about. An elderly couple were struggling to move a heavy cupboard with a mirror. A man with a pinched, drawn face drove past on a cart bearing a beautiful concert grand piano. All the shops, hairdressers and savings banks had their windows broken and there was broken glass all over the place.

The Germans were going around in groups and singly, and they also were carrying all sorts of junk. They didn't bother anybody, and people didn't pay much attention to them. Everybody grabbed what he could for himself; they all had serious business to attend to—it was a sort of redistribution of property throughout the city.

The nearer we got to the Kreshchatik the more officers we came across. They walked in a military manner, keeping in step, with their heads held high, all wearing caps with silver braid and peaks which came low over their foreheads.

There were red German flags hanging out. They looked strikingly similar to the Soviet ones except when they were opened out by the wind. The red flags of the Soviets had a hammer and sickle on them. The red flags of the Germans had a swastika. I was rather puzzled by those red Fascist flags.

In some places, alongside the red flags hung the blue-and-yellow striped flag of the Ukrainian nationalists. The yellow stood for corn, and the blue for the sky. A nice, peaceful flag.

It was a beautiful day. It was autumn, the chestnut trees were turning colour and the sun was still warm. Grandma pottered steadily along while I rushed about in all directions like a little puppy-dog. In this way we passed the Kreshchatik, where men were shifting whole rows of seats out of the cinema, and climbed up to Pechersk, which was swarming with troops. Then, suddenly, in front of us was the monastery.

The Kiev-Pechersk Monastery has been a place of pilgrimage for many centuries. Nearly a thousand years ago, following the conversion of ancient Rus to Christianity, the first monks moved out of the city and made a monastery in caves which they dug out in the cliffs overhanging the Dnieper. It became a stronghold of Christianity and at the same time of culture in general.

The Kiev-Pechersk Monastery now comprises a whole township, surrounded by ancient crenellated walls—a fantastic town, with churches and domes and more domes, buildings of dazzling whiteness and fanciful architecture, a white bell-tower, the tallest in Russia, the whole of it submerged in a great sea of greenery.

I had time to get to know it and to love it, because in it were gathered together all the principal museums of Kiev. The monastery came to be known as 'Museum-town'.

Within it were frightening labyrinths of caves containing the mummified relics of saints in their coffins under glass, where people were taken on excursions, by the light first of candles and later of dim electric lamps. In one of the coffins under glass lies Nestor the Scribe, author of *The Tale of Bygone Years*, from which we have been able to learn the early history of Russia.

In the centre of the monastery is the eleventh-century Cathedral of the Dormition, and beneath its walls is the grave of Kochubei* who was executed by Mazepa. Long ago Pushkin stood over it and wrote down the verses, traced out in ornamental lettering on the metal gravestone, with which his poem 'Poltava' begins. Even the founder of Moscow itself, Prince Yury Dolgoruki, is buried there.

Grandma and I sat down on the grass and began to look around. Churches, walls, domes—they all shone brightly in the sunshine and looked so beautiful and strange. We sat there for a long time in silence. And I felt myself at peace with the world.

Then Grandma said:

---

* Kochubei, a legendary bandit, executed by the nationalist leader Mazepa.

'Don't put any faith, my son, in people who wear their caps down over their eyes.'

'Why not, Gran?'

'They are bad people.'

'But why?'

'I don't know. That's what my mother taught me.'

'Are you talking about the Germans?'

'About the Germans, about the Russians, about all of them. Just think of all those scoundrels, the militia and the secret police, the way they wear their caps . . . When I had a good look at those Germans today my heart fell—they are enemies! Enemies, my child. There's trouble ahead.'

In Grandma's vocabulary the word 'enemy' covered a great many things—illnesses happened because an enemy had got into a person, and it also meant the Antichrist—'The Enemy is passing over the land.'

'Gramp says there's going to be heaven on earth.'

'Don't listen to him, he's an old gas-bag. Heaven is up above, with God. It never *has* been on earth. And never will be. How many times have people been promised heaven? Anyone who wishes can promise heaven. But the ordinary man, poor devil, still has to labour in the sweat of his brow for a crust of bread as he always did. And they are still promising him paradise . . . Your grandfather remembers the herrings and the cheap cloth, but the way I used to go out laundering for other people from dawn to dusk for fifteen kopeks a day—does he remember that? And just ask him about the way they executed Petlyura's men in Pushcha-Voditsa. Oh, what's the use of talking, I have never seen any good on this earth. Heaven is over there.'

She nodded in the direction of the monastery, and began muttering a prayer.

I began to feel alarmed, not quite myself. I had long been an atheist; after all, I went to a Soviet school, and I knew for sure that Grandma's heaven didn't exist either.

Our business in Zverinets was the following.

Grandma's niece, Aunt Olga, and her husband had built themselves a little house there just before the war. They had been working in the 'Arsenal' Factory and now they had been evacuated along with it. When they went away they let a single woman by the name of Marusya have the house to live in and look after. But they left all the documents and a power of attorney with Grandma, so that she could visit it from time to time and make sure everything was in order.

The house had not been burnt down or looted and everything seemed to be in good order. Marusya made us welcome. There was a cheerful, swarthy, unshaven man sitting with her, whom she introduced as her new husband. Grandma immediately kissed her on both cheeks and congratulated her.

The next-door neighbour Grabarev signalled to Grandma across the fence. She gasped:

'What are *you* doing here?'

'Oh, I'm in a real mess,' Grabarev said. 'You see, Martha, I helped transport the "Arsenal" Factory to the Urals, where I waited and waited for my family and kept on sending them telegrams. But there was panic here: the railway stations were being bombed, and they just couldn't get away. So then I just dropped everything and hurried back, only to find they'd just been evacuated. I wanted to rush off back again, but Kiev was already surrounded. So the family got away and I'm stuck here.'

He was a rather gloomy, bent and elderly man. I noticed that his cap was sitting on the back of his head, and I felt sorry for him.

'Oh lord,' said Grandma, 'but you're a Communist!'

'Don't you realize there are lots of Communists caught in Kiev by the encirclement? What sort of a Communist am I, in any case . . . I joined the party like everybody else, so as to survive. I was on the books and I paid my dues. They expelled me last summer—didn't you hear about it? Only they didn't carry it through to the end—the war came. Anyway, now I'm in occupied territory, there's no argument about whether I was expelled or not.'

Grandma nodded her head in sympathy.

'And what are you going to do?'

'Work. Get a job as a carpenter.'

He filled his cap full of apples and handed them to me over the fence.

We passed the night there. I slept well in the new place, but Grandma woke me in the middle of the night:

'Come on, son, wake up.' She kept tugging at me. 'Get yourself down there under the bed.'

The floor and windows were shaking from artillery fire, and there was the horrible whine of dive-bombers. Grandma and I crept underneath the bed, where there was already a blanket on the floor (what a thoughtful grandmother she was!) and we huddled up close together.

It was Soviet planes that were doing the bombing, and in the pitch darkness the bomb explosions seemed to be particularly near and heavy. The bed trembled and the whole house shook as if it was an earthquake. They weren't trying to bomb us but the railway bridge across the Dnieper near the monastery; but I'm afraid that in the darkness they dropped their bombs at random.

'Afather chart in heaven . . .' Grandma whispered fervently, prodding me at the same time. 'Go on, pray, pray! God will protect us.'

I started muttering:

'Thy Kingdom come. In heaven, as it is on earth. Our daily bread . . .'

Next morning Marusya said to Grandma:

'I have every respect for you, Martha Yefimovna, but I must ask you not to come here any more. This house is going to belong to me and my husband. The Soviets won't be coming back and you don't need it. We'll put it into our name.'

Grandma threw up her hands in dismay.

'That's what everybody is doing these days,' Marusya explained. 'The houses of people who've been evacuated are being taken over by those in need. Especially since this house belonged to a Communist, a parasite. Their day is over! It's no good you showing me your authority—it's Soviet and it's not valid any longer. And don't forget that you are related to a Communist yourself.'

Her cheerful, unshaven husband then appeared and stood in the doorway, his hands on his hips, showing his muscles. Grandma talked about a sense of duty and about God and about lodging a complaint. But he simply stood there with a cheerful grin on his face.

Our journey back was very dismal. Grandma had been utterly humiliated.

At the beginning of the Kreshchatik we were suddenly stopped by a patrol.

'You a Jew?' a soldier asked Grandma. 'Show papers!'

Grandma fumbled nervously in her bosom to get her identity card out. Near by they were checking the papers of an elderly man.

'Yes, I'm a Jew,' he said in a squeaky voice.

'Komm!' the German ordered him abruptly and the old man was led away.

'I'm a Ukrainian, a Ukrainian!' Grandma was saying in a frightened tone.

The soldier inspected her identity card, handed it back and turned away. We hurried off down Vladimir Hill to Podol. A woman told Grandma:

'This morning we saw a Jewish girl running down the street, shooting from a revolver. She killed two officers and then shot herself. Then they started hunting out Jews. They say they are checking up on them and sending them off to take down the barricades . . . Oh lord, first they had to be built, now they've got to be taken down, and it's always the local people who have to do it; they're going round from house to house chasing all the young people off to work on the barricades . . .'

There was a crowd of people standing in front of a hoarding, reading an announcement. I immediately pushed my way through to the front. It contained the first orders issued by the German Commandant. I quote from memory what it said.

FIRST. All objects taken from shops, offices or empty houses must be returned not later than tomorrow morning to the place they were taken from. Anyone not carrying out this order and retaining even the smallest trifle will be SHOT.

SECOND. The whole population must hand over all surplus food. It is permitted to retain only supplies sufficient for twenty-four hours. Anyone failing to carry out this order will be SHOT.

THIRD. All members of the population must hand in all weapons, ammunition, military equipment and radio receivers now in their possession. Weapons and radio sets are to be delivered to the Commandant's headquarters on the Kreshchatik, and military equipment to 27 Kreshchatik. Anyone not carrying out this order will be SHOT.

I really felt my hair standing on end; I turned pale and moved away. I was thinking about the brushes and the weights, the lamp and the buttons I had looted . . .

It was only then that I noticed there were no more looters at all on the streets, only small groups of people reading the orders and quickly dispersing.

Grandma and I arrived home in a very troubled state of mind. My mother rolled up my loot and abruptly ordered me:

'Take it.'

'At least he doesn't have to take the weights!' complained Grandpa. 'We've got our own scales; let them try and prove they aren't our weights; there's nothing written on them to show they came from the shop! And I'll throw the buttons down the lavatory.'

In the end they made me take back only the lamp and the brushes, since the whole street had seen me bringing them home. I was afraid, and ashamed to go down to the market. There was nobody else taking anything down there yet; I appeared to be the first. And I hung around a long time, until there was nobody passing near by. Then, choosing the moment, I stuffed the lamp through the window, threw the brushes in after, and scampered off.

At home they were debating with much concern what to do with the food. They were counting up the bags of peas, millet and dried bread. There was enough for about ten days and my grandfather was ready to go to the stake rather than hand it all over.

'They're only saying that to frighten us!' Gramp shouted plaintively. 'Let people like Shatkovsky, who stole butter by the barrel, take it back! We'll just wait and see.'

In the evening they sent me down to see what was going on. The shops were still in the same state and quite empty. But my lamp was no longer in the window, and the brushes had gone too.

Nobody returned anything or handed anything over. But Grandpa hid the food in the shed under the straw, just in case. Our bundles and cases were in the trench under the ground. And we had never had any weapons or radio set.

Next day a couple of soldiers appeared and alarmed us once again. But they only went round the house, took an old head-scarf of Grandma's and went off without saying a word. We watched them, dumbfounded, as they walked away; we just couldn't get used to them. Grandma said:

'It's true, you see, you really don't need any locks; you might just as well shut the house with a piece of stick . . . The three days are already up and they're still looting.'

'Means they've extended it to five days,' Gramp insisted. 'Kiev's a big city, a capital, it's not so easy to loot, so they've given 'em five days. Just mark my words, on the twenty-fourth it'll all be over.'

He was making a great mistake.

On September 24th it was all just beginning.

The Kreshchatik

On September 19th, 1941, German troops entered the Kreshchatik from both ends. One column came from the direction of Podol—those were the ones we had run into already in Kurenyovka, brash and cheerful, mostly riding in cars. The other column came in from the opposite direction, across the Bessarabka, and they were on motorcycles, straight from the battlefield, grimy, moving in swarms, spreading out across the pavements and filling the whole of the Kreshchatik with noise and petrol fumes.

It was like some colossal, sprawling military parade, with continual hold-ups, collisions and confusion. The local people stood watching at their front doors; others came running up to stare; some lent a willing hand to move the anti-tank barriers away or started pulling Soviet posters off the walls.

Obviously according to a previously arranged plan, troops began to occupy the empty buildings on the Kreshchatik. There were in fact more shops and offices on the street than living accommodations, and practically all the occupants of the flats had been evacuated. It was on this main street of Kiev that all the party officials, officers of the secret police and famous actors had been living—and they, of course, had all departed. The Kreshchatik was deserted.

The German command had taken a fancy to the building on the corner of the Kreshchatik and Proreznaya Street, which had the popular Children's World shop on the ground floor. The German staff occupied the enormous Continental Hotel. The Doctor's Club was converted into a club for German officers.

Everything had been carefully thought out and was put efficiently into practice in the shortest possible time: trailers with electric generators were set up right on the pavements to provide current, and water was brought in tankers from the Dnieper.

It looked like a lively and businesslike take-over by guests who had arrived with a lot of noise, and who were not there to amuse themselves but to get on with their business, and the people of the city watched them expectantly.

It was because of the troops passing through that the looting of the Kreshchatik did not start at once, but later—in fact, at night, when it became clear that the troops were busy with their own affairs. But once the first cautious looters had taken sacks full of things from under the very noses of the Germans, people rushed down to the Kreshchatik from all over the city.

By morning all the shop-windows had been knocked out and figures could be seen moving about the Kreshchatik carrying rolls of carpet and piles of crockery, bundles of children's satchels and even curtains out of the theatres. And there were Germans busy among them as well. They chased the looters away, uttering threats and clouting people over the head, and then started looting themselves. It was like an overturned ant-heap—everybody was carrying something somewhere.

After lunch-time the Bessarabka market suddenly came to life: the first stallholders produced hot pies with peas and boiled potatoes, assuming, quite rightly, that the looters would get hungry. They had no idea what prices to ask: they just demanded a packet of home-grown tobacco and let their customers eat their fill.

Two barber's shops opened up. The enterprising Jewish barbers guessed correctly—the German officers crowded in.

There was such a happy mood about the place, a sort of holiday spirit, and the sun was shining, which also helped to put people in a good mood.

The keys of the locked flats belonging to the party officials and bureaucrats who had fled were in the keeping of the house-managers. The Germans went around the flats with them or a workman, opening them up and taking them over or grabbing anything they took a fancy to.

It was a chance for all the house-managers and people employed in the buildings, the watchmen and lift-attendants, to get their hands on things. They took over the five- or six-roomed flats belonging to officials of the city's party organization, which were full of things most ordinary people could never dream of having (especially if you bear in mind that only recently ordinary people would have had to fight for a couple of days in a queue to get a few yards of cloth!). They were dragging stuff from all parts of the building into their new flats, turning them into store-rooms. There was a tale about one workman who moved from the basement to the first floor and collected twelve grand pianos, stacking them one on top of the other.

Nobody ever returned any of the loot when the Commandant's orders appeared. It seemed rather pointless to do so. For the sake of his twelve pianos the stupid workman might well have been shot, but it was out of the question for him to go and hand them back himself. He just couldn't do it!

But the hated weapons and the dangerous radio receivers were taken back. Maybe one person took his back first and then others took fright and took theirs back too. Especially gas-masks—they took a lot of those back. Once you had returned a gas-mask you felt you had at least partially carried out the order. People threw them down in a pile in the premises of the café and cake shop opposite the Commandant's headquarters, at 27 Kreshchatik, and the mountain of gas-masks soon filled the café right up to the ceiling.

The first people to be called together (from lists of names and addresses found in the personnel department) were the employees of Radio Kiev. The offices of the radio and the studios were on the corner of the Kreshchatik and Institute Street. The German who had just been appointed head of the radio stepped out on to the platform, surveyed the people gathered in the hall and started in a very unusual way:

'All Jews stand up!'

A deathly silence descended on the hall. Nobody stood up; people simply moved their heads a little.

'Jews stand up!!' the German repeated more loudly, turning red in the face.

Again nobody stood up.

'All Yids get up!!!' he screamed, reaching for his revolver.

It was only then that in various parts of the hall people began to stand up—musicians, violinists and cellists, a few technicians, some editors. With heads hanging they made their way to the exit.

The new boss waited until the door had closed behind the last of them. Then, in broken Russian, he announced to those remaining that the world must hear 'the voice of free Kiev'. In the next few days, he said, the radio station must be quickly brought back into operation, and from the following day everybody must return to work. Anyone who refused to work would be regarded as a saboteur. The time for peaceful, creative work had come.

People got up from their places, subdued and perplexed, and began to leave. At that moment the first explosion was heard.

It was on September 24th, at four o'clock in the afternoon.

The building housing the German headquarters with the Children's World on the ground floor was blown up. The explosion was of such a force that it blew out the windows not only on the Kreshchatik but also on the streets running parallel with it, Pushkin and Mering Streets. Glass came crashing down from the different floors on to the heads of the Germans and passers-by, many of whom were injured.

On the corner of Proreznaya a column of flames and smoke rose into the air. People started running, some to get away from the explosion and others, on the contrary, to get closer to it and see what had happened.

In the first few minutes the Germans weren't quite sure what to do, but then they linked arms, cordoned off the burning building and held everyone who happened to be near the house or in its courtyards at the time.

They had dragged out a lanky, red-haired youth and

started beating him up mercilessly; the rumour went round that he was a partisan who had taken a radio set into Children's World, supposedly to hand it in, and the set had contained an infernal machine.

Everyone who had been arrested was pushed into the cinema next door, so that it was soon crammed full of people, most of them injured, beaten up and covered in blood.

At that moment, in the ruins of the very same building, came the sound of a second explosion of equal force. This time the walls collapsed, and the German headquarters were transformed into a pile of rubble. The Kreshchatik was covered in a layer of dust, and a cloud of smoke hung heavy above it.

The third explosion sent the building opposite into the air—the one with the café and cake shop, stuffed full of gas-masks, and the German offices.

The Germans rushed out of the cinema shouting: 'Run for it, get away from here! The whole Kreshchatik is going up!' They dashed off, every man for himself, and after them went the people who had been arrested, including the red-haired lad.

People were in an amazing state of panic. The Kreshchatik was indeed being blown up.

Explosions could be heard at unequal intervals in the most unexpected and scattered parts of the Kreshchatik; there was no pattern to be seen in the way they happened.

The explosions continued throughout the night, spreading into the adjoining streets. The magnificent building of the circus was blown up, and the twisted remains of its dome were hurled right across the street. Next to the circus the Continental Hotel, now occupied by the Germans, was in flames.

Nobody will ever know how many Germans, along with their equipment and documents, or how many civilian inhabitants and their property perished in those explosions and the fire, because neither the Bolsheviks nor the Nazis have ever provided any information on this subject.

The weather at the time was very dry, with the result that the fire which developed could be compared, I suppose, only with the famous fire which swept Moscow during Napoleon's campaign in 1812.

Large numbers of boxes of ammunition and bottles of an inflammable liquid for attacking tanks had been stored on the upper floors and in the attics of the buildings, because the Soviet military command had intended to defend Kiev street by street, which was why the whole city had trenches dug all over it and barricades across the streets. When the fire got to them, those boxes went off with a distinctive dull explosion, something like a sigh, which sent streams of fire pouring over the whole building. It was that which finished off the Kreshchatik.

The Germans, who had entered the city so triumphantly and had settled in so comfortably, were now rushing around on the Kreshchatik like mice in a mousetrap. They didn't understand what was going on and they didn't know where to put themselves or what to try and save.

But it must be said, to give them their due, that they got together teams of men who ran from house to house throughout the centre of Kiev, persuading the people living there to get out on the street and evacuating children and invalids. They didn't have to do a lot of persuading. The people—some of them with bundles which they had managed to grab, others with only what they stood up in—were running to the parks above the Dnieper, towards Vladimir Hill, to Shevchenko Boulevard and the stadium. Many of them were suffering from burns or other injuries.

The Germans cordoned off the whole of the centre of the city. But the fire was spreading: the two parallel streets, Pushkin and Mering, were already ablaze, as were the streets which crossed the Kreshchatik—Proreznaya, Institute, Karl Marx, Friedrich Engels and the Arcade. It seemed as though the whole city was being blown up.

Before the war they had started to build an underground railway in Kiev, and now rumours started to go round that it was not really an underground but just excavations in which to lay enormous mines under the whole of Kiev. Rather more likely were the stories which later began to circulate about the lorries which people remembered seeing driving into the courtyards after dark, and the men in N.K.V.D. uniform who had unloaded something into the basements. But the N.K.V.D.'s cars were turning up everywhere in those days after dark, and they were up to all sorts of tricks! And anyone who happened to see them from

behind a curtain preferred not to notice but to forget. So
nobody had any idea where the next explosion was going to
take place, which is why they scurried away from the buildings and as far as they could from the Kreshchatik.

The Germans quickly had some long hose-pipes brought
in by plane from somewhere, and laid them all the way from
the Dnieper, through the Pioneers' Park, and began pumping
water up by means of powerful pumps. But the water did
not reach the Kreshchatik, because somebody cut the hoses
in the bushes in the park.

Up above the gigantic bonfire, which was what central
Kiev had become, powerful currents of air formed, like tubes,
which swept up burning pieces of wood and paper and
scattered them as far as the Bessarabka and Pechersk. The
Germans, the police, workmen and volunteers were scrambling up on to all the roofs, throwing sand on the burning
pieces of wood and stamping out the fires. People made
homeless by the fire spent the night in the anti-aircraft
shelters and in the bushes on the boulevards and in the parks.

The Germans were unable even to retrieve the bodies of
their own people or of the local inhabitants who had been
killed; they were burnt to cinders. Everything the Germans
had looted had gone up in flames, and so had the six-
roomed flats crammed with pianos, the radio station, the
cinemas and the big stores.

After a few desperate days spent fighting the fire the
Germans gave up and abandoned what was now a furnace in
which there appeared to be nothing left alive, and simply
watched the fire from a distance.

The Kreshchatik, now completely empty of people, continued to burn. From time to time the distant sound of falling
timbers in some building would indicate that a floor had
caved in or a wall collapsed, and then more sparks and more
burning splinters than usual would be seen in the sky.

The smell of burning pervaded the whole city; at night it
glowed red and, according to what they said later, the glow
could be seen hundreds of miles away, serving as a beacon
for aircraft.

The actual explosions came to an end on September 28th.
The main fire continued for two weeks, and during that
time it was cordoned off by soldiers armed with Sten guns.
When the cordon was removed and the Germans went in

again, there were in fact no streets left: buildings had collapsed on both sides of them and blocked them up. It took about a month of intensive work to clear a way through. The scorched ruins went on smoking for a long time; even in December I saw with my own eyes wisps of smoke still coming out from beneath the rubble.

The blowing up of the Kreshchatik and its destruction by fire, which no one has ever described before, ought in my opinion to be recorded as one of the principal turning-points in the history of the war.

To start with, it was the first time in history that an operation of that kind and on that scale had been prepared with such care and discipline. I must explain just what the Kreshchatik meant to Kiev. Comparatively speaking, it was like blowing up the whole of the centre of Moscow as far as the ring-road, the Nevsky Avenue in Leningrad and all the streets around it, or, say, the heart of Paris as far as the great boulevards. Until the Kreshchatik was destroyed it was difficult to imagine such a thing happening at all. But the N.K.V.D. found it possible to imagine and opened, you might say, a new page in the history of warfare. It was only after the Kreshchatik affair that both German and Soviet authorities made it a rule to examine carefully every building they occupied and write on it: 'Checked for mines.' The destruction of bridges and of military and industrial installations in the course of a retreat is understandable. But this was a case of destroying the completely peaceful heart of a city, with all its shops and theatres.

In the second place, many people regarded the Kreshchatik operation as the first demonstration of genuine patriotism on such a scale. Not a single capital in Europe had given Hitler the sort of welcome Kiev gave him. The city of Kiev had no longer been capable of defending itself; the army had abandoned it, and the city itself seemed to be prostrate at the mercy of the enemy. But it destroyed itself by fire under the very eyes of the Germans and sent many of them to their graves as it did so. They had indeed entered the city as they had become accustomed to entering the capitals of Western Europe, preparing to celebrate. But instead they received such a blow that the very earth beneath their feet caught fire. Where had that ever happened before?

On the other hand, to destroy the ancient and beautiful centre of a capital city for the sake of giving the enemy one good patriotic slap in the face and killing a great many civilians as you did it—was that not going too far? And now we come to some very old aspects of the affair.

The Soviet authorities never, either at the time or later, admitted their responsibility for the destruction of the Kreshchatik. On the contrary, they attributed it to the Germans. They declaimed in the press about Fascist barbarism and later, after the war, stuck posters over the ruins and published articles in all the papers saying: 'We shall restore the Kreshchatik, pride of the Ukraine, callously destroyed by the German invaders.'

The whole of Kiev, the whole Ukraine, the whole population knew perfectly well that the Kreshchatik was destroyed by the Soviet authorities. Nevertheless they had it drummed into them that it was the work of the cursed Germans. Which was like saying that the Germans were supposed to have entered a beautiful city, taken over its magnificent central part, and then spent five days planting mines underneath themselves, so that they could blow themselves up. What for? To this there was a clear answer: the Nazis were barbarians. No one would quarrel, of course, with this statement. But the fact remains that the Kreshchatik was blown up by the Bolsheviks.

It was not until 1963 that the K.G.B. issued for popular consumption a 'Report by the Committee for State Security of the Council of Ministers of the Ukrainian Republic concerning acts of sabotage and reconnaissance carried out by a group of underground fighters in the city of Kiev under the leadership of I. D. Kudrya'. This report does not discuss the destruction of the Kreshchatik; it only mentions certain 'explosions', avoiding altogether the word 'Kreshchatik'.

It appears from the report that I. D. Kudrya, known as 'Maxim', was an employee of the security service, on whose instructions he had been left behind in Kiev, along with a group including D. Sobolev, A. Pechenev, R. Okipnaya, E. Bremer and others. Here is a quotation:

Fires and explosions continued in the city, and were especially violent from September 24th to 28th, 1941.

Among the places blown up were the shop containing the radio sets taken from the population, the German military headquarters, the cinema used by the Germans and other buildings. Although nobody can say with certainty who actually organized these explosions, which sent hundreds of the 'victors' to their graves, there can be no doubt that people connected with the 'Maxim' group had a hand in it. The most important achievement was that the explosions let the arrogant Nazi 'victors' know they were not masters of the territory they had invaded.

Later on it is revealed that D. Sobolev died in the course of one of his numerous operations, and that A. Pechenev shot himself as he lay wounded in bed when Gestapo men came to arrest him. Kudrya 'Maxim', R. Okipnaya and E. Bremer were captured in Kiev in July 1942, but there is no reliable account of how they died.

In 1965 *Pravda* published, without any commentary, a decree posthumously awarding I. D. Kudrya the title of Hero of the Soviet Union. It had apparently required more than twenty years of vacillation over this decision to make absolutely sure that Kudrya was really dead and that he hadn't slipped across to the Germans and was working somewhere in the West.

The only institution which could fill in the details of the long story of the Kreshchatik is the K.G.B. But it prefers to keep them to itself. So there are a great many things which remain unclear and unverified. There are plenty of rumours and stories of heroic deeds: of a police agent who threw his life away when he blew himself up in the vestibule of the Continental Hotel—pressing the detonator and perishing on the spot. There is another story about a desperate character who blew up the Shantser Cinema during a film show, when it was packed full of Germans. There are many more like that. It is difficult to check them. But one thing is quite certain: the laying of the mines was well planned and carried out very thoroughly long before the Germans took Kiev, and that the more important mines had a mechanism which made it possible to detonate them as and when required.

There are witnesses still living who saw the explosives being delivered on N.K.V.D. lorries a month or six weeks before they were exploded. It did not occur to them then that mines were being laid, because the Germans were a long way from Kiev and the newspapers and radio stations were full of assurances that Kiev would never at any price be abandoned to the enemy. But the secret police apparently had a better idea of the true situation.

What was the real reason for blowing up the Kreshchatik, then?

I shall give you my opinion, which is the opinion of the majority of people living in Kiev, and you can judge for yourselves.

What was blown up was the centre, which had belonged to the party and government elite, the bureaucracy and the secret police themselves. They had not, of course, wanted to abandon their flats and comfortable armchairs. So they decided to arrange a surprise for the Germans, and then, once they had blown up the Kreshchatik along with the Germans, they were so busy gloating over what they had done that they didn't even have the wit to make it appear like an act of patriotism and put all the blame on the enemy. This is the sense behind the passage in the admission that was later squeezed out of them and which appeared in their report that 'these explosions let the arrogant Nazi "victors" know that they were not masters of the territory they had invaded.'

By blowing up the purely civilian buildings on the Kreshchatik, however, they had inflicted an appreciable military loss, and the fact that three times as many civilians perished in the course of it never bothered the Soviet authorities. Especially since, according to Soviet thinking, people who stayed behind on occupied territory were being disloyal to the Soviet regime, which meant they did not count as people.

The Soviet police agents held on for five whole days, their hands on the detonators, to make sure that as many Germans as possible should move into the Kreshchatik and to decide on the order in which the buildings were to be blown up. The first to go up was the German headquarters. And still those five days made it possible to put all the blame on the Germans.

But there was another, much more sinister, aspect of the Kreshchatik affair: it was intended to infuriate the Germans, so that in their fury they would no longer handle the population with kid gloves. The Soviet State Security organs deliberately provoked the Germans into being ruthless. As it happened, the Germans were good pupils when it came to that.

And the Germans fell for it. They revealed their reply to the Kreshchatik five days later, on September 29th, 1941.

The Germans made no official statement about the Kreshchatik affair; nor did they punish anyone for it publicly. But they began to look very stern and bitter; the smiles vanished completely from their faces. It was rather frightening to look at their grimy, worried countenances; it seemed as if they were preparing something.

The Order

On the morning of September 28th, Ivan Svinchenko from Litvinovka village turned up unexpectedly at our house. He was on his way home out of the encirclement.

He was a peasant, a decent, open-hearted, more or less illiterate man, a tremendously hard worker and the father of a large family. Before the war, whenever he came from the country to the city market, he would sleep at my grandparents'. He never forgot to bring me some simple present from the village, but I was shy of him, perhaps because he had a speech defect: sometimes as he was speaking he would seem to choke and all you could hear was a sort of indistinct mumbling—'bala-bala'. It was a very strange defect.

Like all people who worked on the collective farms in the neighbourhood, he had always turned up covered in mud and dressed in rags and tatters. But now he appeared in such rags and in such a frightful condition we could hardly recognize him. Somewhere he had managed to swap his army uniform for some old clothes.

This is what had happened to him.

Ivan Svinchenko had been defending Kiev along with his unit when the order had come to retreat, and they had crossed over on to the left bank of the Dnieper to Darnitsa. For a long time they wandered about aimlessly through the woods and along the cart-tracks, were bombed and raked with machine-gun fire from the air, and none of their officers had the slightest idea what to do. Then the officers themselves disappeared altogether and the men started shouting that they should go home. Everybody had the feeling the war was over.

But in the depths of the forest they ran into some partisans led by N.K.V.D. officers, well equipped, with transport and plenty of food; and they had a lot of weapons. The partisans warned of the dangers of falling into German hands and made Ivan join them. But he hated the N.K.V.D. and was longing to get home.

'So I hung around a bit—*bala-bala*—till it was dark, and then skipped!' he explained.

He spent several days walking through the woods and open fields and everywhere he went he came across people like himself who didn't want to fight. What were they supposed to be fighting for, they asked—for the collective farms, for the prison camps at Kolyma, to go on being poor? When all around was their native Ukraine and somewhere not far away a home, wife and children? The Ukrainians went off to their homes; the Russians, whose homes were where the Soviets were, wandered about not knowing where they were going, or else they went off in search of the Germans to give themselves up.

Ivan came across a column of a couple of hundred men who had surrendered in that way. There were just two Germans in charge of them and even they had their obviously unnecessary rifles slung over their shoulders. Ivan fell in with them, and the other men welcomed him with much shouting and whistling—they were glad that their fighting days were over and that they were going to relax as prisoners. But Ivan was unlike the others; he did not want to relax; he kept thinking about his family.

'So I went along with them for a bit—*bala-bala*—jumped into a hole and then skipped away!'

My grandmother gave the starving Ivan something to eat and sighed her sympathy. My grandfather went out on to the street for some reason, but almost at once his footsteps could be heard again on the porch and he came rushing into the room:

'I've got great news for you! . . . From tomorrow there

won't be a single Yid left in Kiev. It seems it's true what they said about them setting fire to the Kreshchatik. Thank the Lord for that! That'll put paid to them getting rich at our expense, the bastards. Now they can go off to their blessed Palestine, or at any rate the Germans'll deal with 'em. They're being deported! There's an order posted up.'

We all dashed outside. A notice printed on cheap grey wrapping-paper, with no heading and no signature, had been stuck on the fence:

All Yids living in the city of Kiev and its vicinity are to report by 8 o'clock on the morning of Monday, September 29th, 1941, at the corner of Melnikovsky and Dokhturov Streets (near the cemetery). They are to take with them documents, money, valuables, as well as warm clothes, underwear, etc.
Any Yid not carrying out this instruction and who is found elsewhere will be shot.
Any civilian entering flats evacuated by Yids and stealing property will be shot.*

After that followed the same text in Ukrainian and then, lower down, in very small type, the same again in German. It was a sort of three-level poster.

I read it over twice, and for some reason it made me shudder. It was written so very harshly, with a sort of cold hatred. What's more, it was a cold day with a lot of wind and the street was deserted. I didn't go back indoors but, rather disturbed, I wandered off in the direction of the market, not quite knowing why.

Three plots away from us was the large holding belonging to the collective vegetable farm. It was full of little mud huts, wooden sheds and cow-stalls one on top of the other, and it was there that a great many Jews lived, terribly poor, uneducated and in pitiful conditions. I glanced into the yard: it was in a state of silent panic; people were rushing from one hut to the other, carting things in and out.

The same notice had been put up in other parts of the city. I stopped and read it through again, still not quite grasping its meaning.

* Central State Archives of the October Revolution, Moscow. Fund 7021, index 65, item 5.

In the first place, if they had really decided to deport the Jews as a reprisal for the Kreshchatik affair, why should it affect all of them? Say a dozen people might have been involved in the explosions, but why should the others have to suffer? True, the explanation might be that the Germans could not discover who were the actual incendiaries, so they had simply decided to deport everybody. Cruel, but true, perhaps?

In the second place, there were no such streets in Kiev as Melnikovsky and Dokhturov, whereas Melnikov and Degtyarev Streets did exist. The order had obviously been written by the Germans themselves with the help of bad translators. These streets really were close to the Russian and Jewish cemeteries in Lukyanovka, and next to it was the Lukyanovka railway goods-yard. So they were going to put them on a train? But where to? Were they really going to Palestine, as Gramp suggested?

But again this was very cruel: to expel thousands of people by force from the places where they had been born and transport them to places where they hadn't a thing to their names —how many of them would get ill and die on the way? And all because a few of them turned out to be incendiaries?

Did that mean that Shurka Matso would also have to go? But his mother was a Russian and was divorced from his father, and Shurka hadn't seen his father for ages, like me. Did it mean that Shurka would be taken off on his own? That his mother would stay and he would go? I began to feel sorry for him, sorry to have to part from him for ever.

Then suddenly—to my surprise, sort of spontaneously—I began to talk to myself in my grandfather's words, with that same intonation and malice: So what? Let 'em go off to their Palestine. They've grown fat enough here! This is the Ukraine; look how they've multiplied and spread out all over the place like fleas. And Shurka Matso—he's a lousy Jew too, crafty and dangerous. How many of my books has he pinched! Let 'em go away; we'll be better off without 'em— my Gramp is a clever chap, he's right.

With these thoughts in my mind I went as far as the Kurenyovka police station, where my Dad once worked. It had been taken over by the German police and had a portrait of Hitler posted up in the window. He had a stern, almost sinister look and was wearing a peaked cap with lots of braid on it. And the cap was pulled right down over his eyes.

I could not, of course, miss such a rare spectacle as the deportation of the Jews from Kiev. As soon as it was light I was out on the street.

They started arriving while it was still dark, to be in good time to get seats in the train. With their howling children, their old and sick, some of them weeping, others swearing at each other, the Jews who lived and worked on the vegetable farm emerged on to the street. There were bundles roughly tied together with string, worn-out cases made from plywood, woven baskets, boxes of carpenters' tools . . . Some elderly women were wearing strings of onions hung around their necks like gigantic necklaces—food supplies for the journey . . .

In normal times, of course, all the invalids, sick people and older folk stay indoors and are not seen. But now all of them had to turn out—and there they were.

I was struck by how many sick and unfortunate people there are in the world.

Apart from that there was another factor. The men who were fit had already been mobilized into the army and only the invalids had been left behind. Everybody who had been able to get himself evacuated, who had enough money, who had managed to go along with his office or plant or who had influence somewhere—all those had already left. A shopkeeper from Kurenyovka by the name of Klotsman had managed to get away along with his family even after Kiev had been cut off. I don't know whether it's true, but he was said to have paid a fabulous sum to some airmen who put him and all his belongings into a plane. (When the war was over he turned up again safe and sound in Kurenyovka.)

So those who were left in the city were the really poor people, the sort of people described by Sholom Aleichem, and it was they who now came swarming out on to the street.

How can such a thing happen? I wondered, immediately dropping completely my anti-Semitism of the previous day. No, this is cruel, it's not fair, and I'm so sorry for Shurka Matso; why should he suddenly be driven out like a dog? What if he did pinch my books; that was because he forgets things. And how many times did I hit him without good reason?

Deeply affected by what I saw, I went from one group of people to the other, listening to what they were saying; and the closer I got to Podol the more people I found out on the streets. They were standing in the gateways and porches, some of them watching and sighing, others jeering and hurling insults at the Jews. At one point a wicked-looking old woman in a dirty head-scarf ran out on to the roadway, snatched a case from an elderly Jewess and rushed back inside the courtyard. The Jewess screamed after her, but some tough characters stood in the gateway and stopped her getting in. She sobbed and cursed and complained, but nobody would take her part, and the crowd went on their way, their eyes averted. I peeped through a crack and saw a whole pile of stolen things lying in the yard.

I also overheard someone say that in one place a cabby who had been specially hired to transport the luggage belonging to several families simply whipped up his horse and dashed off down a side-street, and they never saw him again.

The Glubochitsa was thick with people making their way up to Lukyanovka; it was just a sea of heads—the Jews of Podol were on the move. What a place that Podol was! It was the most poverty-stricken part of Kiev, and you could recognize it simply by the smell—a mixture of things rotting, cheap fat and washing hung out to dry. Here from time immemorial had lived the poor of the Jewish community, the poorest of the poor—the shoemakers, tailors, the coal-merchants, the tinsmiths, porters, harness-makers, confidence tricksters and thieves . . . The courtyards were devoid of grass or greenery, with evil-smelling rubbish tips, tumble-down sheds swarming with great fat rats, lavatories which were just holes in the ground, clouds of flies, miserable streets which were either dusty or muddy, houses in a state of collapse and damp cellars—that was Podol, noisy, overcrowded and utterly dreary.

My head was simply bursting from the noise and shouting. From all sides came the questions: Where are they taking them? What are they doing with them?

In one crowd only two words could be heard: 'A ghetto, a ghetto!' A middle-aged woman came up, greatly alarmed, and interrupted: 'Dear people, this is the end of us!' The old women were weeping, though it sounded almost as if they were singing. A rumour went around that some Karaimes had passed through (it was the first time I had heard this name, which is apparently given to a small Semitic people)— very old men wearing robes reaching right down to the ground, who spent the whole night in their synagogue, then emerged and declared: 'Children, we are going to our deaths; prepare yourselves. Let us meet it courageously, as Christ did.'

This caused some indignation: fancy sowing panic in people like that! But it was already known for a fact that one woman had poisoned her children and then herself, so as not to have to go. And near the Opera a young girl had thrown herself out of a window and was still lying on the street covered with a sheet and nobody bothered to remove the body.

Suddenly there was a new cause for concern; people started saying that ahead, on Melnikov Street, a barrier had been put up, and that they were letting people in but not back out again.

At this point I myself took fright. I was tired, my head was buzzing from everything that was going on, and I was scared lest I should be unable to get back and they would cart me off. So I began to force my way back in the opposite direction to the crowd, worked my way out of it and then wandered for a long time through the deserted streets, along which a few latecomers were practically running, to the accompaniment of whistles and shouts from the doorways.

When I got home I found my grandfather standing in the middle of the courtyard, straining to hear some shooting that was going on somewhere. He raised his finger.

'Do you know what?' he said with horror in his voice. 'They're not deporting 'em. They're *shooting* 'em.'

Then, for the first time, I realized what was happening.

From Babi Yar came quite distinctly the sound of regular bursts of machine-gun fire: ta-ta-ta, ta-ta . . .

It was the sort of rather quiet, unexcited, measured firing

you heard when they were training. Our Babi Yar lies between Kurenyovka and Lukyanovka: you have to cross it to get to the cemetery. They had driven from there, from Lukyanovka, it seemed, into our ravine.

Grandpa looked puzzled and frightened.

'Maybe it's fighting?' I suggested.

'That's not fighting!' Gramp shouted plaintively. 'The whole of Kurenyovka is already talking about it. Some folk have climbed trees and seen what's going on. Victor Makedon ran all the way back; he went down with his wife, she's a Jewess, and he only just escaped being taken himself. Oh, Mother of God, Queen of Heaven, what *is* this, why do they do that to them?'

We moved indoors. But it was impossible just to sit there. The firing went on and on.

Gramp went across to Makedon to hear what had happened and found a lot of people assembled. The young man (he had been married just before the war broke out) was relating how, down there, they were simply glancing at people's identity cards and then throwing them straight on to a bonfire. But he had shouted: 'I'm a Russian!' so they had dragged his wife from him and taken her off to the ravine, and the police had driven him away . . .

It was cold outside; there was a biting wind blowing, like the previous day. All the same I went outside and strained my ears. Grandma brought out my coat and hat and also stood listening and wringing her hands and muttering: 'Oh God, there are women and small children there . . .' I had the impression she was crying. I turned round, and she crossed herself and, with her face to Babi Yar, she said:

'Afather, whichart in heaven . . .'

At night the firing stopped, but it started up again in the morning. The word went around Kurenyovka that thirty thousand people had been shot on the first day, and that the others were sitting there waiting their turn.

My grandmother came from the neighbours with some news. A fourteen-year-old boy, the son of the collective-farm stableman, had come running into the farmyard and was telling the most frightful stories: that they were being made to take all their clothes off; that several of them would be lined up, one behind the other, so as to kill more than one at a time; that the bodies were then piled up and earth thrown over them, and then more bodies were laid on top; that there were many who were not really dead, so that you could see the earth moving, that some had managed to crawl out, only to be knocked over the head and thrown back into the pile. They hadn't noticed him; he had managed to sneak away and had run all the way home.

'We must hide him!' my mother said. 'In the trench.'

'Come on, son,' exclaimed Grandma. 'Quickly. We'll hide him away, feed him and take care of him.'

I hurried across to the farmyard.

But it was already too late. At the gate there was standing a cart drawn by a spindly horse, and a German soldier with a whip was sitting in it. Another soldier, his rifle under his arm, was leading a white-faced boy from the yard. In fact he was not even leading him; they seemed to be walking side by side.

They went to the cart and climbed on to it, one on each side, and the soldier moved the hay aside to make the boy more comfortable. He put his rifle down on the straw, and the boy lay on his side resting on his elbow. He eyed me with his big brown eyes quite calmly and indifferently.

The soldier cracked his whip, urged the horse on, and the cart moved off—all as simply and with as little excitement as though they were going off to the fields to make hay.

The women in the yard were arguing loudly with each other and I went up to listen. Some were protesting, others argued:

'She did right. Finish with the lot of 'em. That's for the Kreshchatik.'

It was a Russian woman who lived on her own on the collective farm, working with the cows.

She had seen the boy run into his own home. She had gasped with alarm, listened to his story, put a jug of milk on the table and ordered him to sit quietly and not to go outside so that no one should see him, and then she had gone off to the police to give him away. What's more, when she got back she watched over him until the Germans came with the cart.

There was one woman, Dina Mironovna Pronicheva, the mother of two children and an actress at the Kiev puppet theatre, who managed to escape from Babi Yar itself at that time. She is the only eye-witness to come out of it, and I am now going to tell her story, as I wrote it down from her own words, without adding anything of my own.

Babi Yar

She went down to see the order for herself, read it through quickly and went away; nobody stayed very long at notice-boards or got into conversations.

Throughout that day and into the evening they discussed the situation and what to do about it. She had a mother and father, both very old and frail. Just before the Germans arrived her mother had come out of hospital after an operation, and everybody wondered whether she would be able to travel. The old folk were quite sure that at Lukyanovka they would be put aboard a train and taken off to Soviet territory.

Dina's husband was Russian, so she had a Russian name and moreover didn't look at all Jewish. In fact Dina looked far more like a Ukrainian woman and she spoke Ukrainian. They argued, speculated, pondered and finally decided that the old folk should go, but that Dina should take them and see them on to the train and then stay behind with the children. Then they would see what happened.

Her father was a glazier, and he and her mother lived at 27 Turgenyev Street. Dina lived with her children at 41 Vorovsky Street.

She arrived home late, tried to go to sleep, but instead lay awake the whole night. People were running about making a lot of noise all night: they were trying to catch a young girl from the same block. She had taken refuge in the attic and then tried to get down by the fire escape, and men's voices could be heard shouting: 'There she is!'

Actually, before the Germans came in this girl had been heard to say:

'They'll never get into Kiev, but if they do I'll soak the house in paraffin and set fire to it.'

What happened was that the yard-cleaner's wife had recalled those words and, fearing the girl might really set the place on fire, informed the Germans, who were trying to catch her that night.

It was a dreadful, hellish night of tension. Dina was trembling all over. She never got to know whether they caught the girl or not.

When it began to get light she washed herself and did her hair, took all the documents and went down to her parents' house close by on Turgenyev Street. There was an unusually large number of people out on the street, all of them hurrying in one direction or another with their possessions.

She reached her parents' home just after seven o'clock in the morning. The whole house was awake. Those who were leaving were saying good-bye to their neighbours, promising to write, entrusting them with their homes, their possessions and their keys.

The old people couldn't carry a great deal and they had no valuables, so they simply took with them the bare necessities of life and something to eat. Dina put the rucksack on her back and just after eight they set off.

There were plenty of people on Turgenyev Street, and Artem Street was completely jammed. People with bundles, with prams, all sorts of trolleys and carts and occasionally even lorries—all standing there, then moving forward a little, then standing still again.

The noise of raised voices and the crowds made it seem like a demonstration, when the streets are similarly jammed with people; but there were no flags, no banners and no cheers.

How odd it was to see the lorries; where on earth had they got them? In some cases people from a whole block of flats had got together and hired transport for their possessions, and the people themselves would keep clustered around their cart or lorry. Among the bundles and piles of cases old people were lying and children were sitting in groups. In some places people were pushing two or three infants in one pram.

There were a great many people seeing others off: neighbours, friends, relations, Russians and Ukrainians, helping to carry the bags, giving a hand to the invalids, even carrying them on their backs.

This whole procession moved very slowly, and Artem Street is very long. In some of the gateways German soldiers were standing and studying the people, especially the girls, as they went by. Apparently Dina took their fancy, because they beckoned her into the courtyard, indicating that the floors needed cleaning:

'Komm waschen!'

She dismissed them with a gesture. It went on and on and on, till the people were quite dazed by it all; that noisy procession, that 'demonstration', with all the pushing and shoving, the unbroken sound of people talking and children crying. Dina was wearing a fur coat and it was getting too hot for her.

It was not until after midday that they reached the cemetery. She remembers seeing on the right the long brick wall of the Jewish graveyard, and the gateway into it.

At that point there was a barbed-wire barrier across the street and anti-tank obstacles, with a passage left between them, and there were rows of Germans wearing badges on their chests, as well as Ukrainian police in black uniforms with grey cuffs.

At the entrance a very striking figure, a tall, energetic man in a Ukrainian embroidered shirt, with a long Cossack moustache, was giving instructions. The crowd swept through the gap past him, but nobody was coming out again, except cabbies who from time to time would drive back with empty cabs. They had got rid of their loads somewhere and were now making their way through against the crowd, shouting and waving their whips, and causing even more pushing and swearing.

It was very difficult to grasp what was going on. Dina sat the old folk down near the gateway to the cemetery and went to see for herself what was happening up in front.

Like many others, up to this point she had thought there was a train standing there. Some shooting could be heard not far away, a plane was circling low overhead, and there was a general feeling of alarm and panic in the air.

Dina overheard snatches of conversation in the crowd:

'It's because of the war, the war! They're moving us away from it, somewhere quieter.'

'And why are they only taking Jews?'

Some elderly woman suggested in a tone of great authority: 'Well, it's because they are related to the Germans as a people, and they have to be got away first.'

Dina had difficulty in pushing her way through the crowd and was getting more and more concerned, when she saw that out in front they were putting all the people's possessions to one side. All the baggage—the bundles and cases—was being put into a pile on the left, and all the food-stuff on the right.

But the Germans were moving the people a few at a time: they would send off one group, wait, and after an interval let some more through, counting them as they went, and then . . . stop, in the same way as queues of people were let into the shops in batches of ten to buy material.

There was more talk among all the noise and racket:

'Ah, our things will come along in the luggage van; we shall sort them out when we get there.'

'How are we ever going to sort out a pile of things like that? They'll simply divide them up equally between all of us. Then there won't be rich and poor any more.'

Dina was now really scared. It was nothing like a railway station. She wasn't yet sure *what* it was, but she sensed with her whole being that these people were not being sent away. Whatever was happening, they weren't being sent anywhere.

The oddest thing about it was the occasional sound of machine-gun fire near by. She couldn't admit to herself that it was the sound of people being shot. For one thing, there was such an enormous mass of people! Such things didn't happen. And then again—what was the point?

It can be said with certainty that the majority of people felt just as Dina did, that something was wrong; but they clung on to the idea that 'We are being deported,' perhaps for the following reasons:

When the order was first published nine Jews out of every ten had never heard a word about any Nazi atrocities against the Jews. Right up to the outbreak of war Soviet newspapers had been doing nothing but praising and glorifying Hitler as the Soviet Union's best friend, and had said nothing about the position of the Jews in Germany and Poland. It was possible even to find among the Jews of Kiev some enthusiastic admirers of Hitler as an able statesman.

Again, the older men used to tell stories about the Germans in the Ukraine in 1918; how they hadn't touched the Jews then, but on the contrary had treated them very decently, because their language was very similar and so forth . . .

The old men used to say:

'There are all sorts of Germans, but on the whole they are cultured, decent people; not your barbaric Russia, but Europe, with a European respect for order.'

There was something else, which had happened quite recently. Two days previously some people on Vorovsky Street had seized a flat belonging to a Jewish family. Some relatives who had stayed behind in the same building went along to the headquarters of the nearest German unit and complained. An officer came down straight away and ordered them out of the flat at once, saying to the Jews with a bow: 'There you are, everything is in order now.' That was literally only a couple of days before; everybody had seen it happen and stories about it quickly went around. And, after all, the Germans were consistent and logical people; whatever else they might be, they had certainly always been known for their consistency.

But, if it wasn't deportation, what on earth was going on?

Dina says that at that moment she felt only a sort of animal terror and her eyes seemed to cloud over—a state such as she had never known before.

They were taking people's warm clothes off them. A soldier came up to Dina and, in a trice and without a word, he deftly removed her coat.

At that point she rushed back. She sought out her old folk at the gate and told them what she had seen.

Her father said:

'Listen, daughter, we don't need you any more. Go away.'

She went across to the barrier, where quite a lot of people were trying to get back out, while the crowd was still streaming down in the other direction. The man with the moustaches and the embroidered shirt was still shouting and giving orders. Everyone called him 'Mr Shevchenko', like the Ukrainian poet. Maybe that was his proper name, or maybe somebody had dubbed him that because of his moustache, but it sounded rather frightful, like 'Mr Pushkin' or 'Mr Dostoyevsky'. Dina managed to push her way through to him and began to explain that she had been seeing people off, that her children were left behind in the city, and that she begged to be let out.

He demanded her identity card. She handed it to him.

He took one look at the entry after 'Nationality' and exclaimed:

'Hey—bloody Jewess! Get back!'

At that point Dina at last understood everything: they were being executed.

She started convulsively tearing her identity card up into little pieces and scattered them to left and right. Then she went back to the old people, but told them nothing, so as not to upset them before it was necessary.

Although she was already without her coat, she began to feel stifled. All around her were lots of people, tightly packed together, their breath visible in the cold air. Lost children were howling, while some folk were sitting on their bundles, eating. 'How on earth can they eat now? Do they still not realize what's happening?'

Then the people in charge started giving orders and shouting, making those who were sitting down stand up and moving them on, pushing the ones in the rear forward, so that some sort of straggling queue was formed. Some of the people's belongings were put down in one place, others in another; there was much pushing and shoving. In the confusion Dina lost track of her parents; she looked around in time to see them being sent off in another group farther on, while Dina's queue came to a halt.

They stood there waiting. She was straining to see where her mother and father had been taken, when an enormous German came up to her and said:

'Come and sleep with me and I'll let you out.'

She looked at him as if he were off his head and he went away. At last they started letting her group through.

The talking stopped; everyone fell silent, as though they had been struck dumb, and they marched on for some time in silence, between rows of Germans. Up in front could

be seen rows of soldiers with dogs on leads. From behind
Dina heard:

'My dear, please give me a hand; I'm blind.'

She put her arm round the old man and went along with
him.

'Where do you think they're taking us?' she asked him.

'We are going, my child,' he said, 'to pay our last debt to
God.'

At that moment they entered a long corridor formed by two
rows of soldiers and dogs. It was very narrow—some four or
five feet across. The soldiers were lined up shoulder to
shoulder, with their sleeves rolled up, each of them brandish-
ing a rubber club or a big stick.

Blows rained down on the people as they passed through.

There was no question of being able to dodge or get away.
Brutal blows, immediately drawing blood, descended on
their heads, backs and shoulders from left and right. The
soldiers kept shouting: 'Schnell, schnell!' laughing happily,
as if they were watching a circus act; they even found ways
of delivering harder blows in the more vulnerable places, the
ribs, the stomach and the groin.

Everybody started shouting and the women began to
scream. It was like a scene in a film; for one brief moment
Dina caught sight of a young man she knew from her street,
an intelligent, well-dressed lad, sobbing his eyes out.

She saw people falling to the ground. The dogs were immediately set on them. One man managed to pick himself
up with a shout, but others remained on the ground while
people pressed forward from behind and the crowd carried
on, walking on the bodies and trampling them into the
ground.

Everything seemed to go black in Dina's head at the
sight of all this. She straightened herself up, carried her head
high and marched on, stiff as a board, unbending. It seems
she must already have been badly hurt, but she felt and
understood little of what was happening; she simply kept
saying to herself: 'Don't fall, you mustn't fall.'

The poor people, now quite out of their minds, tumbled out
into a space cordoned off by troops, a sort of square over-

grown with grass. The whole of this grass plot was scattered with articles of underwear, footwear and other clothes.

The Ukrainian police—to judge by their accent they were not local people but from the Western Ukraine—were grabbing hold of people roughly, hitting them and shouting:

'Get your clothes off! Quickly! Schnell!'

Those who hesitated had their clothes ripped off them by force, and were kicked and struck with knuckledusters or clubs by the Germans, who seemed to be drunk with fury in a sort of sadistic rage.

All this was obviously being done so that the great mass of people should not come to their senses. There were many naked people covered in blood.

From the direction of a group of naked people who were being led off somewhere Dina heard her mother calling to her and waving her hand:

'Daughter, you don't look like one! Try and get away!'

They were herded off. Dina marched determinedly up to a policeman and asked him where the commander was. She told him she had been seeing someone off and had got mixed up with the crowd by chance.

He asked for her papers. She started fumbling in her bag, but he snatched it from her and looked through everything himself. There was money, a labour book, and a trade-union card, which do not show the nationality of the holder. The surname 'Pronicheva' convinced the policeman. He did not return her bag, but pointed to a hillock on which a handful of people were sitting.

'Sit there. We'll shoot the Jews first and then let you out.'

Dina went across to the hillock and sat down. Everybody there was silent, crazed with fright. She was afraid to look up: somebody might recognize her, quite by chance, and cry out: 'She's a dirty Jewess!' These people would stop at nothing to save their own skins. For that reason she tried not to look at anybody, and nobody looked at her. Only an old woman sitting next to her in a fluffy knitted scarf complained quietly to Dina that she had been seeing her daughter-in-law off and had got caught . . . But she herself was a Ukrainian, she was no Jewess, and who ever thought it would come to this?

They had all been seeing people off.

So there they sat, and in front of them, as if on a stage, a nightmarish scene was enacted: one group of people after another came staggering out of the corridor, screaming, battered, each of them to be seized by a policeman, beaten again and stripped of clothes; this was repeated over and over again.

Dina declares that some of them were laughing hysterically, and that she saw with her own eyes how several people went grey on the spot in the time it took for them to be stripped and sent to be shot.

They made the naked people form up into short lines and led them through the gap which had been hurriedly dug in the steep wall of sand. What was beyond it could not be seen, but there was the sound of shooting, and the only people who returned from the other side were Germans and policemen, to fetch more people.

The mothers in particular kept fussing over their children, with the result that from time to time some German or policeman would lose his temper, snatch a child away from its mother, go across to the sandstone wall, swing back and fling the child over the wall like a piece of wood.

Dina sat on there for a long time, feeling as though she was imprisoned in hoops of iron, her head sunk between her shoulders, and afraid to glance at her neighbours because new people kept joining them. She was no longer capable of hearing either the shouts or the shooting.

It started to get dark.

Suddenly an open car drew up and in it was a tall, well-built, smartly turned-out officer with a riding crop in his hand. He seemed to be in charge. He had a Russian interpreter at his side.

'Who are these?' the officer asked the policemen through the interpreter, pointing to the hillock, where there were about fifty people sitting by this time.

'They are our people, Ukrainians,' the policeman replied. 'They didn't know; they ought to be let out.'

The officer started shouting:

'Shoot the lot at once! If even one of them gets out of here and starts talking in the city, not a single Jew will turn up tomorrow.'

The interpreter translated this word for word to the policeman, while the people sat on the hillside and listened.

'Come on then! Let's go! Get yourselves up!' the police-man shouted.

The people stood up as if they were drunk. Maybe because it was already late the Germans didn't bother to undress this group, but led them through the gap in their clothes.

Dina was in about the second group. They went through the gap and came out into a sand quarry with sides practical-ly overhanging. It was already half-dark, and Dina could not see the quarry properly. One after the other they were hurried along to the left, along a very narrow ledge.

On their left was the side of the quarry, to the right a deep drop; the ledge had apparently been specially cut out for the purposes of the execution, and it was so narrow that as they went along it people instinctively leaned towards the wall of sandstone, so as not to fall in.

Dina looked down and her head swam, she seemed to be so high up. Beneath her was a sea of bodies covered in blood. On the other side of the quarry she could just distinguish the machine-guns which had been set up there and a few German soldiers. They had lit a bonfire and it looked as though they were making coffee on it.

When the whole line of people had been driven on to the ledge one of the Germans left the bonfire, took a machine-gun and started shooting.

Dina did not see so much as feel the bodies falling from the ledge and the stream of bullets coming closer to her. The idea flashed into her mind: 'Now . . . now I . . .' And without more ado she jumped, holding her fists tight as she went down.

It seemed to her that she fell for ages—it was probably a very deep drop. When she struck the bottom she felt neither the blow nor any pain, but she was immediately spattered with warm blood, and blood was streaming down her face, just as if she had fallen into a bath full of blood. She lay still, her arms stretched out, her eyes closed.

All around and beneath her she could hear strange sub-merged sounds, groaning, choking and sobbing: many of the people were not dead yet. The whole mass of bodies kept moving slightly as they settled down and were pressed tighter by the movements of the ones who were still living.

Some soldiers came out on to the ledge and flashed their torches down on the bodies, firing bullets from their revolvers into any which appeared to be still living. But someone not far from Dina went on groaning as loud as before.

Then she heard people walking near her, actually on the bodies. They were Germans who had climbed down and were bending over and taking things from the dead and occasionally firing at those which showed signs of life.

Among them was the policeman who had examined her papers and taken her bag: she recognized him by his voice.

One SS-man caught his foot against Dina and her appearance aroused his suspicions. He shone his torch on her, picked her up and struck her with his fist. But she hung limp and gave no signs of life. He kicked her in the breast with his heavy boot and trod on her right hand so that the bones cracked, but he didn't use his gun and went off, picking his way across the corpses.

A few minutes later she heard a voice calling from above: 'Demidenko! Come on, start shovelling!'

There was a clatter of spades and then heavy thuds as the earth and sand landed on the bodies, coming closer and closer until it started falling on Dina herself.

Her whole body was buried under the sand but she did not move until it began to cover her mouth. She was lying face upwards, breathed in some sand and started to choke, and then, scarcely realizing what she was doing, she started to struggle in a state of uncontrollable panic, quite prepared now to be shot rather than be buried alive.

With her left hand, the good one, she started scraping the sand off herself, scarcely daring to breathe lest she should start coughing; she used what strength she had left to hold the cough back. She began to feel a little easier. Finally she got herself out from under the earth.

The Ukrainian policemen up above were apparently tired after a hard day's work, too lazy to shovel the earth in properly, and once they had scattered a little in they dropped their shovels and went away. Dina's eyes were full of sand. It was pitch dark and there was the heavy smell of flesh from the mass of fresh corpses.

Dina could just make out the nearest side of the sand-pit and started slowly and carefully making her way across to it; then she stood up and started making little foot-holds in it with her left hand. In that way, pressed close to the side of the pit, she made steps and so raised herself an inch at a time, likely at any moment to fall back into the pit.

There was a little bush at the top which she managed to get hold of. With a last desperate effort she pulled herself up and, as she scrambled over the edge, she heard a whisper which nearly made her jump back.

'Don't be scared, lady! I'm alive too.'

It was a small boy in vest and pants who had crawled out as she had done. He was trembling and shivering all over.

'Quiet!' she hissed at him. 'Crawl along behind me.'

And they crawled away silently, without a sound.

They went on crawling for a long, long time, very slowly, coming up against obstacles and turning back and crawling on, apparently, right through the night, because it eventually started to get light. Then they found some bushes and crept in among them.

They were on the edge of a big ravine. Not far away they could see some Germans who had come to sort the people's belongings out and pack them away. They had dogs on leads running around with them. Occasionally a lorry would drive up to take the things, but more often it was just plain horses and carts.

When the dawn came they saw an old woman running, followed by a boy of about six who was crying: 'Granny, I'm scared!' But the woman brushed him aside. They were overtaken by two German soldiers and shot, first the old woman and then the boy.

Then, on the far side of the ravine, six or seven Germans appeared leading two young women. They went down into the ravine, selected a level place, and proceeded one after the other to violate the women. Having satisfied their desires they stabbed the women to death with their bayonets so that they shouldn't cry out, and left the bodies there as they were, naked, with their legs spread wide apart.

Germans kept passing by, sometimes above where they lay and sometimes below, chatting to each other, and all the time shooting was going on near by. In fact there was so much shooting that it began to seem to Dina that it had been going on for ever and had never stopped, even during the night.

She lay there with the boy and they kept dozing off and waking up again. The boy told her his name was Motya, that he had nobody left, and that he had fallen into the pit along with his father when they had started shooting. He was a good-looking child with lovely eyes which looked at Dina as though she was his saviour. If they managed to escape, she thought to herself, she would adopt him.

Towards the evening she began to have hallucinations: her father, her mother and her sister came to see her. They were in long white robes and they kept laughing and turning head-over-heels. When Dina came round, Motya was sitting over her and saying plaintively:

'Don't die, lady, don't leave me.'

She had the greatest difficulty in realizing where she was. Since it was already dark again they dragged themselves out of the bushes and crawled on. While it was daylight Dina had made a note of the direction: across the big meadow to the wood which she could see in the distance. Occasionally she would forget where she was and try to stand up, but Motya would hang on to her and force her back down.

She must have been losing consciousness, because at one point she slipped down into the ravine. They had had nothing to eat or drink for more than twenty-four hours, though they didn't give this a thought. They were in a state of shock.

So they crawled their way through another night, until it began to get light again. In front of them was the undergrowth in which they had decided to hide, and Motya went ahead to spy out the land. They repeated this procedure several times; if the coast was clear Motya was supposed to shake a bush. Suddenly there was a piercing shout:

'Don't move, lady, there's Germans here!'

And she heard shooting. They killed him on the spot.

As luck would have it, the Germans had not understood what Motya had shouted. Dina crawled back and found herself on a patch of sand. She made a little hole, carefully filled it up with sand and made a little mound above it, pretending to herself that she was burying Motya, her companion, and then burst into tears. She was already a little light-headed.

When daylight came Dina found she was sitting, rocking from side to side, right on the roadway and that to her left was a fence, a lane and a rubbish tip. She crawled quickly across to the tip, made a hole for herself in the rubbish, covered herself over with bits of rag and boxes and put an old basket over her head so that she could breathe inside it.

And there she lay, scarcely breathing. From time to time Germans would pass by, stop and light up cigarettes.

Right in front of her on the edge of a garden she could see two green tomatoes. To get them she would have to crawl across to them. And it was only then that she began to feel thirsty and to have hunger pains.

She tried to think of something else, closed her eyes, argued with herself and tried to force herself not to think. Still her head kept turning, drawn like a magnet in the direction of the tomatoes. But she did not crawl out; she lay there until it was dusk.

Only when it was absolutely dark did she extricate herself, find the tomatoes with her hands, eat them and crawl away again on her stomach. She had already done so much crawling, she seemed to have forgotten how to walk properly.

She went on crawling for a long time, then fell into a trench with barbed wire and lost consciousness. Towards morning she awoke to find herself near a cottage with a barn behind it, which she decided to enter. It wasn't locked, but she had hardly gone in when a dog started barking. Then all the neighbours' dogs started yapping as well. It seemed to her that hundreds of dogs were barking, and noise was the last thing she wanted.

A woman came sleepily to the door and shouted:

'Quiet, Ryabko!'

She glanced into the barn and caught sight of Dina. She did not look particularly well-disposed, so that when she started asking Dina who she was and what she was doing there, Dina decided to lie, saying that she was on her way back from digging trenches a long way away, that she had lost her way and decided to spend the night in the barn. She asked how to get to the town commandant.

'Where have you been then?'

'Near Belaya Tserkov.'

'Belaya Tserkov? You trying to tell me this is the road from Belaya Tserkov? Come on, come on . . .'

Dina was, of course, looking frightful. She was covered in dried blood, mud and sand, she had lost her shoes back in the quarry and her stockings were torn to shreds.

The noise brought out the neighbours, who slowly gathered round Dina, looking her up and down. The woman summoned her son, a boy of about sixteen.

'Vanko, go and fetch the Germans; we'll show her the way all right.'

Dina stood there and realized that she could not run away—she hadn't the strength and in any case the women would start shouting and send the dogs after her. The woman who owned the barn was called Elizabeth.

The Germans were apparently quite near, because Vanko returned with an officer almost at once.

'Look, sir, a Yid!'

The officer inspected Dina, and nodded:

'Komm.'

And he walked off ahead along the little footpath, Dina following behind. He said nothing, only looking round from time to time to make sure she was following. She walked with her arms folded across her breasts, all hunched up, she was cold, her right arm ached—it was covered in blood—and her legs were hurting from all the cuts and bruises.

They entered a single-storey brick-built house in which a couple of dozen soldiers were having breakfast, drinking coffee from aluminium cups. Dina went to sit down on a chair in a corner, but the officer shouted at her and so she sat on the floor.

Soon the Germans started picking up their rifles and going outside. Only one soldier stayed behind on duty. He went around tidying up and signed to Dina to sit down on the chair—not to worry.

She moved herself on to the chair. The soldier looked out of the window and handed Dina a rag and indicated that she should clean the glass. It was a large window covering almost the whole wall, with lots of small panes. And it was then that Dina saw that she had crawled right round Babi Yar and finished up in the very place she had run away from.

The soldier started saying something to her in a quiet voice. She understood what he was saying, but he thought she didn't and tried very hard to make her understand:

'Try to get what I'm saying. The officers have gone. I've given you a rag so that you can beat it. Keep wiping the window, look through it and pick out the way you've got to run. Do you get me, Dummkopf, you stupid woman!'

There was a certain sympathy in his voice. Dina came to the conclusion that it wasn't a trick. But at the time she was in such a state that she couldn't take anything in. Just in case she shook her head as though she did not understand.

Annoyed, the soldier thrust a broom into her hand and sent her to brush out the next house, where there was nobody at all. Dina hung around a little, ready to flee, when she heard more noise and weeping.

An officer appeared with Vanko, Elizabeth's son, leading two girls of about fifteen or sixteen.

The girls were shouting and sobbing and throwing themselves on the ground, trying to kiss the officer's boots and pleading with him to do anything he liked with them, to go to bed with them if he wanted, so long as he didn't shoot them.

They were wearing identical clean dark dresses and their hair was done in pigtails.

'We are from the children's home!' they cried. 'We just don't know what nationality we are. We were brought in as infants!'

The officer looked at them lying on the ground and drew his feet away. He ordered them and Dina to follow him.

They came eventually to the clearing where the people had been undressed. There were still piles of clothes and shoes lying about. And alongside the piles of things there were thirty or forty old men and women and sick people sitting. They were presumably the very last ones who had been rounded up when the houses were searched.

One old woman was lying there quite paralysed, wrapped in a blanket.

Dina and the girls were made to sit down with them. The girls were sobbing quietly.

They were sitting beneath a sort of ledge along which an armed guard was marching up and down. Dina studied his movements carefully without raising her head, watching how he first moved away and then came closer again. The guard noticed this, began to get nervous, and then blurted out impatiently in German:

'What are you watching me like that for? Don't look at me! I can't do anything at all for you. I've got children, too!'

A girl in a soldier's tunic and greatcoat came and sat down by her—she had seen Dina shivering from the cold, and laid her coat over her. They talked quietly together. The girl's name was Lyuba, she was nineteen, had been working as a nurse and got caught in the encirclement.

A lorry drove up with Soviet prisoners on it, all of them with spades. The old men were horrified: surely they weren't going to bury them alive? But one of the prisoners saw them from afar and said:

'You're in luck.'

They then proceeded to make them all get up and pushed them into the back of the same lorry. A couple of soldiers took the old woman in the blanket and lifted her like a plank of wood on to the lorry, where others took her in their arms.

It was an open lorry, with high sides to it. One German sat in the cab, another at the back, while four policemen placed themselves at the sides.

They were being carted off somewhere.

It was difficult to discern in this any of the famous German logic or consistency: some had had their clothes taken away, others hadn't, some were killed outright, others were left to die slowly, some were taken in one direction, others in another . . .

The lorry arrived in Melnikov Street, where there was a large transport garage. Around the wide courtyard were doors leading into garages and workshops. One pair of doors were opened and inside were people, packed tight like sardines, who came tumbling out shouting and gasping, when the doors burst open. Among them was an old woman who went at once to relieve herself outside the door. A German shouted at her and shot her in the head with his revolver.

They lifted the paralysed woman, wrapped in a blanket, out of the lorry and passed her into the garage right over people's heads.

With much difficulty, to the accompaniment of shouts and screams, the Germans strained and pushed and finally closed the doors again, having rolled the dead woman's body inside. Then, very concerned, they began to tell each other that there really was no more room.

They had herded this crowd of people in there from the streets at night, and had left them there for several days, awaiting their turn to be shot.

Dina understood German, listened to what was being said and wondered what was going to happen next.

The lorry started to back out of the yard. One German jumped off the end, leaving four policemen behind, two in the driving cab and two on the sides at the back; but they were not sitting right at the back end, more towards the middle. They looked tired but not vicious.

Dina and Lyuba began to make plans: they would have to jump for it. If they were shot at—who cared? It would at least be a quick death; they wouldn't have to wait in a queue.

They were moving fast. Lyuba protected Dina from the wind with her greatcoat as they swayed through the winding streets. They went through Shulyavka, going in the general direction of the Brest-Litovsk highway.

Wrapped up in the greatcoat, Dina tumbled over the back flap and jumped off at full speed. She fell, cutting herself badly on the roadway, but she wasn't missed from the lorry. Perhaps they didn't care?

Passers-by soon gathered round her. She began to mumble that she had been riding in the lorry, that she should have got off at the market, but the driver hadn't understood and she had decided to jump . . . They only half believed her, but at least she saw sympathetic, human faces around her. They led her off quickly into a farmhouse.

Half an hour later she was with her brother's wife, a Polish woman. They spent the whole night heating water and soaking off her body the vest which had congealed into her wounds.

*

Even after these experiences D. M. Pronicheva came very close to death on many more occasions. She hid in the ruins of Kiev, in Darnitsa, and then went from village to village under the name of Nadya Savchenko. Some people took care of her children, whom she sought for a long time and found at the very end of the war. In 1946 she acted as a witness for the prosecution at the trial in Kiev of Nazi war criminals in the Ukraine. But because of the outburst of anti-Semitism which followed soon after she began to conceal the fact that she had escaped from Babi Yar and also that she was Jewish. Once again it was her surname 'Pronicheva' that saved her.

She went back to the Kiev puppet theatre, where she works to this day as an actress and puppet-handler. I had tremendous difficulty in persuading her to tell the story of how she, alone of all the seventy thousand Jews executed in September 1941, managed to escape: she did not believe that it could ever be published or that it would serve any good purpose. It took her several days to tell her story, which was interrupted by a number of heart attacks. It was in an old, decrepit room in the very same house on Vorovsky Street which she had left to go to Babi Yar. It was not until 1968 that D. M. Pronicheva succeeded in persuading the authorities to let her have a small flat in a new building, and she sent me a letter saying that after this book had appeared another inhabitant of Kiev came to see her and told her that he had also escaped from the Yar. He had been only a small boy at the time and had scrambled out as Motya had done. He had been hidden by a Ukrainian family, whose name he had taken, so that his identity card now showed him as a Ukrainian, and he had never told anyone that he had escaped from Babi Yar. To judge from the details he gave, his story was true. But he simply sat for a while, told his tale, and then went off without giving his name.

A Chapter of Reminiscences

1. *Cannibals*

The worst famine in the Ukraine's long history occurred
under Soviet rule in 1933. It is the first thing I can remember
clearly in my life.

My grandmother was mixing a corn mash in a wooden
bowl and I was standing by her in case she should drop
some. My father, drawn and tired, was sitting on a stool,
telling his story.

He had just returned from near Uman, where he had
been helping put through the collectivization of the farms.
When he had returned home on previous occasions he had
brought with him flour and pots of honey, but later brought
less and less, and this time he had brought nothing at all.

'So we forced the peasants to join the collective farms
at the point of the gun,' my father was saying. 'But they
refused to do any work. They simply hung around doing
nothing, with their hands in their pockets. The cattle died
off and the fields were left unsown and overgrown with
weeds. It was simply impossible to talk to the people or get
any sense into them. They went silent, stubborn, keeping
themselves to themselves; they weren't like normal people at
all. If we made them attend a meeting they would simply sit
there with their mouths shut; when we ordered them to
disperse, they would just walk away in silence. In short, we
were up against it. So we told 'em: "Either the collectives or
death." They replied: "We'd sooner die." They said: "Lenin
promised us land, that was what the revolution was for."
And they would keep repeating the same thing over and
over again and wouldn't give in. It was a sort of senseless,
crazy peasant strike, and there was nothing left to eat . . .'

'Good lord,' Grandma gasped. 'So what did *you* eat then?'

'We Communists were issued with rations of food, so
that we would keep alive, and the village activists were

93

also given a little. But what *they* eat—that is beyond belief.
There are no longer any frogs or mice about and not a
single cat is left. They cut the ordinary grass and stubble
for food. They peel the bark off the pine trees, grind it
down to a powder and cook pancakes from it. And there's
cannibalism everywhere.'

'Cannibalism? Lord! What do you mean?'

'It's quite simple. We're sitting in the office of the village
Soviet, say, and a village activist comes in and reports: In
such and such a cottage they are eating a young girl. We
jump up, take our weapons and go to the cottage. The whole
family is there with the exception of the daughter. And they
are sitting there, rather drowsy and with full stomachs. And
there's an appetizing smell of cooking in the cottage. The
stove is well stoked up and there are pots standing on it.

'So I start interrogating them: "Where is your daughter?"
"She's gone into town." "Why has she gone there?" "To
buy some material for a dress." "And what's that in the
pots on the stove?" "That's soup . . ." I tip this 'soup' out
into a basin and there I see meat and more meat and a hand
with fingernails floating in the fat. "Get your things, let's
go."

'They gather their things together, meekly, like drowsy
flies, without any sense or feeling. And off we go. But what
do we do with 'em then? Theoretically they should go
before the courts. But there's nothing in Soviet law to deal
with cannibalism. They could be tried for murder, but that
involves such a lot of fuss for the courts and, in any case,
isn't the famine a mitigating circumstance? In fact, we had
orders from above to decide these things on the spot. So we
would take them away from the village, turn off into the
fields somewhere, find a little gully, shoot 'em in the back
of the neck and throw a bit of earth over 'em, so that the
wolves would eat them up later.'

It was a man-made famine, brought about by Stalin.
The peasants who resisted collectivization had all their stores
requisitioned. The population of many villages starved to
death, to the very last person. Thousands of peasants who
had run away from the villages in search of bread lay
swollen and dying at the railway stations. On the basis of
the figures of the population census the testimony of witnesses and other evidence, scholars have concluded that

the number of people who perished exceeded seven million. Speaking about the total number of victims of collectivization in a conversation with Winston Churchill, Stalin said that he had had to dispose of ten million people.

2. *Who Gave Us the Fir Tree?*

When I was a child there was nothing but falsehood on every side.

I began going to school in the first class in the historic year of 1937. (At that time we started going to school at the age of eight.) The school building was old and decrepit; there were fifty children to a class, and lessons had to be organized in three shifts.

We sang a little song about a goat and started to learn the alphabet. My mother had taught me to read and write at the age of four, so I was bored in class; at Reading I used to rattle away like a machine-gun, and I had already read Victor Hugo's principal novels and Zola's *Fruitfulness,* in which I was particularly impressed by the fact that the surgical interruption of pregnancy prematurely ages a woman.

On the day when we celebrated the twentieth anniversary of the revolution we moved into a new school. It was built near us in Kurenyovka among the crooked little houses and old merchants' villas, looking like Gulliver among the Lilliputians. It had huge windows, tall columns, wide staircases, was a true symbol of the new society and a striking example of the concern felt for us by the Party and 'Comrade Stalin personally'.

We had this drummed into our little heads in all our lessons. We moved into the new school with flags flying, drums beating, and singing songs about our beloved Stalin. They took us in a lorry to take part in the demonstration, where we screamed our rapturous hurrahs!

Every Saturday there was a free film-show in the school hall. We in the first class used to have the best seats, on the floor right underneath the screen, and we used to watch the films with our heads bent back and our jaws hanging down.

Nobody ever knew in advance what the film was going to be, because the boxes with the films were delivered only at the very last moment. For this reason things occasionally got very mixed up. The story of one of the first films we were shown is a case in point.

A young man, an exemplary worker and a member of the Komsomol,* marries a middle-class girl with out-of-date views. He becomes a member of this middle-class family. Stormy scenes follow, depicting the battle between middle-class and Communist ideologies. The young husband walks out and goes to spend the night with a friend. Meanwhile the heroine's aged father wipes away her tears and then sleeps with her, as a result of which a child is born. The young husband learns of this while he is at the factory bench where he is a model worker. He wonders whose child it is, and this causes him to do his job badly and fail to carry out his set quota.

I no longer remember the name of the film or the way it ended, but I know that it made a profound impression on all of us sitting there in the front rows on the floor.

Opposite the school they opened a children's agricultural centre, and all sorts of old dears used to come along to try and persuade us to join the junior naturalists and learn how to produce record harvests according to the new ideas of Academician Lysenko. Zhorik Gorokhovsky and I immediately put our names down, and we were each given a patch of land and a packet of ground-nuts. Unfortunately we tried eating the ground-nuts and we couldn't stop until we had finished the lot. We took one look at each other, and without another word ran away and never came back, thus abandoning a career as followers of Lysenko.

In one of the old villas they started a children's handicraft and hobby centre which had classes for photography, wireless and aircraft modelling. We joined the photography class. The first work the instructor gave us to do was to make a photograph of a bust of Stalin.

At one point they laid asphalt on the footpaths of our winding, ugly street, which was a real marvel for those times.

The papers announced that an outstanding comrade-in-arms of Stalin's, Postyshev, had proposed the introduction of a new national holiday—the New Year, complete with a

---

* The Communist League of Youth. [Tr.]

fir tree. Until then, ever since the revolution, there had been
no fir trees, so that for us small children this was really
something new. The fir tree was set up in the new school
building, the little girls dressed themselves up as snowflakes,
and I recited a poem about Jack Frost surveying his domains.
And we finished up with a song which had appeared in the
newspaper and which ended with the words:

> And it was Mr Postyshev
> Who gave us our lovely tree.

Grandma said:

'This is Christmas. It was Jesus who gave us the tree.'

I argued with her:

'No, it was Postyshev. There is no Jesus Christ and there
never was! Soviet rule gave the children fir trees.'

'You little puppy,' Grandma said, and we had a violent
quarrel. But my mother said:

'My goodness, what a lucky boy you are, Tolya. You've
only just started school, and they've built you a new school,
started a farming centre and a handicrafts club, introduced
the fir tree again, and even asphalted the footpaths. All you
have to do is work. Make the best of it all and work hard;
only read more, read everything you can—there is wisdom
in books.'

It soon became apparent, however, that not everything
in the books was wisdom. In class one day we were ordered
to open our textbooks at the page with a portrait of Postyshev on it and tear it out—Postyshev had turned out to be
an enemy of the people.

So he was executed, even though he had introduced the
fir tree. It was a big shock for our little minds, but we
weren't given a chance to think much about it. It immediately became a matter of routine, something quite
ordinary and usual. Sometimes we would be ordered to tear
out other pages, on other occasions to cross out with ink
certain sentences or names. Making a mess of our textbooks
was really quite a pleasant occupation which we all liked
enormously.

On one occasion in the middle of a lesson the classroom
door burst open and the headmaster entered in a state of
great agitation, along with his deputy and the party organizer,
who ordered us:

'All notebooks on desks!'

The covers of our notebooks had a decorative bouquet of flowers printed on them. All notebooks with these flowers on them were immediately removed from us and taken off to the boiler room, where they were destroyed in the furnace. The school telephone nearly fell off the wall from calls from the education office inquiring whether all the notebooks had been duly withdrawn. It turned out that someone had discovered a Tsarist crown hidden in among the flowers. It was like one of those puzzle pictures, 'Find the hunter'; a lot of little leaves and lines and curls, but if you turned it upside down and went over some of the lines with a pencil you could, if you tried, make out a crown in the roughly drawn bouquet of flowers. Or you could discover a horse . . . It was said that many people had been arrested because of that beastly notebook and had disappeared never to return.

3. *Burning the Books*

'Now then,' my mother said, 'just tear up those books, put them in the stove and burn them.'

We had a lot of books—my mother used to collect them and was always buying new ones. But now she started going through them carefully, stack after stack of them, putting them on the fire. Books take a long time to burn completely and we had to keep stirring them about with a poker. The weather at the time was warm, and it became so hot inside from the red-hot stove that we soon had to open the window; all the same it was stifling.

I had already read a good many of our books, like Zola's *Fruitfulness*, for example, but there were even more I had not had time to get through. I was particularly sorry to see destroyed the beautifully illustrated and bound volumes of *Inostrannaya Literatura** for each year from 1890 to 1910, *Russkaya Istoriya v Kartinikh†*—a Tsarist edition—not to mention Gorky's books.

'Those books are harmful and dangerous,' my mother explained.

---

* *Foreign Literature.* [Tr.]
† *Russian History in Pictures.* [Tr.]

It stood to reason. If school notebooks were being burnt, then dangerous books should have been thrown on the fire long ago. It was not long since Gorky had died, but everybody was already whispering that he had been poisoned. First they had murdered his son, then they started to 'treat' the writer himself in the Kremlin Hospital. And if that was the way things were going, better not have his books in the house.

But I literally screamed when my Japanese fairy tales were condemned to be burnt:

'Don't, mummy, *please* don't!'

That was the book I came to like most in my childhood, the one I learnt to read by. It consisted of the most gripping and highly instructive stories of things that happened to a little boy and a little girl called Taro and Takei, and it had pictures of little ponds with goldfish and little Japanese houses set among dwarf pine trees. I clutched the book to me, but my mother proceeded to pull it away from me; she proved the stronger, and my Taro and Takei landed in the fire. It had a very heavy, lacquered binding which took a long time to start burning. It lay there among the flames— a marvellous children's book—and just wouldn't burn.

'The Japanese are capitalists and our enemies,' my mother said. 'We mustn't keep Japanese books in the house.'

To stop me bursting into tears she gave me a pair of scissors and told me to cut up the family photographs. She put a cross on the faces of those people who had to be cut out, because they were enemies of the people, and I carefully cut round them. It seemed to me that we had a suspiciously large number of enemies of the people among our acquaintances.

When I had finished my job the photographs looked really very funny. There was, for example, a large group picture with rows of very stern-looking men and women with 'Teachers' Conference 1935' written on it. But now, after my work with the scissors, the rows were full of empty holes in the shape of the human silhouette, as if they had not been real people but ghosts. They had all turned out to be enemies of the people, and now they were no longer with us and had to be forgotten.

And then there were the nights.

My mother had practically no sleep at all at night. She would go from corner to corner, listening carefully to every noise. If she heard the sound of a car outside she would jump up, turn pale and start rushing about the room. It would usually turn out to be just a car going past the house.

When she came home from work she would tell us how difficult things were in the school—such-and-such a teacher hadn't turned up, another was missing, and she had to handle two classes at the same time, and every day more classes were being run together and there was continual reorganization going on because they kept on arresting more and more of the teachers . . . She was expecting her own turn to come.

Grandma would weep and say:

'But you haven't *done* anything, Marusya. There's nothing to arrest you for!'

'And what are the others being arrested for?'

'Oh, Mother of God, why are we being punished like this?'

Old Zhuk, my grandfather's friend, was a quiet and inoffensive old chap, who cleaned up the street regularly, kept the fences painted, rushed off to vote at six o'clock in the morning when required and always hung out the red flag for November 7th and other national holidays. And one day he was standing in a queue for some material.

In those days all textiles were extremely scarce and hard to come by. You could buy them only by standing for days on end in a queue. And the queue was enormous, with thousands of people in it. It did not form up in front of the shop but—so that it couldn't be seen from Kirillovskaya Street, where government cars and foreign visitors passed by—along the fence round the square, right opposite our gate. The people in the queue were terribly noisy—they would eat their lunch and dinner there and sleep on the ground through the night.

The police introduced a system by which they would take the first ten people in the queue and conduct them into the shop. It was funny to see them going in—each one holding tightly to the next, one behind the other, like children playing trains. That was so that an eleventh person should not sneak in. They looked exhausted and terribly untidy, but happy and excited—at last they had made it! The police would count them again as they went into the shop—everything was very well organized, perfect order was maintained, and they were admitted to the shop as if they were going into a cathedral. What they would get once they were inside nobody knew. If it happened that a lorry-load of material had just been delivered, then there would be an 'issue' of a few yards for each person and the lucky ones would leave the shop all carrying absolutely identical pieces.

Zhuk, it appears, had been standing in the queue and had said something, and somebody had overhead him, and maybe for reporting it had been given a few yards of material from under the counter. That night there was the sound of motor-cars outside Zhuk's house and they took him off. After that happened my grandfather could no longer sleep. He turned over in his mind all the things he had said against the Bolsheviks, trying to recall which of his friends would remember.

My grandmother prepared two baskets, putting clean underwear, dried crusts of bread, a piece of soap and a tooth-brush in each. She too would start up at the sound of motor-cars passing by. Those were troubled, horrible nights.

My mother again went through all our papers, sheet by sheet, and once again the stove was ablaze and all the work I had done went for nothing—my mother decided not to keep any of the photographs with the holes cut in them, and simply threw them all into the flames. All we had left were the most thoroughly approved Soviet publications and a six-volume collection of Pushkin's works.

That was the second most awful happening in my life after the cannibalism.

*

I cannot restrain myself at this point from adding a short commentary on the question of what people knew about what was going on in those days.

Almost as soon as Kirov* was assassinated in 1934 people

* Sergei Kirov (1886–1934), a Bolshevik leader, head of Leningrad party organization from 1926, who was said to have opposed Stalin's dictatorial methods. His assassination in December 1934 was used by Stalin as the excuse for unleashing a fierce wave of repression and 'purges'. [Tr.]

started saying he had been murdered on Stalin's orders. The same happened in the case of Ordzhonikidze.* When Gorky died they said outright that he had been poisoned because he had been in disagreement with Stalin. Nobody ever made a distinction between Stalin and the N.K.V.D. Vyshinsky† was sent to Kiev by Stalin, took up residence in the October palace and set about putting his signature to sentences of death at the end of long lists of names. Many were executed on the spot, right there in the same building, and their corpses were thrown out of the windows into the gully beneath. Everybody in Kiev was perfectly aware of all this, and even backward, remote Kurenyovka was right up to date with what was going on.

Consequently, when many years later Khrushchev took it upon himself to 'expose' Stalin, there was nothing new in it for people living in the Soviet Union. The only new aspect was the actual policy of 'exposure' and the unending series of monstrous details that were given.

At that point various 'honest Communists' started beating their breasts and declaring that as it happened they had not known anything of what was going on. Or that they had known but believed that the people being liquidated were real enemies. Or that they had thought that the N.K.V.D. was to blame for everything and that our beloved Stalin knew nothing and that the party was sacred. A lot of books appeared by such 'honest Communists', anxious to dissociate Stalin and the party from crimes which they attributed to Yezhov or Beria.

Hypocrites. If they told the truth, they all knew and understood perfectly well everything that was going on. Only a person who DID NOT WANT TO KNOW remained 'unaware'. And such a person would go on playing the hypocrite and saving his skin by that means, remaining steadfast in his hypocrisy and surviving by means of it, and finishing up by being so deeply imbued with it that even today he still goes on lying, trying in effect to argue that millions of party members were mentally retarded.

---

* Sergo Ordzhonikidze (1886–1937), a member of Stalin's Politburo until his death in mysterious circumstances in 1937. [Tr.]

† Andrei Vyshinsky (1883–1955), prosecutor in the three principal show trials of the great purge in the 'thirties. Deputy Minister of Foreign Affairs of the Soviet Union 1940–49, Minister 1949–53. [Tr.]

In just the same way, following the defeat of Hitler, certain 'honest' Nazis declared that they had not known about the monstrous crimes committed in the death camps, or that they had believed that the Gestapo alone was to blame for everything. Hypocrites. Once more I repeat: The only people who did not know were those who did not *want* to know.

Because if one were for a moment to believe them and admit that the so-called 'honest Communists', who have taken it upon themselves to tell the rest of the world how to behave, understood what was going on around them as if they were five-year-old children, then it would be even more frightful.

4. *Pioneering*

Because I could already read and write when I started school, I found the lessons very easy, had four good reports one after the other and was chosen to be chairman of the council of the Pioneer troop.

It was a piece of utter bureaucratic idiocy specially arranged for children: we held conferences, just like grown-ups, and we learnt to use all the dreary official language. Every now and again we had to parade, and the group leaders would have to report to me like this:

'Chairman of the troop council: Group number one; ten men on the nominal roll, nine men present on parade. One absent on account of illness. Group leader Zhorik Gorokhovsky reporting.'

During which procedure I felt a fool, Zhorik felt a fool, and all the others simply stood there stock-still. The banner was brought out and the banner was carried back again, and then the troop leader would teach us how to be good young Leninists, like the famous Pioneer Pavlik Morozov, who informed on his own parents and was killed by the rich peasants.

Fortunately our troop leader, Misha, was a very agreeable Jew, who was fond of children, used to take us round the museums at the monastery, and sometimes took the whole lot of us bathing in the Dnieper. We travelled to Pushcha-Voditsa for the military manoeuvres, took part in athletic competitions, and we all belonged to hobby circles. This side of my life remains for me full of light and happy sounds and sunshine. It really seemed as if the future was wide open to us. People used to come to visit the school from various colleges and do their best to persuade the boys in the senior classes to go and study with them.

Being members of the photography group, Zhorik Gorokhovsky and I spent our time preparing a 'Pioneer Chronicle' and taking pictures of various activists and outstanding students. Our photo-montage, dedicated to Stalin, won us a place in an exhibition.

This was organized in the foyer of the October Cinema, and we had to be on duty at our exhibit all day long lest anything should be stolen. It was marvellous! One of us would stay by the stand while the other rushed off into the cinema to watch the film for nothing.

Every film was preceded by a showing of a news film, *V. M. Molotov's Visit to Berlin,* which was a big hit at the time. I saw that film so many times that I knew it all off by heart.

What emerged from it was that the Soviet Union had no better friend than Hitler. The Soviet people had their Stalin; after him came Hitler. And here was Molotov, off to conclude a pact of friendship and non-aggression with Germany. In Berlin they greeted him with bands, flowers and much cheering. How marvellously the Nazi troops marched! How moving were the military marches! Hitler welcomes Molotov warmly like a long-lost brother, keeps shaking him by the hand; they are immediately immersed in conversation, and the photographers crowd around with their flash-guns busy. Then there were German soldiers marching again with marvellous precision, with their banners unfurled to show the swastika, symbol of strength and friendship.

I would simply gasp with delight as I watched that screen: I so wanted to be able to march like that. If only our Pioneer troop could learn to march like the Germans, then our games of soldiers would be like the Germans' military operations in Europe! . . . Oh, the speed and style with which those Germans operated! The Soviet Union could only produce a rather clumsy imitation.

Then an absolutely fabulous war with Poland broke out. With Hitler coming from the west and us coming from the east, there was soon nothing left of Poland. Of course, for the sake of appearances we called it 'the liberation of the Western Ukraine and Byelorussia' and put up posters showing a ragged Ukrainian embracing a brave Red-Army man—his liberator. But that was the usual thing. Anyone who attacks is always liberating somebody from something or other.

Zhorik Gorokhovsky's father was called up into the army and took part in that war, and on one occasion when he had had a drop too much to drink he told us the sort of welcome they really got in Poland. In the first place they all, from the most senior officer down to the lowest man in the ranks, burst into the textile and footwear shops and started stuffing sacks and cases full of loot. Lord, the things our brave soldiers brought back from Poland with them. A certain political officer brought out a case full of patent-leather shoes which were found to fall to pieces as soon as you took a few steps in them. It turned out that he had got his hands on some shoddily made footwear intended only for dressing corpses. And Zhorik's dad even managed to bring home a lot of bicycle bells. We ran around with them, making a terrible noise and shouting happily:

'Poland's finished!'

And 'bourgeois' Lithuania, Latvia and Estonia were also done for. We seized Bessarabia and took it away from Rumania. It was great to be strong. But this was nothing compared with the sort of feats that Hitler was performing.

Every day my grandfather demanded that I should read to him what the papers were saying about Hitler. Wherever the Germans went they were victorious. They bombed cities, sank ships of thousands of tons and occupied whole countries and capital cities with no apparent effort. The slow-moving and slow-thinking British might last a few more days; Belgium was finished, France was done for.

When Grandpa was resting, I used to draw up to him and we would play a very amusing game. Gramp would make his hand quite flat and hold it hovering in the air, and then making a noise like an aeroplane and crying 'Bombers!' he would dive on me with it. I laughed and laughed.

5. 'If it's war tomorrow . . .'

My generation grew up with a song on their lips. I can't think of the pre-war years without recalling it—

If it's war tomorrow, and we have to fight,
And the forces of darkness attack us—
As one man, the whole Soviet people
Will rise to defend their land.
On land, in the skies and at sea
Our song rings out strong and fierce:
If it's war tomorrow, and we have to fight,
Be ready for battle today!

The song was out of a film which appealed to people to be ready for war with a rather vague enemy, some kind of 'bourgeois' monster, who had invaded us. A fine Soviet soldier was shown, to the accompaniment of belly-laughs from a delighted audience, clouting him over the head with the butt of his rifle.

The machine-guns will fire and the aircraft will swoop
And the tanks will come rumbling in.
The trucks will start up and the troops will move off
And the dashing gun-carts will flash by.

These 'gun-carts', drawn by horses and with a machine-gun mounted on them, had been used in the Civil War period and had since become an inevitable feature of all parades until the real war started.

There were three of us in our gang on Peter-Paul Square—three friends, three musketeers, three tank-drivers. What drew us particularly close together was the fact that we had all been abandoned by our fathers and brought up by our mothers.

BOLIK KAMINSKY was the eldest. He used to clout us over the head; we used to tease him and call him 'Bollibatty', but at the same time were utterly devoted to him.

He was a tall, thin lad, with a gentle, soft face, like a girl's. He would only go to films in which there was lots of fighting: he had seen *Chapayev** twenty-five times, *Shchors* twenty times, *If it's war . . .* seventeen, and *Bogdan Khmelnitsky* ten times over.

---

* Vasili Chapayev (1887–1919), a Red Army hero of the Civil War, about whom a well-known film was made in 1934. [Tr.]

We were all mad about war, but Bolik was a fanatic on the subject. He was so carried away by the whole idea that he could talk about it for hours on end. For him even a game of chess was a form of warfare—a rook was a cannon, a knight a gun-cart, a bishop was a machine-gun and a queen a dive-bomber. You can imagine the sort of battle-sounds we produced in the course of a game of chess.

In the barn, up in the loft, Bolik had set up a machine-gun nest, the sort of thing Chapayev had in a bell-tower. We would poke sticks out of the little window in the roof and pretend to be firing on those undefined enemies who, 'if it's war tomorrow . . .'

Bolik went off to an industrial training school and started to look down on us because he had become a member of the working class, one of the lords of the land, if you were to believe the Constitution. But then the real war broke out, and he was mobilized and sent off to labour on the construction of defence works—on the trenches, as they used to say then—and he was lost from sight altogether.

SHURKA KRYSAN was the same age as myself, small and lightly built, quick on his feet, very enterprising and an unbelievably good companion, ready to go through fire and water for the sake of his friends. In the military operations which took place regularly on our street between our gang and the neighbouring 'leather-lads' (another gang of warriors who lived near the tannery) Shurka would perform incredible feats of heroism but used always to suffer more than the rest.

For him the film *If it's war . . .* was the one he liked most of all, and, of course, the song as well.

He used to be called 'Shurka Matso', and I always called him that, because, after all, you've got to call a chap something, but I was so naive that I had no idea that *matzo* was what Jews eat traditionally at the Passover. In my simplicity I thought that it was a way of teasing Shurka for his way of speaking fast, as if he was just repeating tsa-tsa-tsa . . .

At that time we were not in the least interested in the question of our origins and nationality. We all went to a Ukrainian school, and Ukrainian was our native tongue.

It was only later that I came to distinguish who was what and to realize that we were hybrids—one half-Polish, one half-Jewish and one half-Ukrainian. We later found out that one of our playmates, a girl called Lala who lived near by, was half-Finnish. I was very fond of her, but she wouldn't join in our war games. She was just a girl—what could you expect?

In fairness I have to say that I used also to be teased; not very often, it's true, but it deeply offended me. They nicknamed me 'Semerik, troo-too-too—three buckets of milk, because of my grandfather.

6. Kill Your Officers Yids and Wops

One day in beautiful weather Shurka Matso and I went swimming. There was a little lake, down by the meadow, called the Kovbanka which when translated out of the Kurenyovka dialect means something like 'Froggypond'.

It was after the outbreak of war and there were military vehicles moving across the meadow, Red Army men chasing about, anti-aircraft guns in position and covered with green branches, and anti-aircraft balloons being inflated.

And just by our Kovbanka a couple of Red Army men were sunning themselves.

'Listen, kids, you'd better get out of here, it's too dangerous,' they said.

We felt hurt and put on long faces, but we didn't go away. We swam across to the other side and back, just to show off and demonstrate how well we could swim. In fact we swam like puppy-dogs, and on the way back, I got tired, started gasping for breath and beating about with my tired arms. My head began to swim, and I saw one of the soldiers on the shore watching my marathon efforts with interest. At that moment I felt the bottom with my foot and staggered out on to the shore, only to look round and find that Shurka was missing.

The soldier dived into the water just as he was, in his breeches and boots, and disappeared leaving only ripples on the surface. He re-emerged dragging with him a white-faced Shurka looking like a kitten, put him on the bank and then shook him so that the water came out of Matso's stomach.

'See what a nuisance you make of yourselves?' he said. 'Now get off home or I'll hand you over to the police.'

At that we beat it at such a rate that the reeds rustled in our wake. We hid ourselves in a little hole in the ground and compared experiences.

'Yeah,' said Shurka, 'he got in my way. You see, I had dived and was swimming along the bottom to the edge.'

German planes appeared in the sky, about thirty of them. The anti-aircraft guns quickly raised their barrels to the sky. The first shell-fire deafened us and the blast banged our faces against the ground.

There was absolutely nowhere for us to hide on that level meadow, so we stayed clinging tightly to one another in our little hole, listening to the sound of either shrapnel or bullets dropping around us: shpok, shpok, shpok.

Lying there completely exposed to the blue sky above, across which planes with black crosses were zooming, I had for the first time a physical sense of the vulnerability and helplessness of the frail human body, which only needed one of those 'shpoks' to land in it, as in a dish of jelly, to finish it off.

The anti-aircraft guns didn't hit them, and the bombers went away without doing any damage. But thousands of sparkling white leaflets came floating down from the sky. The wind had obviously not carried them as far as the city and they were coming down right on top of us in the meadow. We rushed out to grab some of them, and found that every one had printed on it in big letters:

KILL YOUR OFFICERS YIDS AND WOPS
SLOSH 'EM IN THEIR UGLY CHOPS

It was without any punctuation. Underneath in small letters it was explained that this was the password for anyone who wanted to give himself up as a prisoner. All you had to do was say those words clearly and distinctly on meeting a German soldier.

Men of the Red Army! (the leaflet's appeal read). The Red Army has been smashed. The rule of the Jewish-Bolshevik commissars in Russia is at an end. Arrest your commanders and commissars, lay down your

arms and give yourselves up as prisoners. You will be
treated well and you will all return to your homes to
take up peaceful occupations. Those intending to sur-
render should take with them a change of underwear,
soap, a bowl and a spoon.

I was very impressed by the leaflet, especially by the bit
about the bowl and spoon. I began to feel how hungry I
was after our swim, and I could just imagine what tasty por-
ridge the Germans were cooking and ladling out generously
to everyone who gave himself up.

Then I felt something was wrong and turned round.
Shurka was sitting there, holding the leaflet, but pale, with
terror in his eyes.

'Tolik,' he said. 'But I'm—a Yid.'

7. *A Second Tsaritsyn?*

For several days we waited at home, our cases ready
packed. The only people being evacuated were those connected with particular enterprises, and it was practically
impossible for private individuals to get away.

My grandmother's nephews had promised to take us along
with the 'Arsenal' Factory. They had plenty of room on the
flat trucks, and were even able to put some of their furniture in among the machines.

But when Uncle Peter came to say good-bye he told us:

'We are on a special train, and the N.K.V.D. has forbidden us to take outsiders along.'

Grandma burst into tears and pushed a pot of lard into
his hands, saying: 'You can eat that on the way,' then ran
after him at the gate and pressed a little cushion on him:
'You can use it to rest your head on on the train.' Nobody
ever went away from her empty-handed.

Meanwhile there was still no reply to the telegrams my
mother had sent my father.

Mother and I picked up our cases and to the accompaniment of Grandma's sorrowful lament caught a tram and
set off for the railway station. The city had a strange look:
all the windows were criss-crossed with strips of paper; sand-
bags were piled in front of the shop windows, and more

were piled across the roads as barricades, with only narrow gaps, reinforced with wood, left for the trams. On all sides there were posters saying: MAKE KIEV A SECOND TSARITSYN.*

We travelled one stop and the tram came to a halt: a young man had been badly hurt in an accident somewhere ahead. There was only just enough room for the tramcars to pass through the gaps in the barricades; one tramcar had been very full, and the young fellow had not been able to squeeze through. He had been squashed up against the boards, twisted round and his arm had been ripped off. They carried him off to the hospital, his arm still hanging by a shred of skin, dragging along the ground.

Very slowly the tram managed to get as far as the new school on the Petrovka, which had been taken over two days previously as a hospital. People with their heads in bandages were peering out of the windows. Then suddenly the hooters wailed—an air-raid alarm. Wardens with red arm-bands ran along the tramlines.

'Everybody out! Into the shelters!'

But my mother and I ran off along the empty tramlines. There was some shooting and bombing going on somewhere, but not over our heads, and we got as far as Nizhny Val, where we hoped to get on a No. 13 tram for the station. But we found that trams were no longer going that far.

Again the sirens wailed. People were running about all the way down the street, and distracted air-raid wardens had no idea where to direct people—there were no air-raid shelters, only holes dug in the courtyards of buildings. It was not long since they had been singing 'If it's war . . .', but the idea had been to fight on someone else's territory.

My mother and I ran from one house to another. She was simply beside herself and shouted at the wardens: 'This is our house, let us in!' In this way we ran the whole way to Andrew's Hill, where there were no wardens and lots of people were hurrying up the narrow twisting street, taking advantage of the fact that it was not blocked.

I could see no point in having all those barriers when there were no air-raid shelters. The city was wide open to

* Tsaritsyn, a city on the Volga, the scene of a battle in the Civil War in which Stalin was said to have played an important part. It was renamed Stalingrad in 1925, destroyed in the Battle of Stalingrad in 1942–3, and renamed Volgograd after Stalin's death in 1953. [Tr.]

the bombers, and the defenceless people were rushing around in it like mice.

As we came near Bogdan Khmelnitsky Square the bombers appeared overhead, and we dived into a gateway jammed with people. The sound of shooting and explosions echoed down the shaft of the stairway, pieces of plaster came tumbling down, children were crying and the inhabitants were bringing water for people to drink. It was terrible to think that a bomb might land on the building and bring it crashing down on our heads.

When things became quieter we started running, still with our cases and quite out of breath, towards the Kreshchatik, from where trolley-buses went to the station. Again the sirens screamed and we were pushed along with a whole stream of people into a dimly lit basement piled high with boards and barrels. The din from the street still reached us down there, and what looked like a very insecure ceiling kept shaking violently. An old man said to Mother: 'If this lot comes down on us, it'll be for keeps.' My mother couldn't stand it and started making her way through the crowd and up the steps.

But they weren't letting anyone go out of the gateway and the wardens were saying that the station was being bombed, that there was no transport going in that direction, that thousands of people were there already, that whole trains had been set on fire, and that the October Hospital was already crammed full of injured brought from the station.

There were a lot of other people in the gateway like us, with their cases, and the story then went around that you could still get on to the barges that were being sent off down the Dnieper. So when the all-clear was sounded we started running back again to Podol, but before we reached it there was another alarm. It was like a nightmare.

They chased us into the building of the lower station of the funicular railway. This time it was a raid on Podol itself—a fantastic din, pieces of glass flying everywhere, a fire breaking out somewhere, and on the other side of the Dnieper a plane coming down in flames.

Pale and anxious, the old women sat there on their bundles, and beside them stood a middle-aged Jewish woman who was saying:

'All right, so they say the Jews have to get away, but what for? Did we ever hear anything bad about the Germans before the war? Now they are putting stories around, but why do we have to believe rumours? Even if we wanted to get away, tell me, how would we do it? Do we have a lot of money? No, we've got no money. And without money you can't get on a train; you can't even get away on foot. Some folk from our house went off, got as far as Darnitsa, lost all their things, ran out of food and had a terrible time and finally came back to Podol. Now the papers say that the Germans will hang yellow stars round our necks and send us off labouring. All right, so we shall work. What else have we seen but work up till now? Only trouble. The Germans are bound to understand that. We are not aristocrats and we're not rich, we're just poor people, we've been working hard all our lives and things can't be any worse. We've decided to stay where we are.'

The women nodded their heads sorrowfully. It was true that until the war started only good things were written about Hitler, and nobody had heard he treated the Jews badly. So let the party officials and secret police and factory managers run for it, but what had poor people to run away from? As for the yellow star, it was obvious that they were lying, and so were the stories about the Germans maltreating the Jews—that was all newspaper lies. If not, why had they not written about it before? They had gone on lying to the very limit, that was the trouble. My mother listened to all this talk and then suddenly took fright lest the Germans should drop a bomb on the funicular, so we dashed off across the Post Office Square towards the river landing stage. The approaches to it were black with people all carrying their baggage. Policemen were shouting and whistling and trying to force the crowd back. A man in a white suit and a straw hat was announcing in a very hoarse voice:

'Listen everybody, enterprises and organizations are being evacuated first. Go back home and don't crowd together in one place. The public will be kept informed and everybody will be evacuated just as soon as we get the enterprises on their way. So go away! We're not taking anybody!'

Frustrated by all this, we sat and rested a little in the crowd and then went away. No trams were running. They were saying that the school which had been turned into a hospital on the Petrovka had been bombed out. It was amazing how the Germans had found out—it was only a couple of days since it had become a hospital . . .

A lorry came down the Nizhny Val with a soldier aboard giving out copies of *Pravda*. I managed to get hold of one. The bulletin issued by the Soviet Information Office said that there had been no substantial change in the situation at the front. That meant that things were going badly for us.

The Petrovka had been cordoned off: The bomb had not fallen on the hospital but on a single-storey house next to it. Only a small section of one wall was left; all the people living in it had been killed and their bodies were just being dug out. But the school had been damaged, windows and window-frames had been blown out, and people were evacuating the wounded, carrying them out and putting them in ambulances.

8. *Bolik Comes Back*

All this time I was bemoaning the fact that I wasn't older, so that I could join the volunteers or, like Bolik, at least go to work on the defences, and then I could have stayed there to help man them.

Then one day the news went round our gang that Bolik had come back.

I rushed down to see him. I found his mother fussing over him while he was stuffing himself with potato, half choking as he told his story:

'We were digging an anti-tank trench, a damned long one, right across the fields. There were thousands of people there, all sorts of professors and girls and that. I saw a Messerschmitt dive on us and machine-gun us and then I saw my professor lying there with no lenses in his glasses . . . I hid in a pile of hay.'

Then German tanks appeared and the people ran off in all directions. Bolik had gone off through the woods and across the fields and finally took refuge from the 'Messers' in the marshes. He trembled when he talked about them; he hated the Germans so much that he started stuttering:

'He'll dive right at you, aiming at you, as if he's after you personally, trying to get you, and there's nothing you can do, doesn't matter whether you shout or cry or fall down'. . . Anyway, listen chaps, I'll let you into a secret. We'll get hold of a machine-gun and set it up in the attic, and when they come, boy, we'll let 'em have it—whee-ee-ee-ee-ee!'

Aunt Nina, his mother, was crying from joy that he was alive. She washed him clean, fitted him out in a clean suit and gave him money for the cinema. So Bolik and I went off together to the cinema on the Kreshchatik to see a funny film called *St Jorgen's Day*. We laughed till tears ran down our faces at the antics of Igor Ilinsky, despite the fact that we could hear the sirens going and bombs exploding outside: the programmes were not interrupted during a raid.

We left the cinema, bought ourselves ice-creams and strolled down the Kreshchatik. We felt fine and knew nothing of what was really going on—that the decision had already been taken to abandon Kiev without fighting; that we were seeing the Kreshchatik for the last time, and had been watching a comedy film in a building which had already been mined; that the next day Bolik would be evacuated along with the rest of his school, and that he would vanish again without even having said good-bye.

The loudspeakers on the Kreshchatik were proclaiming in triumphant tones: 'This is Kiev speaking; this is Soviet Kiev speaking! Kiev calling Russia—do you hear us? Kiev is and will remain Soviet!' Moscow's reply to Kiev was: 'You have revived the immortal traditions of the heroic era of the Great October Revolution and the Civil War. You do not stand alone. The Red Army is with you. The whole Soviet people is with you.'

Words, words . . .

We went home in the opposite direction to a stream of troops who had obviously been on the retreat for a long time. The Red Army men were utterly exhausted, dust and sweat caked on their faces. On an old farm-cart drawn by bullocks a tough-looking lad in a fur hat, a dead-pan expression on his face, was sitting playing a gay tune on the accordion.

Meanwhile the women came streaming out on to the pavements to watch, arms folded, sighing, sniffing and sobbing. A frail old man with a stick was standing near a post, weeping, and he called out to the young man playing the folk dance:

'Come back, lads, come back . . .'

Many of the people were crying as they watched their menfolk retreating.

The little garden in front of our house was crammed full of tired Red Army men sitting and lying around. One of them was working on a 'Maxim' machine-gun, so we sat down by him and watched carefully what he was doing. He said:

'Listen kids, I'll give you a rouble: go and bring me a drink of milk.'

We dashed off down to my grandmother's. She was full of sympathy, wouldn't take the rouble, but gave us a jug of milk. The Red Army men held out their cans and we poured the milk into them, but it was only a drop in the ocean.

My grandfather was carting bread down the street.

There was no longer any bread to be bought in the shops, it was being distributed according to lists that had been drawn up. Every household had to make themselves a bag and write their name on it in ink. Then in the shop they divided the bread up among the bags, and Grandpa was given the job of taking them around on a little cart. Eager to be doing something, we quickly took over the job of pushing the cart, knocking on the doors and emptying out the bags. It was a tricky business weaving our way through the marching soldiers.

'So it's all over, lads, is it?' said my grandfather. 'Kiev is being abandoned.'

'Kiev is to be a second Tsaritsyn,' we said indignantly. 'You just wait, Gramp, you don't know the sort of fighting there's going to be!'

'Don't talk about fighting,' Gramp said with an impatient gesture. 'Just look at 'em—how do you think they're going to fight?'

Tired, scraggy old nags were drawing military carts, weapons and rickety farm-carts. The Red Army men were ragged, bearded and wounded. Some who had walked till their feet were bleeding were going barefoot with their boots slung over their shoulders. Others had no boots or shoes at all. They moved along without any sort of order, like a herd of cattle, bent under the weight of their kit-bags, greatcoats and weapons, their tea-cans rattling in a very unwarlike way.

'Oh, those poor soldiers of ours,' my grandfather mumbled, taking off his hat.

A Chapter of Original Documents

ORDER

It is forbidden for anybody living in the city to be out of doors between 1800 hours and 0500 hours, German time. People failing to observe this order may be shot.

*Commandant of the city of Kiev**

Extract from an announcement:
All males between the ages of 15 and 60 are to present themselves at the housing office in their district . . .†

Title of a feature article in a newspaper:

THE YID—THE PEOPLE'S WORST ENEMY‡

Entry into the city by persons not resident in Kiev is strictly forbidden. Any person who arrived in Kiev after September 20th must leave the city immediately. Anyone who has a good reason for remaining in the city must obtain permission to do so from the city Commandant. Such permits are issued at the permit department, at 8 Komintern Street.

Anyone remaining in the city without permission after October 15th, 1941, will be liable to severe punishment.

City Commandant§

From an article entitled 'Tasks for the Ukrainian Intellectuals':

---

* *Ukrainskoye Slovo*, September 29th, 1941.
† Op. cit., September 30th, 1941.
‡ Op. cit., October 2nd, 1941.
§ Op. cit., October 9th, 1941.

Our task is to restore the national culture of the Ukraine, destroyed by the Jewish Bolsheviks.*

Announcement by the Commandant:

As a reprisal for an act of sabotage, 100 inhabitants of the city of Kiev were executed today.

This is a warning.

Every inhabitant of Kiev will be held responsible for every act of sabotage committed.

Kiev, October 22nd, 1941

                                   City Commandant†

ORDER

All pigeons in the city and suburbs must be destroyed immediately.

Anyone found still keeping pigeons after October 26th will be EXECUTED as a saboteur.

                                          EBERHARDT
                                   City Commandant‡

Day after day the newspaper gives special prominence to the following appeal:

The Führer of the German people has said:

'Millions of German peasants and workers are carrying out their obligations in exemplary fashion.'

Ukrainians! You too must carry out your obligations and work hard!§

Our Führer Adolf Hitler said on October 3rd, 1941

'We shall make the whole continent play a part in our battle with Bolshevism.'

The place of every Ukrainian is at Germany's side in the battle for a better Europe!¶

Announcement by the Commandant:

---

* Op. cit., October 10th, 1941.
† *Nimetsko-fashistski okupatsini rezhim na Ukraini (The German-Fascist Occupation of the Ukraine)*—a collection of documents and facts (Kiev, 1963), p. 45. (In Ukrainian.)
‡ *Ukrainskoye Slovo*, October 25th, 1941.
§ Op. cit., October 22nd, 1941.
¶ Op. cit., October 25th, 1941.

Cases of arson and sabotage are becoming more frequent in the city of Kiev and oblige me to take firm action. For this reason 300 inhabitants of Kiev were executed today. For every additional case of arson or sabotage a considerably larger number of inhabitants of the city will be executed.

Every inhabitant must immediately inform the German police of anything arousing his suspicions.

I shall maintain order and calm in Kiev at any cost and by all the means at my disposal.

Kiev, November 2nd, 1941

EBERHARDT
Major–General
*City Commandant**

All felt boots now in the possession of the civilian population, including children's sizes, are to be requisitioned immediately. The use of felt boots is forbidden and will be punished in the same way as the use of weapons without permission.†

Announcement by the City Commissar:

In accordance with an understanding reached with the city Commandant, the population of the city of Kiev is informed that civilians have the right to be on the streets only from 0500 hours to 1730 hours.

City Commissar‡

Announcement by the Commandant:

Means of communication in the city of Kiev (telephone, telegraph and underground cables) have been maliciously damaged. Since it is no longer possible to tolerate such hostile activity, 400 MALES HAVE BEEN EXECUTED IN THE CITY. This should serve as a warning to the population.

Once again I demand that the German police or Ger-

---

* *The German-Fascist Occupation of the Ukraine* (Kiev, 1963), p. 46.
† *Kiev—Gorod-Geroi (Kiev—Heroic City)*, a collection of material on the achievements of the people of Kiev in the Great Fatherland War (Kiev, 1961), p. 234.
‡ *The German-Fascist Occupation of the Ukraine* (Kiev, 1963), p. 55.

man military should be informed of all suspicious incidents, so that the criminals may be punished as they deserve.

Kiev 29.xi.1941

EBERHARDT
Major–General
*City Commandant**

By German Time

A hundred hostages, three hundred hostages, four hundred hostages . . . It was now a war on the whole population of the city.

The destruction of the Kreshchatik and the fires that followed it were the work of agents left behind in the city by the N.K.V.D. But the people executed for those deeds were just ordinary people picked up at random. The purpose was achieved—the Germans became more violent. And the fact that they could not get their hands on the real culprits served only to make them still more violent. It was as though they had been punched on the nose by a professional boxer, but were venting their wrath on the first child who came along. Having shot all the Jews in Babi Yar in the course of a few days, they now set about taking Russians, Ukrainians and people of other nationalities off there.

They would take the hostages at night, by simply cordoning off some district at random and seizing the number of people stated in the official announcement. On one occasion they simply arrested people in broad daylight as they walked down the pavement on the Kreshchatik. The Kreshchatik itself was still smouldering, but it had been reopened to pedestrian traffic. At the very end of it there was a small area which had miraculously escaped damage, including the building of the Duma on Kalinin Square, which looked like an opera house. Then, belatedly, that building too was blown up and

---

* *The German-Fascist Occupation of the Ukraine*, p. 60.

burst into flames. The Germans proceeded to arrest everybody who happened to be on the Kreshchatik at that moment, put them into lorries and sent them off to Babi Yar.

In Kurenyovka, just at the top of Babi Yar, is the large Pavlov Psychiatric Hospital. Its buildings are spread about in the lovely Kirillov wood, where there is also a little twelfth-century chapel, quite forgotten and long out of use, which has fallen gradually into ruins. We boys used to clamber into it and scramble around inside right up into the domes, where we could just make out the last frescoes painted by Vrubel which very few people knew about.

On October 14th a detachment of Germans with a doctor in charge drove up to this little chapel. They were equipped with mobile gas-chambers, which had never been seen before.

They packed the hospital patients into the gas-chambers in groups of sixty or seventy, then ran the engines for some fifteen minutes so that the exhaust gases went into the vans. Then the suffocated people were taken out and dropped into a pit. This work went on for several days, quietly and methodically. The Germans were not in a hurry, and took regular hour-long breaks for meals.

The patients in the hospital were not all mad; there were many who were simply being treated for nervous disorders. But they were all buried in the pits of Babi Yar. Most remarkable of all was that after the first horrible days of Babi Yar the destruction of all the patients in an enormous hospital went practically unnoticed and was even taken as a matter of course . . . It is indeed true that everything in this world is relative.

The Germans hunted down gypsies like wild animals. They were due for the same immediate liquidation as the Jews.

A person's identity card was of decisive importance. Every Soviet identity card contains, as if it were something quite natural, an entry giving the holder's nationality—the so-called 'fifth paragraph'. Nobody ever thought that it would one day prove fatal for masses of people. I must say that I never could understand, then or later, and presumably I never shall understand, why it should be necessary to indicate a person's nationality in his or her identity papers.

The Germans used to check everybody's papers and comb through the houses, rounding people up and stopping on the street anyone whose appearance aroused their suspicions. Even if a man had 'Russian' written in his identity card, the Germans were not always convinced and they might still haul him off for an expert opinion. People with dark hair and long noses found it better not to show themselves on the street.

The gypsies were taken off to Babi Yar, whole camps at a time; and it appears, moreover, that they too did not realize until the last moment what was happening to them.

One day a German soldier approached the old yard-cleaner at our school, Ratuyev, and made the old man take a spade and follow him. They went to the local recreation park, where another soldier was standing guard over a Jewish girl from whose appearance the old man gathered that the soldiers had been raping her.

They ordered the old fellow to dig a hole. When it was ready they pushed the girl down into it, but she started screaming and struggling. Then the soldiers proceeded to hit her over the head with the spade and shovel earth on her. But she got up into a sitting position and they struck her over the head again.

Finally they covered her up and stamped the earth down. The old man thought the same thing was going to happen to him but they let him go.

The curfew imposed by the Commandant cost many people their lives. Shooting went on all night, first in one part, then in another. In the Bessarabka my grandmother saw a young woman lying dead in the street, with glassy eyes, right across the pavement so that everybody had to walk round her. They said she had been hurrying home in the evening after the curfew, had been shot by a patrol and left to lie there so that everyone should see.

Quite a lot of people also met their deaths later in Babi Yar because of the ban on keeping pigeons. That was because the order came into force the very day after it was published, before everybody had had time to read it in the newspapers.

In the early days orders were posted up in three languages —Russian, Ukrainian and German. Later they appeared in only two—in large type in Ukrainian and in small type in German. Later still it was the other way round—the German in big letters and the Ukrainian in very small script . . .

Everything of importance was concentrated in these orders and announcements; your very life depended on them, and after the tragedy with the pigeon-fanciers, the only question was: What's the latest order?

At the same time as they were rounding up the few remaining Jews and gypsies they also started arresting Communists and Soviet officials. What is more, they arrested them on the word of the first informer to come along, without any attempt at checking, a procedure with which the population had been quite familiar since 1937, so that the foreign Gestapo turned out to be exactly the same as the home-grown N.K.V.D. You were in trouble if you had a personal enemy or someone who envied your position. In the old days he would have written a report to the effect that you were against the Soviet system, that is to say an 'enemy of the people', and you would have disappeared. Now he could write that you were opposed to German rule, which also meant that you were an enemy of the people, and you could expect to fetch up in Babi Yar. The Germans even used the same term— 'enemy of the people'.

Notices were posted on the hoardings saying that anyone who informed the German authorities about Jews or partisans in hiding, about important Bolshevik officials who had not reported for registration as Communists, or about other enemies of the people, would receive ten thousand roubles in cash or in the form of foodstuffs or a cow.

There were plenty of people in hiding—in basements and store-rooms. One Russian family saved their Jewish neighbours by cutting off part of a room with a false brick wall, leaving a narrow cavity with no light and practically no air in which the Jews lived for two years.

But that was unusual. In most cases the hidden people were discovered, because there were plenty of people glad enough to have the money or the cow. Near our market in Kurenyovka, for instance, there lived a certain Praskovya Derkach. She would nose around until she found out where some Jews were hiding and then go to them and say:

'Aha! So there you are! So you don't want to go to Babi Yar? Out with your gold! Let's have your cash!'

They would hand her over all they had. Then she would make a statement to the police and demand another reward. Her husband Vasili had a horse and cart and they usually took the Jews off to the Yar on it. On the way Praskovya and her husband would be snatching clothes and watches off the people, saying:

'You won't need these any more!'.

They carted off sick people, children and pregnant women. It was only at the beginning that the Germans paid the reward. Later they stopped, but Praskovya was satisfied with what she managed to grab, and then, with the Germans' permission, she would search the home the people had left, taking all the best things, and Vasili would cart the rest off to the German stores with a certificate saying: 'We, the undersigned, have confiscated the following articles for the needs of the German army.'

*

It is a curious fact that Praskovya continues to flourish to this day. She lives on Menzhinsky Street and has never been punished in any way, maybe because she did not betray any N.K.V.D. agents or Communists, but just a few Jews. She is, of course, older now, but only in her body, not in her mind. The neighbours often hear her giving her views: 'You think that's the end of the war? Oh no, not yet. The Germans will come back from over there, and the Chinese will come from over there—then we'll give the Yids something worse than Babi Yar!'

Burning the Books

'Come on, let's have all your certificates,' my grandfather said. 'All Soviet publications and all portraits of party leaders —let's get 'em all into the fire. Come on, Marusya, get busy.'

On the left-hand side of my school certificates was a portrait of Lenin and on the right a portrait of Stalin. My grandfather, who had never previously shown very much interest in books, now set about getting them into the stove, whole bundles at a time.

At first my mother tried to argue against it, but then she gave up. People had already been arrested for having the Soviet flag, for having a portrait of Stalin lying about in the house, and for telling jokes.

People started repeating a jingle: 'The Jews are done for and so are the gypsies. Next on the list are the Ukes.' Grandma heard it down at the market and when she got back she repeated it with a grim smile to Grandpa. He said nothing, just stood there blinking his eyes—it really looked as if it was coming to that. Then he quickly set about burning the books.

This time it was cold outside, and the books got the stove burning well. My mother brought a little shovel, cleaned out the ash-pit and gathered up the ashes dumbly and thoughtfully. I said:

'Never mind, one day we'll have lots of books again.'

'No, never,' she said. 'That will never be. I have no faith any more. In this world there's neither goodness nor peace nor good sense. The world is governed by evil-minded idiots. And books are always being burnt. The library at Alexandria went up in flames, the Inquisitors had their bonfires, Radishchev* was burnt, books were burnt under Stalin, there have been bonfires in the squares under Hitler, and there will be more and more of them burnt. There are always more people to burn books than to write them. You have your life ahead of you, Tolya, so just remember that this is the first sign of trouble—if books are banned, that means things are going wrong. It means that you are surrounded by force, fear and ignorance, that power is in the hands of barbarians. My God, just to think . . . It's bad enough when bands of vandals start throwing books on to a fire in the main square, but that's not the worst that can happen. It's always possible that there is only a limited number of them—the vandals, that is. But when every single person in every home starts shaking with

---

* Alexander Radishchev (1749–1802), writer and thinker, regarded as the founder of the revolutionary tradition in Russia. [Tr.]

fright and burning his own books . . . to reduce a whole
nation to that level! That takes some doing! I ask myself why
on earth did I ever have you? To have to live in such a
world . . .'

I have never forgotten those words of hers all my life.
Maybe she didn't use exactly those words, but I have conveyed the exact sense of what she said—about the library in
Alexandria, and about the Inquisition, about which I thus
learned in a very practical manner, because in fact a bridge
had been built directly from those events to the stove in our
house.

They took the ashes out and spread them on the garden
to improve the soil. The only books that Grandpa spared
were the six-volume collections. He didn't quite know *what*
to do with Pushkin: on the one hand, he was a Russian poet
—that is to say, a bloody Russian; on the other hand, he
wasn't anti-German and he hadn't said anything against the
Bolsheviks. So in the end, out of all our books, we kept only
Pushkin.

Having taken over the school for their own purposes, a
German military unit spent several hours throwing the desks,
instruments, globes and books out of the windows.

They threw the books from the Kurenyovka district library
straight into the farmyard. There were also books lying
around in the streets, trampled underfoot like rubbish.

When the soldiers were withdrawn and departed from the
school I went in to have a look. Apparently they had turned
the whole of the ground floor into stables. The floor of our
classroom was covered in a deep layer of straw and manure,
which my feet sank into, and iron hooks had been driven into
the walls to tie the horses to.

In the classrooms on the first and second floors there were
plain bunks covered with straw, and the floors were scattered
with bits of newspapers with pictures of naked women, bandages and contraceptives.

On the playground outside they had built a soldiers' latrine.
They made these by simply digging out a long trench and
putting beams along the whole length of them, on which you
would always see a long line of soldiers sitting with their
trousers down and their bottoms stuck out in full view,
noisily relieving themselves. They would always be reading

newspapers and magazines, which they would leaf through slowly as if they were in a reading-room, and then use the pages for other purposes.

The mountain of books thrown out of the library had already been badly damaged by the rain: the volumes on top were sodden and their pages stuck together. I scrambled up on to the top of the pile and started to dig down into it. The books inside the pile were wet, slimy and warm—they were becoming mildewed.

Huddled away from the wind I sat on top of the pile, sorting through the books, found Hugo's *Bug-Jargal* and became absorbed. I couldn't tear myself away, and when it finally got dark I took it along with me.

Next day I got hold of a sack and took it with me to the pile of books. I sorted out the ones which had suffered least and which had the strongest bindings, brought them home and stacked them away in the shed, behind the firewood. I thought up a story to satisfy my grandfather: 'We haven't got much firewood, but these books will dry out and then we can use them in the stove,' I said.

He pondered this a little. On the one hand they were books once again, but on the other they were not ours, and we could always explain where we found them and that we had only taken them for fuel. 'All right, smart boy,' he said. 'Only don't bring any Lenin or Stalin here.' But I wasn't interested at all in Lenin or Stalin—what I wanted most was to gather together as many novels and science fiction stories as possible.

We had run out of paraffin. The electric lamps hung life-less from the ceiling. So I made some long splinters of wood and stuck them in the split end of a stick and lit them. It turned out to be not such a bad light—after all, our ancestors had lived their whole lives by the light of such tapers. They burn well and you can read by them, using one hand to adjust the taper from time to time and occasionally removing a burnt-out one and lighting another. What's more, they give off a pleasant smell of pine and even provide a little warmth.

I made a place for myself on the stove, which was prac-tically cold because Grandma was being very careful with the wood. My cat Titus would join me and we would keep each other warm while I read. I got through an astonishing number of books in those days!

But my grandfather would carefully gather them up for fuel as I finished reading them, and in fairness to him I must say he would always ask:

'Have you finished with this one? Be careful, or you'll ruin your eyes.'

I would remain engrossed in my reading late into the night, until my bundle of tapers was finished. My mother would come out, clasping and unclasping her hands, and looking at me strangely.

'Why don't you sleep?' I would ask her crossly.

'I can hear a car outside, I can't sleep,' she would reply.

Hunger

Then a very strange situation developed. The shops were deserted, their windows broken, and nothing was being sold anywhere except at the market. But, even if the shops were to open again, what would there be to buy?

Before the war, bread in the shops cost ninety kopeks a kilogram. Now you could sometimes get home-made bread at the market for ninety *roubles* a kilogram.

That was almost as much as my mother was paid for a month's work. And now we hadn't any money left at all.

My grandparents decided to sell a few things. They went through their drawers looking for things to get rid of, but everything was worn out. Under Soviet rule the purchase of a pair of shoes or an overcoat was a major event in your life, and every article of clothing was worn down to the last thread, then patched up and later turned. Grandma took some old clothes to the market to sell, stood there with them for two whole days, but nobody wanted to buy them; everybody wanted to sell.

My mother and grandmother scraped together all our stores of food and dried peel, brushed up every crumb of food, scratched their heads trying to work out exactly how much we should eat each day, devised ways of making pancakes from potatoes and peas. They had to fry without any fat. My grandfather was furious when he remembered Uncle Peter:

'What did you want to go and give that scoundrel a pot of lard for? He's got a good job with the Bolsheviks and he'll be able to eat his fill out there in the Urals, and yet you went and gave him our last pot of lard!'

And so we started to economize.

It was a new word in my vocabulary, and I rather liked it. I had a little box hidden away on the stove in which I began to build up my own private reserves. I never ate the whole of anything that Grandma gave me, especially if it was dried bread. I used always to hide a bit of it away against the day when there would be nothing at all left and I would be able to offer everybody food from my store.

There was an old nut tree with long, overhanging branches growing next to our house. Every autumn Grandma used to pick a whole bag of nuts and keep them on one side for Christmas. This bag now became our emergency rations and our last hope.

My grandfather and I climbed the fence and set about digging the land belonging to the vegetable farm, from time to time coming across a few potatoes that had been left in the ground. I would simply scream with delight whenever I found one.

On Peter-Paul Square we combed through the little garden and managed to collect half a sack of chestnuts. Those wild horse-chestnuts are sharp and bitter to the taste, but when they are dried and roasted they are not so bad. If you're really hungry they are even quite tasty; it's all a matter of getting used to them. At the time I was reading Sholokhov's *And Quiet Flows the Don,* and as I read I ate the chestnuts that had been dried on the stove. As a result I have associated Sholokhov's book ever since with the taste of chestnuts. Despite the passing of the years, and the number of times I have re-read it and seen it as a film, and even written examination papers about it, the taste of chestnuts still lingers on!

One morning, as she was washing herself, my mother commented:

'How extraordinary—I can feel all the bones in my face.'

I started to probe my own face, and found I could feel

how the thin skin was drawn so tightly over it that I could study the whole bone structure. As I kept on poking and probing I began to feel quite ill at ease.

'Eat, eat.' For days on end the little worm of hunger was gnawing away inside my stomach. 'What would you like to eat?' At night I dreamt of real meals, of luscious, luxurious dinners; but I was very strong-willed and I would go for days eating hardly anything but the chestnuts. Grandma used to wash the potato peelings and grate them down to make pancakes. They were sort of bitter-sweet, but they made a good meal.

We kept a flat brick in the pantry to put frying-pans and saucepans on. Scores of times I made the mistake of thinking it was a loaf of bread, and finally I threw it out. I simply couldn't bear to see it in the pantry any longer.

Suddenly the word went around that the authorities in Kurenyovka were opening a canteen for starving children. My mother hurried off to see about it, and I was issued with a special card. The first time I went along there was with Lala.

The canteen had been set up in Bondar Lane in what used to be the nursery school. We entered the large building, full of ragged, skinny children of all ages, from the very youngest up to thirteen years old. But it was terribly quiet there; the only noise was the cook's ladle knocking against the bowls.

We stood in a queue to be served and each of us received a plateful of real hot soup. We carried our plates across to the table, sat ourselves down and, so long as we ate, we were happy. I lingered over every spoonful, held the soup in my mouth and strained it through my teeth before swallowing it, feeling each mouthful as it went down inside me and produced a lovely sense of warmth, although there was nothing in that soup but water and wheat grains, nothing at all. And the children would sit there so quietly, none of them making a fuss, some of them rather shamefacedly licking their plates with their tongues.

We started going down every day for our plate of soup as if it were some miraculous gift from above, and I went down regularly all through the winter, always trying to get there just before it closed, because towards the end the soup was thicker at the bottom, and I used to watch greedily to see how deeply the woman serving the soup dipped her ladle in.

Lala's mother worked as a forewoman in the canning factory and was a good friend of my mother's. When she went out to work she used to leave her little girl with my grandmother, and I used to look after her like a sister when we were very young. Later we went to different schools and I acquired a lot of rowdy friends among the boys, while her friends were all girls. But with the opening of the canteen we again became inseparable.

Lala's mother was a party member and was evacuated on her own, leaving her daughter behind with her sister, an elderly, bad-tempered and unsociable spinster who taught German. They bore the oddly non-Russian name of Engstrem. But there are plenty of names like that in the world, I suppose.

On one occasion after we had been to the canteen we dropped into Lala's home. There to my astonishment I saw a big loaf of real fresh bread on the table, a pot of jam and carrier-bags.

I was literally struck dumb.

'We have it issued to us,' Lala said.

'Where?'

I very nearly ran off at once shouting: 'Granny, how come you didn't know they're giving food out and we're not getting any; go down there at once!'

Lala showed me a circular they had received. It said that Volksdeutsche were to report on such-and-such a day to a certain shop, bringing with them their shopping bags and pots.

'What's that mean—Volksdeutsche?'

'It means we're half German—almost Germans.'

'Are you really Germans?'

'No, we are Finns. But the Finns are an Aryan people, Volksdeutsche. My aunt says that I am going to attend a school for Volksdeutsche and become a translator like her.'

'So you've got yourselves nicely fixed up,' I muttered, still not quite grasping the complicated situation—I had always known Lala as a friend, almost a sister with whom I had shared everything, and now, all of a sudden, she was an Aryan, and I was something lower . . .

In the old days it had been the party elite who had lived well, received all they wanted from special shops and never had to stand in queues. Now it was the same for the Aryans. Then it was the Communists; now it was the Aryans. I felt ready to burst with a mixture of rage and hunger. So the shops were all closed for us, so we had to munch horse chestnuts, while they were doing all right!

'So that's it, eh? Volksdeutsche,' I said solemnly. 'And you still keep going to the canteen for starving children, you little horror!'

Off I went, slamming the door so violently that I felt a little ashamed. But I went on hating her for many a long year, although somewhere deep inside me I understood that it wasn't really Lala's fault.

I Go into Business

By this time everybody knew that Shurka Matso had not been sent to Babi Yar, that he was at home but never went out anywhere; his mother was keeping him hidden. She was Russian herself, but had been married to a Jew, which made her son a little Jew.

When Matso finally decided to run the risk of leaving his house, the first thing he did was to rush round to see me, and I hardly recognized him: he was as skinny as a stray kitten, suffering from terrible hunger, with a bluish look about him, and his eyes glistening like little lamps. You could see that they were really in a bad way.

'Let's go down the market and sell matches. You come with me, 'cos I'm scared to go on my own'—he shook his little bag full of boxes of matches. 'Mum asked me to say that you shouldn't call me Matso. My name is Krysan. Alexander—from the Greek Alexandros or Alexandris. I am Alexander Krysan—please don't give me away . . .'

'All right,' I said. 'So we'll call you Alexandrat, chairman of the dead rats.'

He smiled weakly, and I dashed off to my grandmother.

'Give me some matches. We're going down to the market.'

Grandma had a stock of about fifteen boxes of matches, and, after some hesitation, she handed over ten of them. After all, she could simply keep the fire going all the time, or she could slip next door for a hot coal—there was no real need for matches.

It was very cold out of doors. Shurka was shivering in his light overcoat and kept looking around him like a hunted thing, as if he were in a zoo with the wild animals loose.

The market was almost empty. The price of matches was well known—ten roubles a box. We set them out in nice tidy piles on the bare counter of a market-stall and stood there waiting.

Next to us an old woman was selling saccharine. She had it wrapped up in little packets, like the ones they sell powders in at the chemist's, and people did not yet understand what it was. But the old woman was singing loud its praises, saying it was sweet, better than sugar and that one packet was enough for four cups of tea. Goodness only knows where it came from or how so much of it appeared all of a sudden, but throughout the war and for several years afterwards I never saw any sugar, but only saccharine.

Somebody bought a box of matches, and I received for it a crisp ten-rouble note—and that was the end of me. I had money. Money! Real money, with which I could already go and buy enough saccharine for four cups of tea. Shurka was cold and miserable, but I started to feel warm and I waited eagerly for more and more people to buy from me. For the next box I got one German mark, and at last we were able to examine real German money. The exchange at the time was one German mark to ten Soviet roubles. The mark was a small, yellowish-brown note with eagles and swastikas, half as big as our yellowish-brown rouble, on which the stars and hammer and sickle already began to look rather out of place.

By the time it was dark we had managed to sell all our matches and we had money. Our teeth were chattering from excitement and we eyed greedily the potatoes in piles of three on the stalls and the tumblers full of flour. We each bought a couple of pounds of bread and a packet of saccharine.

That evening we had a party at home—everybody was drinking tea with little crystals of saccharine in it and had

real bread to eat. I was bursting with modest pride. I already
knew what I would be doing the next day—selling nuts.

Shurka had nothing left to sell, so I went down on my own.
I just guessed the price to ask—three roubles a nut, or thirty
pfennigs—and people started buying them off me . . . Not
many, but they bought.

Then a boy from next door appeared, Vovka Babarik, once
a friend of mine but later my enemy. He slapped a three-
rouble note down on the counter and chose himself a nut.
A minute later he was back again.

'Change it. It's a bad one.'

'And how do I know; maybe you had a bad one in your
pocket,' I said, because I was greedy for every single rouble.

'Look here—that's one of your nuts!' and he shoved the
two halves under my nose; it certainly was rotten inside.

'You can still eat it!' I argued, holding on to my precious
bag of nuts with trembling hands.

'Change it, Semerik, you greedy devil, or give me my three
roubles back.'

'Not me! You bought it, and that's that,' I said desperately,
although deep inside I felt I was being pretty mean.

He made a move at me with his fist. But I was ready for
him and dived underneath the counter. He came after me. I
dashed off between the rows of stalls, ducking under the
counters, holding my bag tightly, and I was ready to run as
far as Podol rather than give up the three roubles. Vovka got
tired of chasing me, stopped and, eyeing me with great scorn,
said:

'All right, Semerik, troo-too-too—three buckets of milk—'
there was loathing in his voice—'you skunk. We shall meet
again.'

It was indeed our fate to meet again, and at the end I'll
tell you about it . . .

At that time you had to be careful how you moved about
the city, but I was enjoying a sudden feeling of greed and
satisfaction at having obtained three roubles for nothing at
all.

At one time Vovka Babarik and I had been good friends,
though he was somewhat older than I was. Our friendship
came to an end when I let his birds out. He was a keen bird-
fancier, and I used to go along with him and help him and

spend hours looking at his goldfinches, siskins and tits. But later on I started urging him to let them out. I would say: 'All right, why don't you just catch them, keep them for a while, and then let them go. Otherwise they have to stay in their cages for ever until they die. I'm sorry for them.' But he couldn't bring himself to let them go. So one day he hung the cages out in the trees in the garden. Just as I came along he had gone off somewhere, and I opened the doors of all the cages and then ran away. He spent two weeks looking for me everywhere, trying to catch me and give me a hiding.

I had very few nuts left when Shurka came running up.

'I've got hold of some papers. Do you want half?'

He had a basketful of cigarette papers.

'A man I know got them in the looting and doesn't know what to do with them—doesn't smoke himself. He's selling them at ten packets for a rouble, and we can sell them for a rouble apiece! He let me have them on tick for the time being. I thought there's a lot of smokers, they're bound to buy them.'

I took half of them from him on the spot and began to feel that I was really a great businessman. After all, 900 per cent profit on every packet of cigarette papers—it was enough to turn your head. And it was so easy—all you had to do was to stand there and shout: 'Who wants cigarette papers? A rouble a packet!'

The papers were in little booklets of a hundred leaves— you simply tore one out and rolled yourself a fag from cheap tobacco. But the damned ignorant smokers of Kurenyovka had already got into the habit of rolling their cigarettes from the pages of *Ukrainskoye Slovo,* and business was very slack. Only a rouble, ten beastly little pfennigs, yet they were too mean, only glancing at us and walking past. Stingy devils!

To try and attract attention I constructed a little house from the packets, with their fancy labels on the outside. A woman was walking past with a little boy, and when he saw what I'd done his face lit up:

'Mummy—buy me one!'

She had a look and stood there hesitating. I pleaded with her to buy one. The little boy thought that the papers inside the booklet were just as pretty and he was going to be disappointed. But I didn't care; all I cared about was the rouble.

'No, it's a waste of money!' his mother said and led him away.

I watched her go off with hatred in my eyes.

On the first day Shurka and I managed to sell only ten packets. But that was enough to buy us a hundred grammes of bread each, which we ate right there in the square, and I again had a great sense of pride at being able to earn my keep.

'And we can sell newspapers and clean shoes!' Shurka said, trying to think up other ways of making money. His eyes glistened with the fever of starvation.

And it was on all this that we spent our time, busy at the market from morning till night. My grandfather was right: a new life really had started for me.

Bolik Comes Back

Water won't flow under a rock, and if you want to do business you have to keep on the move. You can't afford to let the grass grow under your feet. So we split the market into spheres of influence and, to the best of our ability, restricted our operations to our own halves, hanging around the stalls and pestering people at the entrance.

'Here you are then, cheaper than mushrooms, top quality cigarette paper! Come along now, roll up, let's see your money! Here you are, sir, buy yourself a smoke—good for young and old, once you light up the smoke'll come out your arse! Ugh!—mean old bastard from Kurenyovka . . .'

Business was terribly slack; we barely managed to scrape enough together for a chunk of bread. But I was still going down for my plate of soup at the canteen, so it was just enough to make sure I didn't die of hunger.

One day I was standing at the entrance to the market, trying to sell my wares, when I saw a strangely familiar figure staggering down the street dressed in rags and tatters.

'Shurik!'—I let out a scream that covered the whole market. 'Bolik's back!'

It really was Bolik. My God, he could hardly drag himself along. And the way he looked—thin as a rake, cuts and scratches all over him and covered in dirt from head to foot.

He had returned from an unsuccessful attempt at being evacuated. He seemed every bit as tough as our cat Titus—no matter where you took him he'd always get back home—

We went back to his home with him, where Aunt Nina burst into tears and a plaintive stream of words: 'Oh dear, oh dear, my only little boy, my precious darling, what have they done to him!' The little darling stuffed himself with potato and crusts soaked in water, shaking and shuddering the whole time, while he told us how his train had been bombed and the whole thing had caught fire, and then German tanks had appeared ahead of them, and he had abandoned the train and set off back home along the tracks.

He had been sleeping in haystacks and fed by kind-hearted women in the villages, and here he was again.

'Why didn't you bring a machine-gun back with you?' I asked.

Bolik dismissed this with a gesture of his hand.

'Listen, lads, we'll try and find the partisans. And if we don't find 'em the three of us can be partisans ourselves.'

We were delighted—this was the old, fighting Bolik we knew; he'd had a rough time, but his spirit was undaunted. So all was well, and off we went round the streets.

The railway lines on the embankment were already covered with yellow rust, and in between them we found lots of spent cartridge cases. At this the three of us became excited, and we went off along the embankment, carefully examining the ground under our feet.

Bolik was the first to come across a complete unused clip of cartridges. But then we found in the bushes two full belts of machine-gun bullets. At this we quite lost our heads and started rushing about all over the embankment collecting bullets. They were Soviet bullets which had been left behind by Red Army men defending that spot. But there wasn't a single rifle to be found.

'A machine-gun, oh for a machine-gun,' Bolik was practically praying.

But we didn't find a machine-gun either, and if my grandmother had known about it she would have said that God was watching over us.

We gathered up every single bullet we could find and buried them all in the side of the embankment in the proper way, carefully pacing out twenty steps from a big marker stone.

Kharkov Falls

The newspaper kiosk which had previously been so colorful, hung all over with magazines, was now broken down and filthy. The woman who looked after it was protected from the wind by a piece of ply-wood and she sat there alone, like a spider, with her pile of *Ukrainskoye Slovo*.

She was as usual glad to see us, and counted out a hundred copies for each of us to sell.

'What's the news in 'em?' Shurka inquired.

'Oh, they've taken Kharkov . . . and they say they're advancing around Leningrad. Their "advances" have been going on for three months now.'

We rushed down to the market, shouting:

'All the latest news! Kharkov falls! Colossal advances at Leningrad! Read all about it—those who can!'

But the market was deserted, and the few women who were there selling things took little interest in the printed word. We managed to sell only four copies.

So we went on to the next stage—selling along the streets, Shurka along the left side and myself on the right, badgering all the passers-by, until we came to the tram terminus close to Babi Yar where we had a bit of luck. There was always a crowd down there, because people stood around waiting for the occasional goods tram. Whenever such a tram left the terminus people would jump on to the trucks and the driver would collect money from them and take them to Podol or Pushcha-Voditsa, according to where he was going.

People differed widely in the way they took the papers

from us. Some would take the paper with a contented smile, others with a very serious, impenetrable look, and some would snatch them angrily. One man, wearing a very good overcoat and carrying a brief-case, said:

'Well, that's that. We shall soon hear about Moscow and then the war will be over.'

An old woman sighed bitterly:

'A fortune-teller down in Podol says the war will come to an end when the potatoes come into flower.'

'I reckon it'll be before that,' replied the man with the brief-case.

Some of them eyed his expensive overcoat angrily, but nobody seemed to want to get into an argument.

I was very hungry and often felt dizzy, as if the slightest thing would knock me over. The bundle of papers was heavy, and my arms and legs hurt me. Shurka was still operating around the entrance, but I sat down on some stone steps and was soon lost in my thoughts.

Before the war I had once been to Moscow with my mother and could remember the city very well. And now, it seemed, the Germans were going to take Moscow, and they would be travelling on the underground and walking along Hunter's Row. They would presumably remove Lenin's tomb from Red Square. They would post up decrees and start executing the Jews. Then the gypsies and all sorts of hostages . . . Then the potatoes would come into flower and Hitler's reign on earth would at last begin; everybody would proclaim him a 'genius', the 'father of the people', 'our wise leader and teacher'; the Aryans would ride around in motorcars, and the queue for textiles would form up again in our square . . . I could see it all so clearly that I went quite cold inside from the hopelessness of the situation.

And selling newspapers is the sort of business, you see, at which you don't get a penny piece until you've sold the lot, and on the same day: they are, so to speak, very perishable goods. So you have to get busy, because the money won't come to you; you have to squeeze it out of people. But that day I just didn't have the strength to get up, but went on sitting on the ice-cold steps until I was chilled through and through; and, with hope still nagging at me, I studied from afar each potential customer who approached.

Then Shurka and I caught sight of an enormous crowd of people moving slowly from the direction of Podol, blocking the whole of the Kirillovskaya—a dark river of people, a sort of spontaneous procession. There was something ominous about it, but we didn't sense that immediately, and dashed off towards the crowd with our papers. Only then did we see the German escorts. It was prisoners being led away. Thousands of them.

They moved along in a crowd, without any order, stumbling and bumping against each other, like a herd of cattle being driven to the slaughter. In fact, that is what they used to say—prisoners were 'driven', not 'led'.

They were filthy and unshaven and their eyes gave the impression that they were utterly without feeling or sense. Their soldiers' greatcoats hung off them in tatters; some had wrapped their feet in rags, others had nothing on their feet at all, and only a few had knapsacks. The air was full of the sound of their movement; they all took short, mincing steps, staring dumbly ahead, and only very rarely would one of them throw a frightened glance at me and Shurka, while the well-shod boots of the smartly turned-out escorts rang out on the roadway and the Germans exchanged comments in their own language.

Frightened faces appeared in the doorways and windows. Somebody standing on the pavement threw the prisoners a cigarette. I just managed to see the white stick as it fell among the crowd and there was a sudden, silent scramble around it. About a dozen men were on the ground, but they quickly gathered themselves up and it wasn't clear whether anybody had managed to get the cigarette or if it had simply been torn to pieces.

Everything else went out of my mind. I dashed home like a mad thing, overtaking the column as I did so. I jumped straight over the fence, dropped the newspapers in the garden, and dived into the cellar where we kept our precious potatoes. I grabbed about a dozen of them and scrambled back on to the top of the fence, trembling with the effort and the excitement.

The escorts came past just beneath me and the whole street was blocked by the mass of moving prisoners. I threw one of the potatoes at random in amongst them.

The prisoners dived after it and once again there was a

silent scramble. But I managed to see which one had got the potato: he started greedily gnawing at it, raw as it was, cowering over it and holding the others off with both his arms. But no one went for him and none of them looked round to see where the potato had come from, as though it was just a matter of course that potatoes sometimes drop out of the sky . . .

I threw a second potato; there was the same scramble, and again one of the prisoners quickly devoured it raw. It made me shudder to see him do it. Then I tossed all the potatoes in one by one and felt myself to be taking part in some unreal dream or nightmare. I stayed sitting on the fence until the tail-end of that incredible procession had passed—made up of the ones who limped along, leaning on their neighbours' shoulders, scarcely recognizable as human beings. But nobody actually collapsed on our street and there was no shooting.

I clambered down and gathered up my papers from the garden. It was getting dark, and there was no further purpose in going out on the street. So I was left with twenty copies of the paper, with its triumphant account of the taking of Kharkov to remind me of the day.

A couple of days later one of the escaped prisoners hid himself with us. He was from Saratov and he was called Vasili, but I can't remember his surname. It took him the whole night to tell his story. It was about Darnitsa.

Darnitsa

Darnitsa was a working-class suburb just across the Dnieper opposite the Kiev-Pechersk Monastery. The name derives from the good old Slav word *dar,* 'a gift'.

Very few of the admirers of the *Good Soldier Schweik**
in the Soviet Union know that there exists a continuation of

---

* Jaroslav Hašek, *The Good Soldier Schweik* (London, 1930). [Tr.]

Hašek's inimitable work, written after the author's death by his friend Karel Vanek. The only translation of it that I could find in Russia was published in 1932 in Minsk in the Byelorussian language.

The Good Soldier Schweik gets taken prisoner by the Russians and finds himself near Kiev, in Darnitsa. During the First World War there had been a gigantic prisoner-of-war camp in that very place, and this is what it looked like:

There were prisoners as far as the eye could see. Some of them were lying under the trees with the unseeing expression on their faces of maltreated animals, others were sitting on their half-empty knapsacks, or else they were huddled together in tight little groups and crowding round the cauldron though the Russians drove them away with big cudgels. And finally there were also those who were crawling round on all fours picking the scarce blades of grass which they put in their mouths with a comic expression of greed, savage hunger and revulsion.

Anyone who had to spend even a single day in Darnitsa became the most ardent anti-militarist for the rest of his life . . .

Eighty to a hundred men died there from hunger and exhaustion every day.

Karel Vanek goes on to describe with grim humour the fight that took place around the soup cauldron when some Austrian was pushed into it by the crowd and was boiled alive. The Russian guards chased the prisoners away with sticks, dragged the Austrian out, and then the crowd threw themselves on the cauldron, and in a few minutes it was absolutely empty with only the unfortunate Austrian's cap lying on the bottom, licked clean of the very last morsel of food.

If the assertion that history moves in a spiral is correct—that the same events are repeated but at a different level—then it certainly applies to Darnitsa. The Germans had no knowledge of what happened at Darnitsa before and had never read Vanek, but they organized on the very same place one of the largest prisoner-of-war camps. Only on this occasion it was the Russians who were inside the camp and Germans and Austrians who had the big sticks.

Darnitsa's historical cycle took exactly twenty-five years to complete, and history really was repeated on a different level: on this occasion there was no grass at all left in the camp, and the men died off every day, not in hundreds, but in thousands.

The units of the South-Western Front which were surrounded had first been given the task of holding out in Kiev to the last man. But later they received an order from Stalin to abandon Kiev and break through to the east. They left Kiev by the bridges across the Dnieper and reached Darnitsa, where, on the left bank of the river, the Germans cut them to pieces from the ground and the air, ground them down, scattered them and took them prisoner. The vast army which had been defending the centre of the Ukraine ceased to exist.

The Germans then enclosed a vast territory at Darnitsa with barbed wire, drove the first sixty thousand prisoners into it and brought thousands more along every day.

As they brought them in, however, they picked out as many of the officers, political instructors and Jews as they could manage to identify and put them in a separate enclosure, making a sort of camp within a camp. Many of these people were seriously wounded; they had to be carried in and laid down on the ground. Extra guards were put round the enclosure.

It was an enormous mass of people: sitting, sleeping, wandering about and waiting for something. They were given nothing to eat.

Eventually they began to pull up the grass to get at the roots, and to drink the water from the puddles. In a few days there was no grass left and the camp was turned into a vast area of bare, trampled-down earth.

The nights were cold. Freezing, and steadily losing the appearance of human beings, the men huddled together in groups; one would rest his head on another's knees, and he in turn would rest his head on the next one, and so on, making a tightly packed group. In the morning, when the group began to move and gradually fall apart there would always remain a few who had died during the night.

But then the Germans brought huge cauldrons and began cooking beetroot which they dug up just outside the camp. There were big collective-farm fields all around with beetroot and potatoes which had not been dug, and if anybody had been interested the prisoners could have had all they wanted to eat. But it was apparently part of the plan that the men should die off from hunger.

Each prisoner was entitled to have one ladle of beetroot water a day. Those who were weak from hunger were forced with sticks and shouts to get into the queue, and then they had to crawl to the cauldron on their hands and knees. This was arranged so as to 'control access to the food'.

The officers, political instructors and Jews who were in the inner enclosure were given nothing. They had scratched over the whole of the ground and eaten what they could. By the fifth and sixth day they were chewing on their belts and boots. By the eighth or ninth day many of them were dying and the remainder were half crazed with hunger. By the twelfth day there were only a very few left, quite out of their minds and their eyes clouded over, who nibbled and chewed on their nails, looked for lice in their clothes and stuffed them into their mouths. Those who held out best were the Jews; the others showed scarcely any sign of life after two weeks, while the officers and political instructors died off sooner than the others. It was frightful to see them die.

'And we were moving around right next to them,' Vasili said. 'We could see them, and we were starving, half animals ourselves, but we couldn't bear to look at them sitting there behind the wire, no longer able to understand what was going on. And a guard stood there with a gun to make sure nobody threw them anything.'

Word soon got round about the camp.

Women started making their way to Darnitsa from Kiev to inquire after their menfolk. Long lines of them came along the roads, carrying bags and bundles of things for them.

At first there was some confusion and muddle: if a woman found her husband, sometimes they would release him and sometimes not. Later they stopped releasing them altogether.

The Germans accepted the parcels but took them first into their own guard-room where they removed the best of the contents and sometimes everything. For that reason the women tried to bring only potatoes and carrots or mouldy bread. They also tried to throw things across the wire themselves, but the guards would shout and even fire at them.

Most of the parcels had no addresses on them: if she did not succeed in finding her husband, a woman would hand over her basket just the same, so as not to take it back again when there were rows of half-demented skeletons standing behind the wire. But even if the man for whom the parcel was intended was there the guards did not always hand it over to him. They would just bring it out of their guard-room shouting: 'Bread! Bread!' and throw it on the ground. A crowd of men would rush up and dive on it— starving men would fight each other, snatch bread out of each other's hands, while the guards stood and laughed.

Correspondents arrived to record these scenes on film. I later saw pictures from Darnitsa in German magazines— frightful-looking, barefoot, unshaven men, and beneath them this sort of caption: 'Ivan, the Russian soldier. With soldiers like these the Soviets are hoping to defend their collapsing state.'

The guards soon got bored with this game and began to devise variations on it. They would bring a basket out of the guard-room and shout 'Bread! Bread!' and then announce that anyone who touched the bread before the order was given would be shot. The crowd of men would stand there motionless. The German soldiers would talk and smoke for a little then turn on their heels and walk away. At that moment the prisoners would rush at the basket, but the guards would swing round and start firing from their automatics. Dozens of men would be left dead on the ground, the crowd would retreat in fear, and this game would go on until the Germans would say that the bread could be taken.

'I used to rush in with all the rest,' Vasili said. 'You just don't stop to think when you're in that state; you see the bread and you make a dash for it without thinking whether you'll get killed; it's only when you see them falling around you that you understand . . . So we would stagger back and stand there, licking our lips and staring at that bit of bread. But when they gave the word then we'd dive on it, snatch it out of dead men's teeth or out of their mouths with our fingers . . . None of us there was really human.'

Among the guards there was a sergeant-major by the name of Bizer. He was passionately fond of shooting, and he used to bring out a small-calibre rifle and go hunting in the camp. He was a brilliant marksman—he could pick off a sparrow and then swing round in a flash and shoot a prisoner. One shot for the sparrow, and one for the prisoner, and he would always get both of them. Bizer would sometimes shoot twenty or thirty prisoners a day, and when he went out hunting everybody rushed away into corners.

Vasili lost count of the days and all sense of time. He admitted that he survived because he used to go to the rubbish tip near the German kitchen, where there was always a crowd gathered picking out potato peelings and onion skins. The Germans took pictures of that too and jeered at the 'Russian pigs'.

Later they began to introduce a sort of prison regime and the men were driven out to work. At six o'clock in the morning the alarm would be sounded on a piece of metal rail, the men would come crowding out of the barracks (which were slowly being constructed), N.C.O.s would select people to form work-parties and send them off to fill in ditches, repair roadways or dismantle ruined houses. No work-party ever returned complete: anyone who collapsed from hunger, worked badly or tried to escape was shot, and there were cases where a hundred men went out and only ten came back.

They also set up a camp police force out of the prisoners themselves. A former lieutenant, Konstantin Mikhailovich Tishchenko, was made the head of it. This man, appointed from his 'own' people, turned out to be more brutal than the Germans themselves. He beat many a man to death with blows from a stick; he forced men to crawl about or sit on their haunches until they lost consciousness; and the sound of his raucous voice alone was sufficient to reduce the whole camp to a state of terror.

The prisoners scribbled notes, wrapped them round stones and threw them over the wire. The women who were constantly crowding around the camp would gather these notes up and distribute them throughout the whole of the Ukraine. The contents were always the same: 'I am in

Darnitsa. Bring some potatoes. Bring my papers along and try to get me out.' And an address.

These notes were passed from hand to hand. Women would go around the market calling out: 'Anybody here from Ivankov? Here's a note: take it!' If there was no one from Ivankov, then they would give it to someone from Demidov, and from there to someone from Dymer, and so on until it reached its destination.

I can't remember how many times I handed on such messages, practically illegible and torn from much handling, so that in some cases I had to go over them again in ink.

This kind of spontaneous postal service never failed, and there was no one so mean as to throw such a note away or too lazy to deliver it.

Once they had received the message the relatives, wives and mothers would, of course, hurry off to Darnitsa, but by no means all of them found the man who had written the message still alive, and even if he were alive, what could they do for him?

Vasili was put to work burying the dead outside the wire and he and a man from Kiev picked a likely place, got hold of an iron bar, crept out of their hut at night and started to dig a passage under the wire.

They covered each other with sand so as not to be too easily seen and dug their trench in a place where the searchlights threw least light.

Of course, it made no difference really; they were quite obvious, especially once they had crawled through the first line of wire and were in the area where the earth had been dug up.

'I was shaking like a lunatic,' Vasili recalled. 'I knew I had to move cautiously, and yet I was running. I saw that I could just squeeze through; I heard my tunic being ripped, the barbed wire scraping down my back, but I got through and ran for it! When I looked round I saw that my chum was missing, and I guessed that he was broader in the shoulders than me and must have got stuck. Then they started shooting . . .'

Anyway, that's the story as Vasili told it. His comrade perished: obviously he had not been able to crawl through quickly enough, had tried to dig his way out and been noticed. It is possible that the guards decided that he was on his own in the escape, or else they didn't want to go chasing after someone across the dark fields. Vasili heard them shouting and swearing, then went on his way.

He managed at last to find a potato field. The earth was frozen on the surface, but Vasili started to dig away at it with his fingers, got some potatoes out and gnawed at them, earth and all. He realized that he had to keep constantly on the move, but he had to eat his fill. Then he committed a great stupidity: he stood up and ran for it. He could not remember how long he went on running and staggering along until he collapsed into a hole and covered himself up with beet-tops.

He spent two whole days in the fields, like an animal, skirting round the villages and feeding himself on potato and beet—he wished for no better food.

He stumbled into a battlefield, covered with rotting corpses, piles of military equipment and weapons. People had already been there in search of loot: there were no boots on the bodies, their pockets had all been turned inside out, and in many cases they were completely naked. Vasili also took what he needed: he chose himself some clothes that were not too ragged and equipped himself with a revolver. In the woods he found a black horse limping around, caught it, mounted it and went on his way. Then he saw a two-wheeled cart in a ditch, harnessed the horse to it and rode on the cart.

Finally he summoned up courage to ride into a farmyard, where the women fed him and gave him some civilian clothes. When he looked at himself in a mirror he saw an old man with a beard, emaciated and in rags.

The women advised him to keep on the move in any direction, so long as he didn't stay in those parts: the Germans were still snooping around, hunting for prisoners. His dead comrade had told him a lot about his family in Kiev, and Vasili could remember their address. And he thought it would not be difficult to get lost among the people of a large city.

He did not dare travel along the main roads but wound his way round the cart tracks until he finally came out on

the bank of the Dnieper. He was driving along the river,
thinking he would have to get rid of the horse and cart and
swim across, when he came to a ferry. He paid for the
crossing with the revolver, which was going to be no use
to him in Kiev anyhow.

Fate was kind to him. All the way to Kiev he did not see
a single German. This made him rather bolder, and he came
to the conclusion that they went about only in groups, units
and whole armies along well defined routes, and that there
was a great deal of space around and plenty of room to hide
in.

He drove into Kiev itself full of confidence. At that time
there were so many old men driving carts that nobody paid
the least attention to him. But he arrived at the address only
to find the house burnt to the ground—it was near the
Kreshchatik.

Vasili carried on driving right through the city, and when
he arrived in Kurenyovka he didn't know what to do next.
Catching sight of my grandmother over the fence he asked
to be allowed to sleep the night and Grandma ordered me
to open the gate. When he told us who he was and where
he had come from, Grandma crossed herself in her amazement.

'You have come from the other world . . .'

Investigations have established that sixty-eight thousand men
perished in Darnitsa. There were similar camps in Slavuta,
in Kiev itself on Kerosinnaya Street and in other places.
The Germans did not treat the prisoners of any other
country in such an inhuman manner as they did the prisoners
they took in the Soviet Union. And those men were without
any protection whatsoever, even the purely formal assistance
from the International Red Cross, because Stalin had placed
the Soviet Union outside its sphere of operation.

When I tried to find out what had happened later to the
people who had been in charge of Darnitsa, I discovered
that not one of them, not even Bizer, had appeared before
a court.

Even more astonishing, however, was the fate of the
Soviet prisoners after Germany's defeat. On Stalin's orders
all those who had not died in German camps were arrested

and sent to Siberia. Out of German concentration camps and into Soviet ones.

REMINDER: Please tear yourself away for a moment and turn to the very beginning of this book, the chapter entitled 'Ashes', and refresh your memory of its first words.

A Beautiful, Spacious, Blessed Land

It was my grandfather's idea and I think he was right: Vasili could not remain in the city; he ought to go away as far into the depths of the countryside as he could, where a man, and especially a man with a horse, was now worth his weight in gold.

I went with him to show him the way.

The road to Dymer used always to be full of life, but we drove along it now without meeting a single soul, and there was nothing but the clatter of the wheels, as big as me, of our army cart echoing in the wood.

Here and there between the cobbles were bits of straw trampled down, horse manure and yellowing scraps of newspaper. Flowering grasses were pushing up between the stones. Some time or other people had used that road, but that was long ago, and the people had disappeared; they had died off, and there was only myself, Vasili and the black horse.

There was still the world itself. So vast and with so much life always surging up. The tall old pine trees of the dense Pushcha-Voditsa forest towered into the sky, rustling quietly and swaying to and fro against the blue heavens, full of peace and wisdom.

I lay face upwards in the straw, watching the tree-tops float by, sometimes catching sight of a brown squirrel or a brightly coloured woodpecker, and thinking, I suppose, about everything at once: that the world is a vast place; that Vasili turned out to be right, that the murderous, all-destroying locusts kept to the main roads and centres, such as our city, where goodness knows what was going on—Babi Yar, Dar-

nitsa, orders, starvation, Aryans, Volksdeutsche, book-burn-
ing; yet close at hand the fir trees were swaying gently in
the breeze as they had done a million years ago, and the
earth, vast and blessed, was spread out beneath the sky,
neither Aryan, nor Jewish, nor gypsy, but just the earth intended for the benefit of people. That was it—for PEOPLE.
My God, either there aren't people in the world any more,
or else there *are* some somewhere but I don't know about
them . . . How many thousands of years has the human race
been living on the earth, and people still don't know how
to share things out.

If only there was something worthwhile sharing. But in
fact one beggar would hang out his old socks to dry and
another beggar would come along and murder him for
the sake of those socks. Can it really be true that the only
thing people have learnt to do to perfection in the whole of
their history is to murder each other?

When we came to the end of the Pushcha-Voditsa we found
ourselves on the top of a hill and we could see for twenty
or thirty miles ahead. Beneath us the blue Dnieper wound
its way through the valley, but there was no sign of any
ship or even a boat on it. Everywhere was deserted, utterly
deserted; nothing but fields and fields, right to the horizon,
with the white line of the road, overgrown with grass, running as straight as if it had been drawn with a ruler and
leading, it seemed, to the sky.

We noticed two crosses standing at the side of the road
among some pretty bushes—simple, wooden things, with
German helmets hanging on them. Flowers had been put
on the little mounds of earth, but they had long since faded
and withered away. Somewhere in Germany, no doubt, some
mothers were weeping or children had been left without
fathers. Their fathers would never return with cases full of
loot or even bicycle bells. Had it been worth while making
such a long and difficult journey just to finish up rotting
beneath a rusty helmet? Is there really anything at all in
the world for whose sake it is worth rotting beneath a rusty
helmet? Century after century, people are killed and rot in
the earth, now for one thing and now for another, and later
it turns out that everything was in vain and that they ought
to have died for something quite different . . .

Vasili was dozing the whole time and sometimes fell right off to sleep, and then our poor lame nag, obviously utterly fed up with limping along not knowing where he was going, would gradually reduce his pace until he stopped altogether. Then Vasili would wake up and use the whip on his belly, and the horse would start up eagerly, moving his head vigorously up and down, as if to say: All right, all right, now I know what you want!

The first village on our route was Petrivtsy, and we passed through it like men from Mars or people from another world. Women and children ran out to stand at their fences and stare at us in astonishment, and the whole village stood looking after us until we were once again in the open country and out of sight along the lifeless highway.

By the middle of the day our livers and spleens had changed places because of all the shaking on the cobblestones, and we turned the horse off to the sandy track at the side of the road. But it was harder work for him there and he didn't like it very much. So he stopped looking at the road and kept turning his head, apparently praying to his particular god that Vasili would doze off. And when he did the old nag would turn with obvious pleasure back on to the hard road, not realizing that Vasili would be awakened by the bumping and shaking.

After he had taken us another three or four miles, full of misunderstandings, conflicts and insults, the black horse went on strike.

We unharnessed him, hobbled him and let him graze, while we munched some dried crusts, piled up some hay beneath a bush, laid a worn-out raincoat and an equally tattered jacket on top of it and lay down there to sleep. We were in no hurry to get anywhere, and that was one of the best sleeps I ever had in my life.

After the crosses with the helmets on them we were reminded once again of war by a bridge across the river Irpen, near the village of Demidov, which had been blown up in a most picturesque manner. There was no village left: there were only ashes, with the remains of the brick stoves standing out starkly among them, their chimneys pointing like fingerposts up into the sky. Which meant that there had been a battle here between one lot of benefactors to humanity and another—and all, of course, for the greater happiness of the whole world.

The Irpen was not a very pleasant little stream, but very fast-running. To ford it, the German units had laid brushwood and logs on the river bed, across an arm of the river, but they had treated them so roughly that we very nearly lost our heavy cart as we made our way over. But once we had entered the ruined village and then turned off the hard road on to a cart track our destination was very near.

I liked our army cart, with its steps down the outside, its handles along the sides, locks like on a lorry, and compartments under the seats. Everything on it was so well thought out, with the exception of one small detail—its wheels were not the same width apart as the ruts in the country roads.

All farm-carts are built with exactly the same distance between their wheels. Anyone who fails to observe this most important rule had better not try and travel on our roads. After all, what are the roads that cross Mother Russia? They consist either of dried mud with deep ruts, in which a cart runs as if on rails; or of real, deep mud, so that if you get out of the rut you are in it up to the axles. At best it is two deep ruts, almost ditches, worn across a meadow with fields and frogs all around. Ruts everywhere.

One of the wheels of our cart went in the rut, the other jumped about all over the place, catching on every bump and ridge and pothole, so that we drove along with the cart tipped right over to one side and very nearly overturning. If we had been carrying shells, which is probably what the cart was intended for, we should have tipped right over from their weight. Two or three miles travelling like that were far more exhausting and five times as difficult as the distance we had covered in a whole day. I understood what Vasili meant when he said that if we were beaten in the war, a modest contribution to that defeat would have been made by whoever it was who designed our army carts.

When Leskov's hero Levsha visited London what most struck him was the fact that the English did not clean their weapons with powdered brick-dust. Back in Petersburg, and dying in a police station, he asked that the Tsar should be informed that it was because Russian weapons were con-

stantly being cleaned that the bullets were loose in the bores
and the guns were therefore—'may God preserve us from
war, no good for shooting with'.

We had such a lot of extremely vigilant people, who were
even capable of detecting a crown among flowers on a
schoolboy's notebook, but no one appeared to be disturbed
by the fact that none of our army carts—'may God preserve
us from war'—were any use on our roads.

Ivan Svinchenko lived at the far end of Litvinovka, in the
'settlement' across the weir, next to the burnt-out remains
of an old mill-house. He received Vasili without hesitation
like a brother, only crossing himself when he recalled that
he himself had escaped practically by a miracle from
German hands.

There were a whole lot of Svinchenkos there, and it was
Ivan's sister Gapka who took me in.

Hers was a typical Ukrainian shack; a very low building,
seeming to grow out of the ground, with tiny little windows
peering out beneath the thatch, which had holes in it where
it had rotted. Inside it was like a cave, with an uneven earth
floor on which lay some old rags and dolls made of straw,
and children and kittens were crawling about. In the middle
stood a stove built of plain bricks, and next to it a sort of
wooden shelf, with some old rags thrown down on it, known
as the 'floor' on which they all slept side by side. The
atmosphere in the hut was strange and heavy for someone
coming from the city. It was, after all, the village, and the
sort of place most collective farmers lived in.

Gapka had lost her husband in the war and had been left
with a lot of children. Her next-door neighbour had children,
too, and they were all crawling around the shack and the
yard outside like cockroaches, with bare bellies, dirty faces
and running noses, in worn-out vests and dresses, and the
smaller ones in nothing at all.

Sitting on the stove and rather frightening to me at first
were a mysterious-looking old man and woman, matriarch
and patriarch of the Svinchenko line. The old man was almost transparently thin, and kept coughing and spitting, but
the old woman would clamber down from the stove and
shuffle slowly round the yard, scarcely able to walk but trying
all the time to do something. She was hunchbacked, bent

nearly double, so that she walked around looking down at the ground right in front of her as if she was looking for a lost kopek.

My mother had told me before I left home that Gapka was a most unfortunate and hard-working woman, and that the old grandparents were terribly kind-hearted people who had spent their whole lives doing nothing but good to others. But at first I could not shake off a strange sense of fear.

Gapka inquired how we had been getting on in the city, gave vent to her horror and concern and then proceeded to tell us about her own life.

They had had, it appeared, some good luck—there were no more collective farms. They had simply collapsed, and good riddance to them.

There were no more farm bosses, nor any of the various officials and hangers-on who had made an easy living off the farms at the expense of the peasants. As for the Germans, once they had passed through no one had seen them again. There was just the village of Litvinovka and there were the peasant families, just as they were, and they didn't belong to the landowners or the Soviets or the Germans. Good God, when had things ever been like that before?

So everybody started to live according to his own ideas. All around were fields which had not been harvested, and everyone selected a patch of land for himself, cut the corn, dug the potatoes and carried the hay. There wasn't enough room to store it all. And they ate and ate and ate. Even the old folk could not recall it ever happening before that the village of Litvinovka had eaten its fill.

They laid in stores for years ahead; the cellars were bursting with vegetables, the attics were piled high with apples and pears, and strings of dried fruits hung under the eaves; nobody forbade anybody to do anything, nobody took anything off anybody and nobody forced anybody to go anywhere . . . The old folk crossed themselves and said the end of the world must be at hand.

In the evenings they would gather in the light of a taper for a get-together, chewing sunflower seeds till they were drowsy, and distilling spirit from beet. In the daytime you could hear the sound of chains clanking; the old men and women, the girls and the children were busy threshing the wheat. Then they would grind the grain between two big stones and pass the flour through a hand sieve. The village of Litvinovka was simply revelling in its good fortune.

Gapka boiled up an enormous pan of potatoes, tipped them out on the scrubbed wooden table, and the whole family sat around with me among them—leaving me to take as much as I liked, dip the potatoes in the salt, and wash them down with sour milk. I ate and ate, to the point when my head was going round and I was swaying like a drunk, so that by the time it came to the ripe red apples I had lost my appetite.

It was true that men and horses were in great demand in Litvinovka. Vasili and Ivan drove out into the fields the next day to shift potatoes and they didn't get a break till Sunday. They went 'half and half' with Vasili for carting from the fields—for every two sacks he carried he received one. He stored these riches in the Svinchenko's yard and was busy from morning to night, while I loafed around.

The Svinchenko children took me out into the fields where there were lots of little craters, in almost every one of them the tip of an exploded mine sticking up, a sort of little wing from which you could make an excellent water-wheel.

We clambered around the long, dark farm stables, trying to find hidden hen's nests, and when we found some eggs we sucked them dry at once. We put on some warm clothes, made some censers out of old tins and filled them with hot coals to keep off the mosquitoes, mounted the horses and took them out to graze at night, while I galloped around on my own lame mount.

There was a broken-down tank standing in the fields, with black and white crosses on its armour-plating, which had been completely stripped inside but still had its seats and vents in order. While the horses were grazing we would play at war: some of us would clamber into the tank while the others attacked it with stones. It made an unbelievable row inside, making our ears ring, and giving us a great deal of pleasure. The tank made a marvellous toy for the village children.

Finally Ivan and Vasili loaded up the cart and we set off back to the city. They wanted to get to the market; I was going home. As my share I was given a sack of potatoes, half a sack of grain and a pile of other gifts. That whole day I strode along the empty highroad, thinking my thoughts, full to the brim with the strangest and most contradictory emotions. Sometimes I wanted to shout, sometimes to cry. I arrived home as a sort of saviour of the family.

The Kiev-Pechersk Monastery

This time Maruska did not even let us into the house, and my grandmother and I went to Grabarev's house to sit down and rest before returning home.

'Oh God,' said Grandma in a very worried tone. 'What on earth am I going to tell Olga now? It's just daylight robbery.'

'They are in the wrong,' Grabarev said unemotionally. 'They will yet have cause to regret what they've done.'

'Olga put all she had into that house, and they have simply grabbed it like thieves.'

'Don't worry, everything will come right,' Grabarev said. 'Thousands of people are losing their very lives, and here are you fussing about a blessed house.'

Grabarev was planing a plank of wood, making a coffin to order. He had decided that this was the most profitable business for the time being.

'It will all come right, Martha,' he repeated. 'Olga will come back, and Maruska will be thrown out and will have to answer for it.'

'But the law's on her side at the moment.'

'Well, it won't always be.'

'Will the Bolsheviks come back?'

Grabarev shrugged his shoulders.

'If only I knew . . .'

'You know all right,' Grandma blurted out.

'I know no more than anybody else. That, at all events, Moscow has not been taken, and that beyond Moscow, Martha, lies the vastness of the Russian land.'

We scarcely paid any attention to a heavy rumbling in

the distance. There were so many crashes and explosions all
around in those days. We simply heard the sound of an
explosion. And we went off home, my grandmother lost in
her thoughts until she looked up and said:

'No, there's some reason for him staying behind—he's
been made to do it because he's a Communist, and he's made
up that story about the misfortune with his family so that
it should seem all right. But he's a good man. May the
Lord preserve him.'

We came to our favourite spot, and there was the monastery
spread out before us. It was ablaze.

All the openings in the monastery's main bell-tower were
lit up with a bright orange light, as if it were being illumi-
nated, but there was very little smoke. The Cathedral of the
Dormition had already gone: it was just a heap of rubble
with what was left of the walls and their frescoes sticking up
out of it. All the museums and the whole township enclosed
by the monastery walls were burning.

Grandma sat down there where she was. We could see
people running out of the monastery and they were all saying
that the Cathedral of the Dormition had been blown up. It
had been a storehouse of ancient manuscripts and books. The
burning pages were swept up by the wind and came raining
down, setting everything alight. The Germans were doing
everything they could to put the fires out, but there was
no water. As for who had caused the explosions, who had
found such an act necessary, nobody knew. The same people,
no doubt, as had blown up the Kreshchatik. It was quite clear
now that it was not the Jews who had destroyed the
Kreshchatik.

That was on November 3rd, 1941. I watched the monastery
burning.

My grandmother was very deeply affected by it all; she sat
on there for a long time, crossing herself from time to time,
and I had difficulty in persuading her to return home. It was
as though something had snapped inside her; something had
broken that was never mended to her dying day.

Only when she reached home did she start fussing round
the stove in her usual way, and, as she ladled out the soup,
she said:

'How could God let it happen? They destroyed the Desyatinnaya church, and St Michael's Monastery, and they made a factory out of our Peter and Paul, where I had you baptized. And now they've wrecked the monastery itself . . . And you, my child, will see more in your short time than many another sees in a whole lifetime. May the Lord take care of you, you poor little thing, in this great world.'

If you ever happen to visit the Kiev-Pechersk Monastery, try asking the guides whether it is true that it was blown up by N.K.V.D. agents, of whom the principal one was posthumously awarded the title of Hero of the Soviet Union —and just watch the expression on their faces as you ask it.

Russia was converted to Christianity in the year A.D. 988. It was the Prince of Kiev, Vladimir the Baptist, who built the magnificent Desyatinnaya church and Prince Yaroslav the Wise who built the Cathedral of St Sophia. The Monastery of St Michael was founded in the city, while just to the south of it, on the steep slopes above the Dnieper, was built the Kiev-Pechersk Monastery and its lovely Cathedral of the Dormition.

It was in this monastery that the monk Nestor started his chronicle *The Tale of Bygone Years*, which laid the foundations for the writing of our history, and it was from there that literacy and the arts spread.

That was before Moscow existed. In the middle of the twelfth century a Kievan prince, Yury Dolgoruki, founded the little settlement of Moscow in the course of one of his campaigns, and he is buried there at the centre of our culture of those days—in the Kiev-Pechersk Monastery.

Until 1917 the Kiev-Pechersk Monastery was a magnificent city, a sort of Vatican or Jerusalem of the Orthodox Church, where the Tsars went to pay their respects and millions of pilgrims gathered every year. The libraries of the monastery contained priceless volumes, a printing press produced books, the walls of the churches were decorated with unique frescoes and mosaics, and ancient treasures were stored in its vaults.

After 1917, to the slogans of 'Religion is the opium of the people' and 'Destroy the old and build anew', the first building to be destroyed and flattened to its foundations was the Desyatinnaya church. All that can be seen of it today are a few bricks preserved in the Kiev historical museum.

Dozens of other churches of less historical significance were pulled down, while others were turned into storehouses, clubs and workshops. In 1934 the Cathedral of St Michael was demolished, and historians were able to save only a few small twelfth-century mosaics, which can also be seen in the museums today.

The monastery was too big to be pulled down. So they treated it differently: they turned it into a group of anti-religious museums, putting all the principal museums of Kiev inside its walls.

During the defence of Kiev the museums were closed and the monastery remained deserted. They managed to evacuate some of the museum exhibits eastwards.

And six weeks after the entry of the Germans the monastery was mysteriously blown up and burnt to ashes, with the Germans trying desperately to put out the fires.

Shortly after that Molotov appealed to the whole world and accused the Germans of destroying historical and cultural treasures.

Soviet experts drew up a 'Report of the Special State Commission of Research into Crimes Committed by German-Fascist Invaders', which says, at one point:

'On the order of the German Command military units looted, blew up and destroyed that most ancient cultural monument, the Kiev-Pechersk Monastery.'*

The same statement appears in guide-books and books of historical research. The most widespread explanation is given in a book by K. Dubina, Director of the Institute of History of the Ukrainian Republic:

It was established that the Fascist vandals had laid mines beneath the Dormition Cathedral and other build-ings some time previously and waited for a convenient moment to detonate them. On November 3rd, 1941, the monastery was visited by the Slovak traitor Tiso. This served as a suitable moment to carry out the act of provocation. As soon as Tiso had left the territory of

---

* *Kiev—Gorod-Geroi (Kiev—Heroic City)*, a collection of material on the achievements of the people of Kiev in the Great Fatherland War (Kiev, 1961), p. 369.

the Monastery the explosions took place. As we have already said, the Germans tried to attribute these crimes to Soviet patriots who were supposed to have prepared an attempt on Tiso's life. But even such a hardened war-criminal as Scheer was forced to admit that it was the work of the German Fascists themselves.*

Such is the official version, confirmed by the sworn evidence of a hardened war-criminal. But it is sufficient to glance through the newspapers published at the time to see that the Germans made no propaganda capital out of the destruction of the monastery. It is true that they blew up and burnt down a great deal, but that was when they were retreating in 1943. In 1941 it was only the Russians who were blowing things up as they retreated.

These are general reflections on the subject. The true facts and documents, if indeed they exist at all, are unlikely ever to be published.

But there are still witnesses living—people who had been living in the few dwelling houses on the territory of the monastery. Here is what they remember; here is what actually happened.

As the former centre of the Orthodox faith, the monastery itself was a thorn in the side of the Soviet government. They had succeeded in driving the monks out of it, in taking savage reprisals on them, in stripping the monastery of its riches in the name of nationalization, and in turning it into an anti-religious museum. But when war broke out and the Germans entered Kiev the surviving monks started preparing to revive the monastery, and the word began to go round that 'Once the Germans are here the monastery will arise again in all its glory.'

The day before the Soviet forces abandoned Kiev, according to the people living there, the deserted monastery was cordoned off by N.K.V.D. troops. Nobody was allowed to enter it. Lorries were seen entering and leaving. Then the cordon was removed.

On September 19th, 1941, the Germans entered Kiev, went

---

* K. Dubina, *Gody Tyazholykh Ispytanii (Years of Endurance)* (Kiev, 1962), pp. 96–7.

straight to the monastery and started ringing out long, excited peals of triumph on the bells.

They then proceeded to open up all the buildings, museums and cells and to take away the carpets, silver vessels and articles of worship. But the German command immediately stepped in and the local people saw the frightened soldiers being forced to take their booty back.

The monastery stands on the highest point in Kiev and is surrounded by high walls, so that it is an excellent fortress to defend. The Germans had gun emplacements there, including anti-aircraft guns to protect the Dnieper crossing, and soldiers were billeted in the numerous cells.

Six weeks passed. The Kreshchatik had already been blown up and destroyed by fire and the last Jews were being executed in Babi Yar. Then suddenly there was a powerful explosion in the monastery. A section of the defensive walls collapsed right on to the guns, though apparently none of the gun-crews suffered. It was obviously an act of sabotage.

The Germans had hardly had time to realize what had happened when there was another explosion, this time in the huge building, shaped like a bunker, that stood at the monastery's main gates. In recent years it had served as a munition store for Soviet troops, and it seemed as if the munitions had been left there since they could be seen exploding in the fire. The building began to burn so furiously and such fountains of sparks and embers went up from it that fires were started throughout the monastery.

The Germans hastily ran their weapons out of the monastery and rushed around trying to extinguish the fires that broke out all over the place, but there was no water. Then suddenly they dropped what they were doing and scattered in all directions, shouting: 'Mines!' They organized a team of people to run round the houses urging the people to leave them. 'Get out, quick! The Soviets have mined the monastery!' Later, it is true, it was established that there were no mines underneath the dwelling houses, but at the time the people living there fled for their lives just as they had done on the Kreshchatik. It appeared that the Kreshchatik affair was being repeated.

What happened in fact was a third resounding explosion, which caused the very earth to tremble. It went off inside the Dormition Cathedral. But the cathedral survived the first explosion. It had been built in the eleventh century from a special kind of flat, red clay brick, which was so tough you couldn't break it with a hammer. The layers of mortar were thicker than the bricks themselves, and in Kievan Russia they knew how to make that mortar even stronger. That brickwork had been meant to last for thousands of years.

After a short interval (exactly as had happened with the German headquarters on the Kreshchatik) there was another explosion in the cathedral of such a force that those flat red bricks went flying half a mile away and landed all over Pechersk, and the cathedral itself collapsed into a heap of rubble. According to what one old man recalls: 'When that happened the first three explosions seemed to have been just child's play; the fourth one was really frightful!' I wonder how many lorry-loads of explosive it took?

The whole territory of the monastery was then covered with pieces of mosaic, frescoes, altar screens, burning pages of ancient manuscripts and volumes with heavy brass bindings ripped and torn to pieces.

And everything was ablaze—the Refectory church, the baroque Archbishop's House, the ancient printing house, all the museums, the libraries and archives and the bell-tower.

After waiting a little to make sure that the explosions had finished, the Germans again rushed in to try and put the fires out. By some miracle they succeeded, by shifting the burning beams in the roof, in putting out the fire in the bell-tower, because it was made of stone with high openings. The top tier which carries the bells, escaped. But that was all they managed to save.

Night

They herded the sailors into Babi Yar one very cold day, when there were even a few snowflakes in the air. According to rumours, they were sailors from the Dnieper river fleet. They had their hands tied together with wire, but not all of them, because some of them could shake their fists in the air. They marched along in silence (maybe they were shot if they shouted), but from time to time a clenched fist appeared above the crowd, as one of them drew himself up and pretended to stretch his shoulders.

Many of them were barefoot, some of them were stripped to the waist, and a few were just in their underpants. It was frightful to see the way the ones in front marched—in a row close together, looking straight ahead, marching stiffly as though they were made of stone.

They went on shouting and protesting even when they were in Babi Yar itself, when they could no longer doubt that they were going to be executed. They shouted: 'Long live Stalin!' 'Long live the Red Army!' and 'Long live Communism!' They believed they were dying for the good of mankind, and the Germans cut them down with machine-gun fire in the same cause.

A strange report, lacking the usual screaming headlines and exaggerated boasting, appeared in the newspaper which I sold on November 23rd:

FURTHER SUCCESSES IN BEND OF DONETS AND ON CENTRAL SECTOR OF EASTERN FRONT ENEMY FAILS IN ATTEMPT AT BREAKTHROUGH BEFORE LENINGRAD.
The Führer's Headquarters, November 21st
The Supreme Command of the Armed Forces reports:
In the course of battles in the bend of the Donets and in the central sector of the Eastern Front further successes have been recorded.
Attempts on the part of the enemy to break through near Leningrad have been repulsed by German artillery.*

Extract from an article in the same newspaper, beneath a modest, unrevealing headline:

THE NATURE OF THE WAR IN THE EAST
. . . The army of the Bolsheviks has in the main been

---
* *Ukrainskoye Slovo*, November 23rd, 1941.

routed; millions of Russians are now in German hands as prisoners, and as many again have perished, and the men the Bolsheviks are now sending to the front are only good for cannon fodder . . . It is not numbers or adherence to particular tactics that win wars but the spirit inspiring the men, because it is not the equipment or the numbers of men which fight and win battles, but each man and his morale. From this point of view nobody and nothing in the world can be compared with Germany, which is why Germany is unbeatable.

On that day I seem to have sensed for the first time, far too soon, the approach of manhood.

I was sitting, miserable and cross, beneath a stall in the market. The wind managed somehow to be blowing from all directions at once; my hands and feet were frozen stiff; my boot-polish had gone so hard as to be quite useless, though I no longer hoped for anyone to want his boots cleaned because it was getting dark, the last peasant women were going away and it was nearly the time when everybody had to be off the streets. I was making no more at cleaning people's boots than I had made selling cigarette papers or newspapers, but I didn't want to give it up, always hoping for something better to come along.

Then I looked around me in surprise, and it seemed as though the curtains, dusty and grey, had fallen away from my view of the world, never to be replaced. I realized that my grandfather, that great admirer of the Germans, was a fool. That there is in this world neither brains, nor goodness, nor good sense, but only brute force. Bloodshed. Starvation. Death. That I was alive and sitting there with my brushes beneath the stall, but no one knew why. That there was not the slightest hope, not even a glimmer of hope, of justice being done. It would never happen. No one would ever do it. The world was just one big Babi Yar. And there two great forces had come up against each other and were striking against each other like hammer and anvil, and the wretched people were in between, with no way out; each individual wanted only to live and not to be maltreated, to have something to eat, and yet they howled and screamed and in their fear they were grabbing at each other's throats, while I, a little blob of watery jelly, was sitting in the midst of this dark world. Why? What for? Who had done it all? There was nothing, after all, to hope for! Winter. Night.

No longer able to feel my fingers, without thinking what I was doing, I began to gather up my boot-black's equipment. I heard the sound of horses' hooves on the roadway: it was a column of Don Cossacks passing through the square. Even they did not really attract my attention, although it was the first time I had seen the Cossacks dressed up: with their moustaches, red faces, the braid down their breeches and their elaborately decorated swords, they looked like people from the days of the Civil War of 1918 or the shooting of an historical film about the revolution. It looked as though City Commandant Eberhard had called for assistance . . .

I hurried off home, because it soon got dark. The air was heavy with the smell of stables from the Cossack horses; dogs were barking from hunger in the farmyards; and from Babi Yar came the sound of machine-gun fire.

Part Two

Man Lives to Eat

In the books I had read a great deal was said about love and suffering, expeditions and great discoveries, the feats of revolutionaries and the struggle for a better future. But for some reason they rarely spoke of where people found the food they needed day by day to enable them to go on struggling, making discoveries, travelling, suffering and loving. The heroes of most of those books, it seemed, derived their nourishment from the skies. They must presumably also have found time to sit down and eat somewhere somehow, and only afterwards did they carry out the deeds of derring-do which won them such fame. But if we could leave the great exploits for a moment—how *did* they manage to get their meals?

No matter how you look at it, the majority of people are primarily concerned in this life with what they are going to eat. And with what they are going to wear. And with having somewhere to live. A great many people are completely taken up with these cares and have no time left for anything else, so difficult do they find the struggle for existence. And it's not because they prefer it that way, but because there is no other way for them.

A wise man said: Man eats to live. But another added bitterly: And he lives to eat.

Oh yes, of course, in the old days the butler would announce: 'Dinner is served,' and the aged, eccentric count would offer his arm to the countess, her face still bearing traces of her past beauty, and the company, still chatting politely, would move slowly to the table. But that was before the October Revolution.

So many pages in books are taken up with descriptions of the feasts held by all sorts of kings and gallant men in the distant past which were certainly worth writing about and which I read with interest in much the same way as I read about the mythical exploits of Heracles.

But I must confess that I found the outcast Sholom Aleichem much closer to what I knew. His people struggled desperately for every crust of bread, prepared home-made ink to make themselves some money, just as I had done with the cigarette papers. I used to read and re-read with a feeling of unbounded affection and gratitude every line written by Taras Shevchenko, whose mother used to have to go out to reap corn in somebody else's fields, leaving her child under the hedge with some poppy seed tied in a bit of rag as a dummy to stop him howling. And how well I understood the whole sense and complexity of the problem of Akaki Akakievich's greatcoat in Gogol.

Books also tell us that we have to fight and perform great feats so that everyone can have enough bread and greatcoats. Yet my grandfather could remember that before the revolution there was plenty of dried fish and that textiles were on sale in rolls and pieces. How was it that the more battles and exploits there were the less there was of bread and greatcoats?

No, I'm wrong—there *are* more greatcoats. Khaki-coloured, grey-green, black, brown, grey and blue.

But there's no bread. And man is such a demanding creature: no sooner is he born than he immediately starts wanting to eat. My God, when you come to think of it, you have to eat to live every day, every single day!

I started saving up. I would skip my lunch, thinking that if I ate none there would be more for dinner; and if I had no dinner that meant there would be more for the next day. But then my grandmother noticed that my hands and feet were beginning to swell, and she and my mother practically stopped eating and gave their bits of food to me.

I had somehow to get enough to eat. Every day the same thought kept going round in my head: how could I get something to eat? I went round poking and probing, looking into the pantry, the barn, the cellar and out in the yard. Nothing but stones, chips of wood, broken pots, rubbish and dirt . . .

The old maths teacher at our school, Balatyuk, died of hunger. Towards the end he had tried to work as a labourer. The factories were reopened and workers were given a wage of 200 roubles a month.

A loaf of bread in the market then cost 120 roubles, a

tumblerfull of unground wheat 20 roubles, a dozen potatoes 35 roubles, and a pound of lard 700 roubles.

When he left for the army (never to return, with or without cases full of gifts), Zhorik Gorokhovsky's father, who had been a fitter at the canning-machine factory, had left all his tools behind, and Zhorik took over his father's workshop in a garden shed. The shed was piled from floor to roof with all sorts of old iron, because Zhorik had made it a rule always to pick up and store away in his treasure house every bit of iron he found lying around.

Having sat for four years at the same desk in school we had become close friends. Zhorik was a serious lad, who believed that man lived not by bread alone, but that he had an even greater need of iron. And he proved it; he taught himself to make cigarette lighters out of spent cartridge cases. His younger brother Kolka and I could only stand and stare in open-mouthed admiration at the skill with which he handled a soldering-iron.

Kolka was the exact opposite of his elder brother; he was not only a happy-go-lucky, lazy layabout, but liked destroying things. If he came across an electric light bulb its fate was sealed—it would have to be smashed against a stone. Every fire-extinguisher had to be put into action as soon as it was discovered.

There was more than enough material at hand for his purposes: just behind his shed was the tall building which housed the anti-aircraft training school. The Germans had taken it over and had immediately spent a couple of hours throwing out of the windows all the instruments, equipment and books which they found in their way.

My first anti-Fascist operation was connected with that building and Kolka. The standard latrine-trench had been dug in the courtyard of the school, so that the Germans sat there reading their newspapers on the poles with their backs to us. We got hold of a good catapult, selected from Zhorik's collection the roughest old nuts and bolts, climbed up on the fence and, aiming at the largest of the exposed backsides, opened fire. Zhorik used later to describe the awful row we had caused in the 'reading-room' and how one German had taken the trouble to climb over the fence and start looking for us to let us have a piece of his mind.

After the military unit had been withdrawn, the school building was turned into a canteen for old people. Hundreds of old men used to totter along there on crutches, carrying their dishes and spoons. The people in charge doled out potatoes to those who were dying, swollen from hunger or living alone. The old folk would crowd around the serving hatch, trembling and quarrelling, to receive a ladle of thin soup each which they would gulp down right there at the table, licking their lips with great relish, and occasionally choking and getting it all over their beards.

Kolka and I would move dejectedly around the tables, eyeing the old folk with something like hatred and looking into their bowls, which they would cover up jealously with both hands.

Then one day the cook called us:

'Will you go and fetch some water to fill the tank, kids? I'll give you some soup if you do.'

We almost yelped with delight, grabbed the largest saucepan by the handles and dashed off to the tap. We went on carting water until the canteen closed, then sidled up to the cooks, looked them straight in the eye, and they poured us out a bowlful of soup each. Proud and contented, we spent as long as we could over it, spinning out the pleasure and praying that the cooks would want us to carry water the next day and the day after.

My grandfather also tried to obtain a meal ticket. They wouldn't give him one, saying that he was still capable of working, but he was so downcast that they took him on in the canteen as a night watchman. He took a sheepskin coat and a pillow and went off for his first night's work, and I went along with him. A very bold plan was forming in my mind.

While Gramp was grumbling at the cooks and dishwashers for not leaving him any soup, I sat quietly in a corner. Once they had slammed the doors and everyone had departed, Gramp put a metal bar across the main entrance and proceeded to make himself a bed from some wooden benches, muttering crossly to himself: 'Blasted cut-throats, they've gone off home with their bags full, the vipers.'

I decided to begin with the second floor. The building had

long corridors and lots of doors opening into lecture halls and study rooms, and Gramp and I were the only people in the whole enormous place.

The lecture halls were full of trestle tables, the floors covered with straw, bandages and bits of paper, and there was a strong smell of soldiery. I began feverishly rummaging through the straw and feeling about beneath the tables. Nothing but cigarette-ends and magazines.

The pictures in the magazines were beautiful, all printed on glossy paper: Germans standing looking at the cathedrals in old Smolensk; people smiling happily, dressed in Russian national costumes, offering a general the traditional bread and salt; a typical Russian beauty with long tresses, looking like one of the women from the Russian state choir, but naked and big-bosomed, sitting with her bottom in a bath-tub near a wall made of logs, with the caption: 'Russian Bath'. I slipped the picture under my shirt to show to Zhorik and Kolka on the quiet.

I gathered up all the flattened-out cigarette-ends and put them in my pocket. I had such a yearning for food that I kept feeling faint. I had heard that pirates used to chew tobacco, so I started chewing the cigarette-ends, but they tasted very bitter and burnt my tongue, so I spat them out.

It wasn't until the tenth or twelfth room that I came across some dried bread. It was about half the size of my hand and mouldy, but it was real white bread. I started nibbling at it, without scraping it clean, so as not to lose a single crumb, and it made my mouth run with saliva. Then I broke it up on the window-sill and put small pieces in my mouth, sucked them until they were soft, then passed it round my mouth with my tongue, relishing the taste. I was in no hurry to swallow it down, and I felt a strange feeling all over my body. I thought to myself: Dogs are very stupid—throw a dog a piece of bread and he'll bolt it down in one go, but men use their heads, they prolong the pleasure and seem to get more out of it.

Elated by my success I went farther—to the chemistry laboratory, where there were so many shelves and glass cup-boards and instruments that the Germans had apparently been too lazy to throw them out but had simply smashed everything and drained all the spirit from the spirit lamps.

I scarcely knew where to look—there were so many different test-tubes and pots of chemicals, and I didn't understand a single word that was written on them. I opened the pots, shook them, sniffed at them. But there seemed to be nothing edible among them.

In a metal cupboard that had been broken open there were rows of flasks labelled MUSTARD GAS and LEWISITE and I started trying to work out what they were. The Lewisite was an unpleasant beetroot colour, but the mustard gas looked like black coffee and I started imagining it really was coffee, with sugar, and my whole body began to tremble with a longing for coffee, to open the glass stopper and taste it. What if it turned out not to be mustard gas but something used for teaching—perhaps they had simply put coffee in it and shown it to the students. After all, it could happen. Even if there wasn't any sugar in it, it would still be drinkable . . . I had great difficulty in forcing myself to put the flask back in its place. I wouldn't take the risk.

Then I opened the door into the next room and stopped in my tracks.

In the middle of the room stood the figure of a man, all covered in blood, without legs or arms. My first thought was that he had been tortured by the Germans. But then I noticed the anatomical charts on the walls: it was the anatomy room.

The head and chest of the human model on the table were riddled with bullet-holes, and the diagrams on the walls had also been shot up, especially the eyes. Apparently the soldiers had been practising using their revolvers. But the dummy's stomach was untouched and you could see inside it by opening a little hinged door. I undid the hooks and took out of the dummy, as if out of a cupboard, its liver, stomach and kidneys, all made from papier-mâché, and studied them for some time, recalling the cannibalism my father had talked about . . . Then, in a moment of blind fury, I flung them on the floor, proceeded to rip the anatomical charts down from the walls and stamped on them, my face distorted with rage. I went on stamping on them and tearing them until I got bored.

In the hall which had been used for amateur theatricals there was a wrecked piano. It looked as if someone had gone to work on it with a heavy instrument, a sledge-hammer or an axe, because the lids were smashed, and the keys were pulled out and lying all over the floor, like teeth that had been knocked out. What harm had it done them, to make them treat it like that?

I started trying to lift away the casing and the splinters of wood and discovered that the sounding board and the strings were unharmed and that the keys and the strikers had only jumped out of their slots, so that it was possible to put some of them back again. I set about restoring two octaves, and when I succeeded I sat there for a while strumming on the keys, watching the little hammers jump about and listening to the sound ringing down the empty corridors.

The results of my examination of the third floor were even more slender—a bit of twisted peel about half as big as my little finger. But there was a mysterious-looking spiral staircase going up from the corridor, and I went straight up it, pushed the hatch up with my head and found myself in a tower crammed full of dusty boxes and fire buckets. The wind was howling round the gaping windows. I climbed up on the boxes and looked out of the window.

Beneath me the streets and the roofs of the houses lay clustered together. No smoke was coming from the chimneys because there was no wood for fires, and threatening notices appeared in the papers about handing over all stores of wood and coal. We had no fuel of any kind; my grandmother used to make a fire from all sorts of rubbish once every two or three days.

There was not a soul to be seen in the yard of the Tsepi Gallya Factory, as though it had been shut down. On the streets only an occasional passer-by was to be seen hurrying along; the city looked as if it had been struck by the plague. In the distance I could see a squad of soldiers marching very smartly: they appeared as a long grey-green rectangle moving along the roadway, all carrying identical bundles wrapped in newspaper. They were probably on their way back from the bath-house and were singing, with the same harmony and precision as they worked, a song which sounded like this:

'Ay-li, ay-la, ay-la,
Ay-li, ay-la, ay-la,
Ay-li, ay-la-ay-la,
Ho-ho, ho-ho, ha-ha-ha . . .'

It was already getting dark and I had still not done the most important thing I had to do, so I slid down from the boxes and rushed down the stairs. Gramp was snoring on his trestle bed. I slipped into the kitchen. That was what I was after!

The smell of freshly made soup still hung around the kitchen, but the stove was already quite cold. There were clusters of enormous, dry, clean saucepans on it. The frying-pans had also been cleaned. I poked around on the tables and underneath them and examined every corner, but there was nothing, not a crumb, not even a slop bucket. I had never in my life seen a kitchen so bare and so utterly clean. Yet there was still the fresh smell of cooking to torment me.

In an effort to find at least a grain of corn I started crawling around examining the cracks in the floor. But everything had been brushed up. I could scarcely believe it was true, and started my search all over again. In one of the saucepans something had been burnt, had stuck to the sides and had not been scrubbed off. I scratched it off and chewed on it, and still had no idea what it was. One of the frying-pans seemed to me not to have been properly cleaned. I sniffed at it and found it smelt of fried onions. The beastly cut-throats and vipers had even been putting fried onions into their own soup! It made me whimper, I longed so much for some soup flavoured with onion, and I started licking the frying-pan, either imagining or actually getting the faint taste of onion. I went on whimpering and licking, whimpering and licking.

Enemies of the People

The *Ukrainskoye Slovo* newspaper was closed down in December. The slogan 'Published in the Ukraine in Ukrainian', which it had boldly displayed day after day, was regarded as harmful. They also closed down the literary almanack *The Drum*. This was the explanation:

> A note to our readers.
> As from today the Ukrainian-language newspaper will appear in a new form and will be called the *Novoye Ukrainskoye Slovo*. Extreme nationalists working with elements close to the Bolsheviks tried to turn the national Ukrainian newspaper into a news-sheet for their own treacherous purposes. No attention was paid to the many warnings given by the German civilian authorities that the paper must be neutral and serve only the interests of the Ukrainian people. An attempt was made to undermine the trust existing between our German liberators and the Ukrainian people.
> The editorial board has been purged of traitorous elements.*

How well we understood the sense of that last line!

The editor of *Ukrainskoye Slovo*, Ivan Rogach, and the brilliant poetess Olena Teliga, who had been President of the Writers' Union and editor of *The Drum*, as well as many contributors to both publications, were executed in Babi Yar. At the same time large-scale arrests and executions of Ukrainian nationalists started to take place throughout the Ukraine.

The new paper soon got down to business. It published an extremely violent article entitled 'Scum', in which it lashed out at the idlers—the scum—who didn't want to find jobs for themselves: nobody knew what they lived on; they made

---

* *Novoye Ukrainskoye Slovo*, December 14th, 1941.

money in various doubtful ways and were a disgrace to society. They had to be sought out and punished with all severity.

Another article was headed 'The Whisperers', and was about people who went around telling malicious jokes. Such nasty, crude jokes and sinister rumours were being put about by traitors and enemies of the people, they said, that firm measures would have to be taken to deal with such rumour-mongers and punish them severely.

'Goodness gracious, you're not pulling my leg every now and again, are you?' my grandfather said in a frightened tone. 'Are you sure that's not a Bolshevik paper you're reading sometimes?'

'No, Gramp, it's German! Look—there's the Fascist sign.'

Every day the newspaper's tone became more nervous, and it was full of shouts and threats. Half the announcements were now only in German. And the bulletins from the Führer's headquarters became much drier and briefer, but more alarming: 'Powerful Attacks Repulsed in Bend of Donets'; 'Soviet Attacks Repulsed on Eastern Front'.

My mother said that in newspapers you had always to read, not the words themselves, but between the lines.

That is what I learnt to do.

My grandfather saw the body of a man who had been hanged on Vladimir Hill. It hung there with the snow settling on it, with nothing on the feet, the head crooked to one side and the face quite black: either he had been severely beaten or his face had turned black after he was hanged. There was a placard on him saying he had attacked a German.

A mine exploded in the German headquarters on Dzerzhinsky Street. They grabbed everybody for that—not only young and middle-aged men but the old folk as well, and even women with babies, and it was said that more than a thousand people went to Babi Yar for that one mine. The City Commandant Eberhard no longer issued any proclamations.

By now we were afraid to go out on the streets—you never knew where the next explosion was going to be and whether you'd be taken off and shot for it . . . 'You get yourself into such places,' my mother exclaimed, 'you are so late coming home; they'll take a pot-shot at you one day, like shooting a rabbit; don't you dare go out any more!'

It was terribly difficult trying to observe the curfew imposed by the Germans. There was no radio, and our clock went only when the spirit moved it, so that before going out my grandmother would go next door to find out the time, then look over the fence to see whether anyone was passing whom she could ask.

There were plenty of rumours going round: that they had shot some saboteurs in Babi Yar; that they were executing Ukrainian nationalists; that they were shooting people who infringed the black-out; shooting layabouts; shooting rumour-mongers; shooting partisans; shooting, shooting, shooting . . . The machine-gun chattered away in the ravine every day.

'What on earth is happening?' my mother asked as she listened to the sound of the shooting. 'What is the world coming to?'

'The Enemy is at hand. Be silent!' said Grandma.

'They keep killing off their "enemies of the people", so that in the end there won't be any people left. Then they will have achieved their ideal—there'll be no people and no enemies, just peace and quiet.'

'It's true, Marusya, what it says in the Bible—that the Enemy shall consume himself.'

'They're shooting again, can't you hear it?—they're executing people . . . Will people never come to their senses?'

'Marusya, my dear, we'll all be dead long before that happens!'

Wounded on the Stairs

I knew they'd be waiting for me and I was frightened long before I reached them. I took some crusts of bread out of my box, broke up a couple of boiled potatoes, wrapped them up and put them into the basket my grandmother had got ready.

It was fabulously valuable, that basket. There was a pot of fruit jelly in it, a little flask of milk, and even a tumbler full of fresh butter. I had forgotten what such food tasted like; it was like precious stones—beautiful to look at, but not to be eaten.

Near the market I jumped on the back of an empty lorry and squatted down against the cabin in the hope that the driver would not look out of his back window. He didn't, and he drove so fast that I bumped about like a wooden doll, but he turned off near the tram terminus and I had to jump down. I had done so much jumping on and off those lorries I was like a cat. Most important was to catch them as they went round a corner, and if you had to jump off when they were going full speed the thing was to push yourself away from it with all your might so as to reduce your own speed. I learnt to do this perfectly after having landed once smack on my face in the roadway.

At the tram terminus I got on to a goods car and tucked myself away in the corner of the platform. The conductor came around collecting money, but I turned away as though I hadn't seen him. I hadn't any money to give him, in any case.

I hopped off in Podol and walked down Andrew's Hill, which was lined with beggars all the way. Some of them were whining and begging openly for money, others exposed their amputated limbs in silence. There were other, quiet, intelligent-looking elderly men and women, some with spectacles and pince-nez, standing there; they were professors and teachers of various kinds, like our maths teacher who had died. In the case of some of them who sat there you couldn't tell whether they were alive or dead. There had always been plenty of beggars about even before the war, but now there were so many it was simply frightful. They wandered all over the place, knocking on people's doors, some of them people who had lost their homes through fire, some with babies, some of them on the run, and some swollen with hunger.

It was bitterly cold and the people walked down the streets with grim expressions on their faces, hunching themselves up from the wind, worried, in ragged clothes, in all sorts of strange footwear and threadbare coats. It was indeed a city of beggars.

St Andrew's church stood on the very top of the steep hill, dominating the whole of Podol. It was built by Rastrelli;* blue and white, delicate, reaching to the skies. It was also besieged by beggars and there was a service going on inside. I straightway forced my way through and stood there listening and studying the paintings of famous masters on the walls. The inside of the church was richly decorated, with lots of gilding, and next to it, in unlovely contrast, was that ragged, starving, whining crowd of devout women beating their brows against the icy stone floor.

I couldn't bear it for long, and climbed up into the tower. From there I had a bird's-eye view of the Dnieper, Trukhanov Island and a long stretch of the left bank, including Darnitsa. Below me was a sea of roofs. To the left was just bare ground, where the Desyatinnaya church used to stand. That was where the legendary founders of Kievan Rus were buried and I wondered whether, if the foundations had been preserved, perhaps the bones of Princess Olga or Prince Vladimir had also by some miracle been preserved, and were still lying there and nobody knew about them. I so wanted to think about all these things. The church tower was a place where I always wanted to rest my elbows on the parapet and think.

A German officer who had clambered up through the snow to the top of the hill was taking photographs of the church from a rather odd angle below it and I, knowing a little about photography, watched how carefully he chose his spot. I was the only human figure to include in his picture and give it a little life.

Instead of moving away I stared straight at him and thought: So you click your shutter, then you'll develop the film and make some prints and send them home to your family, so that they can see what your war has brought you. You photograph it as though it were your own property: you acquired the right to do so by shooting. But what have you to do with St Andrew's church, or with Kiev itself? The fact that you came here shooting and murdering? Like a highway-robber? What is this banditry going on all over the world? First one gang appeared, with their red banners and

---

* Count Bartolomei Rastrelli (1700–1771), the architect who was responsible for major palaces in St Petersburg (Leningrad). [Tr.]

their fine slogans, murdering, robbing and destroying. Now another has arrived, also with red banners and fine slogans, also murdering, robbing and destroying. You are all bandits. Some people build and work and labour in the sweat of their brows, then the looters come along, who have never created anything since the day they were born but who know how to shoot. And they grab everything for themselves. It is you, and only you, the ones who do the shooting, who are the real, genuine enemies, whatever banners you choose to posture under. HENCEFORWARD AND TO THE END OF MY DAYS I SHALL HATE YOU AND YOUR MISERABLE WEAPONS, MAYBE I SHALL DIE FROM HUNGER IN ONE OF YOUR PRISONS OR FROM ONE OF YOUR BULLETS, BUT I SHALL DIE FULL OF CONTEMPT FOR YOU AS THE MOST LOATHSOME THINGS ON THIS EARTH.

I left the church, breathing heavily from impotent rage, and came to myself only when I reached Bogdan Khmelnitsky Square, across which a strange column of skiers were making their way. They had no idea at all of how to get along on skis: they put their feet down awkwardly, slithered about and got their skis all mixed up. The square was full of the noise they made, and the soldiers looked rather pathetic, expressions of pain and annoyance on their faces. They had obviously been forced to try to master that rather difficult skill so that snow should no longer be an obstacle to their evil progress across the world. The officer was shouting at them and getting very cross. They shuffled along slowly in the direction of Vladimir Hill, and I very much wanted to go and watch them breaking their necks on it, but I was already late.

In the middle of the city, the trams were running. People were standing in the wind at the tram stop, among them a very undersized German in a light greatcoat and boots that were too small for him, wearing a soldier's cap and woollen ear-muffs. He was badly chilled and quite blue in the face. His hands were shaking and he couldn't keep them in his pockets as he kept fidgeting and jerking about, banging one foot against the other, wiping his face with his hands; then all of a sudden he started to dance about, kicking his feet out like a wooden clown, and he seemed to be on the verge of letting out a piercing howl, no longer able to bear the biting cold.

The fact that he looked rather silly could not have entered his head, because there were only local people standing around and for Germans that was as if the place was deserted. They moved about among us as though they were on their own, quite ready to let their trousers down, blow their noses with their fingers, or urinate openly on the street.

Two lorries drove out of the gateway of St Sophia's cathedral, carrying something covered over with tarpaulin: once again they were carting off some loot. It was very odd: every tenth word they used was the word 'culture'—'the centuries-old German culture', 'the cultural revival of the world', 'the whole culture of mankind depends on the successes of German arms' . . . It sounded fine; it was amazing what you can do with words.

This culture of theirs consisted, in effect, in their clearing every single thing out of the museums, using the manuscripts from the Ukrainian Academy for wrapping paper, taking pot-shots with their revolvers at statues, mirrors and gravestones—indeed at anything that offered itself as a target. That, it appeared, was the revival of culture.

And then there was the humanism. German humanism was the greatest in the world; the German Army was the most humane army, and everything it did was only to further German humanism. No, not just humanism, but GERMAN humanism, the most noble, intelligent and purposeful of all possible humanisms.

Because, it appears, there are as many humanisms in the world as there are murderers. Every murderer has his own, private and most noble brand of humanism, of course, just as he has private ways of reviving culture.

We had had SOCIALIST culture—'we shall destroy the old and build the new'—and in its name they flattened the Desyatinnaya church to the ground, laid lorry-loads of explosives beneath the Cathedral of the Dormition, sent scholars off to Siberia and poisoned Gorky. There was also SOCIALIST humanism, in whose name the secret police went prowling around in their cars at night, murdered people, threw them into the ravine from the windows of the October Palace, and covered Siberia with whole settlements of concentration camps.

That, it now appeared, had been wrong. GERMAN humanism was now put forward once again as the opposite of that universal, diffuse, ineffective and therefore hostile humanism, for which there could be only one place—Babi Yar.

Soviet humanism, German humanism, Assyrian humanism, Martian humanism,—there were so many of them in the world, and the primary aim of each one of them was to kill off as many people as possible; they all began and ended in Babi Yars. Babi Yar—that is the real symbol of your cultures and of your humanisms.

It was very early in my life that I had first to delve into these concepts of culture and humanism with all their nuances, because from my very childhood my principal occupation was to try and avoid becoming the object of their attention. That has remained my preoccupation all my life, and remains so to this very day . . .

When the tramcar drew up, the crowd scrambled in by the rear entrance while a German entered by the front. The tramcars were divided—the rear part was for the local population, and the front was for Aryans. When I had read about the Negroes in books like *Uncle Tom's Cabin* and *Mister Twister* I never imagined I would one day have to ride in a tramcar in the same way.

The tram went past shops and restaurants with large, bold signs posted up—UKRAINIANS NOT ADMITTED, GERMANS ONLY. Outside the opera was a theatre bill written entirely in German. The German flag with a swastika on it was flying over the building of the Academy of Science, now the main headquarters of the police. All in complete accord with GERMAN culture and GERMAN humanism.

The fire in the Kreshchatik had spread as far as the Bessarabka market and stopped outside it. Consequently one side of the square was nothing but frightful ruins, while the other side was bright with shop-signs and the lights of shop-windows, while the pavement was crowded with people, mostly German officers and their ladies.

It was very awkward and rather frightening to walk among them; it made you feel as though you had pushed yourself in somewhere where you had no right, and I will tell you why.

The officers—well-groomed, clean-shaven, with tightly fitting tunics and their caps down over their eyes—walked along without even noticing the local people; or, if they did glance at them, then it was just casually, like farmers looking round their cattle-yard and deciding what ought to be rebuilt, how to make the place more profitable and which animals to send to slaughter. And if a pair of searching eyes did happen to rest on you with real interest, then you were in trouble: it meant that you had attracted attention because you stood out in some way, and they might decide to get rid of you. Heaven preserve you from the attentions of those in authority.

The women, too, were beautifully turned out: in furs from head to foot, they moved like queens, many of them with smartly trimmed sheep-dogs on leads. However much I try to persuade myself, I have never since been able to rid myself of a feeling of cold resentment for those clever animals. I know it's stupid, but those German sheep-dogs which are used to intimidate human beings in concentration camps all over the world automatically evoke in me a feeling of hostility, and there's nothing I can do about it.

I walked on. At the covered market there was a long queue of people, about two thousand of them, waiting to receive their rations of bread. With the approach of winter ration cards had been issued—workers were to receive less than two pounds of bread a week, other people only half a pound.

My grandparents, my mother and I had four cards between us, each for half a pound, and I used to spend a whole day fighting in the queue to bring back less than one whole loaf of fresh bread. We had never seen such bread before.

It was an ersatz bread: very crumbly and dry, with a crust like cardboard covered with millet husks. It was baked from some flour substitute made from maize tops, millet husks, barley and horse-chestnuts. It was gritty to eat and had a bitter-sweet taste. It was difficult to digest, but, of course, I treasured it, dividing my half-pound up into seven pieces—just over an ounce a day—never touching my next day's ration.

My grandfather and I could not forgive ourselves for having gathered so few chestnuts in the parks before the snow began to fall. The city authorities now issued a printed appeal encouraging people to use chestnuts for food and explaining with scientific precision just how many calories and how much protein and starch they had in them. But we had been eating chestnuts for ages. The Germans were really extraordinary people—fancy trying to teach us Ukrainians what to eat, when we had lived through the famine of the 'thirties . . . We could teach anybody that business.

My grandfather fell sick. What my grandmother and mother did to find a doctor and what it cost is a whole epic in itself. Gramp was found to have stones in his bladder, and he was operated on in the October Hospital beyond the Bessarabka market.

What happened to this hospital was a very strange story. Hospitals were usually taken over to serve as barracks and the patients were simply shot, but for some reason they left the October Hospital alone, and it went on functioning until the summer of 1942 when at last they shut it down. Even stranger was the fact that the wounded Red Army men who had been admitted under Soviet rule remained in it, and the Germans for some reason or other did not touch them.

The hospital kept going by using up the old supplies of medicaments, but there was nothing to eat. Once a day the patients were given a ladleful of hot water with a few grains of something floating in it. Patients from the city lived on what their friends and relations brought in for them, and the wounded soldiers lived on what was handed on to them. It was my job to take Gramp his food parcels and this became a real nightmare for me.

Even as I entered the hospital building I found myself in the doorway surrounded by patients. They didn't rush at me, nor did they shout or snatch at me; they simply stood there in silence, craning their necks and looking. I would push my way through them, take a white coat from the hook and go on up the stairs.

Wide and ornate, the staircase led up to the second floor, and there were patients standing in a line all along the wall, looking like skeletons, with waxen faces and bandaged heads, many of them on crutches and none of them saying anything. They simply stared with their feverish, half-crazed eyes and from time to time shyly stretched out a grey, cupped hand.

I would shake my parcel and push into their hands microscopic bits of crust and potato, loathing myself as I did it—such a small benefactor among those grown men. Then, when I reached the ward at last, my grandfather would guess immediately and start wailing:

'What the devil do you think you're doing, giving stuff away, pretending to be so well-off. Don't you give those crooks anything; they're going to die anyway, and here am I dying too!'

I no longer knew what to do. Gramp really did look like a living corpse. They had already operated on him and inserted a little tube through his stomach, for his water, with a bottle attached to the end. Gramp was so weak he could hardly stir, but he could swear like a fit man, and he clutched on to the basket, stuffed the food into the little cupboard, moved a stool up against the door and for safety's sake kept his hand resting on it.

In the next bed lay a patient who had lost his legs. He had a black beard and an expression of suffering on his face, like the Christ on my grandmother's icon.

'He's a wicked old man, your grandad, son,' he said in a hollow voice, turning only his eyes towards me. 'He's already managed to quarrel with everybody in the ward . . . But come over here a minute, I want to tell you something.'

I went across to him, only sorry that I hadn't kept him a crust.

'Gather up the fallen leaves,' he said, 'dry them well, clean them off and bring them here. I am longing for a smoke.'

I nodded: whatever else was lacking, there were plenty of leaves to be had.

'The leaves of the cherry tree are the best,' he said wistfully. 'Cherry leaves.'

Back home I spent a long time scratching about in the snow, scraping up the blackened, frozen leaves, sorting out the ones from the cherry trees, drying them on the stove and cleaning them off. But when, a couple of days later, I again arrived with the food parcel, it turned out that the legless man had already died. I cannot tell you how guilty I felt . . . Had I known I would have made a special journey sooner so that he could at least have had a smoke before he died.

The other patients eagerly took the little bag of leaves from me, and later on I brought them more. But I've no idea what happened to those patients after the hospital was closed down.

Business Becomes Dangerous

I used to start my normal working day by taking a sack and going down to the corner of Kirillovskaya and Syretskaya Streets, where a dozen or so other traders like me would already have gathered. The trams carting peat to the canning factory turned off there, and we would leap on to the wagons like locusts, throw off pieces of peat, then gather them up and divide them between us.

A tram drawing goods wagons came down the road, with a guard in a long fur-lined coat and felt boots sitting on the front platform. We leapt on to the step and then saw that the wagon was not carrying peat but beetroot.

We really descended on them like young wolves. They were frozen hard, landed with a thump on the roadway and bounced about like little footballs. I managed to hang on in a good place and stayed throwing them off longer than the others, until I saw the guard standing over me in his coat and I slipped away from under his very hands.

But while I was running back a fight had started up on the roadway. The mere sight of the beetroot had made the others wild, and they had forgotten about dividing them up. The more dishonest ones had not thrown any off, but only gathered them off the roadway, and there was nothing left for fools like me. I was so hurt by this that I really lost my temper, because I had thrown off more than anybody. I let out a filthy swear-word—for the first time in my life, I believe—and rushed into the fray. I snatched a beetroot away from a small boy and stuffed it under my coat, but then I got such a punch in the eyes that I saw stars and for a moment was unable to see anything. Then someone tripped me and I fell to the ground, where I covered

my head with my hands, while somebody kicked me viciously in the side trying to make me turn over to get the beetroot
off me. If at that moment I had had a knife or a gun, I
would have murdered the lot of them; I would have murdered them, screaming like a little animal. I don't know how
it might have ended if another tram had not appeared.

I picked myself up, trembling and quite alone in the
world, like a young wolf, with only myself to rely on, and
immediately saw what to do. While all the others were hanging along the sides of the wagons with the guard swearing
at them, stumbling across the beet, hitting at their hands
and trying to drive them away, I hopped on to the front
platform which he had abandoned.

The steps up to the platform were very awkward, no wider
than my hand, and instead of handles they had a thin iron
rail welded on. I seized hold of the rail and, with one felt
boot on the step, I stretched out as far as I could and
started knocking one beet after the other off the wagon—
and at that moment my foot slipped. I hung there, holding
on to the rail by my hands, watching the grey steel wheel
rolling along the grey steel rail and my legs dangling in
front of it. I had no feeling in my hands—they were numb
from the ice-cold rail—and I hadn't a drop of strength left
to pull myself up by. Way up above me I could see the
guard who had turned towards me; I let out a thin, brief
shout: 'Help!'

He realized at once what had happened, grabbed me by
the arms and drew me up on to the platform. Then he
pulled on the rope to separate the pole from the overhead
wires. The tram ran on a little and came to a standstill.

With a sudden jerk I twisted myself out of his hands,
jumped down on to the roadway and ran as I had never
run before. The tram-driver and the guard shouted to each
other and cursed but I did not turn round. I ran all the
way home, burst into the barn, bolted myself in and sat
there on a box until I had recovered. Then I went indoors
and triumphantly laid three beetroots before my grandmother. She threw up her hands in amazement.

I had a little rest and then got out my sledge, a little chopper
and some rope, and set off for Pushcha-Voditsa.

It was a beautiful, well-kept pine forest, in which every

single tree used to be cared for. It was considered to be a health-giving forest, and there were lots of nursing-homes in it, especially for people suffering from tuberculosis, as well as enormous country houses in the best parts of the forest belonging to government officials.

The Germans had started cutting the forest down. Not the Germans themselves, but workers who were paid a pound of bread a week for doing it. They were felling the trees along the tramline, so that they could be easily transported, and there were already big clearings which had been cut in the forest with stacks of logs in them. The saws rang out, the tractors chugged away, and the tops of the fir trees trembled and shed their snow and then came sailing down, to hit the ground with a crash like an explosion.

A great number of old women and children were swarming around with their sledges. In the clearings everything had been cleaned up; they had even gathered up the pine needles, and only the thick, strong-smelling stumps of the trees remained sticking up. Every time a tree was felled the women and children rushed at it from every side, while the workers swore at them and tried to drive them away.

Having made sure in which direction the next tree was going to fall I rushed through the deep snow towards it and managed to be first on the spot. There was no need for my chopper—there were so many branches broken off— and I had just grabbed hold of the biggest when I heard a shout and saw the top of another fir tree descending out of the grey sky right on top of me, getting bigger and bigger every second. The reason why I had been first was that no one had been allowed to go there yet.

I dived into a bush, fell and rolled over, trying to get my body as far away as possible; then came the explosion, and the sound of the branches and cones falling like shrapnel, and for a second I could see nothing for the snow that hung in the air.

'What are you trying to do—you nearly killed someone!' a woman called out.

'That'll teach him not to go there,' the workmen replied. 'Now, you little devil, get out of there or you'll cop it!'

I dragged my sledge out of the mass of branches; by sheer luck it was undamaged, and I scrambled around the clearing. The workmen were shouting at me, but I couldn't leave the place with empty hands. I had learnt my lesson, however, and I didn't dash in first, but snatched the branches from under the women's noses, got wet through in the struggle, and gathered such a pile of branches on my sledge that I could hardly move it.

Still, it was only difficult in the deep snow: it would slide all right on the roadway. I pulled and tugged, too greedy to take off a single branch, grabbing hold of bushes and tree-stumps to help me along, moving only a few feet at a time. When I finally dragged it out on to the tramline steam was rising from my body and my hands were shaking like a paralytic's. A pathway had been beaten down between the rails, and it took me some time to drag the sledge across the rails on to it. But then it became far easier to pull the sledge, and off I went, only hoping that no tram would appear.

At the edge of the wood was the forest-keeper's house. I had forgotten about it and I became aware of the danger only when I caught sight of a pile of wood and two men waiting calmly for me. I looked behind me; but I was quite alone on the tram-track. The others no doubt went round the outside of the wood. The men said:

'Stop. Undo it.'

My heart sank. I undid it.

'Take off that piece. And that. And that.'

I meekly removed the biggest branches, but they left me the smallest pieces and the pine-needles. Then they said threateningly:

'Next time we catch you we'll hand you over to the police.'

Thank God they let me go, at least. So off I went again, thinking to myself: It's an ill wind—the sledge ran very easily now. On the downhill parts I simply let it go, jumped on the pine-needles and had a ride.

At night I went off with the Gorokhovsky brothers to steal Christmas trees. Christmas was getting near, and little fir trees were selling at the market for twenty-five roubles apiece. It wasn't all that much, but it was still half a pound of bread.

There were plantations of young saplings along the edge of Pushcha-Voditsa, beyond Priorka. We tried not to think about the fact that we were breaking the curfew—there was nothing we could do about it, we just had to take a chance. The patrols were almost never seen around Priorka, and we used only the little back streets. Because of our lack of experience we took an axe with us. We would have been better off with a little saw. The sound of an axe carries a long way, and then there's the noise you make when you twist and bend the tree to break it off the stump . . . But everything went off all right; we put the trees on our shoulders and the tops trailed along behind us.

I put my fir tree away in the barn; but then greed began to get the better of me. I felt strong enough and eager enough to go on hauling fir trees the whole night. I found an old saw, listened to make sure that there were no patrols about and set off again, on my own this time. I picked a fir tree that wasn't too big, with the intention of cutting two the same size. I sawed the trunk through with practically no noise at all and then, when it fell, I heard a bark and a shout in the distance:

'Come here, you!'

I seized hold of the fir tree (could I leave such loot behind?) and bolted. I didn't dare look round, but I could sense my pursuers behind me, and the dog's yelping overtook me. The snow was deep and made it difficult to run, but it held back the dog too. I swung the fir tree round, hoping to drive the dog away with it, but it kept running alongside me. I no longer felt any pain, only as if something was hitting me around the legs and knees above my top boots.

I stopped and started swinging the saw furiously about. I felt really vicious, ready to kill the dog with the saw, attack it with my teeth or poke its eyes out with my fingers. But the animal kept out of my reach. I ran on, stopping from time to time, making threatening noises, hurling snow at the dog and then running farther. All dogs are afraid, just like people who behave like dogs, if you go for them or throw something at them. You have to attack them, to go for them, otherwise you are lost. Go straight for them, and they will jump back in their cowardice.

But there was a man chasing me as well. It was only later that I learnt that you had only to give him ten roubles to be able to cut down the whole plantation if you wanted to; but I didn't know and, in any case, *ten* roubles! Better be bitten by the dog. Anyway, it had chased me as far as the first houses, but still hadn't had the courage to bite me, and I hadn't dropped the fir tree.

When I got home I felt my legs and found my trousers were all torn to pieces and my knees were bleeding. But I didn't waste my time being sorry for myself, I sat in the barn resting and thinking about the bright side of things, about my achievements.

It had been a successful day, a very profitable day. In the first place, there were the few ounces of bread I was entitled to on my card. Then there was the plate of soup in the children's canteen. Three beetroots. A sledge-load of fuel. Two fir trees. Goodness, I was a rich man. Of course, on the debit side there were my torn trousers; that really would have been a great loss if I had not been wearing some old trousers which could be patched up anyway. The most important thing was that I was still alive.

What do they teach you in books? That you have to love your fellow men and devote your life to the struggle for a better, brighter future. Which fellow men? What future, if I may ask? Whose?

Death

My grandfather was brought home from the hospital just before Easter. They brought him on my sledge, because he could hardly walk without assistance. He so wanted to be at home for Easter.

Would you like me to tell you what Easter, that most glorious of annual festivals, is like if it is properly celebrated?

In the first place, everything has to be 'no worse than in the best homes'. Preparations begin already in the winter. Money is saved up and put on one side, one kopek after another, and regarded as untouchable, kept near the icons. Then flour is bought somewhere on the black market, in good time before the price rises: it is never to be found in the shops. Then the following problems arise: raisins, vanilla, cinnamon and little packets of colouring. My grandmother used to spend days on end at the market, running from one of her acquaintances to the other and carting home her spoils—some fresh sausage skins, eggs or rice. At home she would keep a sharp eye out to see that no one touched her stores. It was Lent, and my mother and I, although we were not believers, would never break the rules or do anything to upset Grandma.

Then Grandma would always prepare a home-made sausage, smoke a ham and stew some fruit for the occasion, so that the whole house was full of smells that made your mouth water and your head turn.

My job was to rub the poppy-seed and sugar through a sieve, for which I was allowed to lick the wooden spoon. I also helped with colouring the eggs, which left me with fingers all the colours of the rainbow.

For cooking the Easter cake Grandma had a whole row of clay pottery forms stored away in the pantry. She used to bake two big cakes for the house and a whole clutch of smaller ones for taking to the neighbours, giving to the poor and leaving at the church.

With her basket full and covered over with a clean cloth my grandmother would go off to the all-night service, while we would go to sleep on our virtuously empty stomachs. She would return at dawn elated, radiant, not of this world, and wake us with the Easter greeting. Meanwhile everything in the cottage would be spotlessly clean—the walls freshly white-washed, new curtains hung and new mats laid on the clean scrubbed floor. There was something special about everything; it was a very special festival.

The table was moved out and laid with food and paper flowers. But only somebody without manners or education would descend on the food immediately. First you had to wash yourself, in a big bowl with silver coins lying on the bottom, and then dress up in everything clean and new. My grandmother would seat everyone solemnly at the table in his or her proper place and then recite the Lord's Prayer with great feeling and conviction.

'Christ is risen!' my grandfather would say joyfully, licking his lips.

'He is risen indeed!' my grandmother would reply happily,

with tears in her eyes, taking one last look round the table—
maybe it hadn't been easy to do, but it really was·'no worse
than in the best homes'. Then she would give her permission: 'All right, the Lord be with you, let's enjoy ourselves!'

And after the formalities we were able to have a taste of
the good life. That's the way it was in our home in that
happy time of peace, thanks to the fact that if the Soviet
regime did not recognize Easter, at least it did not forbid
it, although, of course, people were not let off from work.

And now, though it was wartime, my grandmother decided
that, come what may, she was going to bake Easter cakes.
We could go without everything else, but she insisted on
having the cakes, as though otherwise she would go to hell.
Could you really celebrate Easter without Easter cake? My
mother had just returned from a long expedition round the
villages exchanging things and had brought back some potatoes and grain.

The first thing we had to do was to get it ground. There
were some people on the other side of the railway embankment who had a mill and who would let people use it in
exchange for a tumbler or two of grain.

My grandmother and I went over there. The mill stood in
a barn and consisted of two big wooden wheels one on top
of the other. You had to turn the top one by means of a
handle, pouring the grain in through a hole in the middle
of it. The two facing surfaces had pieces of metal nailed on
to them to crush the grain and grind it into flour.

My grandmother and I, one on each side, took hold of the
handle and the two of us just managed to turn the heavy
'millstone'. She poured in the grain only a handful at a time,
and even so it was very hard going. We worked half the day,
until we were quite exhausted and out of breath and dripping
with perspiration. There was a cold wind blowing through
the barn, and Grandma was quite concerned lest I should
catch cold.

We set off home, hardly able to drag one leg after the
other, chilled through by the piercing wind. Grandma settled
down to put the flour through a sieve and found amongst it
a lot of razor-sharp shreds of metal from the 'millstone'. I
had to get hold of a magnet and went over the flour, extract-
ing the pieces of metal from it.

Grandma was very upset because she was afraid that our home-made flour would not produce white bread but only grey loaves, but she mixed it and kneaded it just the same and went to bed. That night she had a fever in which she started demanding white flour, raisins and butter.

Next day my mother rushed around the houses trying to find a doctor. An old chap came along, whom we paid with two tumblerfuls of flour, and he wrote out some prescriptions.

'The only thing is I don't know myself where you will get this,' he said.

'Then what are we to do?' my mother asked.

'What can I do?' he said crossly. 'First get the stove going, at least, so that you can't see your own breath indoors. She needs warmth and she needs to drink hot milk and to get some food into her. She is on her last legs.'

My mother gave Grandma drinks made of herbs. She rushed all over the city and managed somewhere or other to get hold of a little bottle of medicine. But Grandma got worse; she couldn't get her breath and kept crying:

'I'm suffocating! Give me air!'

We took it in turns to sit by her and fan her with newspapers, but she found it better, for some reason or other, when we simply blew on her from our mouths. Occasionally she would come round and start worrying about the Easter cakes. My mother had baked them, but they turned out black and sticky, and the grit in them got in your teeth. Grandma took one look at them and burst into tears.

Her friend from younger days, my godmother Alexandra, came to see her along with her blind husband Mikolai. They were such good and inoffensive old folk, probably the most kind-hearted people I had ever met in my life. They had once had a son, their only child, who had been one of the first to join the Komsomol in Kurenyovka and had been sent out to organize the Komsomol in the villages, where he had been killed. That had been in 1919. Not long afterwards Mikolai went blind. Grandma said: 'He has cried his sight away,' although, of course, he had lost his sight through some disease. Alexandra and Mikolai knew absolutely nothing about politics; all they knew was that their one and only Kolya had been a good boy, and they could never grasp why anybody should have wanted to kill him.

In the old days Mikolai and my grandfather had worked

together, but Mikolai was now too senile and helpless. His head was covered with sparse, grey wisps of hair, and for some reason he wore glasses on his nose with a piece of blue glass in the right side. The left lens had been broken and Mikolai had fitted a piece of thin ply-wood in its place.

It was Alexandra who, along with my grandmother, had had me christened. She worked as a cleaner at the children's handicraft centre. Early in the morning she used to go out on to our square and take Mikolai with her. She would sweep the place over with a broom, while her husband would take a rake and, in spite of his lack of sight, would go over the whole ground carefully and systematically, never missing a single bit of paper or rubbish.

They would work together like that for many long hours, because it was a large square, and when they had finished it looked really tidy and you could see the marks left by the rake, like freshly sown vegetable gardens in the spring.

They were Byelorussians, and though they had lived practically their whole lives in Kiev they had never learnt to speak either Russian or Ukrainian.

'Troubles never come alone; there's always something else,' said Alexandra with a sigh as she sat at Grandma's bedside. 'Pull yourself together, Martha, you're still young, you haven't had much fun out of life yet.'

'She will see good things yet, never fear,' said Mikolai with tenderness in his voice. He sat there fanning Grandma gently with a newspaper.

It was difficult to know whether Grandma could hear anything; she was breathing very heavily, she was a yellowish, waxen colour and her face had a glow about it.

Suddenly we heard the quiet but distinct sound of glass breaking: the medicine bottle standing on the bedside table had cracked just above the middle, as if it had been cut through by a knife. Alexandra's jaw dropped and fear showed in her eyes. My grandmother turned her head and eyed the bottle with a thoughtful, strange look.

'Of course that had to happen!' I muttered angrily and grabbed the bottle. 'Nothing's been spilt, I'll pour it into something else.'

I had heard talk of this strange omen—that whenever someone is dying some glass breaks for no reason whatever. But I had never believed it. It was a pure coincidence; but of course the damned bottle would have to go and break at that moment!

I took the bottle out into the kitchen as fast as I could.

My mother was sitting in the kitchen, talking to her friend Lena Gimpel and my grandfather about the topic that was occupying the whole city. The Germans were deporting people to work in Germany.

'They're doing right,' Gramp said, jabbing the newspaper with his finger. 'Everybody's starving here, whereas there they can have enough to eat and earn some money. You'll see!'

It was all explained very persuasively in the paper: under Soviet rule everybody tried to have their children educated so that they could become engineers and professors. But the best education was hard work. If they went off to Germany, with its high level of culture, young people would learn how to work and would gain the experience of being abroad, in Europe. They had to go to Germany as part of the struggle for a better, brighter future.

' "That's the way it always is," ' my grandfather read out solemnly. ' "One generation has to make great sacrifices so that their descendants—their children and grandchildren—can have a better life." Do you hear that—a better life for their children and grandchildren!'

'Oh God,' said Lena Gimpel, 'everything in this world is so relative. Every piece of skulduggery can be explained away and praised. Lenin used to talk about these sacrifices for the sake of a better future, and so did Stalin after him . . .'

Lena's husband, an X-ray technician, had gone off to fight like all the others, and had disappeared, leaving her with a small child. She was desperately hungry and very embittered, and seemed to take a malicious pleasure in rubbing my grandfather up the wrong way.

'You stupid woman, you don't understand a thing!' Gramp shouted. 'To hell with their lousy promises. But don't you go comparing Hitler with Lenin or Stalin. He is at least a clever German, and they were just our own good-for-nothings.'

'They're all as bad as one another,' Lena said. 'It's the same story over and over again: whoever happens to be the latest scoundrel to get into power always declares right away that till he came along everything was wrong, that the struggle for a better future was only just beginning, and that therefore people would have to make sacrifices. Right from the outset—sacrifices! Sacrifices! The scoundrels!'

'I only know one thing,' my grandfather said, unwilling to give in. 'It's right what they say there—young people today have got to be taught how to work. They've got too big for their boots; they do nothing but read books, and who is going to do the hard work? The Germans are right—work is the best training.'

'It simply means that they are short of manpower. They just want to recruit as many people as they can,' my mother commented. 'That's what they ought to say.'

'They can't do that,' said Lena. 'Then nobody would go. They've got to make it sound good. So they use fine words and make their grand appeals. I'd like to see the lot of them dead!'

'You fool, what are you saying?' My grandfather restrained her with a frightened gesture. 'You don't know who may hear you through the window. You don't want to fetch up in Babi Yar, do you?'

'He's right, you know—you must be more careful with that sort of talk,' my mother said, lowering her voice.

'There's a curse on this age and on this country, it's like Dante's Hell,' Lena went on, choking with hatred. 'Oh, Maria, what did we waste our youth on, twenty years of it? We lived day after day with an axe hanging over our heads. We didn't have the right to open our mouths; we had to think over every word we uttered; we were scared of our own shadows and we could trust nobody. Your own father, your husband, your boyfriend, even your own child was a potential informer who might get you into trouble. Sometimes at night I want to shout out—my nerves are simply giving out. I often think: what does it matter where they take you—to Kolyma or to Babi Yar—there's a curse on all of them. I hate them all!'

Suddenly we heard the crack of breaking glass. We all started and turned round to stare at the lamp. It was an old paraffin lamp which hung on the wall and which had not been lit for a long time, because there was no oil for it. That was why it was so clean and polished for Easter. Its glass had cracked, just above the middle, in a clean straight line. My mother got up and removed the top half of the glass and stood turning it round in her hands, rather puzzled. I saw it all with my own eyes and to this very day I don't know how to explain it: you can, of course, say it was just a 'coincidence', but at the time a cold shudder went right through my body.

Alexandra came running in when she heard the noise. She took one look, realized at once what had happened, and proceeded to cross herself vigorously.

'It is a sign from God. Poor Martha, she's dying . . .'

I started to mutter:

'Grandma saw the bottle break.'

'What's all this superstitious rubbish?' Lena exclaimed. 'What is the matter with you, really. You're like little children!'

'It's just an accident, a coincidence,' my mother joined in. 'But it's a bad thing she saw it happen, she's going to think now that . . .'

When I went back to Grandma, Mikolai was still busy fanning her with the newspaper, looking, as all blind people do, straight ahead, as though he was staring into the distance through the bit of ply-wood and the blue lens. I went round the other side and started blowing with my mouth.

My grandmother opened her eyes and looked at me long and thoughtfully, making me feel rather uneasy. It was as though she was seeing me properly for the first time and was making a great effort to understand just what sort of a person I was, penetrating to depths beyond the reach of other people, even me. But perhaps there was a much simpler explanation and that she was simply sorry to be dying and to think that I would be left alone without her and without God while the Enemy prowled across the land.

We took it in turns to sit at Grandma's bedside through the night. She was gasping for breath, perspiring heavily and losing consciousness from time to time. At last the morning came, frosty and glittering, with a rose-coloured sun which bathed the snow and icicles in front of the windows and the whole room in the same pink glow.

And all of a sudden Grandma seemed to be better. She

started breathing easily and deeply and lay back on her pillow, relaxed and apparently content.

'The crisis is over!' my mother exclaimed, turning to me with a radiant expression on her face. 'Thank God, all is well!'

I rushed across to the window and shouted to Gramp, who was out in the yard:

'Gran's better!'

But when I turned round again I saw that my mother was standing there strangely rigid, staring into Grandma's face. It was terribly pale, and Grandma was breathing unevenly and weakly. Then she stopped breathing altogether.

'She's dying!' My mother let out a scream. 'Quick, the coins! Give me the coins quickly!'

My grandmother had had a little box of cotton and buttons in which she kept some old silver and copper coins, and she had always said that when she died her eyes should be covered with these coins. I rushed to the box, as though our whole salvation lay in it, brought it over and pushed it into my mother's hands. But she was too busy calling out, shaking Grandma and rubbing her shoulders, until at last she snatched the coins from me and placed them on Grandma's eyes. And it was all over.

Grandma began to look somehow more distant, more severe and solemn because of those dark, slightly tarnished coins.

There was no money for a coffin. My grandfather took a saw and a plane and some old planks out of the barn, and I helped him to knock together a clumsy, rather rough-and-ready coffin. By rights it should have been painted brown, but my grandfather didn't have any brown paint, only a tin of cheap blue paint. He hesitated a little, thinking it over, then painted the coffin a light blue and put it out to dry in the yard. I had never seen a blue coffin in all my life.

Of course, the house was full of neighbours, mostly old women, who wept loud and long, sang my grandmother's praises, and vied with each other to show the skirts and shoes which Grandma had given them without telling my grandfather and which they now eagerly displayed under Gramp's nose.

'Look, Semerik, what a wonderful wife you had, yet you kept nagging at her all her life!'

Candles were lit in the house, the verger recited prayers, while my mother kept sobbing and going out into the yard and saying: 'I shall never get over it,' while Lena tried to calm her down, saying: 'Take it easy now, we all have to die one day.' It all seemed to me so senseless and pointless, and the old women with their unnatural lamentations so objectionable—their voices were like little drills boring into my ears—and I hung around, not knowing quite what to do, very tense and overwrought.

Bolik and Shurka came along and we sat on top of the fence and started talking about our own affairs, including our buried cartridges (and meanwhile the women went on wailing) and my friends talked to me with sympathy in their voices, as if I were ill. But I suddenly had a desire to show them how unnatural were the women's lamentations and I started copying them and made quite a good job of it. Then I burst out laughing at it all.

I saw Bolik and Shurka looking at me rather strangely, but I went on laughing just the same, and finally they couldn't help themselves either, and we all three felt much more cheerful. We were bursting to do something funny— something really funny! We quickly tied a thread to an old purse, threw it down on the street and then hid behind the fence. When the old women saw it on their way to the funeral and stooped down eagerly to take it, the purse would hop away from them like a frog and we would roll on the ground and hoot with laughter at the sight.

Then the priest arrived with the choirboys and they proceeded to lay Grandma in her coffin. But she was too big for it and there wasn't really room for her. Also the paint wasn't properly dry and came off on everybody. Old Alexandra fussed around anxiously, saying:

'We need more menfolk, more men to carry it!' There just weren't enough men.

At last they managed to lift the coffin and carried it slowly and awkwardly through the door, tipping it as they went. Grandma had a paper ribbon across her forehead with some religious text on it, and in her hands she held one of the little wooden crosses which used to be kept near the icons.

My grandfather, bareheaded and with a look of pain on

his face, helped to carry the coffin on his shoulder along with the others, blind Mikolai taking up his place behind him with his stick under his arm. They put pieces of newspaper on their shoulders so that the paint should not come off on them. Two banners were raised on poles, the priest began his high-pitched lament, the choirboys joined in and they all went through the open gates with Grandma floating majestically above them all.

'You stay here and look after the house,' my mother ordered me. Her face was swollen from crying and she seemed suddenly to have aged and to be no longer beautiful.

I watched the procession move off, closed the gate and gathered up from the ground the fir twigs that had fallen from the wreaths. Everything was now quiet. And it was only then that I really caught my breath and realized at last what had happened. I would never see Grandma again.

'We all have to die,' Lena had said. Grandpa would die, my mother would die, my cat Titus would die. I looked at my fingers, opened them wide and again studied my extended fingers, realizing that, sooner or later, they too would be no more. The most frightening thing on earth was death. It was such a terrible thing when a person died, even a very old person, even if it was the result of illness or just naturally, from old age. Was it not enough to have such a frightful prospect ahead of us in any case, without people continually inventing new artificial ways of bringing death about, arranging more and more of those cursed famines, executions and Babi Yars?

I could hardly stand, and so I wandered off into the house. Everything there was in a terrible state: the floor was trampled down and covered with rubbish, the heavy scent of incense hung in the air, and the stools had been tipped over around the table. Titus, the cat, eyed me attentively from the stove, with his little yellow eyes.

Hitler's Birthday

Some time ago on a day in April, April 20th to be precise, a child was born into this world. As usual, he was red all over, weighed six or seven pounds, measured eighteen inches or so, looked out on the world with little, button-like, unseeing eyes, and kept opening his mouth as though he was yawning, though in fact he was demanding to be fed.

That child evoked in his mother indescribable feelings of tenderness and affection; she had no idea that she was holding in her arms one of the most inhuman monsters of the twentieth century, which fate had for some reason decided she should give birth to. A forerunner of hers (who had performed a similar service to humanity) had been a kind, intelligent and very cultured woman living in a place which nobody had ever heard of called Simbirsk, on the Volga; another one had been the illiterate wife of a cobbler in Gori. But the one I am talking about now lived in Austria. They never knew each other, had never even heard of each other, and no angel came to warn them of what was coming, which was a pity. Maybe they would have sought an abortion. But others would have been found to take their place.

There is, however, always something touching and exciting about the arrival of a child in the world. One repercussion of that touching event in Austria took the form of the following notice posted up in Kiev in April 1942:

ANNOUNCEMENT

On instructions from the City Commissar dated 18.4.42. the occasion of the Führer's birthday will be marked by the issue to the population of one pound of wheat flour per mouth.

The flour will be issued at baker's shops on April 19th and 20th on presentation of coupon No. 16 from the bread-ration cards.*

Novoye Ukrainskoye Slovo, April 19th, 1942.

As soon as it was light, scarcely waiting for the end of the curfew, I rushed off down to the bakery, overtaking many others running in the same direction.

I found, however, that about 1,500 other 'mouths' had ignored the curfew and taken up their places in the queue the night before. Although it was still long before opening time the queue was seething with life; people were pushing and shoving around the door, and a red-faced, perspiring policeman had difficulty in keeping the crowd back.

I fell in at the end of the queue and stood there for a while rather dejectedly, listening to the women saying that the war was coming to an end as soon as the potatoes came into flower, that the Germans hadn't beaten the Russians but that the Russians couldn't win the war, which was why they were going to declare an armistice somewhere along the line of the Volga, and we should simply be left where we were under the Germans.

Even a blind man could have seen that I was going to have to stand in that queue till evening, so I took note of the person I was standing behind, ran off home to get my cigarettes and got down to business.

My friends had all fallen by the wayside. Bolik Kaminsky had been mobilized for work rebuilding the bridge across the Dnieper. He was forced to stay there under guard and wasn't allowed to return home.

Shurka Matso had been taken off by his mother goodness knows where, to live in a different flat. They had been living in a state of constant fear that someone would give Shurka away.

Even my enemy Vovka Babarik was sent away by his mother somewhere into the country to some remote farmstead to try and save him from going to Germany, and I had no longer to be scared lest he should get his own back on me.

Zhorik Gorokhovsky's grandmother got him a job as a server in the church at Priorka, where he used to go around in a long surplice, handing the priest the Gospels or the censer, bowing low with his hands clasped in front of him.

But Kolka Gorokhovsky and I went on selling cigarettes.

It was really a very simple business. We used to go down to the huge 'Yevbaz'. At least, that's what it had been called under Soviet rule—an abbreviation for 'Jewish Bazaar'. Since there were no longer any Jews the newspapers had started calling it the 'Galician Bazaar', but, strangely enough, the name didn't catch on, and people went on calling it the 'Yevbaz'. There we would look out for carts with Germans or Hungarians and start bargaining with them:

'Got any cigarettes?'

'Drei hundert rouble.'

'Nein, nein! Zwei hundert.'

'Nix.'

'Ja, ja! Hey, soldier, zwei hundert, bitte!'

'Zwei hundert—you greedy devil—do you hear? Zwei hundert!'

'Zwei hundert funfzig . . .'

They were out to make money out of anything, selling any old junk they could find, always ready to bargain and argue, but in the end they would hand over a carton of two hundred cigarettes for two hundred roubles. Only very reluctantly.

There is a certain trick in driving a bargain with a German: you mustn't work just with your tongue. You have to get your money out and stuff it under his nose; he will always get excited at the sight of money and will put out his hand to take it without thinking, and once he's taken it you've done a deal.

The first time we got really swindled. When we got back home and opened the packets of cigarettes we found there were about fifteen cigarettes missing from each packet. The Germans had made little holes and hooked the cigarettes out with a piece of wire. After that whenever we bought any we opened the packets on the spot and checked them. There seemed to be such an enormous discrepancy between, on the one hand, bringing about the cultural reform of the whole world, no more no less, and on the other, stealing the dirty underwear from people being executed and hooking cigarettes out of packets.

So we used to hang around in Kurenyovka from morning till night—in the market, at the tram terminus and around the factory gates at the end of the shift, and we would manage to sell a whole carton of cigarettes in about five days, making two hundred roubles profit on it. Three whole pounds of bread in five days—that was a pretty good income.

That was why, at half past six in the morning, I was

already going up and down the queue and all round the market with my cheerful cry:

'Here we are, Levante cigarettes, strong, top quality cigarettes, two roubles apiece. Here you are, mister, buy a fag, don't be mean, you'll die just the same . . . Damn you!'

At the same time I would be gathering up cigarette ends, from which we used to extract the tobacco and sell it by the glassful.

At seven o'clock in the morning the doors of the shop opened. It was impossible to make out exactly what was going on: a terrible crush, groans and screams.

The ones who got their flour first emerged from the shop with clothes all awry, battered and sweating, but with happy faces and clutching tightly their little bags bearing traces of white flour: it wasn't a dream and it wasn't a fairy-tale; it was real white flour.

I went back to my place in the queue, but it still hadn't moved, although there was by this time as long a line behind me as in front.

The women were saying that several men had been executed in Dymer after being caught listening to a crystal radio set; that *Swan Lake* was being performed at the ballet but that there was a notice up saying NO UKRAINIANS OR DOGS ADMITTED.

Dropping their voices, they said the Germans had been brought to a complete halt, that they were lying dead in their thousands around Moscow, that they had not even managed to take Tula, and that a second front was soon going to be opened in Europe. I listened eagerly, so that I could report it all back home. The bush telegraph worked marvellously! What is the use of forbidding people to listen to the radio? You have only to listen to the stories going around among the people ; they nearly always turn out to be true.

At eight o'clock some tramcars came down the road with German children in them. Many of the more important Germans had brought their families with them to Kiev and used to send their children off for the day to Pushcha-Voditsa to a sanitorium, from which they returned by tram in the evening. They were rather special tramcars: each one had a portrait of Hitler on the front, and was decorated with little swastika flags and branches from fir trees.

I ran towards them to have a look at the German children. The windows on the trams were open, and the children were sitting there, well-dressed, red-cheeked, doing much as they pleased and making a great deal of noise. They were shouting and screaming and sticking their heads out of the window like animals in a cage. Suddenly a gob of spit hit me right in the face.

I had not been expecting that. They were small boys, just like me, wearing identical shirts, probably belonging to the Hitler Jugend, and there they were spitting, taking aim and covering me with their spit, with a sort of cold contempt and loathing in their eyes. From the trailing car it was the girls who were spitting. No one reproached them; their teachers simply sat there in their fur coats. (They adored their furs and wouldn't part with them even in the summer.) I stood there quite appalled as the tramcar and its trailer slid past me, like a couple of cages full of furious, screaming monkeys, and I saw them spitting at the queue.

I went across to the stream, my legs feeling as if they were made of cotton-wool. Putting my tray with the cigarettes down on the sand I had a good wash and cleaned up my jacket. Down in my stomach and in my chest, I had a sort of metallic feeling as though I had had some acid or some red Lewisite poured down me.

At eleven o'clock the police managed at last to get things under control. They shut the doors, which had already lost their glass, and were letting people in a dozen at a time, but for some reason or other the queue didn't move at all. It was now getting very warm. At midday German police escorted a couple of young men away under arrest, shoving them in their backs, and, to judge by the way they treated them, with their guns at the ready, it was clear that the young men did not have long to live. But that was a familiar scene which did not evoke any special comments in the queue.

There was very little demand for my cigarettes, so I scratched my head and decided to try a dodge which I had fallen back on more than once. Children used to go round the markets carrying jugs and singing out: 'Cold water, coooold water, who wants cold water to drink?'

I went home and fetched a can and a mug and moved along the queue caling out at the top of my voice. A cupful for twenty kopeks or as much as you wanted for forty. I managed to collect half a pocketful of coins in this way, but it was really nothing, just small change. The German pfennigs were at the rate of one for ten kopeks. They were very unimpressive bits of aluminium, badly tarnished but bearing the eagle and swastika. I changed them all in the market for one crisp new mark. So I hadn't wasted my time.

At four o'clock they started shouting that the queue should disperse: there wasn't enough for everybody. That caused a great fuss. The queue broke up and there was again fighting around the door. Almost howling with disappointment I dived into the scrummage. The grown-ups were struggling with each other, but I crept down between them, squeezing between their legs, wriggling through like a snake, nearly knocking the policeman off his feet, and finally managed to force my way into the shop.

Inside it was relatively easy to move about. The assistants were constantly eyeing the shaking door in some anxiety and shouting:

'No more, no more, that's the lot now!'

But they were still tearing out coupons and handing out bags of flour.

Weeping quietly I got myself right up to the counter, where about thirty people were pressing in. A red-faced man, very distressed, was waving his identity card and shouting:

'I have to leave for Germany tomorrow! I've got it stamped on my card, look!'

'We are issuing it only to people going to Germany,' the manager announced. 'Don't crowd around here the rest of you, you had better go away!'

A few people still received some flour in this way. Still sobbing quietly I went on standing there stubbornly and found myself face to face with an assistant. He looked at me and said:

'Let the kid have some.'

'No, that's the lot now, there's no more flour!' the manager said.

The shelves were empty, with plenty of loose flour lying

about on them but not a single packet. I couldn't believe it
and clung on to the counter, my eyes scouring all the shelves.
Only a moment before there had been packets standing there,
right in front of me.

The police started emptying the shop. I left it in a sort of
daze and went wearily homewards, still seeing in front of me
those white packets which had been given to the lucky ones,
all of whom I hated, with the exception of the last ones, who
were going to Germany. They were to be pitied.

Off to Germany

One of the most tragic periods in the history of the Ukrainian
people, after the invasions by the Turks, the ravages wrought
by Peter and Catherine and the famine and terror under the
Soviet regime, began on April 11th, 1942, with the following
announcement in two languages—German at the top and
Ukrainian below:

MEN AND WOMEN OF THE UKRAINE!
The Bolshevik commissars ruined your factories and
places of work and so deprived you of your means of
livelihood. *Germany* offers you the possibility of taking
up useful and well-paid work.
On January 28th the first special train will leave for
Germany.
During the journey you will be well provided for and, in
addition, at Kiev, Zdolbunov and Przemyśl you will
receive hot meals.
In Germany itself you will be well looked after and
provided with good accommodation. The pay will also
be good: you will be paid at the usual rates, according
to output.
Your families will be well and constantly looked after
while you are working in Germany.
Men and women with experience in all trades, and

especially metal-workers, between the ages of 17 and 50 who wish to volunteer for work in Germany should report to the

KIEV LABOUR EXCHANGE
daily from 8 a.m. to 3 p.m.

We expect Ukrainians to report immediately for work in Germany.

GENERAL-KOMMISSAR I. KWITZRAU
S.A. Brigadenführer. *

The first train for Germany was filled even before it was due to leave, and was made up entirely of volunteers. It set off on January 22nd to the accompaniment of a military band. The newspaper printed a rapturous account of the occasion—smiling faces against a background of goods wagons—and an interview with the man in charge of the train, who pointed out the luggage van full of sausage and ham for eating on the journey. And the headlines: 'Real Patriots', 'Get Trained for Skilled Work', 'The School of Life', 'My Dream', 'We Shall be Useful There'.

On February 25th the second train was dispatched, and on the 27th the third, both of them made up of people who were on their last legs from starvation, who had nothing to lose, or who had been impressed by the words 'good' and 'well' repeated so often in the announcement, as well as by the fantastic luggage van full of sausage and ham. That was a far more successful trick than the fervent appeals to patriotic emotions which were suspiciously like the Soviet ones. They seemed to assume that real patriots must always for some reason leave their native land and go off to hard labour in some other place.

Throughout March the announcements were printed in big letters:

GERMANY CALLS YOU
Go to beautiful Germany!
100,000 Ukrainians are already working
in free Germany.
What about you?†

---

* *Novoye Ukrainskoye Slovo*, January 11th, 1942.
† *Novoye Ukrainskoye Slovo*, March 3rd, 1942.

You should be glad to know that you can go to Germany. You will be working there along with workers from other European countries and by so doing you will be helping to win the war against the enemies of the whole world—the Yids and Bolsheviks.*

Then the first letters began to arrive from Germany, and they acted like exploding shells. Practically everything, apart from 'Greetings' and 'Good-bye', had been cut out of them by the censor's scissors, or had been crossed out with a thick pencil. There was one letter which was passed from hand to hand containing a phrase which the censor had not understood: 'Tell everyone how well we are doing here, and above all tell it to the marines.'

People began to receive summonses at their homes. A labour exchange had been set up in the building of the Art Institute near the Hay Market, and it became, after Babi Yar, the most hated place in town.

People who went there never returned. Amidst continual shouting and weeping, identity cards were confiscated, the word VOLUNTEER was stamped on them, and the people were sent to a transit camp where they waited for weeks to be sent off, while trains were leaving the station one after another to the sound of the military band. Nobody was given anything—no sausage, no 'hot meals' in Zdolbunov or Przemyśl. People who managed to escape from Germany and return home told how they had been sent to work in factories for twelve hours a day, treated like prisoners, beaten, sometimes to death; how the womenfolk were maltreated, and how ridiculous the pay was—enough to keep you in cigarettes.

Some had other stories to tell. They had been taken to a special market, where German farmers walked along the rows of workers, picking them out, looking at their teeth, feeling their muscles, and buying them up at the rate of five to twenty marks a man. They had to work on the farms from dawn to dusk, were beaten for the slightest mistake, and were occasionally killed, because such slaves were worth nothing to them compared with cows or horses, which lived ten times better than the slaves. Moreover, a woman who went to Germany was almost certain to become a prostitute. They all

* Novoye Ukrainskoye Slovo, April 14th, 1942.

had to go around with the word OST on them, which meant the lowest possible category compared with slaves from Western countries.

One of my mother's friends, a schoolmistress, received a brief note saying that her daughter had thrown herself beneath a train. There followed other reports about people who had met a tragic end. The fact was that, apart from those who were simply maltreated or executed, a great many died in the military factories when they were bombed by the Americans or British. The Germans did not stop work during the raids and workers from the East were not sent into air-raid shelters.

Throughout 1942 people from every part of the Ukraine were being driven into slavery.

Call-up notices were being sent round by the thousand. Anyone who did not report was arrested. Raids were carried out in the markets and squares, in cinemas, public baths and in people's homes. The Germans organized a real man-hunt, going after people as Negroes had once been hunted down in Africa.

A woman in Kurenyovka chopped her own finger off with an axe; another entered somebody else's children in her own identity papers and borrowed children from her neighbours when she went before the commission. People put false dates of birth in their identity cards; others roughened their skin with hard brushes and then rubbed in vinegar or paraffin to produce sores; and they gave bribes—at the beginning it cost three thousand roubles to avoid being sent to Germany, but later the price went up to fifteen thousand. And the age at which people were taken kept getting lower—first it was sixteen, then fifteen and finally it was fourteen.

In all the posters and in the newspapers and decrees Germany was always described as 'beautiful'. They printed pictures of the life the Ukrainians were living in beautiful Germany: one showed them, very prosperous-looking, in new suits and hats, on their way after work to a restaurant, a cabaret show or a cinema; another showed a young man buying flowers in a German florist's to present to his girl-friend; another was of a farmer's wife mending a shirt with affection and care . . .

Here is an extract from an article entitled 'Observations on the Reichsmarschal's Speech'—the reference is to Marshal Goering:

> With the exception of a few letters from some spoiled milk-sops, which are often quite laughable, a tremendous number of letters are being received in the Ukraine in which our work-people say how pleased they are. These Ukrainians understand that the war has also had an effect on the food situation in Germnay and they don't think only of their own stomachs . . .
> Here in the Ukraine you may often hear complaints that Adolf Hitler is rounding up people for work in Germany. But, even so, Germany is not demanding, in the interests of ensuring ultimate victory, greater sacrifices from the Ukrainian people than she herself is making on a far, far bigger scale.
> And so, brother Ukrainians, I want to speak to you quite honestly and frankly. I am ashamed of all those who abuse Germany. When I read the Reichsmarschal's speech I felt more ashamed than ever in my life . . .*

Extracts from letters confiscated by the censorship and later discovered in the German archives:

> . . . Anyone who lagged behind or stopped or strayed off to one side was shot by the police. On the way to Kiev a man who had two children jumped out of the truck as the train was moving. The police stopped the train, caught the man and shot him in the back. We were even taken to the lavatory under escort and any attempt to escape meant being shot.
> We remained in the bath-house until three in the afternoon. I couldn't stop shivering and towards the end I nearly lost consciousness. Men and women had to go into the baths together. I was terribly embarrassed. The Germans would go up to naked girls, grab them by the breasts and hit them in improper places. Anyone who wished could walk in and make fun of us. We are slaves and anyone can do what he pleases with us. Of course,

---

* *Novoye Ukrainskoye Slovo*, October 11th, 1942. Signed 'T'.

there's nothing to eat. And there's not the slightest hope of going back home.

... I am now about sixty miles from France in a suburb of the town of Trier, where I live with a farmer. You can guess what it's like for me here. The farmer's got seventeen head of cattle. I have to clean them out twice a day, and I feel sick while I'm doing it. My stomach is swollen, so I can't even cough. There are five pigs in the sty and they also have to be cleaned out. While I'm doing it I can't see for the tears. Then I have to tidy up the rooms—sixteen of them, and everything falls to my lot to do. I don't get a chance to sit down the whole day long. No sooner do I get into bed, the night seems over and it's morning again. I go around as if I'd been knocked over the head . . . The farmer's wife is a real bitch. She hasn't got anything resembling a woman's heart, only a stone in her breast. She does nothing but shout like a person possessed until she's drooling at the mouth.

... As we marched along people looked at us as if we were animals. Even the children held their noses and spat at us . . .

We proceeded to wait in the hope that somebody would soon buy us up. But Russian girls don't cost very much in Germany—you can take your pick at five marks. On July 7th, 1942, a factory owner bought us . . . At six o'clock in the evening we were taken off to eat. Mother dear, the pigs at home don't eat stuff like that, but we had to. They boiled up some radish leaves and put a bit of potato in it. They don't serve you bread with your dinner in Germany . . . Mother, they treat us like animals . . . It seems to me I shall never get back home, Mother.*

---

* Letters from Nina D., Katya P. and Nina K., from a collection of documents entitled, *Listy z Fashistskoi Katorgi* (*Letters from a Fascist Prison*) (Kiev, 1947), pp. 7–8, 15–16.

A Word from the Author

I have driven myself into a dead end.

I have been telling you what happened to me, what I saw with my own eyes, what witnesses and documents say, and I am now at a dead end. What is it all about? What does it all mean?

Is it the dictatorship of madmen in their decline, some incredible, phantasmagoric return to the times of Herod and Nero? Moreover, on a scale never seen before, such as no Herod ever dreamed of?

Thousands of experts, choosing their terms and quarrelling about them—totalitarianism, authoritarianism, national-socialism, chauvinism, communism, nazism, fascism and so forth, explain them away in retrospect one after the other. But does not the very fact that there are so many of these '-isms', springing up like plague spots, first in one place, then in another, point to some universal tendency?

The fate of that unfortunate land, which bears the ridiculous name of U.S.S.R., does not appear to me to be an accident or an exception or something of limited significance. On the contrary, it seems to point clearly to the existence of a tendency to some form of unprecedented barbarism on a world-wide scale.

In the face of such barbarism the most precious achievements of civilization may prove quite ineffective. For example, just as in the ancient world culture was overrun by the barbarians, so in Russia, after all the achievements of philosophy, literature and striving towards democracy, barbarism triumphed again and there was no longer any philosophy, democracy or culture, just one big concentration camp.

Then the neighbouring concentration camp, in which a similar process had taken place and which wanted to extend its possessions to cover at least the whole world, declared war on the other one. The U.S.S.R.'s 'holy' war against Hitler was nothing more than a heart-rending struggle by people who wanted to be imprisoned in their own concentration camp rather than in a foreign one, while still cherishing the hope of extending their own camp to cover the whole world.

There was no difference in principle between the sadism of either side. Hitler's 'German humanism' was more original and more fanatical, but it was citizens of *other* nations and conquered lands who perished in the gas-chambers. Stalin's 'socialist humanism' did not succeed in inventing the ovens, but on the other hand the disaster descended on our own compatriots. It is in such distinctions that the whole difference lies; it is not easy to say which one was worse. But it was the 'socialist humanism' which came out on top.

It took place in the twentieth century, in the sixth millennium of human culture. It was in the century of electricity, radio, the theory of relativity, aviation's conquest of the skies and the invention of television. It was on the very eve of the release of atomic energy and the first expedition into space.

In the course of a dialogue about progress Bernard Shaw's sphinx comments impassively that as long as it has been there, a matter of a few millennia, it hasn't noticed much progress.

If in the twentieth century of our era epidemics of ignorance and cruelty on a world scale are *possible*, if out-and-out slavery, genocide and mass terror are also *possible*, if the world continues to devote greater resources to the manufacture of instruments of destruction than to education and health services, one may fairly ask what sort of progress we are talking about.

It there more justice in the world today? Is there more goodness? Greater respect for the human personality? Just see how much justice, goodness and respect for human beings there is! There is only more *cynicism* and more *sacrifices*. It is like a bottomless pit: stupid politicians keep on demanding them, and they are ready even to turn the whole world into a Babi Yar, so long as they can remain in power. For the rest, what do they care? This is not the time to be thinking about justice or about progress, but rather about *survival*. So much for our progress.

Hitler has been eliminated, but barbarism has not. On the contrary, more and more centres of barbarism are springing up. Dark, savage forces are seething over vast areas of the globe and threatening to break out. Primitively attractive, degenerate ideas, like infectious viruses, are multiplying and spreading. Ways of infecting millions of people with them have been carefully worked out.

Progress in science and technology—apparently the only form of progress of which mankind can boast—leads, however, in these circumstances only to a situation in which slaves are not herded along with ropes round their necks but are taken by electric trains in sealed wagons, and in which people can be turned into idiots by means of injections; the modern barbarism does not kill people with a club but with poison gas or with a technically perfect automatic firearm.

It is said that science aims to extricate itself from its present state of dependence, in which it acts as the obedient servant of the politicians. Perhaps there will then emerge yet another 'scientific-technical' humanism—and we shall have an utterly dreary technocratic barbarism?

Nobody really has the power of prophecy. Nobody knows what is going to happen, and nor do I. But I do know that HUMANISM must at all events be *humane* and not consist of concentration camps and gallows, and that we must not allow ourselves to be turned into idiots. As long as our hearts and brains continue to work we must not give in. And I want especially to remind the young, vigorous and active people, for whom this book is intended, of the need for caution and of their responsibility for the fate of mankind. People, friends! Brothers and sisters! Ladies and gentlemen! Put aside your affairs and your amusements for a moment. Things are not going well in this world.

It is not good if a few rhinoceroses can drive masses of people to their deaths, and if those masses follow obediently, sitting and waiting their turn. If masses of people are forced into slavery for life and meekly allow themselves to become slaves. If books are banned, burnt and thrown on the scrap heap. If millions of people never say aloud what they really think from the day they are born to the day they die. If there is enough energy gathered up in one small cylinder to reduce New York, Moscow, Paris or Berlin to ashes, and those cylinders are being held over our heads—what for? What are these, if not steps on the way to barbarism?

People, friends! Brothers and sisters! Ladies and gentlemen! Stop, think, come to your senses.

CIVILIZATION IS IN DANGER.

No Blessed Land

Once again I was travelling across that beautiful, spacious blessed land. But now it looked rather different.

Near the city boundary just by the 'Cheer-up' sanatorium they had erected a huge, strong signpost which said in German lettering: DYMER—35 KM. We put my bundle of clothes down beneath it and my mother left me because she was late for work at her school.

The Dymer high road, along which Vasili, the prisoner, and I had once travelled like men from Mars, was now full of life: it was busy with cars and people. A little hut had been put up at the side of the road and a policeman stood by it stopping everybody on foot.

'No, why should you take it off me!' a woman shouted desperately, running from one policeman to another. 'I carried it twenty miles and exchanged it for my own things. Please!'

The policeman took her bag into the hut, while the others stopped an old peasant. He was carrying two sacks slung over his shoulder, a smaller one in front, a bigger one behind. They told him to put them down on the ground, which he did in silence.

'Good-bye,' said the policeman with much irony.

The old man turned and set off back along the high road with the same measured step as he had come.

Such was the effect of the order strictly forbidding people to carry more foodstuffs by road than was 'necessary for one day's sustenance'.

A lorry stopped at the signpost and people began climbing aboard it. I followed suit, and we were soon speeding along the road through Pushcha-Voditsa. But this time I had none of that feeling of joy and peace I experienced once before. They were still cutting down the pine trees; there were now clearings in the forest, and big lorries and trailers were carrying long, straight tree trunks.

There were Germans stationed in the village of Petrivtsy, and people were working in the fields. The forest along the banks of the Irpen was also being felled and stacks of logs were piled up along the roadside ready to be carted off.

At Demidov prisoners were building a bridge across the Irpen. Covered in mud, some of them with their feet wrapped in rags, others simply barefoot, they were digging the still-frozen ground and handling the planks of wood, standing up to their chests in water. On both banks there were guards with machine-guns sitting in towers and patrols with dogs standing ready.

At Dymer the lorry driver collected fifty roubles from each of us and drove on. I turned off into the field.

It had not been dug since the previous year, and there were rows of little humps made by the potatoes which had been left in the ground and gone bad. The corn had been beaten down and was also rotten. Yet there had been such a famine in the city at the time.

Everything in the world was terribly mixed up.

For a long time my mother had been watching me get thinner and seedier. Since the X-ray apparatus in the polyclinic had been repaired for examining the people being sent to Germany, my mother managed to persuade them to examine my chest. They found signs of incipient tuberculosis.

At that my mother rushed down to the market and tried to find, among the peasant women she knew, someone who would take me off to a village to feed me up. In exchange for some old things a kind-hearted woman by the name of Goncharenko from the village of Rykun agreed to take me in. That's how I landed up in a village again.

I was quite alarmed myself. To have tuberculosis under the Nazis was like a sentence of death, and I had no desire at all to die. I wanted to survive it all and to live long, and to be very, very old, and for that reason I had to take care of myself. I had already learnt that the only people who survive into old age are those who have lots of luck in life, but you can have luck only if you take good care of yourself continually, day after day.

Goncharenko made me feel really at home right away. She put a jug of milk in front of me, a saucer of honey and some hot bread, fresh from the oven, and I ate until I could eat no more, and still the feeling of gnawing hunger did not leave me.

Watching me thoughtfully, her chin resting on her hand, as I snatched up the pieces of bread and stuffed them into my mouth, she told me how badly things were going in the village. Heavier taxes than ever had been imposed and there were rumours that everything was going to be requisitioned. They had been ordered to drive their cows and horses to the market square for a veterinary examination, instead of which half of them, the best ones, had been requisitioned. So much for the examination.

'You should have seen what happened!' she said, scowling: 'The women wailed and fell to the ground and hung on to their cows . . .'

They had not taken her cow, but issued her with a milk delivery book, and she had to take a bottle of milk every day to the dairy, where it was entered in a book. The German in charge went around in a horse and trap with a policeman, speaking to nobody except the village elder. The village council building had been taken over by the police. All the young people had been signed up for Germany, including her own eighteen-year-old daughter Shura. But her son Vasya was still too young—only fourteen.

Vasya and I, of course, soon found a common language, and he was showing me the bits of mine sticking out of the ground, lumps of TNT explosive, and the nest of the stork which was then away but would soon return from Africa. I thought to myself: why can't we fly away as easily as that? There must be a land without any wars somewhere in the world. If I were a stork I wouldn't come back for any money; I would just live quietly in some peaceful spot—and to hell with everybody.

'There's nothing to make soup from,' said Goncharenko. 'Take a bag and go and get me some sorrel.'

The wild sorrel was growing in thick clumps right in the fields. We nibbled at the juicy leaves and I couldn't resist putting one right in my mouth. It was tasty but bitter, and sent shivers down my spine. The prisoners in Darnitsa would have envied me.

There were lots of lumps of TNT lying around, yellow—the colour of Dutch cheese—which had been scattered by the explosion of a munitions dump. We put the sorrel for soup in the bag, and the TNT for our personal pleasure inside our shirts.

Once we had collected a quantity of it sufficient, in our opinion, to bring about certain changes in this world, we lit a bonfire, filled an old tin with TNT, put in a dynamite fuse, and threw the tin on the fire. It lay there for a little, then there was a deafening explosion and there was nothing left of the bonfire but a grey hole in the ground. After examining the destruction we had wrought, we departed from the scene with a feeling of something achieved.

The long trench had been partly filled in and partly washed away by the spring rains. It was where they had shot the Jews and similar 'enemies' from the surrounding villages, and Vasya had taken me along to see their local Babi Yar. It was just a trench, with fields all around, right to the horizon.

In one place there was something sticking up out of the ground. It was a blackened, moist, human foot in the remains of a boot. We ran away.

Beyond the trench was the beginning, it appeared, of an unfinished military aerodrome. The N.K.V.D. had been building it, and no one had been allowed to come near because it was all secret; only prisoners had been working on it.

The vast aerodrome was now deserted. Long, straight lines of pegs went off into the distance, and long stretches of concrete runway were already finished. Great piles of rubble, stone and cement had gone hard, and wheelbarrows, picks and shovels lay around just where they had been thrown down. It looked as though the work-people had disappeared from one minute to the next.

We walked around this dead world, the only living things among all the machinery and building material. We turned the handle of the cement mixer and unscrewed everything we could. But it was the stone crusher which made the biggest impression on me.

It was a big, hollow drum with blades inside it. The stones would have been shovelled into it from above, then the motor would begin to turn it and the stones inside would begin to dance about like mad things, knocking up against each other in the pitch darkness, being poured from one blade to the other, with absolutely no possibility of escape.

It was an exact copy of our human life. In just the same way human beings are shovelled into something, forced to bang each other about, tossed and turned around, and they cry out, but in the same pitch darkness they are ground down and down and down.

I tried to convey this idea to Vasya, but I didn't succeed. He decided I was trying to amuse him, and he started laughing, picturing to himself how those poor devils would cry out if they fell into the stone crusher.

Children were still running around half-naked in Gapka's shack, and the old woman, bent almost double, was crushing something in a bowl, while the old man wheezed and coughed on the stove. I had gone across the fields to Litvinovka to visit them, but it would have been better if I had not gone.

Gapka was weeping. Her hands were swollen and all the bones in her body ached from hard work. I thought to myself that the serfs at the time of Taras Shevchenko must probably have looked just like that: the very limit of poverty and desperation.

Litvinovka's good fortune had been illusory and very short-lived. The Germans quickly organized a form of village government and started requisitioning things. Everything the villagers had gathered in and threshed, under the impression they were doing it for themselves, they were ordered to give up. Each farm had to pay fabulous taxes; everybody had to work to meet them. Gapka could only clasp her head in despair; to plough the land she needed a horse (where from?) and she needed a plough, a harrow and some grain and then had to sow more land than two strong men could cope with.

'I never had to do so much even on the collective farm,' Gapka said. 'I complained about the collective, and we thought that was bad enough. Now it turns out it wasn't so bad at all. This is terrible! This is the end of us; after all, we agreed to have the collectives!'

'The Day of Judgment is with us.' The old woman muttered her contribution and crossed herself as she worked at her bowl. 'Merciful Lord, have mercy on us . . .'

I came to the conclusion that there probably wasn't a God after all. And, if He did exist, why did He torment people in this way, treating them so cruelly and being so heartless towards old women and little children who had only just arrived in this world? It was a fine form of amusement the Almighty had devised for Himself. If I should ever come across Him I would not think of praying to Him but I'd want to punch Him in the face for what He had done on earth. I couldn't respect such a God. He simply didn't exist.

It was people who made it that way.

From early morning Goncharenko would start bemoaning the loss of her Shura, as though the girl were already dead. She would sit on the bed in her black dress, rocking to and fro, her face all swollen, singing a sort of lament in a low and oddly unnatural voice:

'Oy, my poor little daughter . . . Oy, I'll never see you again . . .'

The same sort of lament went up from all the homes. The police had gathered at the village council offices and the band got ready. Vasya and I dragged ourselves round that weeping, wailing, singing village, not knowing where to put ourselves.

By this time I was much stronger and had got some fresh air into my lungs. Vasya and I worked like grown men, carting manure and ploughing and harrowing the fields. I learnt to harness and hobble the horses and to ride them. My little jacket and trousers were faded and frayed, and I was just like Vasya in every way, with one exception. Goncharenko gave us both the same to eat: it was enough for Vasya but not for me. I had a constant yearning for food in my mouth and throat, but I was too shy to ask for more. What I longed for most was the honey, which Goncharenko kept in the pantry under lock and key and did not serve very often.

The police went round the houses digging out people due

to go to Germany. This served only to augment the lamentations, like pouring oil on flames. Shura tied her case and bag together, slung them over her shoulder and went off to the square with her mother running after her.

My goodness, what scenes took place there! The whole village turned out to watch as they formed the people up. The police shouted: 'Quick march!' and the band, consisting of invalids, struck up. Women ran alongside the marching column, screaming and sobbing and throwing themselves on the necks of their daughters; the police pushed them away and the women fell to the ground. The Germans marched behind, laughing at the scene. And the band kept banging out its jolly march until I could stand it no more . . .

The procession straggled out across the field to Demidov with the whole village running after it. But I stayed behind.

The sound of the band eventually died away in the distance and in its place came a deathly silence. I went slowly into the cottage and there I saw the door of the pantry open, the lock and key lying on the shelf.

I went across the room and sat down by the window, trembling all over from the spectacle I had just witnessed, and then, as if in a trance, I stood up, reached for a spoon and went into the pantry.

The honeypot was covered with a piece of oilcloth and gauze. I peeled them carefully back and proceeded to scoop up the honey by the spoonful and eat it. I nearly choked myself with it, gulping down spoonful after spoonful, without stopping to savour it, realizing vaguely that the next spoon ought to be the last . . . no, the next one . . . no, the next . . . I told myself that Goncharenko was on her way to Demidov and sorrowing, while I was a contemptible creature compared with her, the person who had saved me . . . On the other hand I had to eat honey so as not to have tuberculosis, to take care of myself, and I wanted to devour as much as I liked. Because in this glorious stone-crusher the only way to save your skin was to seize the moment when things went your way, to grab everything you could lay your hands on, that had been left unlocked, that hadn't been noticed, to slip between people's legs and snatch things out of their hands—so long as you survived! Let the others go off to Demidov and not come back too soon: I wouldn't miss my chance. And henceforth, if I'm going to survive, I shall always do the same—I'll take what I can and I'll survive in spite of everything. That will be my laugh.

Excessively Clever People Are Enemies

When my mother received instructions to report at her school she didn't refuse because it protected her from going to Germany. From March 1st they had introduced the *Arbeitskarte*, a labour book which came to be more important than an identity card. It was stamped at your place of work, and had to be stamped again each week. People were stopped on the streets for their papers, and if you didn't have an *Arbeitskarte*, or if it was out of date, there was nothing for it but to be shipped off to Germany.

The teachers turned up at the school and proceeded to fill up questionnaires for the personnel department, just as they had done under Soviet rule. One of the first to speak up was a teacher who had always been a very quiet and meek person. He announced:

'I am a supporter of Petlyura.'

He probably thought that they would appoint him head of the school, but they sent another man along for that job, probably someone who had done more to deserve it.

Then they set about cleaning up the building after the Germans had been billeted in it. They scraped out all the manure, got rid of the broken desks, put ply-wood in the window frames, and then went round from house to house noting down all the children of school age.

There could be no question of starting up classes before the spring because there was no fuel for heating. But then instructions were received to prepare for lessons in the first four classes, taking in children up to eleven. Children older than that were sent out to work.

The size of the teaching staff employed to carry through this limited schooling must be limited . . . All the education officials appointed by the Bolsheviks, as well as all teachers from senior classes, are being dismissed . . . No pensions are payable.

It is forbidden to make use of the curricula, textbooks, libraries and politically tendentious teaching aids (films, maps, pictures, etc.) which existed under the Bolshevik regime. These articles must be kept under lock and key. Until the new textbooks and curricula arrive a system of general education is being introduced. It will be restricted to reading, writing, arithmetic, physical exercise, games and practical work. The language to be used is Ukrainian or, where appropriate, Polish. The Russian language is no longer to be taught.*

All the teachers were then given a copy of a newspaper so that they could study and reflect on an article entitled 'The School'. As I have already explained, everything which appeared in the papers or in the decrees posted upon noticeboards had the force of law, and you had to be careful not to miss anything lest you landed in trouble out of ignorance. My mother and Lena Gimpel read the article together, slowly and with frequent pauses, while I listened and learned. It began with the following quotation:

WHAT WE HAVE TO DO NEXT IS TO CHANGE OUR WHOLE SYSTEM OF EDUCATION. WE ARE SUFFERING TODAY FROM FAR TOO MUCH EDUCATION. IMPORTANCE IS ATTACHED ONLY TO KNOWLEDGE, BUT EXCESSIVELY CLEVER PEOPLE ARE THE ENEMIES OF ACTION. WHAT WE NEED IS IN-STINCT AND WILLPOWER.

(From Adolf Hitler's speech, April 27th, 1923)

And the article itself included this:

. . .Taking as an example the whole way of life of our liberators and in particular their schools, we shall make

---

* From an order dated January 12th, 1942, issued by the Reichskommissar for the Ukraine to all General- and Gebietskommissars concerning the conditions on which primary schools were to be reopened. From *The German-Fascist Occupation of the Ukraine* (Kiev, 1963), p. 71.

every effort to develop in our children the qualities necessary for a regeneration of our whole people without which further progress will not be possible. This means primarily devotion to work and a capacity to work hard; it also means strength of character and high moral standards . . . The 'foundations of science' are very important, but they are not everything and not the most important . . Let us get down to work! We wish the liberated Ukrainian school and the liberated Ukrainian teaching profession every success. The best guarantee of this is the example set us and the help given us by our German friends.*

'So that's it,' Lena said. 'Now we know where we are. The twentieth century needs manpower with some education but not too much. The slaves must know how to sign their names, read their orders and count. But excessively brainy people were always enemies of dictatorships.'

'I'm not going to teach,' my mother said.

'They'll make you, I reckon.'

'They won't make me—I'd sooner they took me off to Germany. Where can I find some other work, quickly?'

'It's really beyond me!' Lena exclaimed, still turning the paper over in her hands in amazement. 'It's here written in black on white and in all seriousness. Sort of grim paradox. After all the renaissances, the great philosophies and the great advances of science, they tell us openly at last that too much education is an evil. The others turned all the truths upside down and taught us lies, but at least they taught us something, whereas these have got to the point of telling us that we shouldn't teach anything. Off you go, children, and work. In the cause of regenerating the nation and further progress and a beautiful future for our descendants.'

'And what about me?' I asked. 'I've already finished four classes . . .'

'You've already had your education, you can go and clean shoes and sell cigarettes. Incidentally,' said Lena, 'there's a notice up saying that children are forbidden to sell things on the streets—you'd better go and read it since you've got an education.'

---

* *Novoye Ukrainskoye Slovo*, May 14th, 1942.

'Did you hear that?' my mother said.

'Oh, I shan't get into trouble,' I said.

My mother learned that the Sport Factory needed someone to work as a messenger and cleaner, so she hastily gave up her job at the school and went to work for the factory. In May lessons started in the first four classes. The children had to learn German and sing German songs.

I used to walk past their windows and listen to them singing about the 'Cuckoo and the Donkey'—

'Die Kukuk und der E-e-sel . . .'

But the lists of children over eleven were handed over by the schools to the local authority, which was why they had been drawn up. I received a summons to report to be placed in a job.

The whole of what used to be the fourth 'A' class in our school went off to learn devotion to hard work. Zhorik Gorokhovsky was sent to the food-machinery factory where his father had worked. He had to cart all sorts of old iron about and went round in old clothes soaked in oil, his hands and face covered with fuel oil, looking small and weedy and rather frightening because of the oil ingrained in his face.

I was sent to work in the brigade in the gardens attached to the 'Cheer-up' sanatorium.

It was in fact no longer a sanatorium but an enormous farm. There were about thirty of us, boys and girls, and we were each given a hoe and sent off to weed the gardens.

I used to get up at dawn and put my aluminium dish, a spoon, a bottle of water and some bread in a bag. I would leave the house at six o'clock in the morning, because I had a couple of miles to walk to work and those who turned up late got no breakfast. At half past six we each used to be given a ladle of hot water with some cereal in it. Then we split up into pairs and the old man whom we called the Gardener led us off to the gardens.

Each of us was given a row of potatoes or cabbage. There was no end to the gardens and the sun was scorching hot. I used to cheat: I just covered the weeds up with earth, although the Gardener would sometimes check up on us and uncover the weeds, and then clout us over the head. On the other hand I often used to finish my row before the others and was able to have a rest at the end of the garden.

In the middle of the day there was a half-hour lunch-break, with a ladle of soup. Then we worked right through to eight in the evening, thirteen hours altogether. I used to be dog-tired and sometimes, when the sun was very hot, collapsed.

But the work also had its advantages—when they put us to work on the tomatoes. They were still green and hard, but we fell on them like locusts. On every side there were also beautifully kept orchards, but we were allowed to move about only in formation and we couldn't break away, so we could only eye the apples from a distance. Fruit was for people of a higher category.

The German in charge started building a rabbit farm and a dozen prisoners were sent from Darnitsa to help him. The grass in the sanatorium was tall and lush with daisies growing in it, and they got down on their knees to it, picking out the most tasty stalks, completely carried away, utterly contented as they munched the grass.

We used to take them cigarette ends and we too would sit round in a circle learning to smoke. I liked it, and I started to smoke like a real working man, because, after all, what working man does not smoke?

I told my grandfather about the Gardener, at which he exclaimed: 'But I know him, he's a friend of mine. Tell him he mustn't wallop you.' Next day, when he had us in formation, the Gardener said: 'Which of you is Anatoli Kuznetsov?' I stepped forward. 'You and two others are being transferred to lighter work.'

He sent us off to pick lime-blossom. We could have wished for nothing better, and went off to climb all over the trees. The limes in the grounds of the sanatorium were tremendous, two hundred years old. They may even have seen the Empress Catherine II; according to the legend, when she drove into the park with Potemkin, who was for some reason rather depressed, she said to him: 'See how lovely it is. Cheer up!'

The best blossom on lime trees is at the very top, at the ends of the branches, and they are not easy to pick. Each of us had a fixed quantity to gather, and if we failed to achieve it we lost our soup ration. So we all tried very hard, and

I used to clamber up to such high places that I dared not look down. On one occasion the tree-top broke off with me on it and I dropped from the height of a six-storey house. I escaped only by sheer luck! On the way down I fell among some intertwined branches which held me like a hammock, though I might still have gone right through if I had not managed to grab hold of them with my hands and hang on, swinging like a monkey. Then I scrambled down to experience the pleasure of hard work.

In this way, at the age of twelve and a half, my official working life began, to prevent me growing up in this world to be too educated or to cause too much trouble to the people who would do all my thinking for me and determine my place in the world to the end of time.

I can only thank my benefactors who made it quite clear to me why I have come into this world—to labour where I am told and to carry out my allotted task in the cause of progress and of a better future for some vaguely defined, good-for-nothing descendants. Lucky descendants.

Potatoes in Flower

The No. 12 tram used to take about an hour to get to the end of the line in Pushcha-Voditsa, and most of the way was through the forest. It went fast, rushing like an express train through the unending green tunnel formed by the pine forest, the branches of the nut trees brushing against the windows.

To do the same journey by foot along the tram track took my grandfather and me practically the whole day. The rails were rusted over, the grass was pushing up between the sleepers, with daisies and cornflowers waving in the wind.

From time to time we met people coming from the other direction, very distressed, who told us:

'Don't go this way: they're taking everything away from people at the children's sanatorium.'

And in fact we found three policemen sitting beneath a

fir tree at the children's tuberculosis sanatorium, with a great pile of bundles and vessels next to them. This was where they had set up their post to do their daylight robbery. All the roads to Kiev were closed and the robbery was perfectly legitimate.

Many years previously my grandfather had worked in the mill at Pushcha-Voditsa. In fact, he had spent his youth there; it was there that he and my grandmother had lived after they were married, and he knew the surrounding country very well.

'So that's what the damned scoundrels are up to,' he said in a worried voice. 'But I know the little footpaths and on the way back we'll miss them by going through the forest.'

Our feet were really sore when, towards evening, we got as far as the fourteenth street, where there is a pond and a weir. By the weir we could see protruding the blackened piles on which the mill had once stood. My grandfather stopped for a moment and studied them thoughtfully.

In the sacks which we carried over our shoulders we had all sorts of things belonging to my grandmother which we hoped to exchange for food: skirts, jackets and some high laced boots.

We spent the night in an empty barn on the other side of the pond, with the old forester who still remembered my grandfather. Then we set off again at dawn with the dew still on the ground and tramped for another whole day along overgrown paths through the forest and were simply dropping from exhaustion and hunger when we came to the River Irpen and the village of the same name.

We proceeded to go from house to house, knocking on the doors and making the dogs bark.

'Can we sell you anything? We've got skirts, and scarves . . .'

The women would come out, feel our goods and hold them up to the light.

'This here is old stuff.'

'It's good quality, it's quite new,' Grandpa would say crossly. 'My wife only wore it once.'

'I'll give you a glass of beans . . .'

'A glass of beans for a scarf!' Grandpa would exclaim. 'To hell with that, it's worth three, you greedy devils!'

We should have looked for a more remote village, because

this, the nearest one, had more than its share of 'barterers' who kept coming and begging, and even stealing. But we didn't have the strength to drag ourselves any farther, so we just went on knocking the doors. At one of them a man came out, heavy with sleep and unshaven, scratching himself, and asked:

'You don't have a gramophone, do you? What's the use of your flea-ridden rags to us?'

We somehow managed to collect two bags of maize, beans and flour. I shall never forget our journey back to my dying day.

We went slowly and painfully, sitting down to rest every mile or so, and no sooner would I doze off from sheer exhaustion than my grandfather would say with a sigh: 'Come on, let's do a bit more.' He went on stubbornly carrying his load, groaning, gasping and sometimes falling: after all, he was already seventy-two, apart from all the hunger and sickness he had been through. To cross the river you had to walk along a couple of shaky poles high above the water. I ran across without any qualms, but Grandpa stopped and just couldn't make himself do it. I had to take his bag across for him, then he crawled across on his hands and knees, nervously holding on to me and the poles. If anyone had seen us they would have died of laughter.

We spent that night in a haystack. In the morning we could hardly move for the aches and pains in our backs, arms and legs. And off we went again, taking even more frequent rests; we just didn't have the strength to stand up. You thought you were getting up, but your body stayed where it was, and your sack seemed full of paving stones.

There was nothing but forest on every side, with an occasional clearing near a farm, with potato tops in full flower, which I saw only through a haze. On one occasion we crept into a field and stole a few potatoes, digging them up with our hands and sticking the tops back in so as to leave no trace. The n we went off and cooked them over a fire and made a meal of it. But they were very small, the size of nuts, and didn't cook very well.

Remembering the thieving policemen posted at the children's sanatorium, my grandfather decided to go round Pushcha-Voditsa to the west of it and that brought us out on a hard forest road. Suddenly we heard the sound of a motor behind us and a lorry with two Germans in the cab passed us, covering us with dust. It braked violently and the driver looked out of his cab and watched us catch up with him. My heart sank.

'Bitte,' the driver said, pointing to the back of the lorry. 'Jump in!'

It didn't look as though he was out to rob us. Anyway, we climbed in and the lorry went careening down the road. I turned my face to the wind and enjoyed the sensation and the rest. In this way we travelled as far as we could have gone on foot by nightfall. When the city came in sight we realized that we had gone around it from the west and had missed Kurenyovka.

Grandpa banged on the cabin, and the lorry stopped in the open country. We climbed down and Grandpa held out a little bag of flour to pay for the ride.

The driver looked at us and shook his head.

'No. You old and small. No.'

We stood there, not believing our ears. The driver laughed and moved off.

'Danke! Thanks!' I shouted.

He waved his hand. Grandpa bowed from the waist at the departing lorry. We slung our bags across our shoulders and set off across the fields in the direction of the roofs of Kurenyovka which were already visible.

'Ah, what a fool he is, that Hitler!' said my grandfather. 'The Germans are not really so wicked. But he's made 'em into scoundrels. How we looked forward to them coming! And if only they had behaved decently Stalin would have been finished long ago. The people would be ready to live under the Tsar or under the rich, so long as it was not under Stalin. Then this monster turned out to be even worse than Stalin. Oh, damn them all . . .' And he spat on the ground.

We went down various side streets, along Beletskaya Street and came out at our bridge, from where it was three minutes' walk to our house. We no longer had any feeling in our feet or shoulders, and we staggered along like long-distance runners at the finishing line.

And at that point we were stopped by two policemen.

'Been carrying it far?' asked one of them ironically.

We stood there in silence, because it was just unbelievable: it just couldn't happen like that.

'Put it down,' said the other one and proceeded briskly to help Grandpa remove his sack.

'Listen, friends,' said Grandpa, quite dumbfounded, in a whisper. 'Listen . . .'

'On your way, now, on your way,' said the first policeman.

'But, friends, listen .. .' My grandfather was ready to fall on his knees.

The police paid no attention to him, but simply took our sacks and put them down by the post where there were several others lying already. They appeared to have set up a new check-point here, on the approach to the market. I dragged Grandpa along by the sleeve, because he was quite beside himself and couldn't believe it had happened. I had difficulty in getting him home, where I simply curled up to rest and get some sleep, because next morning I had to be off to work again. Out of friendship for my grandfather the Gardener had given me time off on the quiet to go and do some bartering. Well, I'd had my time off.

It is a very simple process and it has been done through the ages. You fill up a bag with all sorts of things—potatoes, carrots, with perhaps half a loaf of bread and a piece of fat bacon on top, and you cover it with a piece of newspaper. Then your mother takes you by the hand and you go down to the local authority.

It's a little scaring to go into the place, because it's where all important decisions are taken—about a person's life, his food and work and his death. It is from here that you may be sent to Germany or you may be marked down for the Yar.

There are no Germans there. The people at the desks are Volksdeutsche or 'real' Ukrainians with long moustaches and embroidered shirts. You can't get round them as easily as you can the Germans; they know their own people too well.

Such people are always to be found. They had helped the Bolsheviks to organize the collective farms, to confiscate the property of the richer farmers and to inform on the rest of the population. These people, 'flesh and blood' of their own people, are the main support of the authorities, because they know who had what for dinner and who has got some potatoes hidden in a hole in the ground. After all, who used

to serve on the village Soviets, and who ran the local councils
and the town councils, and the trade unions and the courts?
And now, look, there they were again, the very same people!

They sit there, writing summonses, drawing up lists and
building up files. A thickset, energetic woman with a very
masculine manner, wearing a severe grey jacket and skirt,
strides around the place and says without emotion and with
an air of utter finality:

'If you don't want to work we can hand you over to the
Gestapo . . . If you don't carry out instructions the Gestapo
will deal with you . . .'

Your mother leads you across to the desk of a rather
dishevelled-looking woman who holds your fate in her hands.
She puts the bag down by the side of the desk and moves
the newspaper back enough to leave the bread and the bit
of bacon showing. It's only a tiny bit of bacon, about the
size of a match-box, but you can't see how big it is beneath
the paper, only that it is actually bacon.

With her head humbly bowed, your mother explains that
you have signs of tuberculosis and that it's bad for you to
work in the fields and talks a lot of that sort of nonsense,
while you in the meantime also play your part, standing with
your back bent and doing your best to put on the appearance
of wretchedness.

The woman takes you in with one glance, gives a dis-
approving sniff, looks silently through the lists, finds your
name and crosses it out and then enters it in another list,
saying:

'Seven o'clock tomorrow at the entrance to the canning
works.'

You give an impression of great relief, your mother mut-
ters her thanks, bows and takes you off as quickly as she
can, leaving her bag on the floor beside the desk.

The canning factory was pervaded by a sour, sharp smell
which seemed to bite into you and get right into your nose.
But only a complete fool could go hungry there.

Lorries loaded with pumpkins used to arrive in its vast
courtyard and the group of boys I worked with used to have
to unload them. We would come across pumpkins that had
been split open, and if we didn't then we used to break
some open ourselves, scrape out the slippery white seeds

and stuff our mouths full of them. From then on I ate nothing at home, but kept myself going on those seeds the whole day long. Once I had an accident: I wasn't watching what was going on, the side of the lorry was let down and an avalanche of pumpkins descended on me. They raised bumps all over my head, a piece of one of my teeth was broken off, but I just lay for a moment by the wall and walked away. It was a bit of bad luck.

In the lunch break in the middle of the day we were taken to the canteen in pairs. Here I found a way of squeezing in among the first, getting my plate filled and rushing off into a corner to drink my soup down, without using a spoon and burning my tongue, and keeping one eye on the queue to make sure it didn't come to an end. The people at the end of the queue would be receiving their first helping, but I would be there for the second time. I would turn my face to the wall, quietly lick my plate clean, wipe it with my sleeve and then with a look of innocence hold it out to be filled.

The cook would take my plate and pour half a ladle into it, letting me know in that way that she knew what I was up to, but that she was taking pity on me and wouldn't make a fuss. I used to devour the second helping more calmly, savouring it, letting it pass through my teeth, and licking my lips, and I wouldn't even bother to lick my plate clean, like some of the others who were on their last legs, but went and washed it off under the tap. That was a bit of good luck.

What I hated most was when we were given the job of loading up the jam. It was packed in eighteen-pound sealed tins. We had it there in our hands, but we couldn't get at it. It was for the chosen people.

The production part of the factory was strongly guarded, but on one occasion, after loading up our lorry, we noticed that the watchman had gone away and another boy and I slipped quickly into the factory. It was dark and warm inside and there was something bubbling and boiling away in the vats. We rushed up to the first woman we saw—she was working there in dirty overalls—and said:

'Please, lady, give us some jam!'

'Oh, you poor things, come over here, quick!' She pushed us behind a lot of metal stands and brought us a battered

box half full of hot pumpkin jam. We stuck our dirty hands
into it, dipping our fingers first into the hot jam and then
into our mouths, gulping it down and trying to get as much
of it as possible into our tummies. That was a real bit of
luck!

Then we became even cheekier and slipped into the
workshop where they started boiling the pumpkins. By
means of sticks we each managed to get a piece of pumpkin out of the vat, still uncooked but very tasty. Unfortunately a white-faced, sickly-looking worker saw us and
said:

'Who let you in here?'

We said nothing, simply ignored him, as though to say:
What business is it of yours? He went off, as it turned out,
to summon the foreman. When he appeared, a very strong
man, he first clouted my friend over the head and then
me. My friend started to whine and plead with him, but
I, like a fool, kept silent, so I got more. He beat me so
viciously, with such a professional touch, holding me firmly
by the shoulder, punching me in my ribs and my back, that
my little head nearly came off. Then he let me go and
shoved me away. We went off behind the store and I sicked
up jam with pieces of pumpkin in it. That was bad luck. You
can't have it all your own way.

Our working day lasted twelve hours. When we finished we
were formed up and marched across to the works entrance,
where we were carefully searched and let out one at a time. It
was very well organized, and I reckoned that on the whole
I had more good luck than bad. I used to boast when I got
home, and tell my grandfather about all the good things
there were in the canning factory and how much I had to
eat there. He, poor man, was terribly hungry, and took a
different view of things. He was angry because I didn't bring
anything home.

'There's one clever chap I know,' he said once. 'He's
making sausage on the quiet without a licence and he's looking for a reliable helper, someone who won't talk. Why don't
you let me fix you up with him; he promises to provide food
and to pay in bones.'

'Bones—we could do with some of those,' I said. 'But how
can I get out of working at the factory? I'm on the list.'

'Take a bag along,' said Grandpa. 'If you don't bribe, you don't get anywhere.'

I went on working at the factory for some time, then made up my mind. I took my bag along. I bribed. I got somewhere.

The Dynamo Team: A Legend and the Truth

This almost incredible story took place in the summer of 1942, when the Germans were at the Volga and it seemed as though their victory was already assured. It was a story that shocked everyone and became so well known among the population that at one time, when they spoke about the ravine, they would say: 'That's Babi Yar, where the footballers were shot.' The story became a legend, which was so well told and so complete in itself that I want to reproduce it in full. Here it is.

Before the war Dynamo, the Ukrainian football team from Kiev, was one of the best in the country. The great football battles between Kiev and Moscow were always accompanied by something more than just the excitement of the game itself. It was also a question of honour of the oppressed Ukrainians. That was why the Kiev fans adored their players, and especially their famous goalkeeper Trusevich.

When the city was surrounded the team could not be evacuated. At first they remained there quietly, fixing themselves up with jobs where they could and meeting from time to time. Then they began to miss their football and to hold training sessions on an open piece of land. The small boys and local people soon got to know about this, and in due course it reached the ears of the German authorities.

They summoned the footballers and said: 'Why do you have to use a bit of empty land? There's a wonderful stadium with nothing happening on it. Why not do your training there? We're not against sport: on the contrary.'

The members of the Dynamo team accepted the offer and moved into the stadium. Some time later the Germans summoned them again (note how precise the legend is—the authorities always *summon* people) and said: 'Life is returning to its normal peacetime state in Kiev; the cinemas and the opera have been reopened; it's time to reopen the stadium. Let everybody see how quickly things are being restored to normal. We suggest organizing a match between you and a team picked from the German armed forces.'

The Dynamo players asked for time to think it over. Some of them were against the idea, on the grounds that it would be shameful and unpatriotic for them to play football with the Nazis. Others argued the reverse: 'On the contrary: we'll give 'em a good beating and raise the morale of the people of Kiev.' They finally agreed on the second view, and the team began to make vigorous preparations. They called the team 'Start'.

Eventually posters appeared on the streets of Kiev: FOOT-BALL. ARMED FORCES OF GERMANY VERSUS CITY START.

The stadium was packed. Half the stands were occupied by the Germans, including the top brass and the Commandant himself, all very cheerful, looking forward to enjoying the match. The worst seats were occupied by the hungry, ragged Ukrainian population of Kiev.

The game started. The Dynamo team were in bad condition and short of energy. The well-fed German footballers played a very rough game, committing obvious fouls, of which the referee took no notice, and when the first goal was scored against the Kiev team the German spectators shouted with delight. The other half of the stadium maintained a gloomy silence—the Germans, it seemed, could even wipe the floor with us at football.

Then something seemed to come over the Dynamo team. They were seized by a fury. Goodness knows where they found the strength, but they began to outplay the Germans and they made a desperate breakthrough and scored an equalizer. Now it was the turn of the German spectators to remain silent in their disappointment, while the rest cheered and embraced each other.

Then the Dynamo players refound their pre-war class and with some first-class teamwork pulled off a second goal. At this the down-at-heel spectators in the stands shouted: 'Hurrah!' and: 'The Germans are getting beaten!'

This latter remark went beyond the limits of pure sport.

The Germans started striding up and down in front of the stands and ordering the people to stop shouting—and some shots were fired into the air. The first half came to an end and the players left the field for the dressing-rooms.

During half-time an officer from the Commandant's box came into the Dynamo dressing-room and, very politely, told them the following: 'That's great—you've played some very good football, and we appreciate it. You have done quite enough to uphold your honour as sportsmen. But now, in the second half, don't play quite so keenly—you must understand —you've got to lose. You must. The German Army team hasn't lost a single game yet, certainly not in occupied territory. So this is an order. If you don't lose the game you'll be shot.'

The Dynamo team listened in silence to these words and then went out on to the field. The referee blew his whistle and the second half began. The Ukrainians continued to play well and put a third shot into the German goal. At this a roar swept over one half of the stadium and there were tears of joy in many people's eyes, while the German half was fuming with indignation. Then Dynamo scored another goal. At that the Germans jumped up in their stands and started taking out their guns. Police surrounded the whole playing-field.

The very lives of our team depended on the result of the match, but the public in our stands did not know this; they simply kept shouting with delight. The German players were utterly crushed and downcast. Then Dynamo scored yet another goal, at which the Commandant along with all his staff quit the stands.

The referee cut the game short and gave the final whistle; without waiting for the players to go to their dressing-room, the police seized the Dynamo team where they were on the field, put them into a closed van and took them off to Babi Yar.

Such a thing had never happened before in the history of world football. In that match the Ukrainian players had no other weapon but their own skill at the game, and they performed an immortal feat. They won the game, knowing full well that they were going to their deaths, and they did it to restore their people's self-respect.

In reality the story was not so neatly rounded as that, although it ended in exactly the same way. But, like everything else in life, it was more complicated, if only because it was not just a case of one game but of several, with the Germans' fury increasing from match to match.

Dynamo did not find themselves in occupied territory because they were unable to depart but because they were mobilized into the Red Army and taken prisoner. Most of them went to work as porters at the No. 1 bakery, and they formed a team there.

There was a German stadium in Kiev to which Ukrainians were not admitted. But on June 12th, 1942, posters were put up around the city.

OPENING OF UKRAINIAN STADIUM

The Ukrainian stadium is to be opened at 1600 hours today.

(No. 51 Vasilkovskaya; entrance from Prozorovskaya.)

Opening programme: gymnastics, boxing, light athletics and—as the main item—a football match. (At 1730 hours.) *

In that match, it is true, a team from some German military unit was beaten, which did not please the Germans very much. But there was no serious trouble.

In their annoyance the Germans simply got together a stronger military team—the P.G.S.—for the next match on July 17th. It was utterly routed by the Start team with a score of 6–0.

The newspaper report of that match was priceless:

. . . But the fact that our team lost must not be regarded as an achievement on the part of the members of the Start team. The German team was made up of footballers who are individually very good players, but they could not be called a team in the proper sense of the word. There is nothing surprising in this, since it consisted of players who happened to join the unit for which they play. It was also apparent that there had not been sufficient training, without which no team, not even

---

* *Novoye Ukrainskoye Slovo*, June 12th, 1942.

the strongest, can be successful. The Start team, as everybody knows very well, consists mainly of players from the former champion Dynamo team, and we ought therefore to expect much more from them than the form they showed in this match.*

The badly concealed annoyance and the desire to apologize to the Germans apparent in every line of that report were only the beginning of the tragedy.

On July 19th, a Sunday, a match took place between the Start team and a Hungarian team—M.S.G. Wal. The score was 5–1 in favour of Start. A quotation from the report of that match: '. . . Despite the final result of the match it can be said that the two teams were more or less equally matched.'†

The Hungarians suggested a return match, which took place on July 26th. The score was 3–2 for Start. It looked as though they were on the verge of beating the Ukrainians, and the Germans would at last be happy.

So a match was arranged for August 6th between Start and the German Flakelf team, reputed to be the 'strongest' and 'ever-victorious'. The newspaper fell over itself with its descriptions of the team and comparisons between the enormous number of goals it had scored and the insignificant number scored against it, and so forth. It was in this match that the Germans suffered the defeat which became a legend. But the newspaper published no report of it at all, as though the match had never taken place.

Even so, the footballers were still not arrested. And they were given much longer than the interval between the two halves to think things over: they had three whole days. A few lines in the *Novoye Ukrainskoye Slovo* for August 9th contained the last announcement about football: 'At five o'clock today in the Zenith stadium there will be a friendly match between the two best football teams in the city—Flakelf and Start (Bakery No. 1).'

They were giving the Ukrainian team one last chance. The Ukrainians gave the Germans another good beating in this match, but as for the actual score there are only various fan-

---

* *Novoye Ukrainskoye Slovo*, July 18th, 1942.

† Op. cit., July 24th, 1942.

tastic rumours. It was after this match that the footballers were dispatched to Babi Yar.

At that time, as I said before, the Germans had reached the approaches to Stalingrad.

A Word from the Author

A REMINDER. Well, so you are reading these stories. In some cases, perhaps you have just skimmed through unmoved. In others, perhaps (and that would be my fault) you have been bored and have flicked on to the later chapters. After all, you think, it's only fiction. But I must keep on reminding you that nothing in this book is fictitious.

IT ALL HAPPENED. Nothing has been invented and nothing exaggerated. It all happened with real, live people, and there is not the slightest element of literary fantasy in this book.

There is, of course, a certain tendentiousness. I am certainly biased in my writing because, despite all my efforts to be objective, I remain a living person and not a computer.

My bias lies in my determination to expose every resort to the use of force, every case of murder, of failure to respect individuals and every attempt to humiliate them.

There was a case in one village where the partisans killed two Germans. They were very young, each of them about eighteen, and they lay there partly covered by the snow. The police forced all the inhabitants of the village to assemble in the square, and the peasants thought they were going to be shot. But they weren't. Suddenly an illiterate old woman, whose son had been killed in the Finnish war, started to wail: 'Oh, my little sons! You also have mothers somewhere who don't even know that you've been killed!' And she fell prostrate upon them, lamenting all the time. Her own people from the village dragged her away, whispering: 'Quiet! When our own folk get back here they'll kill you for weeping over some Germans.' But she just went on moaning: 'My poor little sons!'

I have the same bias as had that simple woman. But,

irrespective of my views, I take full responsibility, as a living witness, for the absolute TRUTH of everything I relate.

And as for you young folk born in the 'forties and later, I must admit to you, at the risk of appearing sentimental, that I look at the world at times in amazement and think:

'Just imagine what good fortune it is nowadays to be able to walk down the street whenever you feel like it, at one o'clock at night or even at four in the morning.' You can listen to the radio as much as you like, and you can keep as many pigeons as you wish. If you are awakened by the sound of a car in the middle of the night you may mutter crossly and sleepily: 'The next-door neighbour has come back in a taxi from some party,' and you turn over. I don't like to hear the drone of planes at night; when it starts it seems to turn me upside down inside, but I immediately remind myself: 'Take it easy, those are only training flights; that's not the real thing yet.' And in the morning the papers arrive with their stories of little wars here and there . . . They say we never pay attention to our health so long as we have it and only start to complain when we lose it.

I stare in amazement at this flickering, wobbling world.

Babi Yar: The System

Vladimir Davydov's arrest was a very simple, undramatic affair.

He was walking down the street when he met his friend Zhora Puzenko. They had been to the same school, belonged to the same sports club and gone out with girls together. They got into conversation, and Zhora said with a smile:

'What on earth are you doing, walking about the streets, Volodya? You're a Yid, aren't you? Come on, let's go.'

'Where to?'

'Come on, come on . . .'

'Who do you think you are?'

Zhora simply smiled.

'Are you coming or not? I can show you my papers.'

He produced documents to show that he worked for the police, and he moved a revolver from one pocket to another, letting it be seen 'accidentally'.

It was a fine, sunny day and the street was full of people. They went off together. Davydov asked him quietly:

'Aren't you ashamed of yourself?'

'No,' said Puzenko with a shrug. 'I get paid for it.'

And in this quiet, unemotional manner they arrived at the Gestapo headquarters at 33 Vladimirskaya.

This building is not far from Bogdan Khmelnitsky Square, practically opposite the side gates to the Cathedral of St Sophia. It is a very striking building—huge, and dark-grey in colour, but looking almost black against the buildings near it. With its columns and portico, it rises like a gigantic tallboy above the Vladimirskaya, thick with the dust of ages. There are no cars standing in front of it and no signs on the door. Built before the revolution, it was intended to be the offices of the district administration, but it was never finished and under the Soviet regime it was turned into a Palace of Labour. But not for long—the State security police took a fancy to it.

Right up until the retreat of 1941 the building housed the secret police of the Ukrainian Republic and no expense was spared in adapting it for its new function. Behind the majestic façade were concealed beautifully equipped interrogation rooms, torture chambers, stone cells in the basement, and in the courtyard, hidden away from the eyes of the curious, was a prison, several storeys high, linked to the main building by covered passageways. Sometimes people on the street outside could hear screams coming from the basement. It was generally believed that, as far as ordinary mortals were concerned, they could only enter that building: it was very rarely that anybody came out again.

The Soviet secret police blew up the Kreshchatik with its shops and theatres and also blew up the greater part of the history of ancient Russia in the Monastery of the Caves. But they left their own building unharmed, as though they intended the Gestapo to have at once all the facilities necessary for its work. The Gestapo accepted and appreciated this thoughtfulness, settled in at once behind the majestic façade, and the screams started up again.

(Looking ahead a little, I may add that when the Germans retreated in their turn they set fire to the neighbouring buildings on Bogdan Khmelnitsky Square and the University, but they left number 33 untouched. It now houses the secret police of the Ukrainian Republic, and in it are preserved many Soviet and German records, which this book so lacks, and new ones are continually being compiled, no doubt so that future researchers should not be short of work. But what a marvellous thing it will be if later generations use the building as a museum: 'The destruction of man in the Ukraine and his transformation back into an ape' . . .

Davydov had been serving as a private in the Thirty-Seventh Army. He had been taken prisoner near the village of Borshchi, spent some time in prison camps at Darnitsa and elsewhere, and had finally escaped near Zhitomir. He knew a woman in Kiev by the name of Neonila Omelchenko, a doctor, who had contacts with the partisans in the Ivankov district, and Davydov had been about to set off for Ivankov with some medical supplies when he was arrested in this absurd manner.

It remained a matter for conjecture how much Puzenko knew, but Davydov was put in the most frightful cell, the so-called 'Jewish' one, which was crammed full of people waiting to be sent to Babi Yar. Davydov realized that there was no hope for him.

He was summoned for interrogation, and they demanded that he confess he was a Jew and also tell what he knew about the partisans.

Davydov proceeded to shout that he was not a Jew and not a partisan, and that Puzenko was only working off an old score on him. He was taken in front of a commission, where he was examined by German doctors for signs of his Jewish origin. They used magnifying glasses to seek traces of his being circumcised, but came to a negative conclusion.

Nevertheless they put him back in the same cell, because it was still not the custom to let anybody out of number 33. It was like a conveyor belt: once you got on to it you simply got carried along and there was no way of getting back.

People were taken out of the cell and never returned, but Davydov remained there. Finally, when there were only ten men left, they were led out into the courtyard, where a van was waiting which they recognized at once.

It was one of those mobile gas-chambers, known to everybody in Kiev, which the Germans called *Gasenwagen*. It looked something like the refrigerator vans you see about today. The body of the van was without windows or vents of any kind, boarded over and painted a dark colour. At the back there was a double, hermetically-sealed door. The body was lined inside with metal and there was a removable grating on the floor. Inside there was plenty of room for the ten men, and they put a young girl in with them as well, a very good-looking Jewess from Poland.

They all stood on the grating, holding on to the sides, the doors closed behind them to leave them in complete darkness, and the van moved off.

Davydov took it for granted that they would soon arrive at Babi Yar but that they would never see it, because the driver would let the gas come into the van through the opening.

Believing themselves about to die, the people in the van did not talk, but only awaited the moment when they would say good-bye to each other and, in the pitch darkness, suffocating, their tongues hanging out and their eyes protruding, they would begin the process of dying.

But the van kept moving, bumping about, stopping and starting and then appeared at last to come to a halt. But there was no gas, and Davydov thought that maybe something had gone wrong. Suddenly the door opened with a clang, light streamed in, and a voice said:

'Get out!'

'That means they're going to shoot us after all,' Davydov thought to himself. 'That's better, too—quicker.'

The prisoners hurried to get down, gulping in the air, and, out of habit, standing in a line. They were surrounded by barbed-wire fences, guard towers and buildings. And there were SS-men and police.

A tough, well-built young Russian in fur hat, breeches and highly polished riding boots came up to them (they learnt later that he was the brigadier, Vladimir Bystrov) carrying a big stick with which he proceeded to strike each one of them over the head.

'That's just to initiate you! Listen for the word of command. Physical exercises—quick march! At the trot! . . . Stop! . . . About turn! . . . Lie down! . . . Stand up! . . . Goose-step—quick march . . . Fish-step—quick march! . . .'

The policemen set about the prisoners, raining blows upon them with their sticks and their boots and shouting and swearing at them. It appeared that the 'goose-step' meant going along in a squatting position with your hands out in front, while the 'fish-step' meant crawling on your stomach and wriggling along with your hands behind your back. (It was only later that they learned that all new arrivals were made to do these exercises simply to scare them; they beat the prisoners as hard as they could, and when they broke their sticks on the men's backs the guard went and cut fresh ones.)

They crawled as far as an enclosed space inside the camp, where they were again formed up and a Ukrainian lieutenant by the name of Kuribko delivered the following lecture:

'Right. You know where you are. This is Babi Yar. You know the difference between a prison camp and a holiday resort? Find yourselves somewhere to live in the dugouts, and then you're going to work. Anybody who works badly, breaks the rules or tries to escape will only have himself to blame.'

They took the girl aside and sent her off to the women's part of the camp and the men were led off to a dugout.

There were two rows of these dugouts and they were divided into four types—the ordinary dugouts, the brigadiers' dugout, the 'Jewish' one and the 'hospital' one.

The one that Davydov was taken to was an ordinary military earth-shelter without windows and with a single entrance and rows of two-tier bunks. The floor was bare earth, there was a stove at the far end, and a dim lamp was suspended from the roof. The atmosphere was unbearable, thick, like an animal's lair. Each prisoner was allotted a place, and their camp life began.

Davydov wondered later why the Germans had not turned the gas on or shot them at once, instead of postponing their end by putting them in this strange camp. What was the place for, anyway?

The camp had been built in the early spring of 1942 at the very top of Babi Yar and became a sort of 'check-point' on the way into it. Apparently for the sake of variety, the Germans called it the 'Syretsky Camp', although the Syrets district was really much farther on. Maybe they needed to find a different name because the words Babi Yar had acquired in Kiev the most abhorrent associations. The Germans' name was later used also in official Soviet terminology, which caused further confusion. But the ravine and the camp were essentially, and in terms of territory, one and the same and the ordinary people had always only one name for the whole area—Babi Yar.

The Germans did not arrive immediately at the regime they had in such camps as Buchenwald, Oświęcim and Dachau; they experimented, and in the U.S.S.R. they first simply shot people with machine-guns. It was only later that, like the capable and painstaking organizers they were, they set up in Babi Yar as well a 'death factory', where, before finishing people off, they extracted some further use from them.

The sorting out was done in one of the offices at 33 Vladimirskaya. People delivered in the van to Babi Yar might be sent off to the right into the ravine, or to the left, inside the barbed wire of the camp.

The ravine, Babi Yar itself, continued to function normally with its daily quota of executions. They executed immediately the sort of enemies who would only be a nuisance if they were kept in the camp. Such people would be driven into the ravine along a footpath, laid on the ground beneath the overhanging side of the ravine and sprayed with sub-machine-gun fire. Practically all of them shouted something, but you couldn't make out what they said at that distance. Later on the side of the ravine was dynamited to cover up the corpses, and in that way they worked their way along the side of the ravine. They didn't waste any bullets on people who were wounded but simply finished them off with a spade.

But others, like Davydov and his companions, especially those who looked fitter and about whose guilt there was some doubt, were put first of all into the camp, where they gained a certain postponement. A sort of process of natural selection took place as far as the executions and the type of camp life were concerned. The Germans were in no hurry to shoot those prisoners who persisted in surviving; they knew they would never get away from them.

Every morning at half past five the reveille was sounded by banging on the rails; it could be heard throughout the camp. The prisoners had to move fast; they had only a minute or so to get themselves dressed and, to the accompaniment of shouts from their brigadiers, tumble out of their dugouts, unshaven, scrawny, more like animals than men. They would fall quickly into line, number off and then get the command: 'Quick march, with a song!'

Yes, with a song. Nobody marched anywhere in the camp without a song. The policemen wanted them to sing folk-songs—'Unhook the horses, lads', 'Galya, lovely young Galya', or a soldiers' song about the nightingale and the canary, and they were especially fond of 'Dunya, Dunya, Dunya, my little berry'. The brigadier himself used to sing out the vulgar verses and the whole column would take up the chorus. There were occasions when the marching men would lose their tempers and start singing 'Katyusha', and then they got some rough treatment.

In this way, singing their songs, they would stagger out on to the central parade ground and stand in a queue for breakfast. Each received a slice of ersatz bread and two glasses of coffee, or rather of a sort of lukewarm dirty water.

I asked Davydov what they drank their coffee from. After all, they had to have some kind of drinking vessel. He agreed that it had been a difficult problem for them—one man might have an old mess-tin, another might have found an empty tin in the rubbish, but the most important thing was that people kept dying off, so that their drinking mugs were inherited by others.

After breakfast they were led off by their brigadiers in groups of twenty, again with a song. And what sort of work did they perform?

I will tell you.

1. The inhabitants of the 'Jewish' dugout were sent off to dig soil in one place, load it on to barrows and transport it to another place. Guards armed with sticks were drawn up all

along both sides of the route between the two places, and the prisoners had to run with their loads down this corridor.

They were supposed to put so much on their barrows that they could hardly lift them, and the Germans flayed them with their sticks, screaming and swearing at them: 'Schnell! Schnell! Faster, faster!'—it wasn't work but a sort of wild scramble.

Some would be reduced to a state of complete exhaustion and would fall to the ground. Such 'dropouts' would be led off immediately through the wire and into the ravine to be shot, or simply to have their skulls smashed in with an iron bar. Knowing this, they kept running until they had no strength left at all and they fell to the ground only when they had already lost consciousness. The guards themselves would get tired and be replaced, but the moving of the soil went on until it was dark. In this way everybody was kept busy and the place seethed with activity.

2. On a bare stretch of land some distance from the camp they were putting up some mysterious installation, and some of the prisoners were directed to that. The building work was being carried on in great secrecy, and consequently all those who went to work there said good-bye to their friends. They knew they would not be coming back. (The secret was revealed only later: the Germans had set up in Babi Yar an experimental soap factory for the production of soap from human corpses, but they did not have time to complete it.)

3. Another job was the dismantling of the tumbledown barracks which had been left by a Soviet military unit stationed there before the war. The camp bosses decided that they were ugly and reduced the field of vision. Incidentally, it was here, into the 'nail-pullers' brigade', that they sent the 'dropouts' from the Russian dugouts when they were on their very last legs. They passed the last days before they finally expired pulling out rusty nails and straightening them.

4. So that the whole territory could be kept under close observation, all the trees were being cut down and the roots pulled up inside the camp and around the outside of it. The Germans felt happier when everything around them was bare.

5. A small group of skilled tradesmen—carpenters, boot-makers, tailors and fitters—were employed in the workshops, doing jobs for the German guards and carrying out odd jobs

around the camp. These were jobs which offered many advantages on the side and it was reckoned a great achievement to get one of them.

6. 'Outside' brigades were taken under heavy guard to 5 Institutskaya, where a building was being put up for the Gestapo. Brigades were also sent sometimes to sort out the ruins on the Kreshchatik.

7. The women were used in place of horses—several of them would be harnessed to a cart and they would pull heavy loads or collect the sewage.

The officer in charge of the camp was Sturmbahnführer Paul von Radomsky, a German of about fifty with a raucous voice, smoothly-shaved head, and well-fed body, a thin, elongated face and horn-rimmed glasses. He usually travelled around in a small black motor-car, which he drove himself. In the seat next to him sat Rex, a dark grey Alsatian, well known to the whole camp, trained to rip the flesh, and especially the sexual organs, off human beings. On the back seat was Rein, the interpreter, who was one of the Volksdeutsche.

Radomsky had two deputies: Rieder, known by his nickname 'Ginger', a thorough sadist, and 'Willy', tall and thin, who specialized in executions.

The rest of the administration was made up from the prisoners themselves, some of whom were picked out to be brigadiers in charge of the others. One who distinguished himself particularly in this respect was a Czech by the name of Anton, who was Radomsky's favourite and right-hand man. It was generally accepted that whatever Anton suggested to his boss would be carried out; indeed, Anton inspired more fear than Radomsky himself. The brigadier in the women's part of the camp was the twenty-year-old Liza Loginova, formerly an actress in the Russian drama theatre. She was Anton's mistress, and was his equal in sadism and in the brutal way she beat up the other women.

Davydov gave me a detailed account of this strange life, which was not so much a life as something between life and death, because you could die at any moment of any day. They died mostly in the evening.

After work was finished the prisoners would be brought together (with a song, of course) on the parade ground and

formed up in three sides of a square. Then would take place
the day's most important event: Radomsky went through the
various offences which had been committed during the course
of the day.

If there had been an attempt to escape that meant that
the man's whole brigade would be executed on the spot. If
Radomsky gave the order, they would shoot every tenth or
every fifth man as they were formed up.

They all kept their eyes on the entrance gate. If machine-
guns were being brought in, that meant there was going to
be a 'concert' that evening, or-some 'amateur dramatics', as
the police used to say ironically.

Radomsky would come out into the centre of the parade-
ground with his assistants and might announce that every
fifth man was to be shot.

A furious but silent struggle would then take place among
the first group of men standing at the end—every one could
see where he stood in order. Rieder would begin to count
them out, every one standing there stock still, making himself as small as possible, and, if the 'Five!' fell on him, Rieder
would pull him out of the rank by the arm, and no amount
of begging or pleading would have any effect whatsoever. If
a man kept on importuning and crying: 'Sir, have mercy,
sir . . .' Rieder would simply shoot him with his revolver
on the spot and continue the count.

The greatest mistake was to look him straight in the face;
he might pick on you then and pull you out whatever your
position was, simply because he didn't like the look of you.

Then the ones who had been picked out would be herded
into the centre of the parade-ground and ordered: 'On your
knees.' SS-men or police would go round behind them and
kill each one of them neatly with a shot in the back of the
head.

The prisoners would again march round the parade-
ground, singing as they went, and move off to their dugouts.
Incidentally, according to Davydov's story, it was by being
pulled out like this one day that Trusevich, the Dynamo
goalkeeper, finally met his end. The Germans held him in
the camp for a long time without executing him.

On one occasion a group of prisoners arrived from Poltava. The alarm was sounded in the middle of the day,
everybody was assembled on the parade-ground and it was

announced that some Ukrainian partisans were about to be executed by Ukrainian police. The prisoners wondered why they were putting on such a show: partisans were usually driven straight into the ravine under the cliff-side without coming into the camp at all.

In the centre of the parade-ground about sixty men were kneeling down with their hands behind them. Suddenly a very young policeman started shouting: 'I won't shoot!' It turned out that his own brother was among the partisans and that the Germans had deliberately arranged the spectacle of brother shooting brother.

A German ran across to the policeman, drawing his revolver. Then the young man fired, but he fainted on the spot and they carried him off. He was nineteen and his dead brother had been twenty-five. For some reason or other the remainder were shot with explosive bullets, so that their brains spattered over the faces of the men standing on parade.

The punishment for minor offences was flogging. They would bring out a table specially made in the workshops with a cavity to take a man's body; the victim was laid in it, a board was clamped down on him, covering the shoulders and head, and a couple of toughs from among the camp employees would set to work with a will to flay the prisoner with sticks which were jokingly called 'automatics'. To be awarded two hundred with the 'automatics' was to be condemned to certain death.

When a certain brigade came to be checked one evening they found there was a man missing. One of the dogs quickly discovered him, hiding in a hole underneath the benches in the washroom. Apparently he had intended to wait until it was dark before trying to escape, but it was also possible that he simply lost his reason and curled up like an animal in the first place he came across. The brigadiers put him on the table and beat him until his flesh began to come away in pieces; they beat him even when he was dead, reducing his body to paste.

A young lad of seventeen went to the rubbish tip in search of food. Radomsky himself happened to notice him, crept up behind him very quietly, on tiptoe, drawing his revolver as he went, fired point-blank, put the revolver away and went off with a satisfied air, as if he had just shot a stray dog.

They shot people for standing in the meal queue for a second time; they beat men with 'automatics' for not removing their hats. When the 'hospital' dugout became overcrowded with sick people, they drove them outside, laid them on the ground and sprayed them with fire from submachineguns. And the 'physical exercises' were not even regarded as a form of punishment—they went on all the time: 'Stand up', 'Lie down', 'Fish-step' . . .

Davydov witnessed all this with his own eyes; he was beaten, he joined in the songs, and he stood in line to be counted by Rieder, but the fatal number never fell on him.

There was no prospect that they would ever regain their freedom. Only the brigadiers and those given jobs in the camp might possibly have some faint and very uncertain hope, which was why they strove so hard to please. Davydov was nearly put into the 'Jewish' dugout because it was his misfortune to be rather Jewish in appearance. Dina Pronicheva was helped to survive by her Russian surname and her appearance, although she was a Jewess. Davydov was in fact Russian, but nobody remembered any longer the results of his 'medical examination', and his appearance was his downfall.

By this time Jews constituted only an insignificant proportion of the people in Babi Yar. There was the odd one who had somehow managed to stay hidden through the winter and had then been caught; there were people who were half, or even only a quarter Jewish; there were those who had been converted; and finally there were those who simply looked suspiciously like Jews. Radomsky delayed their end, apparently for his own pleasure, relishing the situation and devising special ways of disposing of them.

For example, one of the ways he had devised was to make a prisoner climb a tree and then tie a rope to one of the top branches. Other prisoners were ordered to start sawing the tree down. Then they would pull on the rope, the tree would fall, and the prisoner on it would be killed. Radomsky always turned up personally to watch this scene, and they say he found it very funny. Those who were not killed in the fall were finished off by Anton with a spade.

Another of Radomsky's amusements was to gallop into a crowd of prisoners when he was out on horseback. Those who didn't manage to get out of the way, who were kicked by the horse or who fell would receive a bullet from Radomsky's revolver, on the grounds that they were not fit to remain alive. More often than not this treatment was meted out to the men living in the 'Jewish' dugout, whom the German guards, with their typical sense of humour, called the 'heavenly host'.

The prisoners were not issued with any clothes. As they arrived in the camp they were stripped of everything that was any good—boots, overcoats, jackets—which the police exchanged in the city for home-made spirits. Consequently everybody tried to get clothes off the corpses, and whenever anybody died in a dugout he was stripped naked in no time.

The food situation was more complicated. Apart from the morning 'coffee', they were given some thin soup in the middle of the day. People doing such exhausting work could not, of course, last long on such a diet, but occasionally they received parcels from outside.

Women were constantly hanging around outside the camp trying to spot their own men. Occasionally they would throw a piece of bread over the wire. If the policeman on the gate were given a litre or two of spirit he might pass a prisoner a bag of cereal or potatoes.

Every morning a special group was sent out under escort to go round the outer wires, which had a 2,200-volt charge in them, and hook out with long sticks the dogs, cats, crows and even, occasionally, hares, which had perished there in the course of the previous twenty-four hours.

They would bring them all back into the camp and then the haggling would begin. A piece of cat would be exchanged for a handful of grain, and so forth. Potato peelings could be extracted from the rubbish tip. They would put them together and boil up their own soup on the stove in the dugout, and it was thanks to this that Davydov and others like him managed to hang on to life.

One of the curses of camp life was scabies. The prisoners lived worse than animals in a hole in the ground, eaten up by thousands of insects, and those who went down with scabies were not given any treatment; they were simply shot. The wife of one prisoner, Trubakov, a carpenter, managed to get some ointment through to him, and that saved many of them from immediate execution.

A group of twenty men got together and planned an escape, but someone gave them away and all twenty were shot. All that is known of the plot is that the leader was a certain Arkadi Ivanov.

That was the way the days passed, and no one, including Davydov himself, had any idea how long the end would be delayed. The desire to live remains with us as long as we can still breathe; that is our nature.

They kept arriving and they kept dying, some on their own, some on the parade-ground, and some in the ravine.

It was a machine which went on working day after day.

Gramp: Anti-Nazi

It was as though we were living in a kingdom of the dead— it was practically impossible to find out what was going on in the world. We couldn't believe the newspapers and we had no radio. Maybe there were a few people who still listened to the radio and knew what was happening, but we didn't. After a certain time, however, we no longer had any need of a radio. We had Grandpa.

He used to rush back from the market full of excitement and report to us which towns had been won back from the Germans and when, and how many aircraft had been shot down. The market was the best source of information.

'Oh, no—Hitler won't last!' he would exclaim. 'Our lads will put paid to those scoundrels—just mark my words. The Bolsheviks have learnt their lesson, they've come to their senses. They're already saying definitely that there'll be no more collective farms after the war, and they are going to allow private property and small-scale private business. After all, they could never get away with it again with the old system, the mess they made of things! Merciful Lord, let me live to see the day.'

After the failure of our last attempt at bartering things my grandfather got seriously scared. He began to loathe Hitler with all the venom of which he was capable.

The old people's canteen was closed down, and there was no point in Grandpa going to work somewhere as a watchman because you couldn't buy anything with what he was paid. So how was he to keep alive?

Suddenly the idea came into his head that my mother and I were a millstone round his neck. He straightway divided up such property as we had, taking the bigger and better part of it for himself.

'You live on your own, on your side of the partition, and I'll go bartering things and try and find a rich widow,' he declared.

My mother only shook her head. Sometimes she would knock on his door and hand him two or three pancakes, which he would seize eagerly and eat; he was obviously terribly short of food. Nobody wanted the old clothes he took down to the market, yet he wanted so much to live to see better times when there would be scope for private enterprise and no more collective farms. For that reason he clung on to life as best he could. He envied me the money I made selling things, and he took up selling cigarettes himself. He dug over every bit of soil, even the little courtyard itself, and planted tobacco, picking the leaves and drying them, stringing them up and then shredding them with a knife. The stalks he crushed in a mortar and sold them off by the tumblerful. That was what saved him.

Occasionally the old Gardener would come and see him. Grandpa would give him unsweetened lime tea to drink and tell him stories of how, under Soviet rule, he had been his own master, had owned a cow and kept pigs for fattening, though they had caught the fever, and what wonderful sausages his wife had prepared for Easter.

'I've worked all my life!' Grandpa would complain. 'Today I could live on my Soviet pension alone, if it weren't for these filthy swine, these thieves and idiots! But our boys'll kick 'em out yet, our lads'll be back, you just mark my words! The folk realize now that it's no good turning to others to help you out. Hitler taught 'em that, and the lesson'll last 'em a thousand years!'

The hungrier he was the more his loathing increased.

Lala's grandfather died from old age, and Gramp rushed round in a state of joyous excitement.

'Aha! There you are! He may have been a Volksdeutsche, but he died just the same!'

In the next house to ours, where Yelena Pavlovna lived, there was an empty flat left by some Jews who had been evacuated, and some aristocratic-looking Volksdeutsche arrived to take it over. Grandpa was the first to notice this.

'Filthy devils, bourgeois swine, such posh people—don't seem to have suffered much under Soviet rule, but just wait— too soon to celebrate yet, their time will come!'

It was fascinating for me to see such a change come over my grandfather—it was as if he had completely lost his memory. What would my grandmother have said to him? I was sorry I couldn't believe in God as she had done . . . I wouldn't have put my trust in anything human, but would have simply prayed quietly to myself . . . What else could you do in this world, what could you put your hope in?

Sometimes I would talk to my cat Titus and try to elucidate his views on what was going on. His replies were somewhat obscure, and our conversations usually went something like this:

'Titus, do some work.'

'I've got a headache.'

'Titus, go and eat.'

'Where's my big bowl?'

'You are a very backward creature. What have you got in that head of yours?'

'Brains.'

'And what's in your brain?'

'Thoughts.'

'And what's in your thoughts?'

'Mice.'

Relics of Empire

I was very curious to know exactly who the 'wicked bourgeois' were who had moved into the house next door. So I
climbed up on to the fence.

In the courtyard was a great pile of their things which
had been unloaded from a cart. A woman, very old and bent,
and a youngish, intelligent-looking man in glasses were carrying the things in, trying rather clumsily to manage on their
own but lacking the strength to move a heavy chest of
drawers and a desk.

I hopped over the fence and offered my services.

'Let me help you. What shall I carry?'

This produced a very strange reaction. They stood stock-
still and eyed me in horror. I stood there, rather put out,
while they exchanged glances and the fear in their eyes
began to pass. Finally the old lady indicated with a gesture
of her slender hand some little footstools and said:

'Those—into the drawing-room, please.'

I grabbed the two stools and carried them into the house,
without having any clear idea where the drawing-room was
supposed to be, but I put them down anyway in the biggest
of the rooms.

'I live right here, just on the other side of the fence,' I told
the old lady. 'You must be the new tenants?'

'That's right,' she said shortly. 'Do you have any parents?'

'A mother,' I said.

'Who is your mother?'

'My mother's a school-teacher, but at the moment . . .'

'Ah, a pedagogue,' the old lady exclaimed. 'So your
mother's a pedagogue. That explains it.'

'A pedagogical upbringing,' the man said, studying me
with a strange expression on his face, 'is hardly an expedient
occupation in the light of a certain *de facto* depression,
although from the practical point of view it is also rather
sad to remark that . . .'

'Mima,' said the old lady, interrupting him, 'the pedagogues are all that is left of the intelligent people. Listen, young man, once we have settled in we shall be very happy indeed to invite you and your mother to visit us, and, for our part, we hope to have the pleasure of visiting you too.'

I was rather taken aback by their highfalutin language, but I dutifully transported everything the old lady indicated. Then I dashed home, fetched some nails and a hammer and helped them to hang up some of their photographs in antique frames.

What I liked most among their things were the wonderful stuffed heads of animals. There was the enormous hairy head of a wild boar with fierce, bloodshot eyes, the heads of a wolf and a deer, and an elk's antlers. They also had a great quantity of books in old bindings, a dinner-set all embossed with monograms, little china statues, but not one new book or any modern article at all.

When everything had been put in its place the old lady thanked me in very refined language and repeated her invitation to visit them.

Next day she caught sight of my mother over the fence. They got to know each other and in the evening we went to call on them.

My mother was introduced very formally to the strange-seeming Mima (his full name, it appeared, was Mikhail), who shuffled his feet, clicked his heels and kissed my mother's hand. We sat on old Viennese chairs at a round antique table.

'I will tell you frankly that what we were most afraid of was having really uncultured people for neighbours,' the old lady said in a confidential tone. 'How lucky for us that you are people of education.'

'Cultured people, as an essential integral in the present situation—' Mima was about to say something, but the old lady broke in:

'Mima, you are right. Culture has remained only with a few individuals. The Bolshevik terror destroyed culture along with the educated class and in their place we have an era of ignorance and the triumph of mediocrity. As for the so-called Soviet cultural workers why, in the old days the servants used to be a hundred times more cultured than they are today.'

My mother and I maintained a rather embarrassed silence. Mother was, after all, the sort of 'cultural worker' she was talking about. But the old lady had apparently lost her sense of time and took my mother for a pre-revolutionary pedagogue.

'We are Kobetses, you know,' she informed us. 'I am the widow of the late Mr Kobets. You have heard of him, of course?'

Yes, we had heard of him. The older people still called the Kurenyovka leather works the 'Kobets' Factory. Its owner had been executed during the revolution.

'We had a large family,' the old lady said, shaking her head sadly, and she started going through the names of her family one by one, adding after each one of them: 'Executed in 1918', 'Killed in action with Denikin', 'Executed in 1937', 'Died in a prison camp in 1940'.

It was as though a procession of dead men had gone past the table.

'I have two sons left,' the old lady said. 'Mima and Nikolya, that's all there is left of us. And here you see all we have to our name.'

She took in the whole drawing-room with one sweeping gesture, but all those old, dilapidated pieces and the moth-eaten animal heads now produced only a feeling of depression.

'Mima was quite a small boy when it all started,' the old lady went on. 'About the same age as your boy, perhaps a little older. He was studying mathematics. The Bolsheviks put him up against a wall and were going to shoot him as the offspring of a bourgeois family, but I went down on my knees and pleaded with them to spare him. They uttered a lot of threats but finally went away without shooting him, but it made such an impression on him that it affected his mind.'

'Insanity as such, for an elementary understanding of the phenomenon, if it is differentiated into . . .'

'Yes, yes, Mima,' the old lady said quietly, without interrupting her story. 'He spent twenty years in the Kirillovskaya Hospital—he is not at all violent and he was allowed out when I went to visit him. It is amazing that God put it into my head to take him home with me when the front line came near. We took refuge in an underground shelter, but then I got to know that they were not providing any food in the hospital, so I stopped taking him along there. They shot all the patients there, and Mima remained with me. He is my only consolation.'

She stroked his head tenderly. I was very moved.

As far as appearance went there was nothing to suggest that Mima was not normal. He had an intelligent, thoughtful and very sensitive face. He wore very powerful spectacles with heavy horn rims. He had very gentle manners, even a little ingratiating, and he would listen to everything people said, even if it were about himself, with attention and the appearance of complete understanding.

'And what about your other son?' my mother asked.

'Nikolya is the only lucky one; he fled abroad. He is now a taxi-driver in Paris. A taxi-driver and a translator from German into French. I had no news of him for twenty years, but now he has got in touch with us again and we have started writing to each other. He even sends us parcels— washing powder, cotton, needles and eau-de-Cologne. You must understand that it's difficult enough for him to make a living there. Here, out of respect for our family, we are regarded as Volksdeutsche, but there he is just a Russian émigré, a taxi-driver and a translator from German to French, and there are plenty of people like that . . .'

'How odd,' my mother said, 'from German into French.'

'It is not the difference between the languages that is strange,' Mima said quietly. 'What is strange is that people are so different, that it is impossible for them to agree with one another or to understand each other, so that there is, apparently, no hope for the world.'

The old lady brought out some heavy albums in morocco bindings, took from a drawer of the chest a great heap of old photographs mounted on thick cardboard with gold edging, and went through them, looking for a picture of Nikolya as a young man. There he was, a sprightly lad, standing beside a motor-car made at the beginning of the century with what looked like cart wheels and an old-fashioned rubber klaxon.

'Sevochka', the old lady said, 'was mad on aeroplanes. There he is with his own plane.'

Another lad—curly haired and well built, wearing overalls

and carrying an airman's helmet—was leaning on the wing of an ancient biplane.

'We bought him that aeroplane,' the old lady explained. 'We had three motor-cars, apart from our horses and carriages. In my younger days I never knew what it was to go on foot. And I was so good-looking! When we arrived in Petersburg they said I was one of the most beautiful women in society. I was expected to enter the Court, and I was presented to the Empress Maria Fyodorovna . . . You are also Maria Fyodorovna, aren't you? It's a nice name. Well, the Empress was a very beautiful woman, despite her age. When she was at the height of her beauty the doctors gave her some injections in the skin of her face, so that it ceased to age and remained for ever dazzlingly beautiful. When I was presented to her and made my curtsey she started to say something very amusing, but I was completely fascinated by her face, which stayed quite motionless. Her mouth was open—a sort of round opening in her face—and I sensed that she was saying something very amusing, but her face remained absolutely immobile, like a mask. It was most strange.'

'Even rather frightening,' my mother muttered.

'There is so much that is frightening in this world,' said Mima sadly, 'that one ceases to react to it. I do not believe in universal good.'

'Mima, better show the people some photographs and not chatter,' the old lady said rather sharply and a little upset. 'And I'll go and make the tea.'

She proceeded to set the table with tiny little cups and saucers, sugar bowls and tongs, and little twisted spoons, gilded but rather worn.

'I use the washing powder for doing the laundry,' she explained, 'but we sold the needles and the eau-de-Cologne, and we also sold our ration of black bread, and used the money to buy some cakes. We decided to have some cakes to celebrate our moving into a new home, as we used to do years ago.'

And, with an air of triumph, she placed on the table an antique cake-stand laden with cakes made with saccharine; my jaw dropped at the sight of such marvellous things. My mother gave me a nudge under the table.

We sat on till late in the evening. Mima talked away all the time, talking a lot of good sense and giving voice to the

most astonishing thoughts. I even began to wonder whether
he had not been putting on a show all these years and had
simply taken refuge in a mental home.

But then something came over him, and what he said
started to make less and less sense—or else I wasn't clever
enough to understand him. The old lady got him to his feet
and took him away, like a child, to put him to bed, and it
was very strange to see her talking to him in children's language and slapping him—such a big, good-looking and yet
helpless man.

Next day I heard the sound of sawing in the neighbours'
shed. The shed backed on to our garden and there was a
crack in it through which I could see Mima sawing wood.
He had put a big log on the sawing-horse and was scratching
at it with a rusty old double-ended saw. The spare handle
was waving about, the saw was bending and jumping out, but
Mima went on scratching away at the rough log, clumsily
but in great earnest. It hurt me to watch him, so I hopped
over the fence and presented myself to him as an old friend.

'Let me help you; it's not so easy on your own,' I suggested in a very down-to-earth manner.

He looked at me in horror and turned quite pale. For a
while he remained silent and then muttered:

'I suppose you can . . .'

I was very good at sawing wood. But on this occasion for
some reason nothing went right. Mima's watchful gaze upset
me and made me feel awkward; behind their thick magnifying lenses his eyes seemed very dark, with huge bottomless
pupils.

It was only with tremendous difficulty that we succeeded
in sawing one log. Mima then leant the saw up against the
wall and said, staring at me rather absently:

'We shan't do any more.'

'No more?'

'No more.'

'But why?'

'I'm afraid.'

Timidly and cautiously I left the shed and clambered back
over the fence. I was feeling rather shaky: it seemed as
though a switch had clicked in my ears and all the noises
going on around me became unbearably vivid—the clatter of

a cart on the bridge, the barking of a dog, the confused hum from the market, the 'ta-ta-ta' from Babi Yar, and from the shed I could just hear the faint, cautious scratching of the saw. I put my eye to the crack. Mima was back on his own, scratching away vaguely at the log.

To Kill a Fish

I have been turning this question over in my mind for a long time, and it now seems to me that the humane and intelligent people who come after us—if anybody is in fact left alive—will find it difficult to understand how it could come about, how man could ever conceive of committing murder, let alone mass murder. Actually to kill someone. How was it possible? What for?

How did this idea come to find a place in the dark recesses of the brain of an ordinary human being, born of a mother, at one time just an infant sucking at the breast and later going to school? The same ordinary being as millions of others, with hands and feet and nails that grow, and cheeks on which, in the case of a man, there are bristles growing, a being which sorrows, smiles, admires himself in the mirror, feels a tender love for a woman and can burn his fingers with a match, and himself has no desire whatsoever to die—in short, ordinary in every respect, except in his pathological lack of imagination.

A normal human being understands not only that he himself wants to live but that everybody else wants to live as well. When he sees the sufferings of others, or only thinks of them, he sees the same thing happening to himself and he feels at least some mental pain. And consequently he would not raise his hand against another.

It is very difficult to kill even a newly born kitten.

If you drown them, some of them will keep moving their paws a whole hour in the bucket of water. Whenever my grandfather had to perform this disagreeable task he used to

send me away so that I shouldn't watch it, and he would
cover the bucket with a sack. I would eye the bucket beneath
its sack from afar, and I would start to tremble: I imagined
to myself that they were swimming around up to their ears
in water, unable to breathe, just twitching their paws convulsively.

That was why, when a cat strayed into our house and
gave birth to a couple of kittens, one of which turned out
to be deformed, with fleshless, twisted projections instead of
legs, and which miaowed desperately all the time, I decided,
out of pity for it, not to drown it but to kill it outright.

It was a moist, warm blob of life, utterly devoid of sense
and as insignificant as a worm. It seemed nothing could be
easier than to dispose of it with one blow. I picked up the
swollen, writhing object between two fingers, took it out into
the yard, placed it on a brick, and dropped another brick
flat on it from a height.

A strange thing happened—the little body seemed to be
resilient, the brick fell to one side and the kitten continued
its miaowing. With shaking hands I picked up the brick
again and proceeded to crush the little ball of living matter
until the very entrails came out, and at last it was silent, and
I scraped up the remains of the kitten with a shovel and
took them off to the rubbish heap, and as I did it my head
swam and I felt sick.

It's not so easy as you might think to kill even some little
blind kittens.

Occasionally fish came on sale in the market. We couldn't
afford it, but I was always trying furiously to think up ways
of getting my hands on some food and it occurred to me to
go out and try to catch some fish.

I had often been fishing with my pals in the old days. It is,
as you know, a tremendously pleasant occupation. True, I
used to be rather sorry for the fish, but we usually put it in
a sack or kept it in a bucket, where it could wriggle about
until it 'went to sleep', and, after all, what wonderful fish
soup it made!

My fishing tackle was rather primitive, consisting of a rusty
hook. But I decided that it was good enough to start with,
dug up some worms the night before, and as soon as it began
to get light I set off in the direction of the Dnieper.

When the river was at its highest the great expanse of meadowland between Kurenyovka and the Dnieper was often flooded right up to our embankment: it became a vast sea stretching to the horizon, and afterwards it would be covered with lush green grasses, the soil enriched with river silt. I made my way for a long time through the long grass, getting my feet wet through, but my spirits were kept up by my hunger and the idea of catching a lot of fish.

The banks of the Dnieper are sandy, with magnificent beaches and steep banks, and its waters are brownish in colour. There was nothing to remind me of the war, of hunger or of all the other horrors, and it made me think that the River Dnieper was just the same then as it had been in the days when Oleg's boats or the floating caravans of merchants on their way along the great route 'from the Varyags to the Greeks' had come sailing down the mainstream, and how many princes, Tsars and political systems had replaced one another since then, while the Dnieper flowed quietly on its way. Such thoughts come into your head many times in the course of your life and eventually become hackneyed. But at the time I was just thirteen.

I cast the line, put the box of worms in my pocket and set off to follow the float as it was carried downstream. The Dnieper is a fast-flowing river, and there are two ways of fishing in it: either to sit in one place and re-cast your line every minute or so, or to move along the bank with the float.

I had probably tramped well over half a mile before I got stuck in an impenetrable willow-bed, but I caught nothing. So I ran back and covered the same ground again, and with the same result. And so I went on, running up and down like a fool, getting ever crosser and more upset. I was clearly doing something wrong—either I hadn't fixed the plummet properly or I had chosen the wrong place and the wrong bait. The sun was already up and had started to warm the air, but I hadn't had a single bite, as though there were no longer any fish in the Dnieper.

Thoroughly disappointed and very near to tears, I realized that the time when the fish are most likely to bite was long past, so I decided to try my luck in a little pool among the willows, although I was afraid my hook would get caught in a piece of old wood and it was the only one I had.

The little pond was some way away from the river. The

current affected it only indirectly and you could scarcely see the water moving round in it. I had no idea how deep it was, so I simply lifted the float up as high as I could and cast it in. Almost at once it began gently to bob up and down.

It had scarcely disappeared beneath the surface when I gave it a sharp tug and pulled out an empty hook: something had eaten my worm. This was not so bad: now the hunt was on. I put some more bait on the hook and cast again, and the same game was repeated in the depths of the pool.

No matter what I did or how I fixed the bait, the hook always came out of the water empty. The fish was smarter than I was. I was now really worked up: I had to catch something, even if it was only a perch the size of my little finger!

Suddenly as I tugged I felt some weight on the line. At first I was horrified, thinking my hook had finally got caught, but at the very same moment I realized that it was actually a fish. Impatiently, not thinking for a moment that it might break away, I heaved with all my strength so that it sailed over my head, and I rushed in triumph across to where it lay flapping about on the grass. 'Aha—you crafty old thing—you lost out in the end! I got you after all.' It was a moment of great happiness. Anyone who has caught a fish even once in his life will know what I mean.

It was a perch, and at first it seemed to me bigger than it really was. A beautiful perch, with green stripes and bright red fins, soft to the touch and with a glazed look about it, it would have made a beautiful still-life.

But I was pursued by failure: the perch had swallowed the worm too eagerly. The line disappeared into his mouth, and the hook had got caught up somewhere in its stomach. With one hand I held down the flabby, twitching fish while with the other I felt around and tried to pull the hook out of its stomach, but it had apparently got caught in a bone. I kept on tugging and pulling and pulling very hard, and the fish went on wriggling, holding its mouth open in silence and looking at me with goggling eyes.

Then I lost my patience and pulled with all my force, the line snapped and the hook stayed in the fish. At that moment I had the feeling that I was having a hook pulled out of myself, and I broke out in a cold sweat on my forehead.

I know perfectly well you will think that it was nothing

but a child's over-sensitivity, and I'm quite ready to be jeered at by any real fisherman. But I was on the river bank alone, everything around me was fine, the sun was beating down, the water was sparkling, the dragonflies were settling on the marsh plants, and I had nothing to go on fishing with.

I threw the perch farther away on the grass and sat down to wait until it was quite dead. From time to time I could hear a rustling and a flapping over there: it was still jumping. Then it lay quiet. I went across and touched it with my foot, and it jerked up again, now all covered in dust and with bits of greenery stuck to it, all its beauty vanished.

I walked away, got lost in my thoughts and waited a long time, until I quite lost my patience and went back to look at it. It was still moving, and it began to get me really upset. I took the fish by the tail and proceeded to bang its head on the ground, but it still opened its mouth, stared at me and would not die: the ground was too soft.

In a fury I swung my arm up and threw the fish down on the ground with all my strength, so that it bounced like a ball, but it still went on wriggling and jumping. I went in search of a stick and found a rough piece of wood which I pressed down on the perch's head—while it went on staring at me with its silly fish-eyes—and I proceeded to squash and hack and dig at that head, until I had gone right through it. And in the end it stayed quiet.

It was only then that I remembered that I had a knife, and it was not without some hesitation that I cut the perch open and poked about in it for a long time, turning my nose away from the revolting smell, and somewhere among the slimy intestines I came across my rusty hook and the undevoured worm. By which time the perch had begun to look as battered and beastly as if it had been dragged out of a rubbish tip, and it seemed strange: here was something that contained such a powerful determination to live, and I wondered why it had been necessary to destroy so crudely a living thing which had been so resilient and so cunningly put together, and so beautiful in its green stripes and red scales. I held the pitiful, smelly pieces of fish in my hand, and, despite my hunger, I knew at once that after what had happened I should not be able to eat it.

That was at a time when I had only just begun to make my acquaintance with life. Later I killed many a living thing, both big and small. Especially unpleasant was the business of slaughtering horses; but there it was, I did it, and I ate them. But that comes later.

. . . It was a sunny day, and while I was busy with the perch over there in the Yar and throughout the continent there were machines at work. I am really concerned least of all with the slaughter of animals. I am talking about the power of imagination which, if you have it, makes it very difficult for you to kill even a fish.

A Chapter of Original Documents

ANNOUNCEMENT

It is strictly forbidden to offer assistance of any kind to escaping Russian prisoners-of-war, either by giving them accommodation or by offering them food.

The penalty for any violation of this order will be imprisonment or death.

STADTKOMMISSAR ROGAUSCH*

Kiev, May 8th, 1942

All able-bodied inhabitants of the city of Kiev from the age of fourteen to fifty-five are obliged to work in places as instructed by the employment exchange.

ABLE-BODIED PERSONS MAY LEAVE KIEV ONLY WITH THE PERMISSION OF THE DISTRICT AUTHORITIES.

People guilty of leaving Kiev of their own accord and of not responding to summonses issued by the employment exchange within seven days of their departure will be punished as for SABOTAGE, AND ALL THEIR PROPERTY WILL BE CONFISCATED.†

MAY 1942   WHAT'S ON IN THE CINEMAS

GLORIA—*That's What Men are Like, The Triple Wedding.*
METROPOLE—*First Love, Wedding Night for Three.*

---

* *Novoye Ukrainskoye Slovo,* May 23rd, 1942.
† Op. cit., May 10th, 1942, 'Order No. 88 issued by the Chief of the City of Kiev'.

ECHO—*Yes, I Love You, A Wedding with Problems.*
LUXE—*A Woman with Plans, Salto Mortale.*
ORION—*Dancing Round the World, Only Love.*

MEN NEEDED FOR SERVICE IN UKRAINIAN POLICE

Qualifications: age—18 to 45; height—not less than 5 ft 6 ins; and a blameless moral and political record.*

OPERA   Season 1942
(For Germans only)
OPERAS *Madam Butterfly, Traviata, The Queen of Spades, Faust.*
BALLET *Coppelia, Swan Lake.*

Re-naming of Streets
The following streets were renamed:
Kreshchatik—to be Von Eichhornstrasse.
Shevchenko Boulevard—to be Rownowerstrasse.
Kirov street—to be Doctor Todt Street.
(Streets had already been named after Hitler, Goering and Mussolini.)

'THE LIBERATED UKRAINE WELCOMES REICHS-MINISTER ROSENBERG.' (Beneath this headline the newspaper gave an enthusiastic and detailed account of how the Reichsminister in charge of the occupied eastern regions attended a lunch given by the General-Kommissar, inspected the principal monuments in the city of Kiev, watched the ballet *Coppelia* and visited a farm on the outskirts of the city) 'where he chatted with the peasants and had an opportunity of convincing himself of their readiness to carry out the tasks facing them'.†

ANNOUNCEMENT
Any person who, directly or indirectly, helps to support or conceal members of gangs, saboteurs, tramps or escaping prisoners or gives any of them food or other assistance will be punished. All his property will be confiscated.
A similar penalty will befall anybody who, being

* Announcement in *Novoye Ukrainskoye Slovo* day after day in the course of May, 1942.
† *Novoye Ukrainskoye Slovo*, June 23rd, 1942.

aware of the presence of gangs, saboteurs or escaped
prisoners, fails to pass information about them immediately to their village elder, the nearest police chief, a
military command or a German agricultural director.

Anyone who by laying such information assists in
the capture or elimination of members of any gang,
vagrants, saboteurs or escaped prisoners will receive a
reward of 1,000 roubles, or priority in the receipt of
foodstuffs, or the right to a strip of land or an extension
of his private garden.

*Military Commandant
of the Ukraine.
Reichskommissar of
the Ukraine**

---

*Headlines from the Bulletins issued
from the Führer's H.Q.*
'Hunger and Terror in Leningrad.'
'Advance Going According to Plan. Destruction of
Important Enemy Units Near the Don.'
'Soviets Continue to Suffer Major Losses.'
'Soviets Yesterday Again Attacked Without Success
Central and Southern Sectors of Eastern Front.'†

Prices on the Market, Autumn 1942
2 lb. of bread—250 roubles.
A tumbler of salt—200 roubles.
2 lb. of butter—6,000 roubles.
2 lb. of fat—7,000 roubles.
Average monthly earnings of factory and office
workers at that time—300–500 roubles.

FILMS SHOWING TODAY
THE TIGER FROM ESHNAPUR
Marvellous full-length adventure film.
For the first time on the screen—THE REAL INDIAN
COUNTRYSIDE.
In the principal role—LA-YAN, popular dancer of
the most unusual beauty.
A SENSATION! GRIPPING STORY! ADVENTURE! DRAMA!
From Friday next in the Gloria and Luxe cinemas.

---

* *Kiev During the Great Fatherland War* (Kiev, 1963), pp. 282–3.
† *Novoye Ukrainskoye Slovo*, July 4th, 7th and 20th, 1942.

THE INDIAN TOMB
In the principal role—LA-YAN.
Even more powerful, more dramatic and gripping—this
film is the second and final part of
The Tiger from Eshnapur.
See it in the Gloria and Luxe cinemas.

Caught in the Round-Up

I went to see *The Indian Tomb* and got caught up in a
police raid. Police vans swept into our square at great speed
and out of them tumbled Germans, dogs and Ukrainian
police. The market-women screamed and scattered in all
directions, baskets were swept off the counters and potatoes
were scattered all over the place. Some folk were quick
enough to get away, others were not so quick, and the crowd
scrambled around first one exit and then another, where
Arbeitskarte were already being checked.

What did I care? I was still under fourteen; I was liable to
be directed to work, but not to be sent to Germany. I sat
down on the step of one of the stalls, huddled up as small
as I could make myself, just in case, and I watched the
proceedings.

It was mainly the women they were after, young girls
who had come in to the market from the outlying villages.
The peasants, of course, had no Arbeitskarte anyway. Even
under Soviet rule they had not been given identity cards;
they were people without rights who went their way until
they were caught. The girls were quickly pushed into the
closed vans, where they screamed and banged on the tarpaulin and stuck their arms through holes in the sides. 'Hey,
Mother, help me, do something for me!' A shabbily dressed
woman unbuttoned her blouse, displaying an enormous white
bosom which she took in both her hands and pushed under
the nose of a policeman: 'I've a baby feeding on me at
home: look—see the milk!'

The police formed a line and combed through the market, driving out the rest of the people, but they didn't bother those who were obviously elderly women, and they took one look at me and again said nothing. The raid ended as abruptly as it had begun. The vans drove off with full loads. The ground was scattered with squashed potatoes and broken bottles and pools of milk.

Such raids were now a daily occurrence, but what was most surprising was that people got used to them and almost at once began to take them for granted. It was as though it was the most natural thing in the world for some people to be on the prowl and for others to be dodging them. Had it ever been otherwise?

Throughout the centuries the unfortunate people of Russia have been hunted down and beaten, sometimes by foreigners and sometimes by their own people, by the Cumans, the Tatars and the Turks, by their own rulers, like Ivan Grozny, Peter the Great and Nicholas, by the Tsarist police and then by the Bolsheviks, and all this seems to have instilled into them such a deeply rooted fear of authority that the most recent—in this case the German—man-hunt seemed quite natural. On the other hand, if there had been no persecution for a long period, that would have seemed somehow wrong and even have made people uneasy . . .

I had my pay in my pocket, in the new Ukrainian money. In a single day Soviet money had ceased to circulate. They announced without any previous warning that Soviet money was no longer valid. In its place appeared 'Ukrainian' money minted in Rovno. I think it must have been one of the most straightforward monetary reforms in the world—you just threw the old money on the rubbish tip and that was that.

The new money was printed on very poor paper which tore easily, with a swastika and some German writing on one side, and with some more German on the other side and only right at the bottom, it said in Ukrainian: 'One Karbovanets'. That is what was known as 'Ukrainian' money.

At the Gloria Cinema, which used to be called the October, I bought myself a ticket and was going inside when I suddenly heard a delighted shout: 'Tolik!'

I turned and there was Shurka Matso . . . I mean Krysan.

He rushed up to me, clutched at me and poked me, and I was also overjoyed to know he was alive and that nothing had happened to him. He dashed off to the vestibule, brought back a bottle of lemonade and two paper drinking cups, and we proceeded to pour it out and drink it right there in the cinema, with the feeling of being real grown-up men, good companions of long standing for whom friendship took priority over everything.

'Down in Podol nobody knows me,' Shurka was saying. 'Everybody treats me as a Ukrainian.'

'What are you doing there?'

'Buying and selling. I deal in silver roubles.'

'By the way, Bolik came back again!' I remembered to tell him. 'He managed to dodge the guards and get away; said he jolly nearly copped it from a machine-gun. Only, soon as he got back home they whipped him off to Germany. But he managed to get out of the transit camp, and he's back home again.'

'They'll never get him down!' Shurka shook with laughter. 'Whatever they do with him he still keeps coming back home. But won't they grab him again?'

'He's hiding away in the cellar, catching mice.'

'Wha-at?'

'He's making mousetraps.'

The lights went down and people silenced us. The film was a documentary: *Come to Lovely Germany.*

There they were—energetic, sprightly young men and women, with their shoulders thrown boldly back and their eyes fixed on some inspiring point in the distance, getting into the goods wagons. The only thing lacking was the march of the young Communists. Instead of that they were singing Ukrainian folk-songs to the beat of the wheels on the rails. And there was lovely Germany—little white houses and everything amazingly clean. Still laughing because of their good fortune, the new arrivals were adorning themselves in new clothes, pulling on new lacquered boots. The young men were already driving well-fed horses, while the girls were putting their arms round the necks of thoroughbred cows. Then it was evening and time to relax. There they were, walking towards the edge of a charming pond, singing enchantingly 'The moon is shining clear above . . .' while the kindly German farmer, a substantial but also cheerful-

looking man, crept up quietly behind them with a tender
smile on his face and listened pensively to the song, just like
their own father . . .

It was ages since I had been to the cinema, not since the
Kreshchatik affair. Consequently every scene imprinted itself
in my memory, especially *The Indian Tomb,* which followed
the documentary.

At first I watched it quite uncritically, especially the
genuine Indian landscapes and so forth. But then I began
gradually to watch the film more closely, and ideas began to
come into my head which the film-makers had not intended.
I suddenly began to choke with rage.

Behind the figures flickering on the screen—of rajahs and
charming German engineers and a dazzlingly beautiful
European woman—I caught sight of the endless columns of
slaves who had built that damned senseless tomb. They could
be seen moving about in the background, but it was enough
to make me shake with rage for the film to lose all its
attraction for me.

They had certainly been to India and filmed her actual
landscapes. But all those folk—the slave-owners, exploiters
and rulers—had their own special way of life, while there, in
the background, were the slaves, divided up into brigades.
That film marked the end for me. Until then I had taught
myself only to read between the lines in the newspapers; but
now I started looking more closely into everything, to see
what was behind it. Especially if it appeared that I was supposed to admire it.

I used to get especially angry if people tried to persuade
me to admire great statesmen. Maybe I missed a great deal
as a small boy because of this. But all the same I never
found myself being carried away by accounts of Alexander of
Macedon or Napoleon Bonaparte, not to mention any other
of our great benefactors. This almost morbid loathing for
dictators, who invariably had their columns and columns
of victims in the background, interfered with my reading and
learning and even prevented me, paradoxically enough, from
appreciating the greatness of such people as Shakespeare
and Tolstoy. When I read *Hamlet* I would try to reckon up
how many wretched servants had to be working for him so
that he could carry on unhindered, torturing himself with

his questions. When I read about Anna Karenina I used to wonder who had to sweat away to ensure that she could eat and drink her fill, and always be beautifully turned out. She was another of those parasites absorbed in her own woes.

Somewhere at the back of my mind I realized that it was rather foolish of me to act like this, but I could not overcome it. One's environment determines one's mental outlook. The only figure in literature who was always and still remains near to me is Don Quixote.

Shurka and I came out of the cinema thoroughly depressed. German soldiers were strolling along the pavements of Podol with their arms round local prostitutes. The young ladies were decked out in the very latest fashion: long and very curly hair falling loosely down over their shoulders, their coats hanging open and, of course, their hands always stuck in their pockets. Two couples just ahead of us had just parted and we overheard the following conversation:

'What did he give you?'

'Two marks, a mandarin and a sweet.'

'I got three mandarins.'

Shurka scornfully shrugged his shoulders.

'They're just amateurs. They have their real tarts in the Palace of Pioneers—the Deutsches Haus, it's a first-class brothel. Number 72 Saxaganskaya is another big establishment . . . Listen, have you got three thousand? There's a pimp around here who wants to sell a whole sack of Soviet money; he's made up his mind they're done for and he wants three thousand for it. Shall we have it?'

'I've got two hundred—that's all my pay.'

'That's a pity . . . Still, never mind, to hell with him and his sack. We still don't know whether the Bolsheviks will ever come back or if we'll be still alive when they do.'

There were some cartoons displayed in the window of the hairdresser's shop. In one of them Stalin was depicted as a falling colossus of clay which Roosevelt and Churchill were trying in vain to keep up.

Another of them also showed Stalin, this time as a hairy, moustachioed gorilla, with an axe covered in blood, with which he was chopping the hands off the corpses of children, women and old people. We knew that cartoon so well! Only in the Soviet version it was Hitler who appeared in the guise of a gorilla.

The caption informed us just how many millions of people Stalin had caused to rot in concentration camps, that he was no worker but the son of a man who owned a little cobbler's shop, that his father had brutally ill-treated him, which was why he had physical defects, that he had arrived at a position of absolute power over the corpses of his rivals, that he had held the country down purely by terror, and that he him- self had gone out of his mind through fear.

We read it through and yawned.

'The Germans hanged some young Communists in the May Day Park,' Shurka said. 'They shouted: "Long live Stalin!" They pinned placards on them saying PARTISAN, but next morning they had been replaced by other ones saying VICTIMS OF FASCIST TERROR. The Germans flew into a rage, like tigers, and put police to guard the place. On the next morning the other corpses had gone and the police were hanging instead . . . All right, then, I'm on my way. Tell Bolik I'll come over and see him!'

'Where are you living?' I shouted after him, surprised at the speed with which he departed.

'Over there!' he waved back. 'Go on, beat it—there's a raid! Say hello to Bolik for me!'

It was only then that I saw the covered lorries racing down the street. People were scurrying into the courtyards and diving into doorways like mice. I flattened myself against a wall, not particularly worried—if the worst happened I could produce my birth certificate to show that I was not fourteen.

How to Turn a Horse into Sausages

Degtyaryov was a thickset, rather round-shouldered and awkwardly built but very active and energetic man of just over fifty, with greying hair, a big, fleshy nose and knobbly fists.

His clothes were always in a terrible state: filthy jacket, dirty, patched trousers, boots worn down at the heels and covered in mud and manure, and a flat cap on his head.

His favourite expressions were:

'A pound of smoke', meaning 'nothing', or 'something of no importance'.

'Perturbations'—meaning changes of political systems.

'Get caught in the devaluation'—meaning to lose everything as the result of a monetary reform.

I turned up at six o'clock in the morning and the first thing Degtyaryov did (and rightly, too) was to give me a really good meal.

He had a very pleasant, clean house; white table-napkins and covers on the furniture; spotlessly white linen on the beds. Amid such cleanliness the master of the house himself looked like some uncouth peasant who had stumbled into a smart restaurant.

I eagerly gulped down the mutton stew, cereals and milk and the pancakes which were put in front of me by his wife, while Degtyaryov, studying me carefully as I stuffed it all down, told me what it was all about.

At one time he had had a small sausage factory. Then, during the revolution, perturbations and devaluations had taken place, and the factory had been taken off him. Next there was the period of the 'new economic policy' and he had again had what was more or less a factory, though it was smaller. They took that off him too. Now all he had was a little private butcher's shop which he had to carry on illegally, because it cost a fantastic sum of money to obtain a licence. That was why they would close it down too.

'Revolutions, systems overthrown, wars and perturbations —but we have to live somehow don't we? I reckon—if your luck holds, you're laughing, and if it doesn't, a pound of smoke! The neighbours know what I'm up to, but I pay them off with bones. There's no need for anyone else to know. If anyone asks what you're doing, tell 'em: "I'm helping on the farm." Like a farm labourer in the old days. You can lead the horses in through the streets, because when I do it they always point at me and say: "There's old Degtyaryov taking another old nag off for sausages." '

I pulled my cap on and we went across the square towards the school. People were getting aboard the two-horse carts driven by cab-drivers, which now did the work of the trams, buses and taxis. Women with baskets, peasants from the villages and educated-looking people in hats were all clambering aboard, arguing with each other, handing up their bags, and arranging themselves around all four sides, their legs dangling down.

We pushed our way in between some baskets of radishes, the driver cracked his whip, and we were off to Podol faster than the wind, at two miles an hour, and the bushes flashed past.

I sat there, bumping up and down, overcome by the thought that for once I was travelling legally (usually I had to hide from the conductor or go by foot, but now Degtyaryov had paid for me like a law-abiding citizen) and with an air of great superiority I looked down on the dreary figures shuffling along the pavements in their shabby jackets and worn-out greatcoats, in galoshes or just barefoot.

The corn market was a sea of humanity and the very heart of Podol (I had read Zola and knew about the heart of Paris). The women at the stalls were shouting their wares, the beggars were whining and children were singing out: 'Who wants cold water?' There was a girl standing at the gate, terribly thin, like a skeleton, selling buns from a plate: 'Fresh buns, very tasty, please buy my fresh buns.'

What a temptation! . . .

Down the Nizhny Val there was an enormous street market, endless rows of people bartering things. 'What's that?' 'An overcoat.' 'What's the use of a coat like that?' 'It's a very good coat! Warm as a coffin.'

Degtyaryov made his way confidently through the crowd and I hung on to his coat-tail so as not to get left behind. I nearly knocked down an old woman trying to sell a single spoon—she stood there holding one steel spoon in her hand. It ought at least to have been silver!

What a sight! . . .

The big market-place was crammed full of carts, manure and trodden-down hay and straw; cows mooed and pigs squealed.

'What do you want for it?' 'Seventy thousand.' 'Go and screw yourself!' 'Gimme sixty then!' Degtyaryov only asked the price of the pigs to remind himself of the good old days, but he got seriously interested in an old, lame, scabby gelding. The animal's lips drooped down, dripping with saliva, his mane was full of burrs, and he stood there with his head hanging sadly down, his unseeing eyes half closed, paying no attention to the swarms of flies which had settled on his head.

'I'll give you five!' 'What did ye say? This is a real working horse!' 'One head, four ears; how about six, cash down?' 'Make it seven, master, he'll pull anything you put behind him, a real fiery steed, you could use him for steeplechasing!'

Degtyaryov haggled fiercely and persistently, waving his money about, smacking his fist down on the palm of his hand, walking away, then coming back again, but the old man was not so stupid as he looked, and eventually they got to within ten roubles of each other. Finally the bridle was put into my hand and we made our way with difficulty out of the seething mass of people. When we got to the cab-rank Degtyaryov gave me my instructions for the journey:

'You can ride him if he'll take you, but for God's sake don't go past the police station.'

I led the gelding across to a mounting stand, climbed up on to his back and stuck my heels into him. His backbone was as sharp as a saw, and he dragged himself along slowly, limping and giving repeated signs of a desire to stop. I urged him on in one way and the other, walloped him with a stick, but finally took pity on him, got off his back and led him by the bridle.

We wandered for a long time through the side lanes, now quiet and overgrown with grass. I called the horse Old Grey and got to like him, because he showed no sign of wanting to kick or bite. I let him graze along the side of the road, sometimes let go of him altogether and then called him:

'Come on, Grey, come on, then—the grass is better over here.'

He would lift his head, look at me and come across as if he understood what I said—he was a quiet, intelligent and good-natured old nag. We became very good friends.

Degtyaryov was waiting for me at Koshitse Street. We stood around there for a long time, waiting until there was nobody about on the street, and then quickly ran with Old Grey into the yard and straight into the barn.

'Give him some hay, so as he doesn't start neighing,' Degtyaryov instructed me.

Old Grey perked up at the sight of the hay and proceeded to munch away vigorously. He had obviously not expected such good things to come his way.

Degtyaryov was in the best of humours and full of energy. He sharpened on a stone a couple of knives made out of strips of steel and bound with insulating tape instead of handles. In the entrance he picked up an axe, a tub and some buckets and we went into the barn, followed by two cats, both excited and miaowing and running ahead, as though we were bringing them some meat.

Old Grey was munching the hay, suspecting nothing. Degtyaryov turned him round, putting his head to the light, and ordered me to hold the bridle firmly. With a grunt he bent down and tied the horse's legs together. Old Grey, who had apparently become accustomed to everything in this life, stood quiet, offering no resistance.

Degtyaryov stood facing the horse's head, moved it a little as a hairdresser does, so that it was quite straight. Then he took a quick swing and struck the horse right above the eyes.

Old Grey didn't stir, and Degtyaryov struck again and again, so that the skull was cracked. After that the horse began to sag, dropped on to its knees, rolled over on its side, and its legs stretched out convulsively and trembled, still bound together by the ropes. Degtyaryov threw the axe to one side, scrambled on to the horse and sat on top of it, exclaiming shortly:

'Gimme the tub!'

I dragged the tub across to him. With both hands Degtyaryov raised the trembling head of the horse and I pushed the tub underneath its neck—and Degtyaryov plunged the knife into it. Underneath its coat could be seen the pink flesh and deeper still the white, slimy throat, still moving convulsively. The knife sliced ruthlessly through the throat tube, the cartilage and the vertebrae, so that the head was practically severed and slumped unnaturally to one side. Blood came gushing out of the neck in spurts, as if from a water-pump, and a red foam formed on top of the tub.

Degtyaryov held on to the twitching body of the horse with all his strength so that the blood should not spill over from the tub. His hands were already covered in blood and his fleshy face was spattered with it. As he sat there on top of the horse, following the horse's movements and clinging on as tightly as he could, Degtyaryov looked rather like a spider that had caught a fly.

I let out an exclamation for no particular reason, and he lifted up his spattered face.

'What's the matter—are you scared? You'll get used to it; you'll see much worse than this in your lifetime. A horse is just a pound of smoke. Gimme that board over there.'

The blood kept pouring out and then suddenly stopped, as though a tap had been turned off. Apparently the heart had stopped pumping. Degtyaryov rolled the horse over on its back and put pieces of wood at each side to support it. The four legs, unbound at last, splayed apart, sticking up in the air. Degtyaryov made incisions right round them at the joints and from them further incisions to the belly, and we set about skinning the animal. The skin came off easily, as if it were simply being unstuck, with a little assistance from the knife, and without the skin the carcass ceased to be a living thing and became meat such as you see hanging on hooks in the butcher's.

At this point the cats crept up and started getting their claws into the meat, each one grabbing what it could, ripping pieces off and growling at each other. Degtyaryov paid no attention to them: he was in too much of a hurry; he didn't even wipe the drops of sweat from his brow. And so between the four of us we proceeded to pull Old Grey to pieces.

Degtyaryov hurled the hooves, the head and the skin into a corner, and with one swift movement opened the belly, scooped out the intestines; the liver went into one bucket and the lungs into another. The legs and the brisket were removed in one stroke of the knife, as though there were no bones at all. Degtyaryov was a master at carving up a carcass. Wet through, with stains all over him and streaks of hair stuck to his forehead, he nodded at the shapeless pile of meat and said:

'Carry it in the house!'

His house was very cunningly arranged: at the front there were the living-rooms and a veranda, but at the back there was yet another room with an entrance through a narrow passage cluttered up with rubbish, and no one would ever guess there was a door there.

We cut the meat off the bones on big tables covered with tin, and smothered it with salt. The knives were as sharp as razors; I cut myself a hundred times and the salt stung fiercely in the cuts. Later on I was always going around with my fingers in bandages. Degtyaryov consoled me, saying:

'This is the way I started; I made my way up from working as a labourer. I'm going to feed you, but no one ever fed me a damned thing; I just worked to learn the trade. You're a smart kid—you learn it too. I'll make a man of you. Once you know the business of making sausages, that's no pound of smoke—with that you'll never be lost; you'll be able to get through all the perturbations and devaluations. Don't try and make yourself a minister—they always get shot. Just be a humble sausage-maker. Learn the trade.'

I learnt it.

Bolted to the ground in the middle of his workshop stood a sausage machine as big as a man, with two handles. Degtyaryov knocked on the wall and his wife appeared, frail and stolid with the pale complexion of a countrywoman. With a sigh she got herself up on to a stool and began forcing the meat down into the funnel with a wooden ram. We got hold of the handles, the machine crunched and squeaked and the ancient gears began to grind. Lack of food had left me without much strength, so Degtyaryov did most of the turning; he worked like an ox, breathing heavily, but he kept on turning with great force. He really punished himself at his work. I got short of breath and at times I wasn't so much helping as being carried round by the handle.

The minced meat flopped out into the buckets. Then Degtyaryov tipped it out into a trough and sprinkled it with salt, pepper and some whitish crystals of dirty-looking saltpetre.

'Isn't that bad for you?' I asked.

'You have to do it for the colour. Goodness only knows: they seem to eat it; nobody's died from it. I don't eat sausage myself, personally, and I advise you to keep off it, too . . . Now, this is what you've got to know—you add water to it, and two bucketfuls of meat will soak up a bucket of water. That's where you get the weight and there's your profit.'

I was really amazed. We put on some aprons and proceeded to work the minced meat in with the water as women work their washing on a scrubbing board. The more we worked it the more water it absorbed.

Once again I felt faint. I jabbed my finger on something in the mince and cut myself: it was a piece of tin.

'The funnel in the machine is losing its plating,' said Degtyaryov in some concern. 'Go and bandage it up so that it doesn't bleed.'

'But are people going to eat that?'

'Be quiet. They don't *have* to eat it, do they? I don't force them. They are free people.'

The sausage filler, which looked like a red fire-bucket on its side, also had a funnel with a handle, some gear wheels and a long tube at the end. Degtyaryov filled it with the minced meat and began turning the handle to build up the pressure, while I put the sausage skin over the end of the tube and tied it off when it was full.

We worked for many long hours as if we were on a factory conveyor and in the end we were surrounded with piles of slippery, raw, rings of sausage. But most unpleasant of all was the blood sausage. The liquid seeped out of the pump, and the blood left in there from the previous time was stale; it had already gone bad, and stank. You couldn't breathe; there seemed no end to the sausage skin, and our arms were thick with blood to the very top. When it was all over I staggered out into the yard and stood there a long time, breathing in the fresh air.

But Degtyaryov worked like a machine. In the corner of the workshop there was a stove with a boiler built into it, full of green, stinking water left over from previous operations. Degtyaryov tipped the sausages into the boiler and when they came to the boil they turned red from the saltpetre. I had always wondered why home-made sausage never looked as attractive as the sausage you saw in the shops. Then we hung the strings of sausages on sticks and carried them across to the curing shed in the garden, which was disguised as a lavatory.

It was late at night when we removed the last sausages

from the curing shed. They were still hot and smelt very appetizing; we packed them into baskets, covering them up with the *Novoye Ukrainskoye Slovo*. I couldn't remember Degtyaryov taking me off and putting me to sleep on a trestle bed. I lay there without moving the whole night, and it was hardly daylight when he was already shaking me and saying:

'Come on now, down to the market! It's the early bird that catches the worm.'

We carried the baskets down to the cab-rank hanging on stout sticks across our shoulders, like the Chinese, and took them to Podol where, in a dark and dirty yard, the women stallholders took them off him. Degtyaryov came away with his pockets bursting with money. Then we returned to the second-hand market, where he carried on whispered conversations with various characters, leaving me standing near a post, and returned with almost empty pockets. He asked me slyly:

'Did you ever see gold coins?'

I had never seen any. He took me round behind a stall and pulled out a big handkerchief tied into a knot. Inside it were four gold ten-rouble pieces issued in Tsarist times. Degtyaryov gave me one to hold.

'Come on, let's go!' he said cheerfully. 'That's all we've managed to earn.'

I stared in astonishment at the tiny little coins into which poor Old Grey had been turned. I was even more surprised at the way Degtyaryov trusted me. Orders had been issued long before about handing over all gold, and the penalty for possessing it, or even simply for not informing about it, was the firing-squad.

'Through all the revolutions and political changes and perturbations this is the only thing, my lad, that will never let you down. All the rest is a pound of smoke,' Degtyaryov said. 'When you grow up you'll understand. You just mark my words—don't bother about other things, and you'll have many an occasion to remember old Degtyaryov . . . And now let's go and haggle over another fiery steed.'

I worked like a slave for Degtyaryov. He handed over to me all the work of delivering the sausages to the stallholders; he had already attracted too much attention to himself with the baskets. He used to give me the fare for the cab, but I used to save it by hopping on a tram and not paying the fare. The drivers used to chase me off, striking at me with their whips. It was very difficult with the baskets. On one occasion I fell off a lorry and a crowd gathered. My clothes were in rags and I was always nervous and restless, like a stray cat.

Once when I was cleaning up the workshop I summoned up the courage to steal a big piece of sausage and hide it in the snow outside the window. I was scared the whole evening, because Degtyaryov always counted them again. But I had pinched it before he counted them. On my way home I went to get it in the snow and found the sausage had gone. At that my heart sank into my boots—Degtyaryov would surely get rid of me. Then I looked more carefully and saw signs of cats walking in the snow . . . Oh, the filthy creatures—I had cheated Degtyaryov, and they had cheated me. Consequently I never tried the sausage. On the first day Degtyaryov gave me four bones from Old Grey, and then gave me some bones from every horse he killed. But there wasn't much fat to be got out of them, especially from the old ones.

Cannibals

They hanged a man for eating human flesh. There was a lot of talk about it in Kiev, and people went along eagerly to watch. I didn't go—I was too busy.

In actual fact he did not himself eat human flesh, but he caused other people to do so. He was a sausage-maker like Degtyaryov. He would go around the market, pick on some likely man or woman, and offer to sell him or her some cheap salt which he would say he had in his home. He would take them home, let them through the door first, crack them over the head with an axe—and turn them into sausages. He got caught through sheer negligence. A woman took some sausages home and sat down to eat them when she came across a piece of a human finger in a sausage. The woman who had sold her the sausage was taxed with it, and through her they caught the man who made them. He admitted working like that for nearly a year. He caused a great many people to eat human flesh.

Degtyaryov commented:

'He was a fool. An old nag costs very little, but he was too mean for that. True, he sold them as pork sausages, and it's a fact that human flesh and pork meat taste the same, so he made plenty of money at it. I knew the fellow, the same women used to buy from him as from me. No, there must be some limit to sharp practice in every trade. Did you ever hear about the graveyard gang?'

I had not heard.

'But how come? It's true they dealt with 'em without a lot of fuss. The keeper of the graveyard was their leader and thought it all up. They used to open up the grave after a funeral and take out the corpse, then turn it into food for pigs. They built up a whole pig farm right there next to the graveyard. Then the pigs went for sausages. It was all very well organized. Even if a corpse today is pretty skinny, it's meat just the same, and what's the sense of letting good stuff go to waste with such hunger about? And nobody would have known about it, but they started quarrelling among themselves, didn't divide up the profits properly, and one of them gave the whole gang away. The main thing is not to know what you're eating. And sausage is very convenient for that reason. You can stuff whatever you like into it so long as you make it a good colour. It was really a great idea, that pig farm; I admired them. If you feed pigs on meat they swell up like yeast. You'll get used to it, I'm telling you—you'll see worse than that yet. Does it still hurt you to have to slaughter horses?'

'Yes, it hurts.'

'Silly little fool, why bother about them? As you see, that's the way life is—not only horses; even human beings go for sausages . . .'

I Always Get Away with It, But I Don't Know Who to Thank

Yes, I reckoned I was very lucky. I had to work hard, but I had enough to eat and I could bring bones home. My mother was much worse off: at the factory she received only a bowl of soup once a day.

But it was my grandfather who hit on the most artful dodge: he decided to marry himself off to a village woman. He spent much time at the market, gallantly offering himself as a husband to the peasant women who came in from the countryside. His main argument was that he was independent and a house-owner. But the elderly women living alone in the villages had their own cottages and no desire to move into the starving city even for the sake of acquiring such a remarkable husband.

Grandpa soon realized this, and decided that if the mountain would not go to Mahomet, then Mahomet must go to the mountain. He speedily fell in love with an elderly spinster by the name of Natalia from the village of Litvinovka, shut up his own room and left to make his home with her in the country.

Grandpa had based his negotiations on the idea that old Natalia would be cooking him stew and pancakes and serving it up to him at table, with a little home-made spirit to wash it down on Saturdays. But he didn't realize that the contract was bilateral. Old Natalia was just as calculating as he was, and she had counted on Grandpa doing the ploughing, sowing, harvesting and threshing in her place. Old Semerik's sojourn in Litvinovka turned into one big misunderstanding and a continual quarrel.

It went on for several months, because Grandpa still clung desperately to the opportunity he had of eating stew and cereals every day, but at seventy-two he was really no longer capable of handling a plough, and old Natalia, deeply hurt, threw him out without more ado. He consoled himself

291

with the knowledge that he had got to know practically everybody in Litvinovka, and that the peasants now stopped more often overnight in his room, some paying with a few potatoes, some with a cup of peas, which was what he lived on. He began envying me again and wanted Degtyaryov to take him on as a second helper, but nothing came of it—after all, what help could he be?

Then, suddenly, Degyaryov vanished.

I arrived as usual early one morning, but his wife, very worried, sent me off home—Degtyaryov had gone away on business and wouldn't be back till the next day. But there was no sign of him the next day or the day after. Then he dropped in on me himself, very agitated, carrying a huge basket.

'Quick—let's get on with the job!' he said.

He had some fresh fish in the basket which he had contracted to smoke. He scribbled out some notes and sent me with them to the market-women in Podol. When I returned the fish was already done and lay in a heap on the table in the workshop, shiny and bronze and smelling quite delicious.

Degtyaryov was sitting there pensively, his face looking rather sunken and tired, while his hands, which had previously looked so strong and capable, lay for the first time lifelessly on the table. I didn't understand what was the matter, but it hurt me to look at him.

'Not turned out so bad, the fish!' I said.

'Bad's the word. I've done them far too much,' Degtyaryov said. 'It's ages since I smoked the damned things, and I've made a complete mess of them. I'm ashamed to take them down there.'

He proceeded to pack the fish carefully in a basket lined with newspaper. I couldn't see what he had done so wrong.

'I'll tell you what, you take it to them,' he said. 'Say that Degtyaryov is not feeling well and couldn't come along. For God's sake don't pinch any of them: they've been counted. You go down through Syrets, past the canning factory and the brickworks, where the road turns off to the left up a hill; keep on up it a long way till you see a military camp with guard towers, and say at the gate: "This is for officer Radomsky." Explain to him that I am sick and couldn't come along. Hand it in, basket and all, don't bring it back again.'

'But it's a new basket . . .'

'To hell with that. And don't say I spoilt the fish; maybe he won't understand. Hand it in and get back home quick. Do you follow me?'

There was nothing really to follow. I humped the heavy basket up on to my shoulder (which always hurt, because it had been rubbed sore carrying things) and off I went. I was exhausted even by the time I reached the Syrets. But I knew that, even when I seemed to have no strength left, I could keep staggering on and always seemed to find more from somewhere.

I sat down to have a rest on the windward side, so as not to smell the tantalizing odour of smoked fish. I passed the canning factory and I passed the brickworks, and the road went off to the left up a hill.

I was so glad, so pleased with myself, when at last I caught sight of the military camp to the left of the road. And it was a pretty big camp at that: I kept walking for a long time without coming across any gate. Notices said: FORBIDDEN ZONE. IT IS FORBIDDEN TO APPROACH CLOSER THAN 15 YARDS. GUARDS OPEN FIRE WITHOUT WARNING.

Because of that I instinctively kept close to the right-hand side of the road, keeping an eye on the guards in the towers. There were three rows of wire, of which the middle one was mounted on china insulators and obviously carried an electric charge, which meant that it was a very important camp, perhaps a secret one.

At last I managed to drag myself as far as the corner where the gate was situated. I decided that here the fifteen-yard zone did not apply and went up to the guard who stood there leaning against one of the gate-posts and looking bored.

'For officer Radomsky,' I said, pointing at the basket.

He nodded in the direction of a long, low building near the gate and said something of which I understood only the word *Wachstube*—the guard-room. I went up the steps into the porch, entered the building and found myself in a long corridor. There was nobody to be seen, but I could hear the tapping of a typewriter and went towards it. The door into the room was half open and there were some girls inside gossiping—our own, local girls, working as secretaries, apparently. It looked the same as any other office—desks stained with ink, counting frames and cash-books with columns of figures. The girls were pretty in the Kurenyovka style: rosy-cheeked, with full figures and curly hair. They all stared at me.

'This is for officer Radomsky,' I repeated my piece.

'Aha—put it down here.'

One of the girls helped me to lift the basket on to the table and immediately put her hand under the paper and broke off a piece of fish.

'Oho—not so bad . . . mmmm . . . very tasty!'

They gathered round the basket and proceeded to pull the fish to pieces with their chubby little ink-stained fingers and stuff it into their mouths. They were just simple, naughty little girls from Kurenyovka. I began to be rather worried, but if they seized on the fish so boldly it meant that they had the right to do so, it seemed to me, and I was delighted that they enjoyed it. Let them eat their fill.

'It's from Degtyaryov—he's ill and couldn't come along,' I said, thus completing my mission.

'Aha—mmm . . . we'll pass it on. Thanks.'

And off I went, a little worried, it's true, that I had not handed it over to 'officer Radomsky' in person, because the girls might gobble up half of it. And a bit later I began to regret that I hadn't eaten at least one small fish myself, because nobody had the slightest intention of counting them.

Degtyaryov was unusually pleased when I returned and gave him a full account of how I had handed the fish over and to whom. He wasn't pleased that I hadn't handed it over to the officer himself, but when I described how the secretaries had eaten it and praised it he jumped up and started striding round the room.

'That's good—maybe even better! Those stupid girls won't understand. And they were licking their fingers? Thank God, maybe this perturbation will pass. I shan't take it along there again, to hell with it. Phew—thank the Lord! Go off home—there's no more work for you.'

I departed, not quite sure why it had all upset him so. Well, supposing he *had* spoilt the fish, just imagine, what a tragedy. I realized, of course, that, as a skilled tradesman he was ashamed to disappoint his German client, apparently a very important person . . .

Then suddenly it struck me: wait, where on earth had I been?

Surely that was the camp just next to Babi Yar, the one they told such awful tales about? Tired and dazed through carrying that basket, I had not grasped that I was approaching it from the back. Cars and lorries going there from the centre of the city went through Lukyanovka, but I had gone through Syrets, round the other side.

So that meant Degtyaryov had been in the camp—and got out again? What for, and how had he done it? For gold, for a basket of fish? And it had been my good fortune that the 'officer gentleman' had not been there. If he had lost his temper because Degtyaryov had not turned up, he might have kept me in there. What a dirty, mean trick, sending me along in his own place! Like sending someone into a minefield.

I started to think about that barbed wire charged with electricity, and remembered seeing some dejected prisoners inside it, but I hadn't studied them very carefully; after all, there were plenty of them around. And I had heard the sound of shooting beyond the barracks, but there was now shooting everywhere. Like a sparrow, I had flown into the cage and flown out again, and I had been lucky.

In any case I have been very lucky indeed up till now, and I don't know whom to thank for my good luck: it's nothing to do with people; there is no God, and fate, that's just a pound of smoke. I am simply lucky.

It was purely a matter of luck that I arrived in this world not a Jew, not a gypsy, not old enough to be sent to work in Germany, that bombs and bullets missed me, that patrols didn't catch me, that I escaped from under a tram by a miracle and fell off a tree without killing myself. My God, what luck!

I suppose it's only people who have a lot of luck who manage to survive in this life. If I had been unlucky I might already have been inside the wire of Babi Yar, quite by chance, accidentally, perhaps just because the 'officer gentleman' happened not to be in a good mood or got a fish bone stuck in his gum . . .

I walked on a little farther down the street, utterly crestfallen. It was already getting dark and storm-clouds loomed heavy and violet-coloured. Once again I felt the strength draining out of me and leant against the fence. I felt such a sickness and such a yearning that I could have stood there and howled.

An unbearable feeling of being suffocated; the silence of the world around; the purple stripes across the sky. I felt myself to be a tiny little ant bricked up in the foundations of a building. The whole world seemed to consist of nothing but bricks and stone, without a glimmer of light showing through; wherever you turned there was nothing but stone and walls and prison.

I was submerged in a sea of desperate, elemental longing. When you came to think of it: the whole world was a prison: restrictions on all sides; everything laid down within precise limits; everything concreted up and divided off; you can go only here, live only like this, think only like this and speak only like this. How can it be, why should it be, whom does it serve, that I should have been born and allowed to crawl around in this world as if I were in prison? We have built barriers not only for the ants but for ourselves as well! And they call it living.

Unhappy people: what have you done to deserve such a fate? You are born like hungry, cold, homeless puppies on a rubbish dump. The rain whips down on you, the frosts bite you, and death threatens you. You can't escape anywhere; there's nowhere to hide. So where is all the justice you talk about, where are you all, clever people of this world?

Just throw the word 'compassion' out of the vocabulary. There is no such thing. There is no compassion on this earth.

Part Three

Escape from Silence

A thousand years ago Vyshgorod was a fine, large city, a rival to Kiev itself, the 'mother of Russian cities'. Later it failed to sustain the rivalry and declined, so that today it is just an ordinary village on the high banks of the Dnieper.

I had ten thousand roubles with me, so I decided to avoid places where lots of people were gathered: the most populous places had now become the most dangerous.

Degtyaryov had bought a stallion off a farmer in Vyshgorod. My job was to take him the money and bring back the horse; it was not the first time I had done it. I didn't keep to the main road, but went across the fields, past the Pochaina river, through the Dubki woods; and I was glad I had, because I did not meet a single soul.

It was rather strange that although as I was halfway through the village I could see some German soldiers in the distance, and felt something was wrong, instead of turning back and taking cover, I carried on as if hypnotized until I reached them. By this time I was in a state of panic and confusion, trying to work out what to do but unable to hit on anything.

They stopped me in their usual matter-of-fact way. One of them took me by the shoulder quite kindly and turned me back, while the other continued going from house to house.

I realized at once what was going on, immediately did what was expected of me, marching obediently into a farmyard where there were a dozen or so farmers, old men and boys, sitting around, some of them on the ground, with calm, indifferent, detached expressions on their faces. Just to be sure I checked with a boy of my own age:

'Is this a round-up for Germany?'

'That's right,' he sniffed. 'They're taking everybody.'

Leaning up against a wall, I started to try and think the situation out: Degtyaryov would now decide that I had run away with his money. True, when my mother went to him

299

and made a fuss, he would understand that I was in trouble, but by then I should be on my way to Europe. It had happened to me at last.

The round-up was carried out very quietly. The soldiers went from cottage to cottage, taking all the menfolk, and they all came quietly and silently, as I had done. The Germans no longer asked for any documents, because dates of birth were of no importance. Everything was quite straightforward and proper: if you got caught, it was your own look-out, and it was best to keep your mouth shut.

Then we were all driven out on to the roadway and something like a column of prisoners-of-war was drawn up. We moved along in one grey mass, raising the dust, with escorts on either side, their rifles under their arms. And without thinking I found myself shuffling along, my eyes to the ground: I really was being driven. I bumped up against the others and felt less like a human being than like an animal in a herd.

We were driven into a collective farmyard surrounded by buildings, and left among the remains of rusty carts and seed-drills. There were only a few escorts, and they were apparently so accustomed to people obeying them and following the crowd that they didn't even bother to come into the yard. Two of them simply stood at the gate to keep an eye on the yard while the others went off somewhere.

The peasants were sitting in a long row beneath the wall of the house, which looked as if it had been the village Soviet. In search of a place to sit I went to the corner of the building where I found a big stone to sit down on. True, it was out in the full heat of the sun, but all the shade had been taken.

However unfortunate I may have been, my clothes still marked me out from the villagers. Their clothes were all faded and torn, and they sat there, silent and utterly passive. The feeling that I too was just part of a herd would not leave me, hard as I tried to dismiss it.

What did it mean—that there was really no difference between a herd of cows and a herd of people? Cattle were driven to the slaughter, guided with big sticks and divided up into small groups, and the herd would obey and be broken up; each individual one would stand in line and move forward, one after the other, head to tail, to receive the fatal blow. If the herd were to rear up and to become conscious of its own strength, it could destroy the whole slaughter-house. Yet still they went to be killed one at a time, quietly and calmly, taking regular lunch-breaks.

And here, close by, just the other side of the fence, was another herd grazing, unheeding, unconcerned. 'Just animals,' we say, 'they don't understand.' Human beings understand everything, and still behave like a herd of cattle. Apparently we haven't advanced very far from the animal stage yet.

What was it like before the war? Year after year our herdsmen used to grab people one at a time or in groups, herd them in droves off to Siberia or shoot them, while the others just went on grazing, looking on, trembling with fright and waiting. So when the Germans drove that crowd of people on to Melnikov Street, and they sat there waiting their turn the next day and the day after, they no longer had anything to lose, and they didn't rear up or tear anything down, they simply wept and marched off in small groups to be dealt with. Yet around them there was what seemed to be a civilized city, in which others, including myself, re-mained, grazing quietly and swinging their tails, seeing, hearing, trembling with fright and remaining silent.

It is beyond comprehension. They slap us in the face, and we only shy back, like a herd—and stay silent. The herds-men have behind them centuries of experience to fall back on: they know that once you have scared people into silence with brazen self-confidence and the aid of sticks and cudgels, you can then do what you like with them. You have only to wave a straw at them and the herd will shy away.

It's the same as with a big bully in school who terrorizes a whole class single-handed. One succeeding the other, brazen scoundrels have reduced the people of Russia to the state of a munching herd of cattle which no longer knows which way to retreat in that land which is so deep in blood, so even and flat as a table that there is nowhere for the herd to hide, and it has no other land to go to.

When the soldiers saw something happening on the street and went to have a look, I got up from my stone and went to relieve myself round the corner. There, amongst the nettles, was a pile of bricks and pieces of iron. Stumbling over them and making more noise than was safe, I managed to reach the fence and scramble over it somehow. I was almost certain that the soldiers would catch me at once and send me back or shoot me.

But so far all was well. There was a lane going down to the left, but to the right it came out on the main street which I had come along. It was quite wide where it joined the street, making a sort of square in the middle of which stood a house with no fence round it. I stupidly walked out on to the main street and went around the house to the left, because that was the way I had come and the way I knew. Actually, I scarcely knew what I was doing and was simply counting on my luck.

And all went well. The guard on the gate did not notice me, although he could have done. But then, just ahead, appeared the soldiers who had left the yard. I picked up a stick from the ground, pulled my cap down over my forehead, made myself as small and insignificant as possible and, sniffing unconcernedly, walked past the soldiers who were busy talking to each other. When I was about twenty yards beyond them they apparently realized what had happened and shouted:

'Hey, sonny!'

I kept on walking, as though I had heard nothing.

'Hey!' they started shouting from behind me.

At that point I broke into a run. The bolts on the rifles rattled, but it was a winding street, and I dashed into a gateway, wide-eyed, my feet clattering on the stones like the sound of a motorcycle. I heard the sound of a shot, a SHOT AIMED AT ME personally, and almost immediately afterwards two more shots aimed at ME. But apparently they were only firing in my direction and couldn't actually see me.

Sensing with my whole body, and especially the back of my neck, the possibility of a bullet hitting me, I ran zig-zag down the lane leading down steeply to a little bridge which I intended to hide under. But while I was still thinking about it my legs carried me on of their own accord and I found myself among the vegetable gardens, and beyond them I recognized the field through which I had come.

Once again—simply because that was the very road I had come by—I ran across the open field. They could have shot me like a hare as I crossed it, but I kept running, because my thoughts couldn't keep up with my feet. I ran on, not looking round, in a state of blind terror, cross with myself only for not being able to run faster.

They did not chase me. I don't know why not. I went on running till I could no longer see properly, all the way to Dubki, where finally I collapsed and lay writhing on the grass, gulping in the air . . . I was safe for the time being.

Vyshgorod was now far behind me, in a bluish haze. I had a good drink of water from a puddle, splashed some over my head and slowly came to myself. I was alive!

Ah—perturbations and devaluations, but I was alive! So you thought you'd got me, you bastards? You've got the guns, but I've got my legs: how marvellous life is—how many times my legs alone have saved me! Thanks be to those life-saving legs! Because I need that life of mine.

No, it seems to me I know now why I am alive, scratch around among the market-stalls, gnaw horse's bones: I am growing up so as to be able to hate you and fight you. That's the task I set myself in my life: to fight against the evil ones who are turning the world into a prison and a stone crusher. Do you hear that, evil ones?

The Earth Ablaze

One night my mother woke me, saying:

'Get out of bed quickly and look out of the window!'

There was a blood-red light in the windows. Sparks were rising up above the railway embankment and pale tongues of flame showed along its whole length. To me, waking from a deep sleep, it seemed fantastic: how could a railway embankment catch fire? There was nothing but stones and rails and the cartridges we had buried there. It was like a nasty dream; but the earth really was burning.

'The factory's on fire,' my mother said.

Everything then fell into place. The Sport Factory was just out of sight on the other side of the embankment, so that only the tongues of flame were visible. We had no more sleep that night, and my mother kept walking about, clasping and unclasping her hands, wondering what would happen next. She looked after the boilers in the factory.

It was an ordinary engineering works which before the war had produced all sorts of sports equipment and beds. It now had very few employees, and the factory was organized on the principle of letting sleeping dogs lie. The work-people would all get together in a corner and gossip while one of them hammered on a piece of iron to let the boss know what effort they were putting into their jobs.

They would tinker with all sorts of junk, mending some things, breaking others. Everybody was working for himself and went away with cigarette-lighters, buckets and pans to use in barter. They would tell the boss that a lathe was broken. He would believe them and they would drag the lathe out on to the rubbish dump. A draughtsman would produce drawings that made no sense; they would construct something, riveting it and welding it together; then it would be discovered that everything had been done the wrong way round and they would do it all over again. This was all because the rather simple-minded boss was not in the least interested in running the factory. He had set himself up with excellent accommodation in the factory offices, where he used to lock himself in with the factory manager's daughter, Lyubka, while the manager in turn was left free to steal whatever he pleased.

My mother's job was to clean out the offices, act as a messenger and look after the boilers, and since she had to arrive before the others her working day lasted fifteen hours. In the winter she used to wake me at three o'clock in the morning and we would take a sledge and go along to the factory, where I would huddle in a corner and wait for her. She would then bring out a bundle of logs which I would drag back home, desperately afraid lest the patrol should set eyes on me. But what could I do? If it hadn't been for that wood we should have been completely frozen up that winter.

The morning after the fire, investigations and interrogations were started. A hundred army sledges had been brought in the evening before to have new runners fitted; they had been dragged inside the workshops, and had caught fire during the night. All the main workshops were burnt down, and nothing of the factory really remained. The boss stamped around in a state of hysteria, and the inquiries went on for several days. But the work-people said nothing. There had been nobody in the factory that night, apart from a senile watchman who had been asleep, and by the time he saw the place was ablaze there was nothing he could do about it on his own.

It was a very common occurrence. It seemed as though hatred for the Germans was in the very air. Moreover, there were rumours coming from the east, one more encouraging than the other: Stalin had changed his policy, the Soviet system was now something quite different, religion was recognized, the churches were being reopened, epaulettes and officers' ranks had been introduced into the army, and the country was no longer called the U.S.S.R. but Russia, as before the revolution . . . People were especially surprised by the business of the epaulettes. So much had happened because of them during the revolution! If a man wore epaulettes, that had meant he was a deadly enemy. When the Bolsheviks took officers prisoner they cut strips of skin on their shoulders in the form of epaulettes, and the officers in their turn cut stars in the bodies of captured Bolsheviks. And now, all of a sudden, the Soviet Army was to have epaulettes and officers' ranks! They were getting along happily with the stars. It should have happened long ago. They'd come to their senses at last. The people would be ready to go through fire and water for such a reasonable government and would forgive all its sins; it would be, after all, their own.

The German news bulletins began to be full of references to 'defensive battles', 'successful counter-attacks', 'shortening the lines' and 'the enemy succeeded in slightly . . .' When they abandoned a town they would make no announcement, but would say: 'Battles are proceeding to the west of Orel.' We understood perfectly well and envied Orel. We rejoiced at the victory in the Kursk bulge.

Whatever the papers write, however they may try to evade telling the truth, however convincing the lies they produce, the truth always gets through in the end. All evasions are in vain and are only a form of consolation for those who write them. The Soviet people have learnt to read between the lines, to hear between the words and over decades have developed their own bush telegraph. Nothing can be kept from it. On September 29th, 1941, for example, every single eye-witness of what happened in Babi Yar was executed, but the people of Kurenyovka knew all about it an hour after the first shots had been fired.

The rumours about Soviet reforms and German defeats gave rise to hope. For the Germans now stationed in Kiev, which was bursting with hatred for them, it was like living on a volcano. Every night something was blown up or burnt down, or some especially hated individual was murdered.

The cattle-cake factory beyond the tram terminus was burnt down, and next morning they said there was a message chalked up on the wall: THIS IS IN RETURN FOR BABI YAR. THE PARTISANS.

The bridge across the Dnieper at Darnitsa was destroyed by dynamite, and quantities of rolling-stock were blown up by mines. In Pechersk an enormous garage belonging to the SS was burnt down. In the musical comedy theatre mines were discovered only fifteen minutes before a gathering of officers in which Erich Koch* was due to take part. First in one place in the city and then in another leaflets would appear, and there was talk about the partisans on all sides.

Beyond Irpen and Dymer the partisans were liberating whole districts and setting up a new and just Soviet administration. The village police and elders came pouring in from the countryside around Ivankov, telling stories about the vast numbers of partisans who were on their way and from whom there was no escape. They organized detachments of the Kiev police and sent them off to Ivankov, and before their departure they got themselves drunk, danced and wept, because they knew they would not return alive.

The Germans and the police started going around only in groups and armed with rifles. Trenches were dug in the courtyard of the Kurenyovka police station and a strong pill-box was put up with its gun-openings facing the street.

They were everywhere, those elusive partisans, but how could I get in touch with them? At night I thought of

---

* The German Gauleiter in the Ukraine.

Grabarev down at Zverinets, but would he be likely to trust me if I turned up and said: 'Give me a leaflet'? He would again fill my cap with apples and laugh. Or what about the people at my mother's factory who had set fire to it? My mother and I were practically certain we knew who had done it, but since the fire they were trebly cautious and they would probably take me for a little spy. Tremendous sums of money were being paid for informing on anyone working in the underground, and the penalty for not informing was death.

Everything inside me turned upside down and I trembled to think that our troops were advancing and that partisans might perish. One day when I was sitting alone in the cottage I dug out a notebook, made some ink, thought a little and wrote the following on a sheet of paper:

COMRADES!

The Red Army is advancing and beating the Germans. Wait for them to come. Help the partisans and strike at the Germans. They will soon be done for. They know it and are scared. And the pollice, their dogs, are also trembling. We will settle accounts with them. Let them wait; we shall come.

Long live our glorius partisans!
Death to the German invaders!
Hurrah!

On the space that was left I drew a five-cornered star, filled it in heavily with ink, and the appeal acquired, in my view, a very heroic appearance. Especially that bold 'Hurrah!' which I had thought of myself—the rest I had copied from real leaflets. I tore a second page out of the notebook and was going to write a hundred copies. But my legs were itching to get on the move and stick the leaflet up somewhere. I already knew where: on the bridge, where lots of people passed by and would read it.

I scarcely waited to finish writing the second leaflet; then I put it on the stove to dry the wet ink on the star, mixed some paste in a tumbler and put it on the back of the leaflet, which I folded in two and stuffed inside my shirt. Holding it with two fingers, I ran off.

It was my bad luck that people kept coming by, so that

by the time the coast was clear the leaflet had dried out and stuck together. Now in a panic, I started to separate it, licked it wet again and stuck it all askew on the concrete wall, and, with my heart thumping violently, went away. That was all. Quite easy.

I opened the door and stopped in my tracks: my mother and Lena Gimpel were standing in the room reading the second example of my work, which I had left on the stove. I walked through to the coat-rack as though nothing had happened and took off my coat.

'Not too bad, on the whole,' Lena said. 'But if you've made up your mind to write leaflets, don't leave them where people can see them. You've got plenty of time to lay down your life; there's no hurry, they'll take it off you in the end anyway. What's the point of dying before you have to?'

'Tolik,' said my mother turning pale, 'are you trying to get yourself into Babi Yar?'

'And what was the point of teaching you to read at school,' said Lena with a shrug of the shoulders. 'The word "police" is spelt with just one "l", and "glorious" has an "o" in it. The star and the "Hurrah!" are silly—you can tell at once it was written by a small boy. They track down little fools like you by their handwriting.'

They didn't go on at me too much, but what they said was serious. They added that people as naive as I deserved only to die for nothing, and that I still had a great deal to understand and study, and that I must grow up—and learn.

I learnt.

At night, when my mother was asleep, by the light of a little lamp I started writing down stories from real life—of how Grandpa and I went off to barter things, and how the cattle-woman betrayed the Jewish boy. I set out to write a very heroic story about a noble leader of a revolt, like Hugo's *Bug-Jargal,* a hero who really beat the Germans at every turn. I hid the sheets of paper covered in writing inside my shirt the moment I heard the slightest noise. Later I used to roll them in a piece of oilcloth and bury them in the shed, in some dry sand in a corner. I don't suppose it would have been any use for publication under any political system because it was all too simply and sincerely set down.

Then bombing raids on Kiev started, and that told us that the front was moving towards us. First would come the hollow thuds of the anti-aircraft guns, and a stream of red tracer bullets would shoot up into the sky. The dark heavens would tremble from the drone of invisible aircraft.

The windows of my grandfather's room looked out on to the fields, so he would rush into our half of the house and we would open the windows and lean out on the sills, waiting for the show to begin; we were never kept waiting long.

The parachute flares lit the sky brightly. They hung in the air, grey smoke streaming out of them, and the whole city—the towers and roofs and the cupolas of St Sophia and the monastery—could be seen. The aircraft would drone away and keep circling for a long time, carefully and slowly selecting their targets, then the bombs would go off. One landed right on the Kobets leather factory.

We were not afraid of bombs, because they fell only on factories, bridges or barracks and never on people's houses, which served to demonstrate once again how good and just the Soviet government was. Everybody knew that before the raids the partisans sent back exact information about the military targets, and signalled to the planes with torches when the raids were on. To do that they had to be right next to the target flashing their torches, attracting the bombs on themselves.

On May 2nd, 1943, an important concert was due to take place in the opera house. Germans crowded round the entrance in festive mood; cars drove up and generals and their ladies got out of them, while the soldiers with their Russian prostitutes filled the gallery.

The raid began as it got dark. One bomb landed right on the opera house, fell straight through the ceiling of the auditorium and into the stalls. But things never seemed to go right with the theatres: the bomb didn't explode. It only killed six or seven Germans in the stalls, though pieces of their bodies landed on the stage and produced a terrible panic. The lights went out, everybody rushed for the doors, scrambling on top of one another, the maddened crowd staggered out of the theatre, and the performers ran down the street, still in their greasepaint and costumes.

This sort of thing went on right through the summer. The number of fires and explosions increased, and it seemed as though everything was infused with a sort of nervous tension, expectation and alarm.

An event of considerable importance to me personally took place on August 18th, 1943—I became fourteen years old, of age, officially liable to be shipped off to Germany and affected by all the orders being issued.

It was at about that time that we first saw the strange, black, heavy smoke rising over Babi Yar.

Babi Yar: The Final Phase

On August 18th, 1943, all the prisoners in the Babi Yar camp were drawn up on the central parade ground, military lorries drove into the camp, and helmeted SS-men with dogs jumped out of them.

Everybody realized that it was the beginning of the end.

A few days previously the camp had been bombed by Soviet planes. The bombs had fallen just round the perimeter of the camp—obviously aimed at destroying the outer fencing. But the wire had been damaged in only one place and was quickly repaired. Now the Germans seemed to think the time had come to wind the camp up altogether.

They brought out a table, lists of names and card-indexes. They made everybody stand in a line which then moved slowly past the table. Rieder studied the lists and ordered some prisoners to go to the left, others to the right. In the first place they selected exactly a hundred men—all of them especially dangerous political prisoners. The SS-men shouted: 'Move on! Quickly! Quickly!' showered blows on them, and the hundred men went through the gates.

'We've left our things in the dugouts!' some of them shouted.

'You won't be needing anything,' the Germans replied.

Once outside the gate they were told to take off their boots, which they left behind, and they marched off barefoot into the ravine. Davydov was among the hundred and was up at the front, thinking: 'Well, so this is the end . . .'

The falls of earth in the ravines had formed terraces, now thickly grown over with grass. The hundred men made their way down to the first terrace. To their great surprise they found a new dugout had recently been constructed there.

There were a lot of people and noise in the ravine. It was literally swarming with Germans, lots of SS-men and be-medalled officers. Cars had even driven into the place, and there were piles of all sorts of tools lying around.

They brought the hundred to a halt and asked whether there were any metal-workers or blacksmiths among them. A few men stepped forward; they were taken aside and led up on to a little earth ridge. The remainder were divided into groups of five, who were also taken up to the ridge. There was no shooting at all.

Davydov began to have hopes that it was still not the time for execution. He looked about as keenly as he could, but could not make out what was going on.

Finally he too was led up on to the ridge. There he saw a long rail and a great pile of chains; each man was having a chain fixed to him. A fat, stolid German was sitting by the rail among the prisoner-blacksmiths and he also was riveting the chains on the rail. He did Davydov's. It was the sort of chain you find in village wells. The German put it round his ankles, fixed on the collar and riveted it carefully together.

Davydov walked away, taking very short steps. The chain hurt him. Later it would bruise and cut his feet, and people learnt to put rags under it and tie it up with string to their belts so that it did not drag along the ground.

When all the chains had been fixed it was announced that they were going to eat, and they were given a good meal. It was proper soup with fat in it, really filling.

Then they were all given spades, and the clanking column of men was marched off into a branch of the ravine and ordered to start digging. They dug and dug, right through to the evening, making a large, uneven trench, without having the slightest idea what it was for, though it was quite clear that the Germans were looking for something. They were watching all the time to see whether anybody had come across anything in the course of their digging. But nobody had.

For the night the hundred men were herded into the dugout. It was pitch-dark inside, but they could hear outside the sound of the voices of the strong guard on duty. A wooden tower had been built in front of the entrance, with a machine-gun mounted on it and aimed straight at the entrance.

Next morning they were again driven out into the ravine. There were just as many people about and the same shouting and swearing. A tall, well-built, very smart officer with a riding-crop was shouting hysterically. He was about thirty-five and his name was Topaide, and, when he listened carefully, Davydov realized to his amazement that it was Topaide who had been in charge of the first executions of Jews in 1941.

Topaide had not been there the previous day. He had only sent a plan of the sand-pits showing where the bodies had been buried, but the Germans on the spot had not been able to make any sense of it and had started digging in the wrong place. He shouted at them hysterically, called them all idiots, said they didn't know how to read plans and had been looking in the wrong place. He ran across and kicked the earth with the toe of his boot, saying: 'Here! Here!'

So they began to dig where he showed them. Half an hour later they came across the first corpses.

The Germans treated Topaide with great deference and among themselves, either seriously or ironically, they used to call him the 'execution expert'. Now he had become an expert in excavations. He spent the whole day going around the ravine, pointing things out, giving orders and explanations. From time to time his whole face was violently contorted into a most unpleasant expression, a sort of tic, and he seemed to be a bundle of nerves, on the verge of hysteria. He couldn't let a minute go by without shouting or rushing about or hitting someone. It was clear that his 'expertise' had not left him unscathed.

The work gathered speed. So that nobody should see what was going on the Germans quickly put up some screens around the ravine, camouflaged them with branches of trees and in some places made artificial plantations. It was quite

BABI YAR 313

obvious that whatever was going on there, it was intended
to be kept the closest secret.

The road from the city to the ravine was blocked. Lorry
drivers had to get down from the lorries well before the
ravine and hand them over to guards who drove them on
into the Yar. The lorries were loaded with rails, blocks of
stone, timber and barrels of oil.

That was the way the final phase of Babi Yar began; that
was the first attempt to erase it from the pages of history.
From the very beginning nothing seemed to go right. Topaide
rushed about the place, raging and fuming, and the Germans
became more and more nervous, beating the prisoners
horribly and even shooting some of them.

New groups arrived from the camp to help the first detachment, and in a few days there were more than three hundred
prisoners at work there. They were divided up into brigades,
and the carefully planned, productive labour of those brigades
was a model of German order and method.

The DIGGERS dug the earth out of the pits and exposed
the bodies; a sort of grey-blue in colour, they had been
squashed down flat and caught up in each other. The job
of hauling them out was the most frightful ordeal. Some of
the bodies, notably those of children, had no injuries on
them at all—they were the ones which had been buried
alive. But the bodies of some of the women, especially of the
younger ones, had, on the contrary, been sadistically mutilated, probably just before they died.

The Germans held their noses on account of the stench,
and some of them nearly fainted. The guards sat on the sides
of the ravine, all of them with a bottle of vodka stuck in
the sand between their legs which they would take a swig
at from time to time. As a result all the Germans in the
ravine were permanently drunk.

The diggers were not given any vodka, and at first they
too felt sick. But they gradually grew accustomed to the
work. They had no choice, anyway, but to keep at it, their
chains clanking around their feet.

The HOOKERS pulled the bodies out and dragged them to
the fires. They were issued with specially forged metal rods
with a handle at one end and a hook at the other. The hooks
had been made, incidentally, to Topaide's own design.

After a good deal of experimenting Topaide had evolved a way of dragging the bodies out without them being torn to pieces. This involved sticking the hook under the chin and pulling on the lower jaw-bone. In that way the whole body came along and could be dragged to its destination.

Sometimes the bodies were so firmly stuck together that two or three of them came out on one hook. It was often necessary to hack them apart with axes, and the lower layers had to be dynamited several times.

The PROSPECTORS, or *Goldsuchern,* as the Germans called them, had pliers with which they pulled out gold fillings and crowns. Their job was to examine every corpse as it went to be burnt, remove any rings or other jewellery and see whether there were any coins or valuables in the pockets of those that had clothes on them. It was all collected in buckets. A guard stood near by and watched to see that no gold was stolen or thrown into the sand.

The CLOAKROOM ATTENDANTS removed from the dead everything that was still whole. Good quality boots which had been buried under the earth for a year or two were removed. Occasionally they came across woollen garments or kit-bags which had survived. The Germans loaded it all carefully into lorries and took it away, though for what purpose no one knew, since it all stank terribly. Anyway, they managed to gather up quite a lot of junk: only the very bottom layers—the Jews—were naked; the middle layers were in their underwear, while the more recently executed were fully dressed.

The BUILDERS had the job of constructing the fires. They were taken under strong guard across to the other side of the ravine to the Jewish cemetery, where the Germans showed them which granite tombstones to break up.

The prisoners pulled the graves and headstones to pieces, carried them into the ravine and laid the flat pieces out in rows. On these surfaces, again under the professional guidance of Topaide, the master of all trades, they built quite well-designed and technically efficient furnaces, with chimneys to make them draw, complicated flues and grids. They were first packed full of wood, and then the bodies were laid on top of it on the grid, heads outwards. The second layer of bodies was laid crosswise to the first, then came a layer of wood, and so on, until the pile was about ten feet high and twenty feet square.

Each pile consisted of roughly two thousand bodies. To complete the pile they laid planks up against it, as is done on building work, and the bodies were carried up them. The completed pile was sprayed with oil pumped from a barrel into a hose.

The STOKERS got the fire going underneath and also carried burning torches along the rows of projecting heads. The hair, soaked in oil, immediately burst into bright flame—that was why they had arranged the heads that way. The stack of bodies then became one gigantic bonfire, and the heat given out became quite unbearable. In the ravine and for a long way around it there was a heavy smell of burning hair and roasting meat. The stokers stirred it all around with long pokers such as metal-workers use, then raked up the ashes and cinders. When the stove had cooled down they cleaned it out, laid the fire again, replaced the burnt-out grid and prepared to load up again.

The CRUSHERS were the ones who dealt with the ashes. Using ordinary wooden rams on granite blocks from the cemetery, they crushed any bones which had not been completely burnt by the fire and then passed them through a wire sieve, again looking for gold.

The GARDENERS were so called because their job was to load the ashes on to barrows and distribute them under escort around the environs of Babi Yar and scatter them over the vegetable gardens. They were better off than the others, because they had a chance to dig up potatoes in the gardens, bring them back to the ravine and cook them in old tins over the heat still remaining in the furnaces.

This was a very important additional source of food to sustain the prisoners. Because after having fed them well the first day, the Germans never did so again, and the prisoners were ravenously hungry.

One of them, for example, unable to bear the smell of roasting meat any longer, started to eat the human flesh, pulling pieces of it out of the fire. At first the Germans didn't notice him, but when by chance they found what he was doing they shot him on the spot, and threw him on the fire. Moreover they were terribly embarrassed by the degree of savagery which he had displayed.

Davydov spent time in several different brigades. He worked at the cemetery, dragged corpses and helped build the fires. He recalls that at first the terrible smell and all the business with the corpses made him feel sick and that he nearly fainted, but that he became accustomed to it as time went on. Apparently a man can get used eventually to anything.

They worked till they dropped during the day, then at night slept the sleep of the dead in the dugout. They shaved their scraggly beards off by fire—a well-tried method of shaving that had been used in Soviet concentration camps. The day was spent in a state of feverish anxiety not to stop a bullet and to get hold of some potatoes. They quarrelled among themselves, made it up again, played tricks and cracked jokes. 'Do you think we didn't tell each other jokes?' says Davydov. 'Whenever anyone went to piss, they would all roar with laughter. The laughter of the gallows. And if the guards saw what was happening they also had to grin. They could also, apparently, see the funny side.'

Meanwhile routine executions went on as before in Babi Yar, except that the dead were no longer buried but thrown straight on the fire. And any prisoner already on his last legs and no longer able to work was also thrown on to it. Alive.

The Germans were in a great hurry. It was nothing but 'Quickly! Quickly! Schnell!' But there was such an enormous number of corpses. Davydov had to work on clearing a pit in which there were exactly four hundred of the hostages who had been shot on Eberhard's orders. He also opened up graves with a hundred and with three hundred hostages. Everything was very precise, and Topaide knew everything; it was he who pointed out the places—he remembered absolutely everything.

(Incidentally, the name of Topaide never featured among the Nazi criminals who were later brought to trial. It is possible that he was killed, although Gestapo men like him, who were working back behind the lines, usually succeeded in going into hiding. Therefore it is by no means impossible that he is still alive . . . I wonder if he has cured himself of his nervous tic? But nobody was in fact tried specifically for Babi Yar, and nobody knows what happened to the German and Russian administration of the camp, headed by Radomsky and Rieder.)

Before the curtain came down on Babi Yar all sorts and kinds of 'enemies' were thrown into the fire, ranging from some crank who had merely told a joke, and such 'saboteurs' as a baker who had kept a loaf of bread aside, to the genuine partisans and the very last Communists. There were some members of the Communist Party who had succeeded in proving that they had joined the party, like the majority of people, for purely careerist reasons—'We were just on the books and paid our dues'—and who for nearly two years had not been arrested. They had simply had to report regularly to the police. But it didn't save them. Now they were all sent to Babi Yar. The Germans killed off even their own servants and hangers-on, because they knew too much.

The process of liquidating people now followed a different pattern. The mobile gas-chambers arrived from the city with people alive in them, and it was only at Babi Yar that the gas was turned on. Stifled cries could be heard coming from the body of the van and then wild banging on the door. The van would stand there, the motor running and the Germans smoking away quite calmly. Then everything would be silent, the Germans would open the doors, and some prisoners would set about unloading the van. The bodies inside would still be warm, dripping with sweat, practically all of them with excreta and urine over them, and some of them might be not quite dead. They would be put on the fire. Davydov recalls that some of them would writhe in the fire and throw themselves about as if they were alive.

On one occasion a gas-van arrived full of women. When the usual procedure was over and the shouting and banging had died down, the door was opened. After the fumes had cleared the van was seen to be packed full of naked girls.

There were more than a hundred of them, pressed tightly together, sitting on each other's knees. They all had their hair done up in scarves, as women do when they take a bath. They had probably been told when they were put into the van that they were on their way to the baths. Many were found to have rings and watches, lipsticks and other small things hidden in their headscarves. The drunken Germans hooted with laughter, explaining that they were waitresses from the Kiev night-clubs, and shouted to the prisoners: 'Take one for yourself! Go on—try fucking one, have a go at her!' When Davydov lifted them and laid them on the stack, covered in filth and still warm, the breath would come out of their mouths with a faint noise, and he got the impression again that they were alive but had simply lost consciousness. They were all burnt on the fire.

Some very important officials drove up in elegant limousines, and shouted at the Germans working in the Yar that the work was going too slowly. There were not enough people to cope with it so on several occasions they simply let the new arrivals out of the gas-vans, put them straight into chains and set them to work.

They started taking the prisoners outside the camp limits, to a near-by anti-tank trench some two hundred yards long. It was crammed full to the very top with the bodies of Red Army officers—the prisoners could tell that from the uniforms, kit-bags and binoculars. There were apparently between twenty-five and thirty thousand of them. Prisoners were also sent to open up the graves at the Kirillov Hospital. The ground in the ravine and all around it for nearly half a square mile was literally stuffed with corpses.

In Babi Yar they could hear the distant sound of gunfire come from the other side of the Dnieper. The prisoners knew that the final fire would be lit for them. The Germans did not in any case regard them seriously as human beings and at the morning roll-call they would report:

'Three hundred and twenty-five *Figuren* on parade!'

Figuren meant what it said—figures, shapes, something which could not be regarded as a human being. That was also a form of humour.

The prisoners did not wash, because they were not given any water; many of them could hardly stay on their feet and were covered with festering wounds, burns and filth from the corpses. Some among them were old enough to have served sentences in Soviet concentration camps before the war, and they said there was no comparison. Compared with Babi Yar any Soviet camp was a health resort.

However, there is no camp in the whole world from which it is impossible to escape. This was, incidentally, the opinion of a former secret police agent, who had been a senior official in the security services, and had had a lot to do with prison camps in the Ukraine. He was so to speak an expert on the subject, and he now worked as a stoker on the furnaces.

They called him Fyodor Yershov. All that was known about him was that he had been in charge of various explosions and acts of sabotage, and had been caught. Who knows —maybe it was he who blew up the monastery. All particulars about him must have been kept at 33 Vladimirskaya, but for some reason the security service did not reveal the name of this particular employee or give him a posthumous award.

In other circumstances Fyodor Yershov would have been a man for the prisoners to fear. But he was now in the same position as they were; he tried fanatically to persuade them to organize a revolt and the others listened closely to what he, as an expert, had to say. He discussed it with the men who were working next to him or who slept on neighbouring bunks in the dugout. Little groups of conspirators were formed who debated the various escape plans at every convenient moment.

Some put forward the idea of attacking the guards in broad daylight, seizing their guns and scattering in all directions under cover of fire. Fyodor Yershov was against this idea. The guards in a concentration camp were always ready for that sort of thing, he said, and moreover the prisoners were all in chains, and too weak to deal with the burly Germans.

Among the prisoners there were some former lorry-drivers. One of them, Vladislav Kuklya, proposed seizing a couple of the lorries which brought wood to the camp, or even a gas-van, and crashing through the guard in them. It was a fantastic plan, and very tempting because of the daring involved. But it would have involved far too long a drive through the ravine and then through the city, with Germans and police everywhere. It would have been simply a very dramatic form of suicide.

The group which had been sent to work at the Kirillov Hospital requested permission to make their dash for freedom independently, because their guard was relatively small. It is possible that they might have succeeded, but Yershov was strongly opposed to it. 'You will get away yourselves, but it will be curtains for the rest of us then. No, we must all act at the same moment.'

In a separate corner of the dugout, however, some young lads put their heads together and, without consulting anyone else, started desperately digging a trench through which to escape at night. They did not have time to finish it in one night, and next day the Germans discovered the whole plot and lined all seventeen of them up outside. One of them turned out to be Kuklya, who denied he had had any part in it. Topaide demanded:

'Was this man with you?'

'I think so . . .' muttered one of the lads.

Topaide didn't understand what he said and turned to another prisoner who knew German and had been an interpreter:

'What did he say?'

'He says he wasn't among them.'

They let Kuklya go back to his work, but the other sixteen were made to kneel down on the spot and were killed by a bullet in the back of the head.

There was also the case of a man who had kept himself to himself, and who carried out a very daring escape in daylight. Nobody knew his name. He was working apart from the others and moved off, apparently to relieve himself. Suddenly he jumped into the ravine, dashed off and hid in one of the gullies leading to the cemetery. The alarm was raised; there was a burst of shooting, work was stopped, and dozens of Germans raced after him, but they did not find him. He had managed to undo his chains and was thus able to run fast. In their fury that day the Germans killed twelve prisoners and shot the officer who had been in command of the patrol and was responsible for guarding the escaped man. After that they mounted machine-guns at the entrances to the gullies.

The various escape plans were dropped one after the other, and it was Fyodor Yershov's plan which was accepted in the end: to break out of the dugout and attack the guard at night. This was also likely to end in disaster, but doing it in darkness offered at least the hope that a few of them might get away.

The dugout was really a deep bunker with a narrow path leading sharply down into it. A machine-gun was aimed straight at the entrance from the tower outside and at night-time there was a heavy guard right round the dugout. It had no windows and the one and only door, serving as both entrance and exit, was made of wire netting, to let in air so that the people inside should not suffocate. From time to time the guards would shine their torches through the wire to make sure everything was quiet in the dugout. The door, or gate, was locked with an enormous padlock.

The drunken guards used to get bored standing around all night and would occasionally make all the prisoners get up and come outside, where they would pretend to be setting up an execution under the floodlights. It was a frightful form of practical joke, because the prisoners would take it seriously. Then the guards would burst out laughing and drive them all back inside. The nights were dark, wet and foggy.

Somebody kept insisting that they should wait until the guards put on the next 'performance', get their irons off and rush them. The trouble was that the chains couldn't be taken off quickly; they needed preparing to the point where they were only just holding. And how could anyone tell which night a 'show' was going to be put on?

It is scarcely credible, but there was an informer even in that dugout. There are informers and traitors everywhere. This one was a former police-chief from Fastov by the name of Nikon. The scoundrel got sent to Babi Yar for some very serious offence; he tried hard to get into the Germans' good books, was ever ready to maltreat the prisoners brutally—he was as strong as an ox—and eavesdropped on all conversations. It is by no means impossible that the deaths of the sixteen young men were his work. If that jackal had got to know about the escape plan he would have betrayed it immediately.

That was why very few people were let into the secret until the last moment. This in itself made it more difficult for everybody to join in the action during the regular 'performance'.

'We've got to undo the lock,' Yershov said, 'then tell everyone to get ready, remove the chains and only then break out. We shall get away with it, lads! Maybe half of us will make it, perhaps only a quarter or even five of us. But someone must get out and get through to our own folk to tell them what went on here.'

The work going on in the ravine by this time resembled a major construction job. The Germans brought in building machinery, an excavator and a bulldozer, which ground away all day long opening up the trenches. The excavator had a grab on the end which was lowered into the trench on wire ropes and, almost like a human hand, gathered up a bundle of corpses and brought them out to the surface, dropping pieces of body and heads as it did so.

(The Germans themselves called Babi Yar a *Baustelle*, meaning a building site. Babi Yar appeared in German official documents under the title of a 'building company', and had a bank account of its own, because all that machinery and equipment had to be financed in some way.)

Another important circumstance ought to be mentioned here. The prisoners used to come across all sorts of unlikely objects, especially on the bodies of the Jews killed in 1941, because they had been preparing for a long journey and, although they had been stripped naked, every single one of them had found a way of keeping something of importance to himself. Some skilled tradesmen were found still to have tools on them which they had not parted with right up to the grave itself. On some of the women were found scissors, hair-pins and nail-files. Pocket-knives occasionally turned up. Somebody once found a bottle of 'Red Moscow' eau-de-Cologne and was going to drink it, but was persuaded to spray the dugout with it instead.

They often found keys, too, in the pockets of the dead people—keys of flats and sheds, sometimes whole bunches of them.

Yershov divided all the people who knew about the plan into groups of ten, each responsible for preparing its own part of the escape. The group which had been given the task of undoing the lock collected keys. They sorted over hundreds of them again and again, trying them out during the dinner-break when they were all herded back into the dugout but not locked in. Some of them would crowd around the gateway while Kuklya quickly tried the keys in the padlock.

On one of those days a prisoner by the name of Yasha Kaper, one of the very few Jews who, by some miracle, had still survived, found a key which fitted the lock. Someone on his way to his death in 1941 had brought it with him to Babi Yar, never suspecting that in 1943 Yasha Kaper would find it and that it would save several people's lives.

Meanwhile others were collecting, bringing into the dug-out and hiding away in the walls everything that might be of the slightest use to remove the chains or serve as a weapon. David Budnik had the good fortune to find a pair of pliers and a hammer. One of the *Goldsuchern*, Zakhar Trubakov, had the pliers issued to him by the Germans themselves for pulling out teeth—he was entitled to them, so to speak.

One day an officer struck one of the prisoners for some minor offence and as the man fell down something rattled inside his shirt. They immediately stripped him and found some rusty scissors. Topaide went for him:

'What are these for?'

'I wanted to cut my hair.'

Topaide did not believe him, and they proceeded to beat the prisoner and kept on asking him why he needed the scissors. The rest looked on, terrified lest he should give the game away. That was a moment when the whole plan might have fallen through. But the prisoner did not talk, and he had already lost consciousness when they threw him on to the fire. And nobody, unfortunately, even knows what his name was.

There was one young man amongst them from the Northern Bukovina—Yakov Steuc, an educated man, who knew several languages and had studied at one time in Bucharest. They used him as an interpreter when something had to be put across to the prisoners, and it was he who had saved Kuklya from being shot. He said:

'It will work out even better than we think. Have courage, lads! You have no idea how cowardly and superstitious the Germans are. We must break out with wild shouts and whistles, and they'll take fright, they'll be scared stiff, you'll see.'

The key was ready, the weapons gathered, night followed night, but a suitable moment never came. As luck would have it, the guard was strengthened and at night they kept coming to the dugout, shining their torches in and checking up. Yershov proposed:

'Tonight!'

But the majority were in favour of making it the next night. 'Tonight' meant going to almost certain death, and nobody wanted to die that day. And supposing a better opportunity turns up tomorrow, they thought.

Yershov agreed. He was a strange, highly-strung, fanatical individual, who encouraged and persuaded all the others but was himself exhausted and weak, and apparently cherished no illusions about his own prospects. On one occasion he told Davydov:

'It's a crazy scheme, Volodya, and it'll do me no good. I'm already over forty. It's the younger and stronger ones who'll get away—you, for example . . .'

It was a pure accident, a coincidence of dates, that the escape took place on September 29th, exactly two years after the first executions had taken place in Babi Yar. Some of the prisoners hoped superstitiously that it would be their lucky day.

The team working at the Kirillov Hospital returned to the camp, Yakov Steuc among them. On the way back he was chatting about nothing in particular with the escort, an elderly, talkative sergeant-major by the name of Vogt. On previous occasions Vogt had tried to cheer them up, saying: 'When the work's finished, it seems they're going to move you to Zhitomir.' But on this occasion the old fellow whispered to Steuc anxiously:

'Morgen—kaput—you're for it tomorrow.'

Why did he warn them? Just out of kindness? In any case the prisoners could see for themselves that the camouflage screens were being taken down and the tools packed away. There was still, however, one brand-new furnace.

That night two large cans of boiled potatoes were brought into the dugout. That also was rather odd. What had happened? Were they going to waste, so the Germans decided to let the prisoners eat them after all?

'I'm opening the gate tonight,' Kuklya announced.

Fyodor Yershov sent the word around: 'We go today. Steady nerves.' He also gave the order for Nikon to be put out of the way. Nikon's neighbour in the bunks, Boris Yaroslavsky, was ordered to kill him. The poor man's hands trembled as he said:

'But look, fellows, I've never even killed a cat in all my life.'

He was a kindly, intelligent man. They gave him a hammer.

They waited for the very middle of the night. Somewhere around two o'clock Kuklya poked his hand through the netting, put the key in the lock and proceeded to open it. He gave it one turn and the lock made a loud click. Kuklya just managed to pull his hand back and retreat, covered in a cold sweat.

The guards heard the noise, started to look about them, came down to the gate and shone their lights in. Everybody in the dugout was lying on his bunk. The Germans walked away, went on talking for some time up above, occasionally striking matches.

The lock needed two turns to open it. Kuklya admitted in a whisper that he could hardly control his hands. The others reassured him, but he muttered:

'Well, lads, I hope at least there's a change of guard. Otherwise, if it clicks a second time . . .'

It was true that the guard was soon due to be changed, and they waited for that. Kuklya pushed his hand through again, turned the key very, very slowly, and the lock made no noise. Kuklya fell back into Davydov's arms bathed in sweat.

'It's O.K.!'

'Wake everybody, get your chains off and get hold of your weapons!' Fyodor Yershov ordered.

A dull thud was heard, a groan and then a second thud. Yaroslavsky had killed Nikon, and that was a sort of signal. Sounds of activity could be heard in the dugout. Many of them found it too much for their nerves; they all started to hurry and there was a lot of scuffling and clattering, scratching and talking. All of them were trying, half crazed, to remove the metal collars from their ankles as quickly as they could with all sorts of chisels, knives and scissors. In the quietness of the camp it seemed as though a real din was going on, the guards rushed down to the gate, demanding:

'What's the matter?'

Yakov Steuc answered for the rest in German:

'They're fighting down here over your potatoes.'

Everybody in the dugout quieted down, and the Germans started to laugh. Of course, they found it funny that the prisoners they were going to shoot the next day were fighting to fill their stomachs with potato.

Twenty minutes passed. Quietly they opened the gates right back.

'Run for it, lads!' Yershov shouted.

And up the narrow exit, ten steps at a time, rushed the crowd of prisoners, uttering savage howls, screams and whistles.

As it turned out, Steuc was right. For the first few seconds there was not a single shot. The Germans were taken completely by surprise, dumbfounded. Dozens of prisoners managed to scramble out on top before the machine-gun began to fire. But the dogs set on them immediately.

It was dark and foggy, and impossible to make out what was going on: someone was struggling with a dog with his bare hands, someone else struck a German over the head with a hammer and they rolled on the ground, locked together.

They did not succeed in capturing the machine-gun. But it was difficult for the Germans themselves to use it, because they were unable to distinguish between their own men and the prisoners. Rockets were fired into the sky, and there was shooting the whole length of Babi Yar. Prisoners were running in all directions, some with chains still dangling from a leg and there was firing on all sides, as if it were the front. Motorcyclists were dashing along the roads and footpaths.

Davydov ran round the dugout, bumped into one German and then another, dashed off into the darkness and, unable to see his way, ran right into the camp. He felt his way along the wire and by the vegetable gardens met Leonid Kharash. The two of them ran in the direction of some cottages in the distance. It was already getting light; the shooting was still going on, there were cars and motorcycles driving around and much shouting and swearing to be heard.

Davydov and Kharash caught sight of a woman doing something outside her house.

'Lady—hide us!'

She looked at them and seemed about to faint.

'God! You must be from the Yar! I've got children; they'll shoot me.'

Then her sister came running out.

'Get into the chicken house under the straw!'

They crept in underneath the straw, but asked her:

'You won't give us away?'

'No, my boys, we'll do you no harm.'

Later she went and made them some soup and brought them a whole bowlful of it—real, delicious Ukrainian *borshch*.

Those two sisters were called Natalya and Antonina Petrenko. Davydov visited them later in Kurenyovka, on Tiraspol Street, where they still live. Only 15 of the 330 prisoners escaped. They later joined the Soviet Army and some were killed at the front. Fyodor Yershov did not succeed in getting out of the Yar, but perished there, just as he anticipated. Boris Yaroslavsky was also killed there. There are today nine people still living who took part in that unique revolt. Vladimir Davydov is working as foreman of a building site in Kiev. Yakov Steuc teaches German and Greek in the Kaluga teachers' training college. Others are still alive and working in Kiev: Vladislav Kuklya, Yakov Kaper, Zakhar Trubabkov, David Budnik, Semyon Berland, Leonid Ostrovsky, and Grigori Yovenko. Every year on September 29th they can be seen, with Dina Pronicheva, at Babi Yar, whither many people make their way unofficially to honour the memory of those who perished there.

A Word from the Author

A former high-ranking officer in the Gestapo declared recently in an interview that there had never been any death camps, ovens or gas-chambers, that all such things had been invented by propagandists. He stated, quite simply, that they had *never existed*. He was not as mad as he might seem. He goes on living and working like an automaton, conditioned by rules based on the principle of 'Keep on lying—

something will stick; call black white, death happiness, the Leader a god, and promise mountains of gold in the future—there will always be people ready to believe you.'

For example, for many long decades there were officially declared to be NO concentration camps in the U.S.S.R. And, officially, *there are none today*. You have just read in this book how the Soviet N.K.V.D. blew up the Kreshchatik and the monastery and announced at once that it was 'a crime committed by the German-Fascist invaders', while the Gestapo organized a complete 'building company' to demonstrate that Babi Yar *did not exist*.

All these systems based on lies and the use of force have exposed very clearly and turned to their own advantage one of man's weakest spots: his credulity.

There is a great deal wrong with the world. So some benefactor comes along with a plan for changing everything. The plan demands sacrifices today against a guarantee of universal blessings when it is complete. A few inflammatory words and a few bullets in the heads of the sceptics, and in no time at all millions of people are carried away with enthusiasm. It's amazingly crude, but it works!

Then, with the very best of intentions and the selfless heroism of devoted young boys and girls, patriotic mothers and grey-haired old men, it all starts—the acts of aggression, the purges, the informing, the executions, the humiliations and the cynicism. And I suspect it doesn't much matter *what* the objective really is. It is quite sufficient to assert, without adducing any proof, that it will be marvellous. They will believe.

I did not write this book simply to recall the past: I am writing *today* about the occupation of Kiev, which I happened to witness and which is well documented; because the same sort of thing is happening now; and there is no guarantee whatever that even more sinister events will not occur tomorrow. Not the slightest guarantee.

Just reckon up what proportion of the world's population is today living under political systems based on force.

The world has learnt nothing. It has become only a more gloomy place. It is crammed with misguided puppets and

unthinking blockheads who, with the light of fanatical conviction in their eyes, are ready to shoot at any target their
leaders may command, and trample underfoot any country
they are sent to; and it is frightful to think of the weapons
they have in their hands today.

If you tell them out loud, to their faces, that they are
being deceived and that they are no more than cannon fodder and tools in the hands of scoundrels, they won't listen.
They will say it is only a malicious slander. And if you
produce facts, they just won't believe you. They will say:
'Such things never happened.'

Ask people who have lived a little longer in this world. When
the first reports came from Germany about the Nazi death
camps, the rest of the world did not believe them. People
were much more disposed to believe the fair words of the
scoundrels. Many of those who ended their days as smoke
from the chimneys of Buchenwald started by believing.

Let us recall that the Jews of Kiev believed that they were
being sent to Palestine, and that even when they could hear
the shooting they went on discussing how their belongings
would be 'divided up equally' when they got there. How
many such Palestines has the world already been promised?

You suggest that something has changed? Only for the
worse. With the fanaticism of a suicidal maniac, mankind
reaches for the poisoned honey, whoever offers it to them;
there really is no limit to human credulity.

People will put their trust in absolutely anybody—in Lenin
or in Stalin, in Hitler or in Khrushchev, in Mao Tse-tung or
Brezhnev, and in all sorts of Fidel Castros lower down the
scale. They excuse the crimes that are committed because of
the grandeur of the ultimate aims; they deny the facts and
put their faith in the mere good intentions.

All right, go on believing . . .

If civilization is in danger today, if it is fated to decline and
perish, it will do so with the enthusiastic assistance of cred-
ulous people. They seem to me more dangerous than the most
brazen leaders, because everything is done with their co-
operation. Meanwhile their numbers are becoming depress-
ingly large, and one can discern in the future such Babi Yars,

Oswięçims and universal Hiroshimas as we have not yet dreamed of.

I would like to be mistaken. I pray that I am.

I tell only the story of how it all comes about.

I do beg you, all human beings, to come to your senses.

Kiev Will Be No More

1. *When Gunfire Is Good to Hear*

The rumble of gunfire reached us from across the Dnieper. Darnitsa, Svaromye, Vigurovshchina and Trukhanov Island were already ablaze. The railway station was crammed full of Germans and Volksdeutsche being evacuated from the city. Refugees passing through from Rostov, Kharkov and Poltava said the Germans left only the bare earth as they retreated.

The bridges over the Dnieper were blown up, along with the people being driven from the other bank who were on them at the time. Their bodies fell into the Dnieper with the girders from the bridge.

At night Soviet reconnaissance scouts appeared out of nowhere on the beach of Trukhanov Island and shouted: 'We shall soon liberate you!'

The last, frantic arrests were taking place. Grabarev from Zverinets was executed: it really had been no accident that he stayed behind.

Everything that could be removed from the factories was carried away; in the offices they even unscrewed the door-handles and window catches and removed the lavatory basins. The Germans were getting out.

Quite by chance, the old mare Mashka had a bit of luck. A German offered Degtyaryov five sacks of grain, and they had to be fetched, so Mashka was harnessed up and I went along as driver.

The German soldier was a very pleasant, smiling character.

The sun was warm, and he unbuttoned his tunic and lay back in the cart.

I flicked Mashka with the reins, but she was determined not to trot. Then the soldier asked me, in sign-language, to let him drive the cart. I moved over.

Obviously knowing what he was doing, he took the reins, whipped up the old mare and off she went at the gallop. The cart began to rattle and bump about, nearly overturning; the soldier stood up, and it was clear that he had worked on a farm somewhere. His eyes sparkled, and he drove the cart with much relish and pleasure, immediately becoming a very ordinary and familiar figure, like some Ivan Svinchenko from Litvinovka.

I was in a good mood too, and I wanted to talk to him, but my German vocabulary was very small. I tried to dig something out of my memory.

'What's that?' I asked in German, pointing to the columns of smoke on the horizon. 'Is it fire—fire, eh?'

The soldier looked at me and smiled, as if to say: What are you asking for, as though you didn't know, and spreading out his arms he said:

'That's the war, sonny. That's the Bolsheviks.'

'Where's the front?' I asked.

'Front here, right here.' The soldier let the whip hang down and his arms hung loosely at his sides. 'Dnieper—front. Dnieper—frontier. Here is peace. Bolshevik there, German here.'

That's the way you'd like it, I thought to myself. So you'd be ready to settle for that now, would you? But you won't get away with it.

'I have a little boy like you.' The German pointed at me and patted his pocket. 'Kurt—very good boy.'

I asked him to show me, knowing that it would soften him up. I never came across a German who didn't carry photographs with him, and when they showed them they always became very sentimental, sad and thoughtful.

The soldier eagerly brought out his wallet. There was his Frau, with an infant in her arms, a very plain-looking woman with a pockmarked face. And there was the little boy, looking rather like Shurka Matso. The soldier was trying to explain something to me by drawing little circles on the picture with his finger; I didn't understand him, but nodded none the less. At that moment we went round a bend, the cart tipped and he put his arm round me to make sure I did not fall off. Just like a father caring for his son. I was very moved by this: I had already forgotten my father long ago.

We drove into the grain store; the soldier confidently produced his papers, carried out the sacks and humped them on to the cart. That was the way to steal! Meanwhile I had thought up some sentences to use on the way back, and when we set off I said haltingly:

'Have you ever killed a man?'

He answered quite simply:

'Ja, ja.'

'How many?'

He used the whip on the mare, nodded his head:

'Plenty. War.'

'Jews? Women? Children?' I pressed him with questions.

At last he understood what I was getting at, eyed me a little, then smiled knowingly and wagged a finger at me, saying:

'Bolsheviks!'

I studied his hands. They were the big hands of a farm worker, with thick, calloused fingers and broken nails. He was obviously a very skilful operator who stole and sold grain belonging to the government, took a whole pile of money from Degtyaryov for it, smiled and went on his way. I never saw him again and never shall see him, but he engraved himself on my memory, perhaps because he put his arm round me like a father. At all events, because of him the whole frightful situation became even more confused for me. Those men who operated the machine-guns in the Yar had probably been the same sort of people, who knew how to handle horses, had unattractive wives and big-eared little boys. They would boil up their coffee on a bonfire, grasp the handle of a machine-gun as if it were the handle of a plough and shoot, and then go back and boil some more coffee and tell each other jokes . . .

Before going out on the street I always looked around carefully. On one occasion I stuck my nose out of the door and ducked back in again at once—a crowd of men, young and old, including some boys smaller than me, were being herded down the road. Off to Germany.

Grandpa took some old clothes, worn-out winter boots and

galoshes down to the market to exchange for a couple of potatoes. A soldier stopped him and took the sack off him. Gramp was very upset and followed the soldier for a time. They came to a group of Germans who had lit a bonfire and were amusing themselves with a little boy, making him shout: 'Stalin kaput!' which he did very willingly, for which they let him lick out a saucepan. The soldier threw the old boots and galoshes on to the bonfire: it turned out he didn't really want them, but the sack.

'What wicked people they are!' said Gramp when he had hurried back home, sobbing. 'From one lot of good-for-nothings to another! It was easier to be poor under our own people than it is with these. Let them perish and rot, let them be struck by God's thunder and lightning!'

Meanwhile the thunder, but Soviet thunder, continued rumbling away. People were stopping on the streets to listen, climbing out on to their roofs, peering across the Dnieper to the east and listening to the powerful, triumphant roar of the guns.

From the direction of the ravine there floated streaks of dark, oily smoke and sometimes, when the wind blew it across, it was difficult to breathe for the smell of burning hair and flesh.

2. *Towns Abandoned without Interference by the Enemy*

Soviet troops forded the Dnieper and crossed to the right bank, the Kiev side. The rumble of guns could now be heard from the north, from beyond Pushcha-Voditsa and Vyshgorod.

GERMAN TROOPS ATTACK SUCCESSFULLY ON NORTHERN AND SOUTHERN SECTORS OF FRONT

Führer's headquarters, September 25th

At many points on the middle Dnieper the enemy attacked bridgeheads to the east of the river. To the north of Cherkass German tank units destroyed some small enemy boats.

On the central sector of the front to the east of the railway junction of Unech and to the south of Smolensk fierce defensive battles are still going on. Without any interference on the part of the enemy the cities of Roslavl and Smolensk have been abandoned after their complete destruction and the demolition of all important military installations.*

TO THE POPULATION OF THE CITY OF KIEV
The west bank of the Dnieper and the city of Kiev will be defended by German forces with all means at their disposal. Parts of the city of Kiev close to the Dnieper will become a military zone.

In the next few days German troops will be taking up their positions there. To avoid unnecessary casualties among the population and to ensure that the military operations can take place without interference the military zone in the city must be cleared . . . I hope that, in its own interest, the population will carry out this order without resistance.

All people found in the forbidden zone after the stated time without a special pass will be severely punished.†

Our house was inside the evacuation zone. My grandfather and my mother debated anxiously whether to leave or not. Grandpa carried into the cellar everything we had left, then we carted bucketfuls of earth into the barn and spread it on the floor, laid out the onions on top of it, trampled it all down and scattered straw and hay on top. Nobody would ever find them.

Then we nailed boards crosswise over the windows. Grandpa took a bag and went to see his friend the Gardener, while my mother and I made a hole in the hay stacked in the corner of the hay-loft and made a hiding place into which we put some dried crusts, a big pan of boiled potatoes and a flask of water. Then we sat back to await developments.

3. *Degtyaryov's Achievement*

Earth has a very pleasant smell. I always enjoyed digging it. It's even pleasant to sit in a trench, breathing in the smell of moist earth and studying the damp walls and the spade-

---

* *Novoye Ukrainskoye Slovo*, September 26th, 1943.
† Ibid. Order issued by Maj.-General Virov, Military Commandant.

marks in them. Especially in the spring, when you walk across earth that has been resting, or start to turn it over with a rake or a plough or a spade: it can make you quite dizzy, the pleasure of that smell . . .

I will make bold to say that people who have never had to burn up last year's garden rubbish, or have never done some really hard digging in the smoke of a bonfire, to whom the smell of earth means nothing and who in all the bustle and care of life have forgotten what it is, are missing something very remarkable.

Consequently, when, as he was about to leave, Degtyaryov asked me to dig him a trench for his belongings, I dug down so deep in the ground that they had to pull me up by the handle of the spade. I also helped him to camouflage the hole with dark earth and stubble, though only time could hide it altogether.

A cart, loaded to the top with all kinds of junk and harnessed to the lucky old mare Mashka, stood in the yard. The old lady was crying, and Degtyaryov was shouting at her to keep her spirits up. He had decided to leave Kiev for the west.

People were trundling two-wheeled carts and children's prams along the streets, getting themselves out of the battle zone. Mashka sadly dragged the cart up the hill past Priorka church, out into the open fields where I had once gone looking for fir trees. Degtyaryov did not dare go through the centre of the city, but made his way round the back ways which he alone knew, so as to come out on the main road a long way outside the city.

'What are you turning your nose up at?' he asked. 'This is all very strange and exciting for you, I suppose. But I've been watching these perturbations all my life, and I know you've got to be quick to change the flags and the pictures. You'll soon have the Reds here.'

'Where are you going?'

'The world is a large place, and sausage-makers can always earn a living. The Hitlers and the Stalins keep on fighting, but who's to make the sausages? If God spares me I shall try and find a place where there are neither Fascists nor Communists. Let 'em all drown.'

'Maybe you should wait a bit . . .'

'Why? What they're writing in the papers is just a pound

of smoke. The Reds are already at Vyshgorod. Hitler's already lost the bloody war, good and proper. Of course, I could stay on if I wanted to—take over some Soviet store or something. But it's better to be your own boss. I'm making for the west.'

We left the outskirts of the city and the cart creaked along slowly through the open country. The line of telegraph poles with rusty wire hanging from them ran straight to the horizon.

'Let's say good-bye,' said Degtyaryov. 'We shall probably never see each other again . . . Cheerio. Look after yourself.'

'*You* look after yourself.'

'Don't you worry about me! See here!'

He threw open the threadbare, baggy jacket he was wearing, and beneath it was a very full shirt covered with bulging patches. At first I didn't understand. But then Degtyaryov shook his shirt and I heard the clank of coins. The patches were arranged unevenly round his chest, underneath his arms and even round his back. That shirt of his was worth millions, even billions in the money then in circulation.

Degtyaryov was grinning intensely at me, enjoying the impression he had made.

'Feel them.'

I touched the patches, heavy as stones. I knew what he meant! He wanted someone to appreciate his wealth, the effort he had put in, his achievement. Those bulging patches contained his sweat, my sweat, the sweat of his wife, all the horses we had slaughtered. At last he could show someone all his gold, because I was staying behind, did not know where he was going and could not inform on him. We would in any case never see each other again, and he could afford to boast to me. Then he gave Mashka the whip and stepped out brightly alongside the cart, down the line of telegraph poles to the horizon.

4. *Caught and Not Caught*

As I was on my way back, lost in my thoughts, I suddenly looked up and found I was in trouble. It was too late to do anything—the street was cordoned off by Germans who were bringing boys and old men out of the houses.

I immediately put on my most successful act: I made

myself as small as I could, pulled my cap down over my forehead and went straight up to the soldiers. I must have looked rather funny because they seemed pleased, as though they had been waiting for me; they even laughed. There was a group standing by the fence and they put me among them.

As they moved down the street the soldiers drove our little crowd along with them. Three of them with rifles watched over us, while the others combed through the houses. We were all silent, and in this quiet, calm manner we passed some six houses. There was a loud noise from the next house: it sounded as if furniture was being tipped up, and a shot was fired. Our escorts became nervous, peering anxiously into the yard.

I dashed off as though I was trying to set up a world record. As I ran to the corner I heard a shot intended for me. Quick as lightning I glanced round and saw the whole crowd running in all directions.

There was much more shooting when I was already round the corner, and I don't know how it all ended, because I kept running for another couple of miles before taking refuge with the Gorokhovskys, rushing into their house and hiding away behind a cupboard. My legs had saved me once again.

Kolya was at home on his own. He listened eagerly to my story and told me that his mother and grandmother had taken their belongings down to the church, where the old ladies from the whole of Priorka had gathered, intending to sit there praying until our own troops returned. His grandmother had taken Zhorik to the cellar of the priest's house to prevent him being caught. But Kolya wasn't yet fourteen and could go around as free as the wind, and he had got hold of some grenades . . .

'Where did you get them?'

'Stole them off the Germans. Careful—they're loaded!'

I seized the grenades greedily.

'Give me a couple.'

'Take 'em, only let's go and pinch some more.'

I stopped to think. I hadn't really recovered from the scare I'd got from the round-up, but on the other hand I very much wanted to have a weapon. And, whatever else, my legs certainly served me well.

'All right, stand up next to me,' I said.

Kolya stood up. We were exactly the same height; he was just a little thinner.

'Could you really tell that I'm fourteen?'

'Not on your life,' said Kolya, encouragingly.

We scrambled quite openly over the fence of the anti-aircraft training school, which was packed with soldiers, and walked across the yard as though it belonged to us.

The soldiers were gazing out of the windows, looking bored: some were trying to get tunes out of mouth-organs; others were cleaning their weapons; nobody took any notice of us. It was one thing when they were rounding people up and quite another when they were relaxing.

At the back door we found a rifle leaning against the wall, and we studied it carefully.

Just round the corner, smoke was rising from a field kitchen and a fat, red-faced cook was stirring around in the cauldron, a cigarette drooping permanently from his mouth. It had burnt right down and was sending acrid smoke up his nostrils, but it didn't seem to bother him. We stood by the kitchen and watched, but he took no more notice of us than he would of a couple of mongrel dogs sitting licking themselves by the stove.

We went right round the house a second time, and the rifle was still propped up against the wall. We walked up to it, snatched it and dived into the cellar, a disused stoke-hole. One of us kept watch while the other hastily wrapped the rifle up in straw and paper. Once we had made a clumsy parcel we took it by the ends, threw it over the fence and climbed over ourselves.

Kolya fetched some cartridges from his store and we went off to a piece of open land where they had been building some houses before the war, but where there were now only trenches and the remains of the foundations from which all the bricks had been removed. We unwrapped the rifle and tried to work out how it worked, and once we had decided we stood a brick on end for a target and proceeded to shoot.

There was always a lot of shooting going on, so we didn't take any particular precautions. The rifle recoiled on our shoulders like a blow from a heavy fist, and I was rather taken aback. Once we had knocked over a few bricks we decided to go and see where our bullets were going when they didn't hit the brick. It turned out that they were landing a long way off, right in a street where lots of people were passing. The good Lord spared them.

We used up about fifty cartridges; our shoulders were swollen and we could hardly lift our arms, but we were very happy to be armed. Then we hid the rifle in the foundations and agreed that the first of us to have need of it should take it.

5. *A Night of Terror*

Even before I reached our house I realized that something was wrong. Weeping women were running round with bundles and children in their arms; soldiers with rifles were standing at our gate; guard dogs were straining at the leash, their tongues hanging out; and my mother was standing in the yard trying to explain something in a tearful voice. On seeing me she rushed up to me saying:

'There he is! Now we'll go at once.'

The soldiers took her at her word and went off to drive out the other people. But we popped into the hay-loft and covered ourselves with hay. My mother scolded me quietly in the darkness. I said nothing, either about being caught in the round-up, or about the rifle, and certainly not about the hand-grenades in my pockets. There was no point in worrying her more; she had already changed beyond recognition because of everything that had happened: she looked much older, was terribly thin and stooping, and her nose seemed to be more prominent; when she walked down the street in a plain woollen cardigan and a black head-scarf her former pupils did not recognize her, or if they did would exclaim: 'Maria Fyodorovna, whatever's happened to you?'

I broke away a few bits of wood to make a peep-hole through which I could see the collective farm garden. It was already getting dark. Then suddenly shooting broke out very near us—and there was a despairing squeal or a scream which didn't sound as if it came from a human being. My mother started at the noise.

A German ran through the garden with a rifle, took aim and fired. His second shot also hit the target: there was a yelp and a sort of grunt, and I saw that he had been hunting down a dog.

As night fell, everything became quiet. We only drank

water and had nothing to eat. I went off to sleep, and when I woke I noticed a faint glow in the hay. I reached out and took hold of a piece of rotting bark which gave off a mysterious and rather beautiful luminescence. Half the night I amused myself with that piece of rotten wood, but then it began to fade through being handled and eventually went out.

Then I heard a faint rustling: somebody was creeping into the loft. It sent shivers down my spine, but I thought it might be Grandpa, back from the Gardener. Then I heard a faint, plaintive miaow, threw back the hay and rushed to pick up Titus. I held him close to me and felt at once a lot happier.

Cats are really amazing creatures. They live among us, they depend upon us, and yet they preserve a high degree of independence and have their own, special, complex life which comes only very slightly into contact with ours. They have their own sense of time, their own special ways of coming and going and their own meeting-places, which are seldom the same as the ones we use. I always respected Titus's private life, but that night I was happy beyond words that it had coincided briefly with mine.

We spent whole days like that in the hay-loft, never going outside. Then one day I awoke in the morning and found that neither my mother nor Titus was there. I swept the hay brusquely to one side. Someone was going down the street. In the Babarik's house opposite, Vovka's mother was moving about and closing the shutters. I felt easier. Then I heard my mother calling out in business-like tones:

'Hand the things out; we're leaving. There's an empty room the other side of the tramlines. They're putting barbed wire right round this part.'

I spent a long time looking for Titus and calling him, but he seemed to have vanished into thin air. So we went off without him. On the square a German was dashing from one post to another, aiming at something. First we pressed ourselves flat against the fence, but then realized that he was shooting at a cat. There were dead dogs and cats all over the place. To myself I said good-bye to Titus, who had doubtless also been found unwanted by Hitler's occupation troops.

All along the tramline prisoners were digging holes, putting up posts and stretching barbed wire between them. There was an announcement on the newspaper kiosk: FORBIDDEN

ZONE. PERSONS ENTERING WITHOUT SPECIAL PERMISSION WILL BE SHOT.

Immediately opposite this notice there was a long, low building with tiny little windows, fit only to be pulled down. On the courtyard side there were five doorways into it, each with a little porch. It had probably been occupied previously by Jews, but now all the rooms were taken by refugees. It turned out that around the corner there was yet another rickety door, with a little room inside, a stove and a stool. We made a bed on the floor, promoted the stool to serve as a table, and I went off to find some sticks for the fire.

6. *Masses of People on the Move*

The last printed communication between the occupying force and the city of Kiev:

TO THE UKRAINIAN PEOPLE!
MEN AND WOMEN!

After two years of peaceful reconstruction in towns and villages war is once again drawing near. The German Command wishes to conserve its forces and therefore does not fear to abandon certain areas.

The Soviet Command, on the contrary, makes no attempt at all to spare the lives of its officers and men, counting irresponsibly on allegedly inexhaustible reserves of manpower.

For that reason the Germans with their reserves will hold out longer, and that is of decisive importance for the final victory.

You will realize that the German Command is obliged to take certain steps which sometimes seriously upset the personal lives of some individuals.

But this is war!

Therefore you must work hard and willingly whenever German officials appeal to you.

GERMAN COMMANDER*

In practice it worked out like this: using the butts of their rifles and their fists, and firing into the air, they drove out

---

* *Novoye Ukrainskoye Slovo*, September 30th, 1943, after which the paper ceased to exist.

on to the streets everybody who could walk and even those
who couldn't. They gave them one minute to gather their
things and then announced: The city of Kiev is being evacuated to Germany; the city itself will exist no more.

It was horribly like the procession of Jews in 1941. Masses
of people were on the move, with howling children, old people and invalids. Bundles hastily tied up with string, broken
ply-wood suitcases, shopping bags and boxes of tools . . .
One old woman was carrying a string of onions hung round
her neck. Babies were taken along, several of them together
in one carriage; the sick were carried on people's shoulders.
The only form of transport was barrows or children's prams.
The Kirillovskaya was already one mass of milling humanity.
The people with their bundles and barrows would all stand
still for a while, move forward a little, then stop again. The
crowd made a great din; it was like some fantastic parade of
beggars. Nobody was seeing anybody off: everybody was
leaving.

My mother and I watched this procession from the window.
The appearance of the trams was something out of this world:
never in my life had I seen a line of tramcars looking so
dreary.

The Germans let them through to speed up the evacuation.
The trams circled the Peter-Paul Square and the refugees
crammed into them. There was much howling and crying as
they clambered in through the doors, handed their belongings
in through the windows and found places for their children.
It all took place just outside our window. The police were
saying sneeringly:

'You wanted to welcome the Bolsheviks, did you? Well,
come on then, get in.'

Without waiting for them to chase us out with dogs we
took our bundles and went outside. And only just in time,
because the last groups were already being driven out. Next
to us near the school a grey-green line of soldiers were
standing shoulder to shoulder across the road and behind
them it was completely deserted—not a living soul to be seen.
We went up to an already overcrowded tramcar.

'Let's try the next one,' my mother said.

We went to the next one.

'Let's try the next,' mother said.

The line of trams started up, moved forward a little and stopped again—there was a hold-up somewhere. We ran from one car to the other and couldn't make up our minds to get in. The Germans were no longer shouting or shooting at people, but just waiting patiently.

My mother seized me by the hand, dragged me back to the shack where we had been, and we slipped into the court-yard. All the doors were hanging wide open and there was not a soul in sight. We dived into our little room and shut ourselves in. My mother sat on the floor, staring at me with terror in her dark, deep-set eyes. We sat there, not daring to move until the last tram had departed.

Darkness fell outside and from time to time we heard the tramp of heavy boots. Peter-Paul Square was absolutely empty, with bits of paper and old rags lying about. About five yards away from our window along the pavement a German soldier stood on guard with an automatic. I could see him only if I squeezed right up against the wall, and I kept stock-still, like a little animal, and even held my breath whenever he turned round.

Next day they chased out some more small groups of people whom they had caught, and they went through the houses again, but the man continued to mount guard at our window, and that saved us, just as ducklings sometimes remain un-molested immediately beneath a hawk's nest.

We hadn't the slightest idea what was going to happen next or what had become of Grandpa: we didn't know even whether he was still alive. But I thought up the following plan. If they found us they would probably not shoot us in the room but take us out into the yard. There we would have to jump in different directions and make a dash for it, not out on to the street but farther into the yard and then through the gardens to the embankment, which was long and over-grown with bushes. Without dogs it would be difficult to find us there, but since they were sure to have some dogs we would have to run farther, across the meadow, weaving about until we could dive in among the reeds in the marshes and stay there. If necessary we would have to put our heads under the water and breathe through a reed as I had read they did in ancient Russia when they were escaping from the Tatars. Then we should have complete, marvellous security.

It was only later that it came to be known that the Germans had indeed loaded the whole population of Kiev into goods trains and transported them to the west. The majority of them succeeded in escaping and dispersing in Poland; many died on the way; some turned up in Germany and some even got as far as France.

A few figures: Before the war Kiev had a population of about 900,000. Towards the end of the German occupation about 180,000 remained, or a great many less than lay dead in Babi Yar alone. One in three of the inhabitants of Kiev was killed during the occupation, and if you add to this figure the number of those who died from hunger, who failed to return from Germany and so forth, then it appears that every second person must have perished.

'War of the Worlds'

When our water came to an end and we had nothing more to eat, the guard was withdrawn and the city was left completely empty and dead. We crawled out, moved aside the barbed wire just beneath the notice that threatened trespassers with death, and made our way home across the square. We came to the conclusion that there would be less chance of being ferreted out in the forbidden zone.

Previously the square had had flower beds and a children's playground with swings. Who would have thought that one day we would have to creep across it at the risk of our lives! We ran across keeping bent down, our eyes skinned, ready at any moment to fall flat on the ground. But the square was deserted and there was not a sound to be heard. The corpses of dead cats and dogs lay rotting everywhere.

My mother threw up her hands in dismay when she saw our house. The gate was wide open, the doors were broken and ripped off their hinges, a window had been knocked out, and books, broken crockery and some of my photographic materials were lying all over the place. Germans had been billeted in the house, and the rooms were full of straw, magazines and empty tins, the doors had been broken off the cupboard and a tin bowl had bullet holes through it.

Beneath the wall of the barn lay an icon which I was quite sure Grandpa had hidden in the cellar. We rushed into the barn. They had not found the onions; they had simply raked the earth away and with a crowbar had forced a hole through into the cellar. Some odd scraps of material were hanging there and a shabby old fox fur was lying with its tail torn off. Mother wrung her hands and gave voice to her feelings.

I crept through the hole, fumbled around and came across an empty trunk and the crowbar they had broken in with. Icons lay all over the barn. The principal one, of the stern-looking Virgin with the adult-looking child, was broken and now at last all its gilt leaves, flowers and other ornaments were in my hands. They turned out to be very primitively constructed of tin; they were cold and rough, and not in the least interesting.

I tried to see what was beneath the *oklad,* bent it back, and found the whole icon painted on wood. It was a complete icon for which someone had later made an *oklad* and covered up everything but the faces and hands of the Virgin and the child. There was nothing else of any interest in the case. In those days we knew nothing at all about Rublyov and early Russian icon-painting; I had been taught that icons were just nonsense and deception. Consequently I swung my arm back and threw the Virgin away, so that she turned over and over several times and landed in the vegetable garden.

At that moment there came from behind the rubbish tip the plaintive wail of a cat. When we returned Titus had apparently kept out of the way and had only just recognized us. He crept out, laboriously forcing his way through, his eyes wide and staring, intoning a mournful, droning lament; he was trying to tell us what a bad time he had had there, all alone, what frights he'd had and how he had laid low. He jumped on to my chest, dug his claws in, pressed his head against mine and kept nudging me—doing everything he could, in short, to show how pleased he was.

I was very pleased myself to find that he had been clever enough not to fall into the Germans' hands throughout the time they were posted near us. Titus's return cheered us up and we set about putting the house in order.

There was a butt full of water standing under a rainwater pipe, so that we were not likely to die of thirst. We poked around in the vegetable garden and dug out a few potatoes that had been overlooked. Some rabbits, already quite wild again, were skipping around the gardens, but they were as fast as hares and there was no way of catching them. My mother decided not to light the stove, because the smoke would be seen coming from the chimney. Instead she set two bricks side by side on the ground and made a fire between them. The trouble was that we had only a few matches left, so we decided to keep a little fire going the whole time.

The neighbouring houses had been turned inside out: windows broken, doors hanging open, the contents lying outside —a stool here, a book there, a bucket, or just rubbish. I decided to investigate the district around us and went first to the Engstrems' house.

As I went in I tripped over tins and saucepans lying around on the floor, examined the shelves on the dresser and in the pantry, even looked under the beds; and I was not disappointed—I found a piece of dry bread that had been dropped.

This inspired me to further effort, and I hopped over the fence and went into the next house, where I found the same kind of mess; somebody had even relieved himself in the middle of the floor. I went down to inspect the cellar. Since there were no matches, I felt around with my hands in the darkness, caught my foot on some slippery boards and found what I was looking for: a pile of old, rotten potatoes, and a few withered carrots. That was real abundance!

As I crossed the road I glanced at the house in which the Kobets family had lived and nearly dropped my loot from sheer fright. Staring at me out of the broken window were the little bloodshot eyes of a shaggy wild boar.

It was the Kobetses' stuffed boar which some German had apparently propped up in the window as a practical joke. When I had taken the potatoes home I went back to the stuffed boar, examined it carefully, poked it in the snout, and it fell into the room. I climbed through the window after it.

Broken glass crunched beneath my feet and the floor was scattered with pieces of paper, old letters and albums which had been tipped out of the desk drawers. I picked some of the things up, examined a little broken porcelain statue, a monogrammed spoon, a book—they were lying in piles in the corners—and threw everything back. None of it meant anything to me.

I picked up the stuffed boar and fixed it up in the window again. Then I found the deer, the wolf and the fox and spent a long time fixing them up in the other windows, supporting them with books, to keep the boar company. I was having a lot of fun, and I decided to go outside and see what the house looked like with the heads of the animals staring out of the windows. It wasn't bad—really quite amusing . . .

Going through the drawers of the chest one after the other I found the collection of photographs which the old lady had once shown us. They were stacked up, as if in a card-index, strictly according to size, and I recognized in them the elegant ladies, the men with their flowing moustaches, the children in their sailor suits, Nikolya next to his motor-car with the cart wheels and Sevochka standing by his aeroplane. It was a precious collection of all the people close to her, and I came to the conclusion that she and Mima must have had to flee in a great hurry if she had left all that behind.

One photograph was very much like another, and they were of no interest to me anyway. But now they meant nothing to anybody; everything had collapsed, and I wondered whether I couldn't find a use for them. So I took the whole collection out into the garden in its box and started flicking the photographs in all directions. They sailed away beautifully, spinning and sailing through the air like plates, some landing in the bushes and others disappearing over the fence into the street.

At last I tired of doing that, dropped the box into a ditch and went into the house of Mishura, the woman who lived next door to us, because I remembered that she had a cellar. Unfortunately, it had already been cleaned out, except for a few old mildewed cucumbers left in the bottom of a tub. I proceeded to take them out, covered in dill and mould, wiped them on my trousers and bit into them. I sat down there in a dark, damp corner of the cellar, munched my cucumbers and reflected that it was like the situation described by Wells in his *War of the Worlds,* when the Martians arrived on the earth and then started to die off themselves, because everything was in ruins and deserted and there were no people left.

Profession—Fire-Raisers

We lived in a state of isolation, with no one at all to talk to. Once or twice German troops passed down Kirillovskaya and some tanks rumbled through, but they didn't come past our house. We occasionally heard the sound of gunfire from the direction of Vyshgorod, but on the whole everything was quiet, as if there were no fighting going on at all.

I investigated all the houses in the vicinity, making holes in the fences so that I didn't have to show myself on the street. My routes, like Titus's, led across the roofs of barns, through trapdoors and windows. I was always looking for food.

Suddenly the street was filled with noise and the clatter of wheels. We cowered down inside in our fright: a German unit had arrived. Some officers strode quickly into the yard, stamped around the veranda, threw open the door, and stepped back in fright. The first one pulled out a revolver and pointed it at my mother, saying:

'A woman and a boy! Why? Everybody evacuated.'

My mother tried to explain, but the officer would not listen, and made as though to shoot us.

We stood there, more dead than alive. But they quickly looked over the house and then signed to us to get out.

The soldiers were already throwing the gates open and a very smart car drove into the yard with a high-ranking officer in it. Nobody paid any attention to us any more, and we slipped quickly into the barn.

Our house became the scene of furious activity. They carried in a telephone exchange and radio receivers; signals troops rushed up, unrolling coils of wire; orderlies cheerfully carted a nickel bedstead, a divan and pots of flowers from the neighbouring house; messengers kept arriving at the gate on horseback.

Then a lorry drove up loaded with belongings, and two Russian girls started bustling about and giving orders. The German soldiers carried out their instructions without question.

The officer had a great collection of things: women's fur coats, winter boots, lengths of material, even a child's wheel-chair—all of which he was apparently intending to send off to Germany. Inside the house the radio was blaring, the cook had wrung the necks of a couple of geese and was cleaning them. It became all very gay and noisy.

One of the girls was dark-haired, the other fair, and both were pretty and rather plump, with attractive voices and lazy movements. They called each other Shura and Lyuba.

'You stayed here all the time?' Shura, the dark-haired one, asked my mother. 'They could simply shoot you. Or maybe they'll just throw you out, depends who deals with you—they're beasts, these Germans. In any case nothing will be left alive here, so don't waste your time hoping. The front line will pass through here for a long time, and the city will be burnt down.'

'Why for a long time?' my mother asked.

'Our general has been ordered not to abandon Kiev at any cost. The front will stop here, you'll see.'

'But what's your job here—translating?' mother asked.

'Ach!' Shura made a contemptuous gesture with her hand and laughed. 'We are just attached to the general. We have been retreating with him all the way from Kharkov.'

'He likes sleeping with two women,' said Lyuba cynically, munching a pie. 'We keep him warm, one on each side. Poor old chap, he gets cold at night.'

They both burst out laughing. A soldier came in and summoned my mother to go and clean some vegetables and cut up some meat in the kitchen, and she went off and was busy there till evening. At one point she slipped out for a minute and brought me some of the general's thick soup.

I decided not to hang around where I would be seen, so I tucked myself away in the hay-loft, took the whole of Pushkin along with me and read *Yevgeni Onegin*. I had tried to read it before a couple of times, but couldn't get on with it. I preferred reading about Pugachov and the novels of Belkin.

But now once I had started it I couldn't put it down, forgetting about the hay-loft and the Germans and letting myself be carried away by the music of the poetry:

> You came to me in my dreams,
> Unseen, you seemed so lovely,
> Your beauty overcame me,
> I heard your voice within me
> Long ago . . .

I went on reading late into the night, for as long as I could make out the words. Then I lay back in the hay and went over the poetry again in my mind, regretting only that Titus was missing. As soon as the Germans came in Titus had once again vanished.

The general remained with us for about three days and then took off as suddenly as he had appeared. They swiftly rolled up the wires, loaded the divan, the nickel-plated bed and the pots of flowers, and the general and his suite departed northwards, towards Pushcha-Voditsa.

But the house remained empty for no more than a couple of hours: some of General Vlasov's troops—Russians fighting along with the Germans—appeared outside, cheerful, noisy, one of them playing a concertina. We were glad to see them because they were not Germans but our own people, all speaking Russian, and after being isolated there for so long we weren't used to hearing our own language spoken. They were not even very surprised to see us. They simply said that our house was in a better state than the others, and they were going to move in.

They quickly installed themselves and started quarrelling about something, shouting and laughing; there was an air of recklessness and tension about the whole bunch. They wound up a gramophone and had a great pile of records to play, but at first the thing seemed not to work properly —only a squeaky voice, which appeared to be a speech by Lenin, coming through the scratching and wheezing. (Before the war it used to be sold on the other side of the tune 'Katyusha'.) One of them went out on to the veranda and threw Lenin over the fence into the road, so that it broke into a thousand pieces, and from the gramophone came the sounds of a Ukrainian folk-song.

'So here we are, my dear, with the job of destroying all this,' their officer, a former Red Army commander, said with a grim smile. 'Tears will make no difference; we've got our orders. We are going to burn all these houses down; this is going to be a no-man's-land, and Kiev will exist no more—you can say good-bye to Kiev. But you'd better get out of the city before it's too late. So long as we're here I'll say you're working for us, but if other people come along it'll be "Bang!" and you'll be no more. It's so very simple. We ought to pop you off too, really . . .'

The first thing the Vlasov men did was to steal a cow from the Germans. This daring operation was carried out somewhere on the other side of the bridge. The Germans got on their tracks and came chasing around our square in a very bad mood, waving their guns about. But a ferocious-looking Vlasov man stood guard at our gate, while his pals were already skinning the cow in the barn.

That evening they had a marvellous feast. They played the accordion, danced till the plaster began to fall off the ceiling, drank recklessly, staggered out into the courtyard and finished up lying all over the place. 'Let's have some fun before we die!' they cried.

But next morning they were as smartly turned-out as guardsmen, and they formed up outside and marched off in the direction of Pushcha-Voditsa.

They did not come back till late in the evening, tired, their faces black with soot and their clothes smelling of petrol. They were carrying whole bales of things they had stolen or picked up.

'We've started on the job,' the officer said to my mother. 'We burnt down about a hundred houses today.'

'What did you do—pour petrol over them?'

'Some we did with petrol, some with straw. Depends how you set about it. Each of us has a quota to fulfil, and we have to make sure everything is burnt to ashes. It's always the wrong way round: when you don't want a place to catch fire, it'll go up on its own; but when you want to burn it down, it just won't catch light at all. What a job!'

'And you found the things there?'

'The things were buried in the ground.'

'What are you going to do with such a lot of stuff?'

'Barter them for vodka.'

And that's what they did: two of them set off at once across the bridge with bundles of clothes, and returned later with a large can of home-made spirit which they had obtained from some Germans. In the meantime others had organized a full-scale hunt for hares and there was nothing but shooting going on everywhere.

Others went round the gardens with long sticks, walking slowly in a long line as though they were looking for mines. They kept their eyes fixed on the ground and could detect immediately where something had been buried: they would poke the stick into the ground, feel around with it and then start digging. Sometimes they would pull out a trunk or a barrel of something, and in this way they got together a whole pile of clothes and linen. They were especially delighted when they came across a gramophone or a guitar.

'The Germans are like second-hand merchants: they'll take anything!'

For the second night in succession they again drank and made merry; they could be heard all over Kurenyovka. They broke one accordion and immediately took up another. We got some petrol from them, and just sat there listening to their goings-on. There was something rather horrible about their merrymaking.

The officer saw our light and, rather drunk, came and sat down with us, holding his head in his hands.

'We're in a fine mess now. We went to fight for the freedom of Russia, and look at that freedom now . . .'

'Are you one of those they talk about who turned your weapons on your own people?'

'Some of us mutinied, some escaped from prison camps, some joined up because they were starving and some because they were dying. But the Germans are no fools: they immediately gave us the dirtiest jobs to do, so that we could never go back. So we're in it right up to our ears. With the Germans we shall get as far as the first crossroads, and if we're caught by the Reds they'll hang us by our balls.'

'Is there really no way out for you?'

'What way out can there be? Where is there any way out today anywhere in the world?'

One of his friends came to fetch him:

'Give over, Mikhail! He's always like this—he has a drop to drink and straight away starts philosophizing. Come on, let's get some more drink.'

Mikhail jumped up, let out a hysterical growl and started tearing the front of his shirt apart, saying:

'Ach—we shall fetch up somewhere like dogs in a ditch!'

'Maybe, maybe,' said his friend easily. 'But why ruin your shirt!'

For several days they formed up in platoons each morning and marched off to their work near the park at the 'Cheer-Up' sanatorium. Then they decided it was too far to go and they moved to the other side of the embankment. We were left alone in the house once again.

We stayed there, quiet as mice. At nights there was a great, silent glow beyond the embankment, all the more ominous for being so completely silent. No-man's-land was drawing nearer.

How Many Times Should I Be Shot?

By the time I had reached the age of fourteen I had committed so many crimes on this earth that I should have been shot many times over. Here is a list of my offences:

1. Not informing on a Jew (my friend Shurka)
2. Concealing an escaped prisoner (Vasili)
3. Wearing felt winter boots
4. Being out after the curfew
5. Concealing a red flag
6. Not returning all my loot from the shop
7. Not handing over fuel
8. Not handing over surplus food supplies
9. Sticking up a leaflet
10. Stealing (beetroot, peat, wood, fir trees)
11. Working illegally with a sausage-maker
12. Dodging being sent to Germany (in Vyshgorod)
13. Dodging the transport again (in Priorka)

14. Stealing a weapon and using it
15. Possessing ammunition
16. Not observing the order regarding gold (failing to report it)
17. Not reporting for registration at the age of fourteen
18. Not informing on underground fighters
19. Being anti-German and encouraging anti-German attitudes (there was a decree about this, too)
20. Spending forty days in the forbidden zone, for which alone I should have been shot forty times over.

Moreover I was not a member of the party or the Komsomol, nor a member of the underground; I was not a Jew or a gypsy; I did not keep pigeons or have a radio set; I did not commit any crimes openly; and I did not get taken as a hostage. I was in fact a most ORDINARY, unexceptional, insignificant little chap in a peaked cap.

But if the regulations drawn up by the authorities had been observed scrupulously, according to the principle of 'If you did it you pay the penalty', then I had LOST THE RIGHT TO BE ALIVE twenty times over.

I persist stubbornly in remaining alive, while the number of my crimes increases in a catastrophic manner, so that I have stopped counting them. All I know is that I am a terrible criminal who has still not been caught.

It is largely as a result of a misunderstanding that I am still alive; it is simply because in all the haste and confusion, the regulations and laws which the authorities draw up are never carried out fully, to the last letter. Just as I always managed to slip through the holes in the net, and get away by pure chance, I might, by the same chance, have been caught. We all hang on a thread; none of us depends on his own will, but on chance, on the luck of the draw, on somebody else's mood, and even to a great extent on his own swift legs.

And on what besides? Today one two-legged scoundrel arbitrarily makes one rule; tomorrow another one comes along and adds a second rule, and so on, until five or ten, and God knows how many more, may be conceived in the murky minds of the Nazis, the N.K.V.D., the royalists, Marxists, Chinese and Martians, and all our other uninvited benefactors whose name is legion.

But I want to live!

To live as long as is permitted me by Mother Nature and
not by the two-legged degenerates. How dare they, what right
have they, to claim to decide the question of MY life or
death—

of HOW LONG I should live

of HOW I should live

of WHERE I should live

of WHAT I should THINK

of WHAT I should FEEL

and of WHEN I SHOULD DIE?

I want to live so long that there will be no trace left of
those people!

I loathe you all, dictators, enemies of life; I scorn you as
the most loathsome things which the earth has ever given
birth to. You are cursed! Cursed! CURSED!

Five Days and Nights of Agony

Monday, November 1st

On the Sunday night I had had a terrible feeling of the
imminence of death for which there was no obvious reason.
It was simply that we were surrounded by solid, impenetrable
darkness in which the city lay dead. I had a sense of fore-
boding within me that my life was coming to an end.

We all have moments when we can foresee clearly our
coming, inevitable death. With some it happens sooner, with
others later, but we all at one time or another realize suddenly, with a chill in our hearts, that the moment must come
when that 'I' will cease to exist. It will cease to breathe and
to think, and these hands, this head and these eyes will be
no more. And each one of us reacts in his own way as he
throws off that obnoxious feeling and seizes that straw of
reassurance that says: 'It's not today; it's still a long way
off.'

I first experienced that feeling when my grandmother died;
but that was nothing compared with what came over me that

Sunday night. The trouble was that I couldn't clutch on to
that 'not today'—in fact, every day could well be 'today'.
felt short of breath.

The utter silence made my head swim. It was like bein;
tied up in a black sack or buried alive deep under the ground
where you just couldn't budge and it was no use wrigglin;
about because there was no way out.

I slid down from the stove, felt around with icy hands fo
the oil-lamp and matches, and went out in the yard, carefull'
feeling my way in the pitch darkness.

I could hardly tell I was outside—it was the same pitcl
darkness, the same black sack, and not a sound to be heard
as though my ears were blocked. I took a spade and crep
under the house.

The house stood on raised brick foundations, and ther
was a gap between the floor and the ground into which
could just squeeze myself. The space between the beams an;
the earth below was less than a foot, but I eased my way
through, lying flat on the ground, my chin digging into th
earth, holding the lamp with one hand and dragging th
spade along with the other. I kept bumping into the woode;
posts and coming across dead rats which had dried out int
parchment. In a fit of annoyance I knocked one of them ou
of the way and it rolled off with the sound of an empty box

Once I had crawled far enough underneath I lit the lam;
and stood it up in the dry earth. My face was covered in dus
and cobwebs, which I wiped off and then, lying on my side,
I started to dig.

At first it was very awkward, because I had to twist round
to get each spadeful out. But when I rolled over into the hole
I had made and could raise myself on my elbows I was able
to dig faster.

The earth was dry and sandy, and the spade scraped
against the pieces of brick in it. I was soon sweating, but by
then I was able to kneel up in the hole. It was uneven,
crumbling, like a rather long crater. I dug up lots of bones,
a square nail and some pieces of newspaper. Everything had
been preserved just as it was when the house was built in
the time of the Tsar. The people who had printed and read
those newspapers and thrown away the broken bricks were
probably already dead.

I wanted the hole to hide in. And I really felt safer in it.

There were only three possibilities of my dying in it: if they used dogs to find me, if a bomb fell on the house, or if the house were burnt down.

I thought I was quite alone and nearly fainted when a pair of green eyes lit up beside me. Titus had turned up and was staring at me with his enormous eyes.

I nearly wept out of gratitude, joy and affection for him. I drew him over on to my lap; he didn't object—on the contrary, he started to nestle into me and purr, and we sat there, the two of us, reading passages from a newspaper half a century old.

We studied closely an advertisement which said that a certain Mr Schmidt was able to offer a large selection of the very best Swiss gramophones as well as the Amour needles, and that you could also obtain from him a marvellous collection of records, all at very reasonable prices . . . For some reason or other he was also in the business of buying up clocks, pearls and antiques. It was amazing to learn that there had been a time when people lived at peace in the world, buying clocks, gramophones and pearls. It was hard to believe. A gramophone was the only thing that Titus and I lacked.

I went quietly off to sleep, curled up in the soft earth. When I woke up light was already coming into the space beneath the house, which meant it was daytime. The cat had gone, I was frozen stiff, and the place no longer appeared to me to be as cosy and safe as it had during the night. Whole curtains of dirty cobwebs hung from the floorboards, which were so low they pressed down on me and seemed almost to crush me. Once again I began to feel nervous: I imagined the house collapsing on top of me with all its weight. I flattened myself to the ground and crawled as fast as I could, as if rats were nibbling at my heels, towards the hole and scrambled out.

To calm down I leant over the rainwater-butt to have a drink. Fallen leaves were floating on the water, but I scooped them off and blew on the surface; it was sweet and pleasant to the taste. I thought to myself: if ever I live to have water properly laid on, I shall still go on drinking rainwater, I like it so much.

At that moment I heard a noise. I started, raised my head

and saw a German soldier coming into the yard carrying a
rifle; then I caught sight of another one on the street outside.
Instinctively and very stupidly I squatted down behind the
butt, though I knew perfectly well that they were bound to
see me.

When I thought they were not looking in my direction I
dodged round the corner of the house, again cowering down
rather stupidly, not looking round and averting my eyes from
them in a sort of superstitious belief that they would not see
me. I heard someone shout 'Hey! . . . Hey!' and I straightened up and stopped.

The soldier eyed me very sternly. He was a dark-haired,
stocky fellow of about thirty, rather awkward in his movements, wearing old, muddy boots. His was a very ordinary,
everyday type of face which had something familiar about
it—he could easily have been a mechanic from the Sport
Factory . . . His cap was cocked on one side of his head, his
dark curls sticking out from under it. In German he said:
'Come here.'

I took a few steps along the wall.

'You'll be shot,' he said sternly and started to raise his
rifle.

It was, apparently, loaded, since he did not shoot the bolt.
Another German came up, took him by the arm and said
something in a very calm and indifferent tone, which sounded
roughly like: 'Don't do it, there's no point.' (That's what I
thought he said.)

The second soldier was rather older, quite an elderly man,
with sunken cheeks. The dark-haired one answered him back
and turned his head away for a moment. In that brief
moment—I realized—I ought to have jumped up and dashed
away. As luck would have it, at that moment my grenades
were in the house. Yet this was the moment I had been preparing for.

There was no time even to cry out: 'Please, mister—wait!'
The dark one simply raised his rifle, turned his head for a
moment, said something to the elder one, and that was the
last moment of my life.

I realized all this, without having time to move an inch. It
was just the same as when you knock a flask or a bowl of
flowers with your elbow and see it tip and fall before your
very eyes: you have time to think that you ought to grab it,

that though it is now whole and perfect in a moment it will be smashed; but you are not quick enough to make the movement, you can only think about it, annoyed and mortified—and it's already smashed to bits.

Right in front of my face—not in the cinema, or in a picture or in a dream—I saw the black hole at the end of the barrel, and had in my nose the unpleasant smell of gunpowder (meanwhile the elder German apparently went on saying something, but the dark one—alas!—wouldn't listen); ages seemed to pass and there was no shot.

Then the end of the barrel dropped from my face to my chest and I realized at once in amazement that that, apparently, was how I was to be killed—shot in the chest!

Then he lowered the gun altogether.

I couldn't believe it, and I thought and expected that he would raise it again. The elder one merely glanced at me, tapped the dark one on the shoulder and left the yard. The dark one said to me sternly: 'We-eg!'

It was only then that I finally came to myself, more dead than alive, and broke out in a cold sweat. I walked off, as in a dream, round the corner on my shaking, frozen, skinny legs, and into the house, where I stood in a corner with my face to the wall, swaying on my feet.

I have thought a great deal about the affair since, and I still cannot understand what happened. Was it a joke? Did the elder one say: 'Stop fooling about; don't scare him?' Or was it meant seriously? And did the elder one say: 'Stop that; he's given himself up?' If it was a joke, why didn't he shoot? He only had to squeeze his finger. I suppose on November 1st every year I ought to remember and thank that finger, the forefinger on his right hand, which let me live.

Tuesday, November 2nd

I am one of those people who definitely prefer strong light. There can never be too much artificial light or too much sunshine for me. This is neither good nor bad but simply, it would seem, a biological peculiarity of my organism. I have never worn dark glasses, because the brighter everything is around me, the more dazzling the beaches and the snowfields, the better I like it and the more cheerful my mood. It never hurts my eyes; on the contrary, they bathe in a sea of light.

My mother used to have trouble with her eyes. She would always be drawing the curtains across the windows; I would draw them back. When everybody was suffering from the summer heat, I would be just starting to enjoy it. And during those terrible, cloudy autumn days, when it suddenly occurs to you that at that very moment somewhere in the Crimea, or in Africa, or on islands in the Pacific, the sun is shining bright and hot, a longing comes over me almost to the point of tears. How fortunate are the migratory birds which can just take off and fly where they please, without any special permission.

I hate it when the clouds stream across the sky and the sun shines through only briefly, and is then hidden for long stretches. I keep watching the beastly cloud, longing for it to pass. Whenever I recall something which happened years ago I am always quite sure whether the sun was shining at the time or not, if it was a dull day.

All this is by the way of background to the fact that I was overjoyed when, after the dull October days, the sun at last appeared.

It was as though my escape from being shot the day before had never happened. I became carefree and self-confident. It was as though, since I had been lucky once, I had decided that fate was looking after me and that I should get through somehow in the future.

Wiser now, I put a grenade in each pocket and kept them with me all the time, checking them from time to time to make sure the caps had not come unscrewed. I kept looking round me vigilantly, like a cat, ready to take cover at any moment. And I was seized with a desire to do something active, so I dug a trench under the house and made another hole there, for my mother.

She came and looked at it, but was not overpleased with the idea. She suggested hiding the trunk in it. I quickly did this, burying it deep down so that it should not be burnt. I had no doubt at all that the house would be burnt down, if not in the fighting then by the Vlasov people: there was no way of saving it. I studied it carefully, so as to remember what it looked like. Once again there were footsteps and voices on the street. I dodged under the house and saw

Alexandra and Mikolai, my godparents, walking very slowly across the deserted square.

The old lady was carefully leading the blind man, keeping him away from the pot-holes and paving stones and talking to him very earnestly. He was wearing his famous glasses with the blue lens and the piece of ply-wood. When they found we were at home they both broke into tears. They had simply been trying to find some human beings.

My mother immediately took them in and fed them. They had not been able to find any food for themselves and had eaten nothing for two whole days.

'We were living in the cellar,' said the old lady plaintively. 'The old man is dying anyway, so we came out to look for people.'

My mother nearly burst into tears. Just imagine what it is to be utterly alone in a deserted city! She persuaded the old folk to spend the night with us, and they agreed that it was better to keep together—to survive together or perish together. They fussed for a time, trying to make themselves comfortable, and were about to go to bed when they suddenly decided that they must go and look after their own flat in the children's technical school, and that it was better for them to sleep in the cellar over there. They were really quite beside themselves and there was nothing for it but to let them go to their cellar.

My mother gave them some potatoes, which they accepted with a deep bow, and they made their way slowly back across the square. I said:

'Have a look around the yards and in the cellars.'

The old lady threw up her hands.

'In other people's cellars? To go and steal? The Lord forgive you, my child!'

For some time I stood watching them go, afraid they might be shot. They were very unusual people, really 'not of this world'. They went off across the square, destruction all around them, arm in arm, chatting quietly to each other.

I was already going to sleep when I heard the sound of a motor. Beams of light played over our windows. Something resembling a tank was rumbling straight across the vegetable garden, its headlights shining straight at our cottage. Without slowing down it crashed right into the fence, sending splinters

flying, and looked as though it was going to charge right into
the house. But it stopped at the wall of the house, at the very
point where my wonderful hole was. It was too late for me
to escape. There was a banging of doors in the yard and the
sound of a lively conversation going on between some
Germans.

As though someone else had willed it, my mother rushed
to light a lamp so that they should see the light and not take
fright as they came in. She did the right thing, because they
even wiped their boots in the porch and knocked on the door.
My mother answered their knock and they walked in, brisk,
smartly turned-out and smiling.

'Guten Abend!'—they indicated by means of gestures what
they wanted—'Schlafen, schlafen—sleep!'

'Bitte,' said my mother.

They moved about the room quite relaxed, arranging their
things, quickly deciding where to hang their greatcoats and
where to throw their cases. They proceeded to bring blankets
and cases in from the vehicle. Meanwhile we rolled up our
own bedding and moved into the other half of the house. I
felt a little easier by this time and went outside to see what
they had driven up in. It was a half-track vehicle, armoured,
it seemed to me, and a gun was trailing behind.

The Germans kept up a lively conversation and in ten
minutes they knocked on the wall and called out:

'Missis, son, come here!'

We went into their room. Apart from the oil-lamp, which
my mother had decided not to take away, they had a blind-
ingly bright carbide light burning, but it was flickering, and
one of them was working on it. The table was piled high
with food and drink. There was wine, in earthenware bottles
with brightly coloured labels, and metal drinking mugs for
glasses. The Germans pointed to the table like the most
expansive of hosts, and said:

'Bitte, bitte! Come and eat!'

One of them handed me a ham sandwich. Staggered at
the sight, I started to eat it, and it made me feel quite dizzy.

There were three of them. Franz was middle-aged, ginger-
haired and very calm. Herman was about seventeen, dark-
haired, handsome and well-built. I did not get to know the
name of the third; he was the driver, who was mending the

carbide lamp. He simply took a bite at a sandwich and collapsed from exhaustion.

Franz, the older one, poured my mother and me some wine, waving the earthenware bottle and saying boastfully: 'France, Paris!'

The wine was sweet, with a delicate bouquet. Mother drank hers and told Franz that they were good Germans, but that there were others about who wanted to 'bang-bang' us.

Franz frowned.

'That not soldier. That bandit—shame German nation. We are front-line soldier, artillery. War—"bang-bang". Mothers, children—no "bang-bang".'

Herman took a mouth-organ out of his side pocket and started to play on it. Franz went on drinking wine and insisted on using his small supply of words, explaining with some difficulty how desperately tired they were. The three of them had first been in Norway, then they had fought with Rommel in Africa, and now they had been withdrawn from the Western Front. Everywhere they went they had to fight.

'Mein Gott! Here—war. There—war. War. War.' This Franz was a serious, hard-bitten, very manly character, who seemed to be permeated with the smell of gunpowder, and I was rather scared of him. But young Herman, who was only about three years older than I was, was as straightforward and as likeable as my friend Bolik, and he was more ready to talk to me.

'Franz is from Hamburg, I am from Berlin,' he said proudly. 'I've been at the front for a whole year!'

'And is it awful at the front?' I asked.

He smiled and said:

'To tell the truth, it's terrible. France not so awful. Russia awful.'

He immediately pulled out a photograph of himself with his father, a very substantial looking gent in a hat and carrying a stick, and next to him stood a shy, bony little boy in shorts with a Berlin square in the background.

My mother asked them where the front was and whether Kiev was being abandoned.

Franz became at once very solemn. No, Kiev would not be abandoned. The front was right there, in the forest. But the Russians would never enter Kiev. There would be a terrible battle. If forces had been transferred all the way from France, it was going to be a real battle! Yes, this was going to be another Stalingrad, only this time for the Russians. He pondered for a while, sitting there, and repeated the word, pronouncing each syllable clearly: Stalingrad.

Mother said:

'November 7th is the biggest Soviet holiday.'

'Ja, ja,' Franz exclaimed. 'Soviet want take Kiev on holiday. October. But they no take Kiev. They die.'

I began to feel rather depressed. He wasn't lying—why should he want to! They were just treating us as human beings. It was a serious conversation. So I asked:

'But if they do take it? Will you retreat?'

'Ja, ja, understand,' said old Franz very seriously. 'You waiting for Soviets, but I say, I am old soldier: you go away, go away, please. Here—you die.'

He went on to explain that we ought to get away somewhere to a village or into the forest, dig ourselves a hole, sit there and wait until the front line moved away, because Kiev was going to be turned into a no-man's-land on Hitler's orders.

Franz jabbed his chest with his finger and said:

'I tell you, old soldier. I fight in Poland. Is all the same—advance and retreat. Russian tired.'

The driver was asleep on the couch with all his clothes on. Herman suddenly became morose and put the mouth-organ aside. Franz was getting drunk. We went to our own part of the house, but could hear that Franz and Herman stayed awake a long time, talking.

That night I was awakened by a shout. My mother was calling in desperation:

'Tolya, Tolya! Help me!'

I heard some scuffling and the sound of a stool going over. Half asleep, I cried out:

'Who's there? Who is it?'

I struck a match and was at first blinded by it, then saw my mother struggling with the ginger-haired Franz. He was very drunk, muttering in German, arguing with her and pushing her about.

I always had tapers ready by me on the stove. I lit one of them, summoned up my courage, and began to let myself down from the stove. Franz turned towards the light, stared at the flame with drunken eyes, eyed me thoughtfully for a moment and let my mother go.

'Krieg, Mother. War, nichts gut,' he said. 'Ach!'

And, completely drunk, he staggered, bumped against the door and left the room.

Still trembling, my mother fixed a piece of wood against the door.

'He's drunk, quite drunk,' she said. 'It was a good thing you lit the light. Go to sleep . . . And—thank you.'

For the first time I really felt myself to be a grown man, who could and had to defend others. I woke up many times before the morning, listening and feeling for the grenades under my pillow. I reckoned up the number of days and hours left. Until the holiday of November 7th there remained only ninety-six hours. All around was silence.

Wednesday, November 3rd

Wednesday, November 3rd, began with beautiful weather. The sky was clear and blue, and when I went out on to the porch I literally caught my breath at the freshness and purity of the air and the brightness of the morning sunshine.

You must know that feeling, when you look at the sky in the morning and it makes you want to make the most of the day ahead. If you are not working it makes you want to get your things together quickly, pack some sandwiches and go off fishing, or just for a walk.

It was the day of the decisive battle for Kiev, and now, when I re-live the way it began, I cannot for the life of me understand why, on this beautiful, blessed earth—among people equipped with brains and the capacity to think, who are not just animals with instincts, among thinking, understanding beings—it is possible for people to indulge in such absolute madness as war, dictatorship, police terror, to kill each other and to humiliate each other sadistically.

I know, of course, that this has all been carefully analysed by experts in all the '-isms,' and that in their view it has all been explained politically, historically, economically and psychologically. Everything has been examined, proved and all is clear. All the same, I DO NOT UNDERSTAND.

Herman and the driver ladled water out of the rainwater-butt
and washed themselves, laughing and splashing about. The
ginger-haired Franz was going round looking rather chas-
tened: he must have had a hangover after the previous night's
goings-on. But he tried to give the impression that nothing
had happened.

My mother made a fire from some sticks and started preparing a meal. In daylight the Germans' vehicle no longer
looked frightening; it was quite an ordinary lorry for going
across rough country, with wheels at the front, a caterpillar
track at the rear and a tarpaulin cover. It was standing
quietly near the house, staring at the world attentively and
questioningly through its headlights, smelling of petrol and
covered with dust.

Franz and Herman lifted the tarpaulin and started unloading sacks of potatoes from the back. I hung around, trying
to work out why they had so many potatoes.

But it turned out that underneath the potatoes were shells.
Either the quartermaster had made them carry the potatoes,
or they had stolen them from somewhere. In any case they
had no intention of bartering them. They unloaded every
single thing, asked for a brush and cleaned out the back of
the vehicle. Herman untied a sack, tipped about fifty pounds
of potatoes out on the ground and signed to me to take
them: they were for us.

Suddenly the earth began to shake.

It was so strange and unexpected that I had no time to be
afraid. The ground simply trembled beneath our feet as it
does, no doubt, during an earthquake; the wood-pile in the
barn collapsed, and the doors banged. Those earth tremors
continued for some seconds in that clear sky and bright
morning, followed by the sound of explosions from the direction of Pushcha-Voditsa.

It was not so much the thud of individual explosions as a
continual roar—a veritable avalanche, a sea of sound. I have
never in my life heard anything like it, and I don't want to:
it was as if the earth itself was exploding and turning inside
out.

Some force threw me out into the middle of the yard, and
I couldn't understand what had happened or why, whether
the whole world was collapsing, or whether there was a

gigantic tidal wave sweeping over the earth. And the Germans also started scurrying about, looking anxiously in the direction of the noise, though there was nothing but the blue sky to be seen beyond the embankment.

The driver quickly climbed up on to the cab and peered around, but he could make nothing out either. At this point the Germans exchanged a few short sentences, and quickly and efficiently proceeded to load the potatoes and shells back on to the lorry. Herman ran into the house and brought out the submachine-guns. Franz got out their helmets and gave them to the others.

Far beyond the embankment, above Pushcha-Voditsa, some planes appeared—just little black points in the sky. They couldn't be heard because of the din; they were just little spots moving across the sky like mosquitoes. The sky around them was immediately filled with white puffs of smoke. They flew quickly over Pushcha-Voditsa and had hardly gone out of sight when a second wave came from beyond the Dnieper, this time rather nearer us. They flew in formation through the exploding anti-aircraft shells, and they were followed by a third wave, even closer to us. They came in, wave after wave, to bomb Pushcha-Voditsa, each time covering a different area, one after the other, right on the target.

Franz, Herman and the driver left their lorry and stood by the barn in their helmets, holding their submachine-guns, looking very earnest and very much on the alert. Another formation of planes flew over the edge of the forest, just over the 'Cheer-Up' sanatorium, even closer . . .

I went over to them and stood by them, listening to what they said. They were talking to each other quietly, never taking their eyes off the furious, gripping show that was being put on in the sky.

'Ilyushin.'

'Yes.'

'There's a trench over there.'

'Put the sights up.'

Franz, the red-haired one, took me by the shoulder and proceeded to say something, very seriously and anxiously, pointing to the garden and to my mother. Run for it, he was saying, take cover.

'Bang, bang. Soviet Ilyushin . . . Schwarzer Tod.'

I nodded my head but didn't go away, I don't know why. Everything within me was strained to the limit. The 'Black Deaths' were getting nearer and perhaps my last minutes of life had arrived.

At that moment one of the planes burst into flames. It flew on slowly, one wing down, and disappeared behind the embankment. A parachute opened, dome-shaped, in the sky —a member of the crew had managed to get clear and the wind was carrying him towards the forest. The tiny figure of a man hung suspended beneath the white circle of the parachute, utterly defenceless against the anti-aircraft fire. I don't think he can have reached the ground alive, and if he did he must have fallen into German hands. The Germans showed no signs of pleasure at the sight. They watched him descend and disappear just as glumly as I did.

The dive-bombers came shooting over the embankment practically at ground level, black against the sky, making a terrible whine. They were both bombing and strafing: it was a hail of fire, and bits of debris, wood and earth were thrown up in the air. The sky was dotted with explosions. The next wave was due to pass over us.

And it did.

They zoomed out from behind the gardens and houses, terribly low, so fantastically low you could almost touch them. The roar of their engines drowned the sound of voices, and they flashed past in threes, their guns firing ahead of them. The last thing I remember is Franz, pressed up against the barn, spread out in an unnatural position, aiming up in the air with a machine-gun which was shaking as it fired. But it was like a silent film—the machine-gun rattled away, but no sound came from it because of the unbroken roar of the engines. And everything was shaking.

I was thrown to the ground and let out a penetrating yell: 'Bombs!' which I couldn't even hear myself and which came out something like 'Bo-ow-ee!' It went dark, then it was light again, earth was thrown up in the air and fell to the ground, and I found myself scrambling along on my hands and knees and nearly banged my head into the porch. Then there were no more planes.

Herman then appeared from behind the barn, his face contorted, covered in earth from head to foot. He grabbed a fresh cartridge clip from the half-track to reload his sub-machine-gun. But he was too slow.

Another group of planes shot out like black arrows from behind the gardens and houses. Herman crept underneath the tracks of the lorry. I dived into the house and only just had time to get inside and press myself up flat against the stove when the whole house, stove and all, rocked. Through the window opposite me I saw a blinding flash in a lilac bush near the entrance and pieces of gate and fence flew in the air. At the same moment a pane of glass in the window cracked in the shape of a star, a cloud of plaster and dust fell on me, and I felt something brush across the hair on the top of my head, like a hand. The planes disappeared, but I could still hear the sound of breaking glass.

I started to clean myself off mechanically in the usual way, shook my head to get the plaster out of it, glanced at the stove and saw, to my great surprise, that a perfectly round hole had been made in it just an inch above the top of my head. Scarcely believing my eyes, I leant with my back up against the stove again and poked my finger into the hole. Now I knew what had brushed across my hair. I went round the stove to look at it from the other side. The other side was undamaged, which meant that the piece of shrapnel had been stopped inside the stove.

Now at last I realized that I would have to take refuge in the trench. I had no idea where my mother had got to. I went outside, looked around and thought: 'Perhaps she's already there,' and at that moment more planes came over from behind the houses.

I must have been in a state of shock, because I dashed off like a hare across the flat, exposed garden towards the trench, knowing full well what a beautiful target I offered and that I should never make it.

With one little part of my mind I saw that the planes were already ahead of me, that alongside me in the garden there was an enormous hole and everything round it was covered with a layer of light earth into which my feet sank, leaving a line of tracks in the sand.

The planes had gone over—that was the main thing. I had seen the pilots' heads and the red stars on the wings, and with the same little part of my mind I had noticed little columns of sand spurting up around me, and felt very hurt

that they should try to kill me, poor little me, taking me to
be a German. I was cross rather with myself and my fate,
because at that speed they couldn't be expected to distinguish
who was beneath them, German or non-German, especially
since they knew the population had left the city.

There were many little columns of sand spurting up, but
I somehow managed to dodge between them. The planes had
long passed over, but I kept on running towards the trench.
I tumbled into it, half-deafened, and dived into the darkest
and farthest corner, bumping right into my mother. What
joy! There she was, alive and well. But then there was
another roar of sound.

The planes shot out from behind the houses and the
earth began to shake as though some infuriated giant was
drumming on it, the beams across the trench started to
tremble, and earth began to pour down on us. My mother
pushed me roughly into the bottom of the trench and fell
on top of me, covering me up with her body, and when the
din subsided she glanced out, muttering as though in prayer:

'That's the way, that's the way to treat 'em!'

She seized hold of me, nearly out of her mind, rocking to
and fro and saying, not so much to me as to 'them':

'Never mind if we have to die, just drop as many as you
can. Hit 'em as hard as you can! Never mind about us, so
long as you get them!'

I am afraid you will not understand this or believe it. The
people in the planes were OUR PEOPLE and they were strafing
and routing the OTHERS, giving them what they deserved.
That was the way to drive them out, the scoundrels.

'Go for 'em, lads, go for 'em!'

That was how it started.

Human beings have an amazing capacity for adaptation. By
lunchtime I could already tell by the sound which way the
planes were coming and how great the danger was. I started
to get accustomed to that kind of life. In the intervals I
would run into the house.

It was a real sight: the walls were pitted with shrapnel,
every pane of glass was out, and the roof looked as though
someone had been shovelling sand on it; there were scorched
bricks lying on it, though the chimney was undamaged. The
hole which the bomb had left next to the house was big

enough to take a couple of lorries. And there were many smaller craters all over the place, as if the earth had small-pox.

The German gunners were now sitting in a slit trench behind the barn, huddled up together, smothered with earth, no longer firing from their machine-guns but obviously thinking of one thing alone—how to save their skins. Their guns were lying in the yard.

Franz waved to me and shouted:

'Get away, get away, boy!'

I dismissed his advice with a gesture, then surveyed the scene and thought: Pity the bomb didn't carry another twenty yards, it would have landed right on the lorry and gun. Of course, then there wouldn't have been anything left of our house.

A very worried-looking soldier came in through the broken-down fence and beckoned the gunners, who crept cautiously out of the trench. But at that moment a plane came over, and they dashed like rabbits back into the trench. 'Aha!' I thought. 'One plane's enough to scare you now.'

After waiting a little they ran after the soldier, and I went along to see what was going on. The house next but one to us, where the Korzhenevskys had lived, was no longer there. In its place was a gaping hole partly filled with boards and spattered with blood.

Next to it stood a poplar tree, all cut about by shrapnel, with the door of the house hanging in the top of it, caught in the branches. That was where the bricks which had landed on our roof had come from.

The soldier and the gunners started pulling the boards out of the hole. On the table in the yard there were some bright red pieces of flesh covered with sand, and some had strips of cloth stuck to them. I thought perhaps they had been killing a cow. But then I saw the Germans bringing more pieces out of the hole, handing them from one to the other and piling them up on the table. There was a piece of a head with teeth sticking out. I felt sick and went away.

I have noticed more than once that bad weather accompanies a heavy bombardment. Perhaps it was only a coincidence that following the din from the direction of Pushcha-Voditsa the sky which had been so clear in the morning started clouding over by the middle of the day, and low, grey clouds made the day dull and miserable. But they didn't interfere with the dive-bombers—the 'Black Deaths'—which flew almost at ground level.

The Germans were standing around the water-butt, cleaning the blood off their hands, when a horseman came galloping down the street. He shouted something in a sharp, guttural voice, and they rushed to the half-track. The motor belched a cloud of fumes and they drove through the gate and turned sharply, the gun bouncing along behind. In the distance other vehicles started up and moved off, clanking down the road to the north, towards Pushcha-Voditsa, into the inferno.

Thursday, November 4th

We thought we should never see them again, but they came back . . . That night the earth tremors and the sound of the guns had subsided. Then suddenly our windows were lit up by headlights, the half-track drove into the yard and stopped by the lilac bush. I thought to myself: 'So that's the way they do it: they go off to battle as if they were going off to work and come back home to sleep at night.'

They didn't come straight into the house but set about camouflaging their vehicle with branches broken off the trees in the darkness. I went outside but they took no notice of me. They unhitched their gun and rolled it out on to the street, pointing the barrel in the direction of the embankment.

The tarpaulin cover was hanging on the half-track in strips. And when they came into the room and lit their lamp their appearance was indescribable: their hands, covered with burns and soot and bandaged up, were trembling. Young Herman looked particularly shaken. He pottered aimlessly about the room and seemed to be on the verge of tears. Franz handed me a kettle and asked me to bring him some water.

'Was it a heavy attack?' I asked.

'Oh!' said Franz, and they all started talking at once, explaining and describing: they needed to get it out of themselves, and they did their best to explain by means of signs and all the languages of Europe just how awful it had

been, impossible to describe—the hail of fire, the inferno . . .
Herman pulled a little dictionary out of his satchel, poked
about in it until he found the word he wanted and then
repeated it several times with a terrible look in his eyes:

'Horror. Horror! Understand? Horror!'

From the stream of words I gathered the general sense:
that France or Africa had been health resorts compared with
that day's battle. The Russians were attacking with Katyusha
rocket guns. The noise and the earth tremors of the morning
had been mainly due to the Katyushas. The Russians had
advanced from the village of Petrivtsy and moved into
Pushcha-Voditsa. The German units had been overrun and
routed, the forest was ablaze and the very earth burning.
They themselves couldn't understand how they were still
alive.

'Oh, my boy, my boy!' Franz clutched his head of red
hair between his hands, shook it from side to side and
stayed like that, resting his elbows on the tables.

It was all so sudden: when they arrived they had been so
full of life, so manly, and now they were behaving like
frightened women.

'Does Franz have any children?' I asked Herman quietly.
'Ja,' Herman replied. 'There are three children. Drei.'

I went outside. The horizon was lit up in several places
in a bright crimson glow, giving the night a sort of blood-
red appearance. From time to time came the sound of gunfire.

Then I heard the sound of motor horns near the school,
of orders being given and hysterical screams. Driven on by
some demonic urge I went out on to the street, keeping
close to the fence, and made my way stealthily towards the
school, with the idea of seeing what was going on and, if I
found a gun lying about somewhere, of grabbing it.

Near the Engstrem house I was halted by a sudden sense
of fear. I turned my head, trying to make out what was
threatening, and in the crimson light reflected from the sky
I could see someone moving inside the wire fence.

It was a man with a bag or a box hanging at his side. He
stood there motionless, looking straight at me. I stood stock
still, as though I had been hypnotized. I still had the impression that he did not see me, or it may have been that he
hoped I did not see him.

After standing for a moment like that I withdrew slowly and nois... ... and ducked into the house, where I found myself shaking all over, as though I had seen a ghost. Only next evening did I realize who the man was.

The glow in the sky kept dying down and then flaring up again right through the night. The German gunners did not drink or play the mouth-organ now—they just slept, quite exhausted.

Next morning Alexandra came running in. She said the Germans had taken over the school, that the playground was full of half-tracks and the first floor crammed full of wounded. They were crying out and dying, the floors were running with blood and there were very few doctors. They had come and taken all Alexandra's sheets and towels for bandages.

She had heard that somewhere near by in Kurenyovka a lot of people had taken refuge in a cave, and she wondered how she and her husband could join them. But where was the cave? My mother again gave Alexandra some potatoes and she went off to feed her husband.

It seemed time for the bombardment to start, and I expected that the planes would come over any minute; but time passed and everything remained quiet. The gunners started patching up bullet holes and saying, not very convincingly, that the Russian break-through had been stopped, though they themselves hardly believed what they were saying. The whole day passed in agonizing silence.

As darkness came, the glow in the sky could again be seen and occasional gunfire was heard. Then suddenly there was the whistle of shells passing over our house. We felt the explosions quite close by. The shells had fallen right in the middle of the half-tracks, which burst into flames, and the ammunition loaded on them started to explode.

I clambered on to the fence and with thumping heart watched the Germans rushing about in the light of the fire till at one point they scattered, falling to the ground and hiding in trenches. The shells were exploding in the fire, throwing out clouds of sparks and sending pieces of shrapnel hissing through the air. It made the same sort of din as a bombing raid. I then realized that the man I had seen the day before must have been a scout who had sent back the exact position of the half-tracks, and I was amazed at the accuracy with which the shells were aimed—there were only two of them.

The Germans started towing the half-tracks out of the school yard. The children's handicraft centre had caught fire from the flying shells. I ran and told my mother all about it; she put a scarf over her head and we hurried down to try and help the old folk, but met them coming towards us on the street.

Alexandra and Mikolai had been sitting in the cellar when they had realized that the place was on fire. The old lady had led her husband outside and then rushed back into the building, but was only able to pick up a saucepan, a kitchen knife and some spoons in the passage-way. And there she was, leading Mikolai with one hand and carrying an aluminium saucepan in the other.

The handicraft centre burnt like a torch all night, and we had no need of any other light. We were now four: the old folk had no choice but to stay close to us. By now we assumed that our own Grandpa had already perished. But in fact he hadn't: at the time he was sitting in the sewer pipes, which he knew so well.

Friday, November 5th

Titus had put on weight. I used to sleep in the hole under the house, and he would come at night and lie on my chest which gave me nightmares all night. I would drive him away, but, fat and heavy as a little pig, he would insist on crawling back to keep himself warm.

The number of rats and mice in the empty houses had increased enormously. Titus went round the barns hunting them and when he had nothing else to do he slept. He was the only one for whom the approach of the front line was an advantage. But he was lonely, because there was not a cat or a dog left anywhere in the neighbourhood.

I was awakened in the morning by the sound of gunfire. Again the dive-bombers came over in waves. It was a repitition of what had happened on November 3rd, but with a difference.

The Germans' nerves couldn't take it. At the first sound of a plane they just scattered wildly. The dive-bombers flew low over the ground and did their job with complete impunity, as if they were spraying the fields with weed-killer.

Once again the gunners were summoned by a messenger, and again they departed for Pushcha-Voditsa. The half-tracks which had escaped destruction were moved away from the school. In the middle of the day some other gunners set up a gun in the vegetable garden and started firing across the embankment. They fired so many shells, it seemed as if they were trying to over-fulfil some quota, but they ran shamelessly in all directions at the sound of a plane. Without showing myself I observed them carefully through a hole in the fence: watching them load, shoot the bolt, and seeing the ringing, golden shell-cases shoot out. I thought to myself as soon as you're out of the way those shell-cases will be mine.

The firing of that gun and of the other ones around now bothered me no more than the noise of a tram. When the 'Black Deaths' came over it was worse, but I would always manage to dive in somewhere, and later I would creep out, examine the freshly-made craters and note with astonishment that our house was still undamaged.

I came across Titus in the barn, taking no notice whatsoever of the war. I picked him up, half asleep, and carried him in my arms to the trench, where I made him comfortable on a sack. He went on sleeping calmly, not even twitching an ear when there was an explosion.

My mother didn't keep fussing me or trying to stop me going out to see what was happening. In the end she was completely confused: how could you tell where you might be hit—everywhere was dangerous. I would run into the trench, and meet her going the other way, from the trench to the house; it was both funny and sad; everything was a matter of luck. She began to take this so much for granted that when, later, I walked boldly in among the minefields and started taking the fuses out of bombs and setting off explosions, she didn't scold me and gave up trying to stop me. It was as though after a life constantly imbued with fear something in her had snapped. She had known practically nothing else throughout her life. I was all she had, and she had worried so much about me in the past, had been through so much, there seemed to be no end to the causes for worry

—and now it seemed as though this had turned into its very opposite. If it hadn't, no ordinary being could have stood it.

Old Alexandra and Mikolai refused point-blank to go into the trench. They stayed in the house and I acted as a runner between them and my mother. The old folk took the spring mattress off the bed, leant it up against the stove and covered it with the eiderdowns to make a sort of lean-to inside the room. They crept underneath it and sat there huddled up together. I used to go in and pull the eiderdown aside, saying:

'Still alive in there?'

'Still alive, son, thank the Lord!' Alexandra would reply. 'Is your mother all right?'

'Everything's in order; it'll soon be time to eat!'

Old blind Mikolai, who had very sensitive hearing, would say:

'Here they come, here they come, two planes flying over . . .'

I would not be able to hear anything at all, but Alexandra would seize my hand and say:

'Come on, come in here out of the way!'

I would scramble into their 'shelter' and, sure enough, two planes would skim over the roof and we would hear the sound of little shells exploding.

'Now they're dragging the gun away,' Mikolai announced.

I rushed out into the yard and found he was right: a half-track was towing the gun away. I was delighted and set off to gather up the shell-cases, but only stamped my foot in anger: the beastly Germans had gathered up every single one and taken them away.

Suddenly I saw Alexandra and Mikolai running as fast as they could across the garden to the trench. She was dragging him along by the hand, but the old chap couldn't keep up and was waving his stick in the air.

'The Germans are there, the Germans!' Alexandra cried.

A number of shiny limousines were driving into our yard. Signal troops were already running around, undoing rolls of red wire. The general was back. The yard filled with officers, messengers galloped up, and the general shouted down the telephone. I thought: our house is no better than the others now, and in any case you won't be staying here long.

'You still alive?' Shura called out through a window.

'Where's the front line?' I asked.

'Nobody knows! Oh, what a fright we had,' she said, her eyes goggling. 'Soviet tanks appeared in the middle of the night, all with their headlights on and their sirens going, making a terrible, heart-rending howl. There were hordes, simply hordes, of tanks and nothing stopped them. And then the fire and the howling and death all round. The Germans were scared out of their wits—ran about like mice. How we managed to get out of it I don't know. They're clearing out of Kiev. Right away. They can't hold it. The general's shouting at them now to blow up the bridges and burn everything down. The final round-up and the fire-raisers will come along right behind us. Run and tell your mother! Go and hide somewhere.'

'Where can we hide?'

'I don't know: try and find somewhere.'

I moved away from the window and decided not to say anything to my mother about it, because there was nowhere to run anyway.

I could make out the figures of German soldiers running along the embankment, setting up machine-guns and taking up position at them. The sound of firing from heavy guns and machine-guns reached us from Pushcha-Voditsa. I awaited the final round-up.

A Chapter from the Future

1. *Whereabouts Not Known*

One day at the beginning of December I went with some other boys to Pushcha-Voditsa to collect some grenades and find some explosive.

The forest was sadly mutilated and many of the trees were down. Beneath the fir trees and among the bushes stood the remains of heavy guns, burnt-out half-tracks, tanks without their turrets and stacks of unused shells and mortars. And there were masses of corpses everywhere. Somebody had already been dealing with them: their clothes had been removed and they were piled up in heaps about ten feet high—pyramids of dead, naked Germans, grey-blue in colour, and decomposing despite the cold weather.

In one village the children used the naked corpses as toboggans, sitting on them two and three at a time and sliding down on them. A stiff, blue-grey corpse with glassy, unseeing eyes becomes as hard as rock in a severe frost. But the frost was only slight at the time, and the heaps stank unbearably.

One of the dead men had red hair. I could see only half the face, but I could have sworn it was old Franz. I couldn't be absolutely sure, however; we didn't go right up to them and turn them over because of the smell, and what did it matter anyhow? I suppose there are many families in Germany who still do not know where and how their menfolk perished. If these lines should ever come to the notice of the children of a missing officer, Franz, from Hamburg, a red-headed, middle-aged gunner, who had taken part in the invasion of Poland and Norway and the capture of Paris, and who had fought with Rommel in Africa, they may now know that their father died in that way in the Soviet Union, along with thousands of other fathers, and that he lay, grey-blue, on a pile of corpses throughout the winter of 1944, to be pushed into the ditches and trenches and covered over with earth in the spring.

The trees in the forests grew again, and today you would never recognize those places.

2. *An Essential Scrap of History?*

As they retreated, the Germans managed to capture Bolik and carry him off with them. He escaped and turned up again a couple of days after Kiev had been liberated. None of his family were left and his home was wrecked, so he lived with us and with our next door neighbour. Then he was called up into the army. So Bolik went off to fight at the front like a real soldier; I reckoned that there he would at last get his hands on a machine-gun.

He next appeared some time in the autumn of 1944, look-

ing the same as ever: rather lanky, with a prominent forehead, but more erect and manly. He even had a rank—he
was a corporal. He had spent seven months on the Finnish
front where he had fallen into some water and been frozen
and had lain sick for a long time in a village. Now there was
something wrong with his lungs and heart, and he had been
sent to Kiev for treatment. He was thin and pale, the sort
of person about whom they say that a puff of wind would
blow him over.

'How was it? What did you do? Where were you?' I showered him with questions. 'How did you fight?'

Sadly he dismissed my question with a gesture, saying:
'Yeah . . . in the medical corps, behind the lines.'

'What about the machine-gun?'

'I never got one. I only took pot-shots at planes with a
rifle. That was a waste of bullets . . .'

I just couldn't recognize Bolik, he was so pensive and
remote. He'd been to the war and didn't want to talk about
it.

'They gave me a medal,' he said casually.

'Show me!'

'It's at home.'

We were standing in our courtyard and it was a cold, grey
day. My grandfather (who had also survived) came along
and looked in astonishment at Bolik. Then he said:

'So you're back?'

'Yeah, I'm back . . .'

'Well, just look what's happened to you! The same would
have happened to Tolik if he'd been a bit older.' Grandpa
eyed Bolik closely, and then said: 'You know, young man,
you're in a bad way. You're going to die.'

'Ha, ha!' replied Bolik.

'You'll see,' said Grandpa and, with a gesture of his hand,
went into the house.

We stayed there, silent, flabbergasted.

'Stupid old man,' said Bolik.

'Don't you take any notice of him; the old chap has been
quite potty since the war,' I said. 'Let's go: I've got a whole
library in the barn; I've been going around everywhere
again with a sack gathering books together.'

Proud of my rich store of books, I showed Bolik the
stained but perfectly readable volumes of travel and Wellsian

science fiction and copies of *Technology for Young People*. But he looked at them only absent-mindedly; he just couldn't stop worrying.

'No, he's not right in the head. How could he say a thing like that? Silly old man!' he muttered.

A few days later Bolik was taken away to a sanatorium in Pushcha-Voditsa. I was pleased for him, because the sanatoria in Pushcha-Voditsa were good and it was always difficult to get into them, but the most important thing was that there he would have enough to eat.

At that time I got completely taken up with my work at school, became interested in mathematics, sat for hours at night working out theorems and rarely gave much thought to Bolik. So it came as a complete surprise to me when my mother ran into the room one day and exclaimed sorrowfully:

'Go and take leave of Bolik. He's being buried today!'

The funeral passed down the street outside. Bolik's uncle walked in front, carrying a little cushion with the single medal on it. Then there were two or three wreaths, followed by the lorry bearing the coffin and about a dozen people bringing up the rear. The coffin was open.

My friend Bolik lay there, his face yellowish, his hands folded awkwardly on his chest, and dressed in a smartly pressed suit. Aunt Nina, his mother, was sitting next to him on the back of the lorry, very small and doubled up, the same yellow colour as her son, from whom she never took her eyes.

There were pot-holes in the road opposite our house; the lorry swayed as it went over them, and Bolik's mother swayed too, hanging on tightly to the side of the coffin. I supposed she couldn't walk, and that was why they had put her on to the lorry.

There was some confusion in my mind; I can't quite explain it. As the lorry was passing our gate a multitude of thoughts flashed through my head, not too clearly and in batches. How had my grandfather known that Bolik was going to die? People said: 'He has the stamp of death on his face.' Had Grandpa seen the stamp? And what did it look like, anyway? Why hadn't they succeeded in curing him in such fine sanatoria, and why had nobody told me he was dead, and why hadn't I been called to him when he lay at home? I knew where they were going to bury him: in the Kurenyovka cemetery, next to the grave of his grandfather, Kaminsky, the Pole. I knew the spot very well, because it was where my grandmother was buried. In a few days I would go down there. But I didn't want to go there at that moment. I just wanted to see Bolik and remember him.

Swaying slightly, he sailed past me with his mother, quite close, so that I had a good look at him. My mother was urging me on, and saying in a tearful voice:

'Go on, go on, say good-bye to Bolik.'

But I stood my ground, silent, stubborn. The procession went slowly on, down towards the market, and I simply watched it till it disappeared.

Bolik had gone away.

3. *A Million Roubles*

It was not under German but under Soviet rule that I first saw people being hanged. Several gallows were erected in the squares of Kiev, each with from five to eight ropes. They hanged Ukranians and Russians who had been collaborating with the Germans and who had not managed to escape. They were driven up on an open lorry, the ropes were put round their necks, the back of the lorry was thrown open and the lorry would drive away, leaving them dangling and swinging about on the end of the ropes. Some of them shouted and struggled a good deal until the lorry moved off, and showed they didn't want to die. Afterwards they hung there, stiff and still, some with quite calm expressions, others with their heads twisted to one side, their blue tongues sticking out. They were left hanging there for a long time, as a lesson to everybody.

All prisoners of war who survived the German prison camps were sent off automatically to camps in Siberia as traitors who had surrendered to the enemy and not fought to the death. The famine continued even after the war, but then embraced the country districts as well. Then in 1948 a campaign against the Jews was started. Not being Jewish or prisoners of war or collaborators with the Germans, my mother and I found ourselves in the category of those who 'had lived in occupied territory,' and from then to the end of our lives that fact immediately put all the questionnaires we filled into the third category. It was to cause me a great deal of unpleasantness and a lot of explaining in the future.

Meanwhile I worked as an extra in the theatre, went on with my studies, reflected on the problems of the world and the brevity of human life, and took to wandering round the streets, lost in thought. In this way I was crossing the Troitsko-Kirillovskaya Square one day when I saw an old woman, bent almost double and as wizened as an old root, drawing water from a pump. To my astonishment I recognized in her the widow of Kobets, the leather manufacturer.

She drew half a bucket of water from the pump and moved away very unsteadily. After a moment's thought I rushed after her, took the bucket from her and filled it right up. The old lady accepted this quite calmly and uncomprehendingly.

'You must remember me,' I said. 'We used to be neighbours. My mother is Maria Fyodorovna, the teacher. When you were living on the Peter-Paul Square under the Germans . . .'

'Yes, we lost everything we had there,' said the old lady, staring at me intensely but obviously not remembering me. 'Yes, yes: very glad to see you again. How very kind of you to give me a hand. I'm already ninety, you know.'

'How is Mima?' I asked. 'Is he well?'

'Mima is in the Kirillov Hospital,' the old lady said. 'When the Germans drove us out we landed up in Poland. It took us a long time to make our way back here, and there was nowhere for us to live. But they give them food in the hospital now, and so I put Mima in there. He's not right in his head, but he's quite harmless. They let him out and he brushes the paths and they're satisfied with him, but he's quite incurable. When he was a boy the Bolsheviks stood him up against a wall because he came from a rich family, but I fell on my knees and begged them to spare him . . .'

'Yes, I know about that,' I assured her. 'We lived next to you and used to visit you. At that time you were still receiving parcels from Nikolya in France.'

'When the Germans drove us out,' the old lady said, 'all contact with Nikolya was broken off, and I fear he is no longer alive. All that is left me is Mima. I don't have even any photographs.'

I said nothing: I knew only too well who had destroyed

her photographs. And so we arrived at an old house, and then at a small cupboard in semi-darkness beneath the stairway, the sort of place where people keep brushes. You could see through the door, which had been knocked together with a few nails. There was scarcely room inside the cupboard for the camp bed with some old rags thrown on top, a little stool and a rough, home-made table. The old lady told me to put the bucket in the corner, covered it with a piece of wood and stood a tarnished, dented aluminium jug on top of it.

'I don't remember you,' she said. 'Don't bother to remind me: I shan't remember anyway. But, tell me, you're not a collector by any chance? You don't collect old money?'

I muttered something to the effect that I didn't, had never thought about it, but that I had a lot of acquaintances and I could ask around.

'The thing is,' the old lady said, 'that I have got some old money. We held on to it in the hope that it might come back into circulation. Good Lord, my husband died because of this money and the valuables. We have got rid of all the valuables in exchange for food, but the money remains. I am tired of carrying it around and I'm ready to sell it. I wouldn't ask much for it. You tell your friend.'

She reached down under the bed and pulled out a small threadbare bag tied up with string. When she undid it I could see it was full of bundles of notes.

'There's about a million here,' she said. 'A fabulous amount of money in the old days. They're all unspoiled and genuine—look.'

I had never in all my life seen a bag of money, and it made me feel quite strange. I took some of the notes and examined them. There were bundles of Tsarist hundred-rouble notes, pale and multi-coloured, with a portrait of Catherine; and there were green five-hundred-rouble notes, with Peter I in knight's armour.

'There's also Kerensky money, and money issued by the troops of the Don,' said the old lady, putting the bundles away again. 'You tell your friend: let him come and have a look. I don't want much for them.'

It slowly dawned on me that she had been looking after that bag of money all those long years; governments had come and gone, her husband and family had perished, her son had gone out of his mind, and there had been many currency reforms—in the course of her life the paper money had been changed many times over—and throughout it all she had never lost hope and had even taken the bag with her when the Germans had driven everybody out of Kiev. It was only now she had come at last to the conclusion that her money was of no value except to a collector.

I left her, promising to send the collector along, but I forgot, and soon afterwards I heard that the old lady had died.

Later on I wrote a short story about her entitled *The Million*, but editors returned it to me saying that it was an unconvincing piece of fiction. They also wanted to know what I was trying to say in the story—what was the point of it? . . . There wasn't one, I suppose. And as for being unconvincing, the reproach ought perhaps to be directed to life itself, which is full of incredible things.

4. *Burning the Books*

As a result of the Germans' building activities the Jewish cemetery at the top of Babi Yar was reduced to a state of chaos. Literally not a single tombstone, vault or grave was left undamaged.

It looked as though whole regiments had been marching round the cemetery practising shooting and doing physical training. Only an earthquake, and one of unusual force, could have caused such destruction.

It had been an enormous cemetery, remarkable for its great variety of tombstones, and picturesque corners. One of the gullies leading off Babi Yar cut into it, and through it they had carted the materials for building the ovens; piles of gravestones, which had been overturned but not used, lay there long afterwards.

The latest dates carved on the stones were in 1941, but just a few of them showed signs of efforts at restoration: the dried dirt had been scraped off, a broken stone clumsily cemented together, or some withered flowers laid.

Young trees had grown up in front of the rusty doors of some of the vaults, so that the door could be opened only if the tree was cut down. Not that there were signs of any-one trying to open them: those families had, apparently, come to the end of their line and no one was left to open the door.

At that time I got into the habit of going down there with a sketch-book. I was fond of painting at one time, though not good at drawing, which was a pity because there were plenty of subjects for sketching if only there had been a competent artist to draw them.

On one occasion Valya, who lived near us, came along with me. On the Repyakhov Yar side the cemetery was bounded by an overgrown and utterly deserted path, no longer used because of the gullies made across it by the rains. Someone had had the idea of using the gullies as rubbish tips, and lorries loaded with rubbish used occasionally to come there from Lukyanovka. I was sketching as usual, while Valya was collecting all sorts of bits of metal, springs and other useful articles from the tip.

Then we noticed a huge bonfire burning. A lorry was drawn up there and some men had unloaded a great pile of books and were burning them.

The instincts of a collector of worthless books were awakened in me, and I thought that I might perhaps pick something up for myself, since they were being burnt to no good purpose. But the men at the bonfire shouted sternly:

'What do you want? Go on, get out of the way.'

'What's the matter with you? We're not doing you any harm.'

'Go on, beat it!'

So that was it. I came to the conclusion that they were probably burning Zoshchenko* and Akhmatova†. There had just been articles on them in the papers saying that they had given a false picture of life in the Soviet Union, and there had been a decree of the Central Committee about raising the ideological content of literature.

Valya and I sat down on what remained of the cemetery wall and watched from a distance the men's efforts to raise the level of ideology. To judge from their appearance the books were still in good condition, of assorted sizes and covers—a good quality publication, you might say.

There were four men, who looked and moved like

* Mikhail Zoshchenko (1895–1958), satirist. [Tr.]
† Anna Akhmatova (1888–1966), poetess. [Tr.]

soldiers but were in civilian clothes. They were poking around in the fire with long poles, stirring up the books so that they would burn better. It was such a shame and such a loss. The Germans simply threw the books out and you could at least dig about in them. But these folk wouldn't even let you near them.

Our presence apparently worried them, and one of the men left the fire and started running across to us, shaking his fist. We slid down off the wall and hid in the bushes to keep out of his way.

5. *Babarik Just Sits*

After the war I was sent all over the country and worked on many different construction sites. Then Stalin died and people who had lived through the occupation were moved up from the third to the second category. I managed to get into the Literary Institute, studied in Moscow and became a writer. One day when I returned home to Kiev my mother said:

'Vovka Babarik is home. He was blown up by a mine near Warsaw; he was in the engineers, and he's only just out of hospital. He's a terrible sight—he can't move, he's lost an arm and he can't see. He didn't want to come back home at all like that, but they persuaded him and brought him here. You should drop in and see him; he's glad when people call on him.'

It was the same Vovka Babarik with whom I had been friendly, and had later quarrelled. He was the one whose birds I had let out of their cages, and to whom I had sold a rotten nut.

I went across the road and knocked on the Babariks' door. It was the same house and garden, and the same trees as Vovka had hung his cages out on. Vovka's mother came to the door and threw up her hands, saying:

'Tolik! How pleased Vovka will be! Come in, come in.'

I went in, rather uneasy, recognizing their entrance, their kitchen and their 'big rooms', which now appeared to me very small. There were brown rabbits jumping about the floor.

Sitting on a chest by the window was a very plump and

puffy-looking man with an ugly crew-cut and only one arm. It even looked as though he was not sitting, but had been propped up on the chest like a bag of flour.

He was blind, with moist holes in place of eyes. His complexion was unhealthy, very smooth-looking and covered with blue spots and stripes, as though someone had scribbled on him with a blue pencil. Through the open neck of his shirt, on his chest near the neck, could be seen the most frightful scars. He was utterly motionless, like a sculptured Buddha, and his only hand, strong and masculine, lay helpless on the edge of the chest.

His mother then did something very strange: she went up to him, took hold of his head abruptly, put her lips to his right ear and shouted into it in an unnatural, thin, penetrating, flute-like voice:

'Tolik Semerik has come to see you! Tolik Sem-er-ik. You remember him?'

I watched in amazement, knowing that it was Vovka but failing altogether to recognize him and realizing that on top of everything else he was deaf. Then Vovka began to get excited, shaking his head and shouting in a thick, rather wheezy voice as he raised his arm:

'Tolik! How good of you to come and see me! Where are you?'

'Sit down like that, on his right side and talk right into his ear,' said his mother, smiling nervously and sitting me down beside him.

I sat down, leaning gently against his plump body so that he could feel me, and I put my hand into his, which had been clutching feverishly at nothing. His hand seized mine, kept squeezing it and never letting go. He held on, sometimes stroking my hand, sometimes gripping it tightly.

'Yes, yes,' Vovka said, 'so you've come to see me. That's very nice of you. I heard you were studying in some institute. You're going to be a writer, they say?'

He turned his ear towards me.

'Yes,' I said, 'I write!'

'They say you're going to be a writer?!' He repeated his question again, and I realized that he hadn't heard me. 'What institute did you say?'

'Literary!' I shouted at the top of my voice right into his ear.

His mother came up, took him by the head and shouted again in her penetrating, thin voice right into his ear:

'He says: literary! He's going to be a writer!'

'Aha, aha,' Vovka nodded his head, satisfied and happy now. 'That's good . . . smart lad. And is your mother well?'

'Yes!' I shouted, at the same time shaking his hand up and down in acquiescence, giving him to understand that it meant 'yes'.

'And Grandpa Semerik?'

'No! He's dead!'

'Grandpa Semerik died!' his mother shouted to him in the same way as before, and Vovka heard her.

'Really? So Gramp Semerik's dead? . . .' said Vovka slowly. 'I didn't know . . . Oh, well. Anyway, I'm glad for you. You can see how I am. I couldn't move at all at one time, but now I'm sort of improving and I sit like this. My hearing apparatus doesn't work, I've only got a tiny bit of a nerve remaining. Perhaps my mother will manage to badger a place in a sanatorium out of them, so that at least she could have some time off . . . So long as she's alive, all is well. Some of the lads drop in on me from time to time. We read the paper together. Still the same old "rapid improvement" in agriculture, eh?'

'Yes, yes,' I shouted, using my hand as well. I held on to his hand as the only channel of communication, and I was sitting close to him, pressing up against that unmoving body, with his face close to mine, but I still could not recognize him at all, except that there was something in his voice and manner that recalled the old Vovka.

His mother left us and went to the kitchen. Pronouncing the words as clearly as possible, I shouted in Vovka's ear:

'Forgive me! For the nut in the market—remember?'

'Yes, yes,' he said, 'that's the way things are. You're a smart lad. Higher education, eh . . . And I can remember when you, you little devil, let my birds out.'

'Yes! Yes!' I screamed, again jerking his hand up and down and then, for some reason or other, from right to left.

'I keep rabbits now,' he announced. 'Mother—hand me a rabbit.

I started shaking his hand backwards and forwards.

'Your mother's not here!'

I looked around, but there wasn't a single rabbit to be

seen—they had hidden themselves somewhere. Vovka waited patiently and then asked, without waiting for the rabbit:

'Do you read about what's going on in the United Nations? About the tension and the rows they're having!'

I moved his hand up and down.

'I wish they'd put me up on the platform there,' said Vovka. 'I'd make 'em a real speech. Listen, is there going to be a war?'

I moved his hand horizontally. He understood but didn't agree.

'There'll be a war all right. We're living on the very brink of it. It's as if we were all taking aim at one another and had dropped the safety catches—that's how we're living now, with rockets aimed at all the big cities, only there's a bit of a hold-up somewhere—but someone only has to press a button and the fun will start . . . Ma, where's the rabbit?'

'Never mind,' I shouted, without, be it said, much hope of being heard, 'maybe there won't be a war: all's well at the moment!'

'So there we are, Tolik,' he said with affection, stroking my hand. 'So your mother's well and you've grown to manhood . . . Mind you drop in on me, don't forget.'

I shook his hand vertically.

'I can't hear with my left ear,' he explained, 'but I can hear with the right one. Just speak clearly into the right ear.'

'Vovka, Vovka,' I muttered, squeezing his hand.

'Don't forget—drop in on me, and then you can describe me just as I am. Let people know what war is really like. Agreed?'

I moved his hand up and down.

So there you are—I have kept my promise, by describing Vovka Babarik, my friend, who now, as you are reading these lines, is still sitting there in Kiev, at 5 Peter-Paul Square —one of the millions who took part in the Second World War and survived it. His mother too is still alive.

La Commedia é Finita*

The general got into his car and the girls scrambled quickly in after him. The whole cortège of shiny limousines started up and drove away literally in a matter of minutes, leaving behind the telephone and all the wires. (My mother went on using them for a long time afterwards as clothes-lines.)

Rather tense, I fussed aimlessly about the yard and kept looking out on the street, down which the troops were still retreating. I had never seen such a mass of distracted, worried people. What they looked like cannot be conveyed in words; it might be possible to give an approximate idea of it on film.

Lorries, half-tracks and carts were hurrying in the direction of Podol, carrying Germans, Hungarians, Vlasov men and police all mixed up together. The drivers kept racing their engines and sounding their horns and running down their own people. The horses were covered in lather and the drivers whipped them like people possessed. The Germans were retreating on our stumpy little horses—there was not a single fiery bay cart-horse to be seen: they had obviously perished, unable to withstand the conditions.

All sorts of things—bundles, even gramophones—were dropping off the carts, and the roadway was littered with junk as well as with cartridges and abandoned rifles; somebody had even left a submachine-gun leaning up against a post.

The windows of the school were lit up, as often happens at sunset, but there was no sun at the time: it was a dull, grey evening and getting dark. The school had an indescribably sinister appearance about it. At that point I realized that it was burning—all the floors were ablaze. As they left it the Germans had poured petrol over the classrooms and set fire

* 'The comedy is over'—closing sentence by Tonio in Leoncavallo's opera *I Pagliacci*.

391

to it. The troops marched past, and the school went on burning slowly, lazily, because it was built of stone and was empty.

A column of black smoke shot up close by, near the market, straight up in the air. It wasn't clear what exactly was burning, but the Germans were certainly fulfilling their quota! Then I really got a fright! There had been shooting and banging from all sides, and it was impossible to follow what was happening; but suddenly there was a violent explosion that shook the house and smashed a mirror to pieces on the wall. I was deafened by it and took cover: it was just as though something had exploded near by in the yard. Then there was another explosion and I cowered down again.

'Oh, horrors! They're blowing up the bridges!' my mother shouted at the top of her voice in the yard.

I looked towards the embankment and there, instead of the bridge, I saw a gap piled high with blocks of stone and sand across which Germans who had been left on the other side were still scrambling, while others were scurrying along the embankment. (When, some time later, they cleared the ruins they discovered that the explosion had caught a lorry with four officers in it. Some people reckoned they were the men who had blown the bridge up, going deliberately to their deaths. Others, nearer the truth in my opinion, thought it was just an accident that the lorry had got mixed up in the explosion. After all, a great many troops had been left on the other side.)

I was stunned by all this, and I wandered around, poked about in the barn, found Titus the cat, took him in my arms and nursed him like a baby.

Night fell, but it did not get dark. Everything was bathed in a red glow. The light was reflected off the clouds as from a screen; the reflections would sweep across the sky, then stop still, as though someone were amusing himself waving a torch in the air. A great deal of the city was ablaze, and it was as if we were in the middle of a bonfire.

And everything became very quiet.

In that quietness from time to time there would be a dull thud from the direction of the school, and sparks would spurt up into the air. That meant part of the roof had fallen in.

Mikolai and Alexandra stayed sitting in the room beneath the mattress, weeping. If a stranger had gone into the room he would have been very scared, because it was empty except for the lean-to by the stove with strange, thin, whimpering sounds coming from under it . . . I had never heard old folk whimpering and whining in that way.

My mother took them by the hand and led them like children to the trench. I also sat there for a while, but I was too tensed up; I felt as though needles were sticking into me from all sides, so I crawled out and again started messing around, going over my plan in my mind—to fight with grenades, taking my gun with me and dashing across the embankment over the fields and into the marshes and perfect safety . . . It was going to cost them something to get me, but I had to be careful not to miss the crucial moment. My mind was really very confused, but I was still determined to live.

There was no question of sleep. Titus the cat wouldn't let me: he came to life only when it was dark, becoming bad-tempered and difficult to hold, and finally going off on his predatory business in search of rats. It meant nothing to him that the political regime was due to change that very day.

Friday, November 5th, came to an end.

I was standing in the porch with a rifle in my hand. On the other side of the embankment a green flare shot up into the air. Then I heard a shot; and then another . . . Then another flare. It was a fantastic scene: the green flares bursting against the background of the crimson sky . . .

I thought that at last the fire-raisers were on their way. I would be very happy to write that at that moment I became quite calm, took my grenades and slowly unscrewed the caps . . .

But it didn't happen like that. My collection of weapons turned out to be quite useless and little hammers began thumping in my head. Through the noise they made I caught the sound of shouting on the other side of the embankment. What was I to do? Where could I hide?

Suddenly a really brilliant idea flashed across my mind—I ought to climb a tree, right to the very top. They would be burning everything on the ground, but the trees would survive as they always did. And if they saw me, I would be in a good position to drop the grenades on them from above, like stones, and before they could shoot me I would at least have a go at them. The shouts from beyond the embankment got louder; I could hear a lot of voices calling out:

'A-a-a-h . . . take cover!'

I leapt into the tree like a wild cat, tearing my nails as I scrambled out on the first branch, then held my breath and listened.

From the embankment came shouts in the purest Moscow Russian:

'Comrades! Come out! The Soviets are back!'

But where were the fire-raisers? Good God, had we really survived it all? Everything swam in front of my eyes.

I mumbled something disconnected, shouted out, slid down from the tree and rushed out into the street. I made my way down the red street beneath the red sky towards the red embankment, noticed that I was still clutching a grenade feverishly in each hand, stopped for a moment and put them down side by side on the ground and ran on.

From close by, especially in that red light, the ruins of the bridge were frightening and sinister. There were a few living creatures, either people or animals, crawling on all fours up the steep side of the embankment. I concluded that they were people who had been in hiding like us, so I rushed up the slope and overtook them, but I was still not the first at the top. There I found people embracing each other and weeping, women howling hysterically, and old women in rags throwing themselves on the Russian soldiers' necks.

Urgently, the soldiers asked:

'Any Germans about?'

'No! No!' the people shouted, sobbing.

There were not many soldiers, just a small group, presumably scouts. They exchanged some words among themselves, and then one of them fired a green flare into the sky. Then another soldier, out of breath, climbed up from the other side, a fair-haired, easy-going lad, a typical Ukrainian, carrying a bundle in his hand.

'Well, did you have a bad time here?' he asked brightly.

'Terrible!' the women wailed in chorus.

'Here you are then: put these up on your houses. For the holiday.'

It turned out that he was carrying a bundle of red flags,

not much bigger than the ones children wave at demonstrations. The woman rushed to grab them. I also went for one, and the soldier shouted:

'Don't take all of them! We need some for Podol too!'

The soldier with the rocket-thrower fired a second green flare and they ran off down the slope.

I didn't run, I simply flew down to our house and burst into the trench, shouting at the top of my voice:

'Our chaps are back!'

Without waiting to enjoy the effect, I dashed out again. I climbed into the attic, felt around in the darkness and found the paper parcel. Grandma had been right about that too. I broke the handle off a rake in the barn and nailed a flag to it in the semi-darkness, banging my fingers as I did it. The whole world outside was crimson red, and in that light the flag itself looked a sort of indeterminate pale colour.

The liberation of Kiev continued throughout the night. There was street-fighting in some places. Buildings were blown up and set alight—the university, schools, warehouses and the enormous dwelling houses opposite the Cathedral of St Sophia. But the cathedral itself, fortunately for history, once again escaped.

The main units of the advancing army entered the city through Kurenyovka. The streets were blocked by the bridges that had been destroyed, and so a road had been made round through Beletskaya Street, from which came rolling the tanks, the American Studebaker lorries, which we had never seen before, the artillery and the transports.

The infantry simply wound their way straight across the ruins of the bridge. The men were covered in stains and smears, exhausted, half-starved, and amazingly like those who departed in 1941, except that now they had epaulettes. They did not march in step, but awkwardly, in their loosely-fitting, grey-green uniforms, to the very prosaic clatter of their mess-tins. Some of them went barefoot, putting their sore, red feet down heavily on the ground already hard from the November frosts.

A Final Chapter: Getting Rid of the Ashes

And here I am, back in Kiev, where my mother, much older now, continues to live in the same house at 28 Peter-Paul Square.

She has trouble with her eyes—she's half-blind, and for that reason she had to give up the school in which she had worked for nearly forty years. Because she had had the misfortune to spend some time under German occupation her salary was never raised, she received no awards and was allotted the lowest possible pension, on which it was impossible to exist. But she has a real talent for buying things a little more cheaply than most at the market.

She lives alone. She is frightened when motor-cars sound their horns on the street or when somebody bangs loudly on the front gate. She asked me always to let her know by letter and not by telegram when I was coming to visit her, because the boys who deliver the telegrams always knock and want a signature. That frightens her.

My mother helped me a great deal with the work on this book, especially in getting the details and facts right. But whenever I started talking politics she would immediately retire into herself, and say: 'But why do you ask me that? What are you up to—gathering political material against me?' At which, in desperation, I would drop everything and go and mend the roof.

Sometimes she drops in to number 38, to call on her friend Nina Kaminskaya, Bolik's mother. Nina is an invalid and bed-ridden; she is nothing but skin and bone, and she can't move her horribly twisted fingers. Both women dread the forthcoming demolition of the houses round the square. The Kinap Factory in the former Peter and Paul church has been 'classified', which means it is a military enterprise and it is now being extended. When houses are knocked down single people are not entitled to receive a separate flat. They get a room in some communal accommodation, usually somewhere on the outskirts of the city where there is no market, and that would be an absolute disaster for my mother.

Building work is going on all over the city. Kurenyovka has changed a great deal: trolley-buses now run down the main Frunze Street (Kirillovskaya) and big Chaika limousines often sweep down it, taking government officials out to their country homes in Pushcha-Voditsa; and along the main road there are now huge nine-storey buildings, white and modern, looking like great ocean liners.

I used to like wandering around Kiev. It has some very lovely parks overlooking the Dnieper and many old streets redolent of the city's ancient history.

But I do not find the centre of Kiev agreeable. It was rebuilt after the war to the slogan: 'We shall rebuild our Kreshchatik, destroyed by the German-Fascist invaders'—so pompous, in the Stalinist style; and, moreover, the buildings look like fancy cakes.

At the corner of the Kreshchatik and Proreznaya, where that first explosion once took place in the German headquarters, is now the Ministry of Culture for the Ukraine, busy russifying what is left of Ukrainian culture. In the name of 'socialist humanism' political trials are going on all over the Ukraine and all freethinkers are being sent to prison camps.

The Church of St Andrew still dominates Podol, as it used to. Schoolchildren are taken on excursions to see the Cathedral of St Sophia. The State Security Committee of the Ukraine is still at 33 Vladimirskaya.

The 'Museum-town' has again been organized in the monastery, the ruins of which make a very depressing sight for tourists, and showcases have been set up in the newly constructed buildings. Before they are admitted to the caves, visitors have to pass through the anti-religious museum. The bells ring out from the bell-tower. There is a notice among the ruins which says: CATHEDRAL OF THE DORMITION (ELEVENTH CENTURY), CALLOUSLY DESTROYED BY THE GERMAN-FASCIST INVADERS, NOVEMBER 3RD, 1941. Next to it, in what used to be the Refectory chapel, charts are displayed showing the development of education in the U.S.S.R., and a Foucault pendulum swings to and fro, demonstrating the rotation of the earth. What is not clear, however, is in what direction it is going.

Babi Yar no longer exists. In the opinion of certain politicians, it never did exist. The ravine has been filled in and a main road passes over it.

As soon as the war ended, people—of whom Ilya Ehrenburg was one of the first—started saying that a memorial should be erected at Babi Yar. But the Central Committee of the Ukrainian Communist Party, of which Nikita Khrushchev was then in charge, considered that the people who had been executed in Babi Yar did not deserve a memorial.

More than once I heard Communists in Kiev saying this sort of thing:

'What Babi Yar are you talking about? Where they shot the Yids? And who said we had to put a memorial up to some lousy Yids?'

In fact, with the spread of government-inspired anti-Semitism between 1948 and 1953, the question of erecting a monument was dropped. After Stalin's death people again started cautiously putting round the view that Babi Yar was in fact not just a Jewish grave and that there were three or four times as many people in it of Russian and other nationalities. Arguments like this always seemed to me quite ridiculous: were they trying to say that only if the proportion reached a certain figure would it be worth while erecting a memorial? How could you possibly work it out in percentages? It is PEOPLE who lie buried in Babi Yar.

But the Ukrainian Central Committee, headed in 1957 by Nikolai Podgorny, apparently worked out the percentages, found them unconvincing and arrived at a Solomon-like solution—to put a stop once and for all to talk about Babi Yar, to destroy it and forget all about it.

That marked the beginning of the second attempt to erase Babi Yar from history.

To fill in such an enormous ravine was a gigantic task, but it was possible, given the vast scale of construction work in the U.S.S.R. The engineers hit on a very clever solution—to fill the ravine not by tipping but washing earth into it by means of pumping machinery.

They built a dam across the end of Babi Yar and proceeded to pump pulp—a mixture of water and mud—into it through pipes from the neighbouring quarries of the brick-works. The ravine was turned into a lake. The idea was that the mud would separate and settle, while the water would flow away through channels in the dam.

I used to go along there and study in amazement the lake of mud which was swallowing up the ashes and the bones and the remains of the gravestones. The water in the lake was evil-smelling, green and stagnant, and the noise of the pulp pouring out of the pipes went on day and night. That lasted for several years. Each year the dam was strengthened and increased in height, until by 1961 it was the height of a six-storey building.

On Monday, March 13th, 1961, it collapsed.

The spring rains had rushed down into the ravine and filled the lake to overflowing; the channels could not deal with the volume of water and it went right over the top of the dam.

At its wide end Babi Yar came out on to Frunze Street (that is, Kirillovskaya), just opposite the tram terminus and the densely populated district around it. There were even houses clinging to the hillside at the very mouth of the ravine.

At first the water flooded the roadway, so that trams and cars were halted; people were hurrying to work at the time, and crowds gathered on both sides of the road, unable to get across.

At 8.45 in the morning there was a frightful roar, and a wall of liquid mud thirty feet high poured out of the mouth of Babi Yar. Eye-witnesses who managed to escape and who watched from a distance affirm that the wall of mud burst out of the ravine with the speed of an express train, that no one could get out of its way and that the cries of hundreds of people were smothered in half a minute.

The engineers had overlooked an error in their calcula-tions: the mud which they had been pumping in for so many years had not been hardening out. It had remained liquid, because it consisted for the most part of clay. The clay slopes of Babi Yar formed waterproof walls which kept the mud liquid. Babi Yar was thus turned into a bath of mud as monstrous as the idea which gave birth to it. Undermined by the pressure of the spring rains, the dam burst and the bath overflowed.

Whole crowds of people were swallowed up instantly in the wave of mud. People sitting in trams and in their cars perished, presumably without having time to grasp what had happened. There was no question of anybody being able to work his way to the surface of that glutinous mass, or of getting free, however much he floundered about in it.

Houses which stood in the way of the wave were swept away as if made of cardboard. A few trams were carried along by it a couple of hundred yards and then buried. So were the tram terminus, the hospital, the stadium, an instrument factory and the whole of the residential quarter.

The police cordoned the whole area off and took care that nobody took photographs. People could be seen stranded on roofs, but nobody knew how to get to them. At one o'clock a MIG-4 military helicopter flew in and began evacuating the surviving patients from the roof of the hospital and taking off any other survivors.

The scene of the disaster was very quickly surrounded by a tall hoarding; Frunze Street was closed to traffic; the remains of the tramcars were covered with sheets of corrugated iron; and civil airline routes were diverted so that planes should not fly over Kurenyovka and no one should take photographs.

The sea of mud which had spread far and wide had at last an opportunity of drying out and hardening as the water gradually seeped out of it in little rivulets down to the Dnieper, and in the late spring it became possible to start clearing it.

The digging went on for two years and resembled the excavation of Pompeii. A great many bodies were recovered —in the houses, in their beds, in air pockets formed beneath the ceilings in rooms. One person had been making a call in a telephone booth, and perished there, with the receiver in his hand. At the tram terminus they dug out a group of conductors who had just gathered to hand over their takings, along with the cashier who was taking the money over. The number of people who perished was never, of course, stated. Babi Yar was never lucky with figures.

That attempt to get rid of Babi Yar turned out unexpectedly, led to further large-scale sacrifices, and even gave rise to new superstitions. The phrase 'Babi Yar takes its revenge' was much on people's lips. The main feature of the Bolshevik character, however, is a reluctance ever to give up.

The third, and most serious, attempt started in 1962. A tremendous quantity of machinery was brought into Babi Yar—excavators, bulldozers, tipping lorries and earth-moving machines. The soil was moved back into the ravine, some of it was spread over the area that had been destroyed, and Babi Yar was finally filled in and a main road carried across it. Then the following works were undertaken.

On the place where the concentration camp had been they built a whole new complex of multi-storey dwelling-houses— built them on bones, as you might say. When they were digging the foundations they kept coming across bones, sometimes caught up in barbed wire. The windows and balconies of the first row of these houses look out over the very place where the mass executions of Jews took place in 1941.

A new tram terminus has been built where the old one was.

In the place where the destroyed residential quarter stood they have erected nine-storey buildings, white and modern, like ocean liners.

The remains of the dam have been planted with a beautiful row of young poplars.

And, finally, the Jewish cemetery was destroyed. The bull-dozers were let into that vast cemetery and proceeded to sweep away the graves and the gravestones, digging out bones and zinc coffins as they went.

In the place where the cemetery had been they started to build new premises for a television centre, equipped in accor-dance with the very latest developments in science and technology—which only goes to confirm once again that science is no obstacle to barbarism.

In the very centre of all this building work, over the places, now filled in, where the executions had taken place, they started to mark out a new stadium and a vast amuse-ment park. I spent the summer of 1965 writing this book by night and walking round and watching the bulldozers at work in the daytime. They worked slowly and inefficiently, and it took time for the newly shifted soil to settle down.

On the twenty-fifth anniversary of the first executions, on September 29th, 1966, to be precise, people from all parts of Kiev made their way to Babi Yar. They say it was a very impressive scene. Without any previous planning a spontaneous public meeting took place, at which Dina Pronicheva spoke, as well as the writer Viktor Nekrasov and the young Ukrainian publicist Ivan Dzyuba—and once again there was talk of erecting a memorial . . .

When they heard of the meeting some cameramen from the Kiev news-film studios rushed down and filmed it, as a result of which there was a great row in the studio, the director was sacked and the film confiscated by the secret police.

But the authorities were apparently somewhat alarmed by all this. A few days later local people were surprised to discover, just to one side of the ravine, a granite plaque on which it said that a monument would be erected there to the memory of the victims of German Fascism. When that plaque had been put there or who had done it, nobody knew. But now, if any foreign visitors insist, they can be taken along and shown the stone plaque, which will have had some flowers laid around it in advance. Once the visitors have departed the flowers are removed.

The plan for building a stadium remained unfulfilled. Nothing is being done now on that cursed place. In between the housing estate, which stands where the camp was, on the one side and the television centre, which stands where the cemetery was, on the other there is now a vast, deserted space, overgrown with burdock and bramble.

And so Babi Yar disappeared after all at the third attempt, and it seems to me that if the German Nazis had had the time and as much equipment they could not have devised a better solution.

It may be added in parentheses that the former secretary of the Central Committee of the Ukrainian Communist Party, Nikolai Podgorny, under whose rule this great feat was achieved, has since risen to even greater heights. He is now Chairman of the Presidium of the Supreme Soviet of the U.S.S.R., which is to say President of the Soviet Union.

Until very recently the old lady who used to look after the cemetery—her name was Maria Lutsenko and she was known as Masha—still lived in the cemetery house just above the ravine. For some reason the Germans had completely overlooked her, and never suspected that she used to make her way quietly through the undergrowth and saw everything they were doing. I used to walk round there with her and she would show me again and again just where it started, where they had dynamited the hillside and how 'Over there and there they used to lay them on the ground. And how they screamed! . . . Oh, Mother of God . . . They would keep on hitting them with spades.' As she said this she would be pointing beneath the surface, deep down, because we were standing over a ravine which no longer existed. It is only people like her who have lived there for a long time who can still point out the shape of Babi Yar, the remains of the dam and other traces of what happened there. But no evidence of the crimes committed remains. If you remember, the ashes were partly blown away; the rest, along with the bones, are now buried deep under the earth, so that nothing remains of the people who perished. How many there were of them we shall never find out. All the officially published figures are only estimates, changed to suit the occasion.

All the same I believe that no major crime against society can remain undetected. Some old Masha who saw everything will always turn up, or else a few people—a dozen, two or even just one—will manage to escape and live to tell the tale. However much you burn and disperse and cover over and trample down, human memory still remains. History cannot be deceived, and it is impossible to conceal something from it for ever.

I started writing this book in Kiev, in my mother's shack. But then I found I couldn't go on with it—I just couldn't sleep. I would hear cries as I lay in bed at night—sometimes I was lying on the ground and they were shooting straight at me, in the chest or in the back of the neck, or else I was standing to one side with a notebook in my hand and waiting for it to start, but they didn't shoot because it was their dinner break. They would be making a bonfire out of books or pumping some kind of slush, and I would go on waiting until it happened so that I could record it all conscientiously. That nightmare pursued me, something between dream and reality, and I would jump up with the cries of thousands of dying people ringing in my ears.

We must not forget those cries. They are not yet history. They are the present day. What will happen tomorrow?

What new Babi Yars, Maidaneks, Hiroshimas, Kolymas and Potmas, in what places and with what new, more advanced methods, lie hidden in the future, just biding their time? And which of us now living is already perhaps marked out for them?

I wonder if we shall ever understand that the most precious thing in this world is a man's life and his freedom? Or is there still more barbarism ahead?

With these questions I think I shall bring this book to an end.

I wish you peace. And freedom.

1969